Travel Discount Coupon

This coupon entitles y[...]
when you book yo[...]

D0659247

TRAVEL NETWORK ®
RESERVATION SERVICE

Hotels ♦ Airlines ♦ Car Rentals ♦ Cruises
All Your Travel Needs

Here's what you get: *

A discount of $50 on a booking of $1,000** or more for two or more people!

A discount of $25 on a booking of $500** or more for one person!

Free membership for three years, and 1,000 free miles on enrollment in the unique Miles-to-Go™ frequent-traveler program. Earn one mile for every dollar spent through the program. Earn free hotel stays starting at 5,000 miles. Earn free roundtrip airline tickets starting at 25,000 miles.

Personal help in planning your own, customized trip.

Fast, confirmed reservations at any property recommended in this guide, subject to availability. ***

Special discounts on bookings in the U.S. and around the world.

Low-cost visa and passport service.

Reduced-rate cruise packages.

Call us toll-free in the U.S. at 1-888-940-5000, or fax us at 201-567-1832. In Canada, call us toll-free at 1-800-883-9959, or fax us at 416-922-6053.

---

* To qualify for these travel discounts, at least a portion of your trip must include destinations covered in this guide. No more than one coupon discount may be used in any 12-month period, for destinations covered in this guide. Cannot be combined with any other discount or program.
**These are U.S. dollars spent on commissionable bookings.
***A $10 fee, plus fax and/or phone charges, will be added to the cost of bookings at each hotel not linked to the reservation service. Customers must approve these fees in advance.

Valid until December 31, 1997. Terms and conditions of the Miles-to-Go™ program are available on request by calling 201-567-8500, ext 55.

JAM123

Frommer's

3rd
Edition

Jamaica &
Barbados

by Darwin Porter
& Danforth Prince

Macmillan • USA

ABOUT THE AUTHORS

A native of North Carolina, **Darwin Porter** was a bureau chief for *The Miami Herald* when he was 21, and later worked in television advertising. A veteran travel writer, he is is the author of numerous best-selling Frommer guides, notably to England, France, Italy, and the Caribbean. He is assisted by **Danforth Prince,** formerly of the Paris Bureau of the *New York Times.* For years they have been frequent travelers to Jamaica & Barbados and have become intimately familiar with what's good there and what isn't. In this guide they share their secrets and discoveries with you.

MACMILLAN TRAVEL

A Simon & Schuster Macmillan Company
1633 Broadway
New York, NY 10019

Find us online at **http://www.mcp.com/mgr/travel**
or on America Online at Keyword: **Frommer's.**

ISBN 0-02-860914-X
ISSN 1061-9429

Editors: Bill Goodwin and Lisa Renaud
Production Editor: Charles K. Bowles II
Design by Michele Laseau
Digital Cartography by Raffaele DeGennaro
Maps copyright © by Simon & Schuster, Inc.

SPECIAL SALES

Bulk purchases (10+ copies) of Frommer's travel guides are available to corporations at special discounts. The Special Sales Department can produce custom editions to be used as premiums and/or for sales promotion to suit individual needs. Existing editions can be produced with custom cover imprints such as corporate logos. For more information write to: Special Sales, Simon & Schuster, 1633 Broadway, New York, NY 10019.

Manufactured in the United States of America

Contents

4   Montego Bay   82

5   Negril, the South Coast & Mandeville   109

List of Maps

INVITATION TO THE READER

In researching this book, we discovered many wonderful places—resorts, inns, restaurants, shops, and more. We're sure you'll find others. Please tell us about them, so we can share the information with your fellow travelers in upcoming editions. If you were disappointed with a recommendation, we'd love to know that, too. Please write to:

Darwin Porter & Danforth Prince
Frommer's Jamaica & Barbados, 3rd Edition
Macmillan Travel
1633 Broadway
New York, NY 10019

AN ADDITIONAL NOTE

Please be advised that travel information is subject to change at any time—and this is especially true of prices. We therefore suggest that you write or call ahead for confirmation when making your travel plans. The authors, editors, and publisher cannot be held responsible for the experiences of readers while traveling. Your safety is important to us, however, so we encourage you to stay alert and be aware of your surroundings. Keep a close eye on cameras, purses, and wallets, all favorite targets of thieves and pickpockets.

WHAT THE SYMBOLS MEAN

✪ Frommer's Favorites

Hotels, restaurants, attractions, and entertainment you should not miss.

⑤ Super-Special Values

Hotels and restaurants that offer great value for your money.

The following abbreviations are used for credit cards:

AE	American Express	EU	Eurocard
CB	Carte Blanche	JCB	Japan Credit Bank
DC	Diners Club	MC	MasterCard
DISC	Discover	V	Visa
ER	enRoute		

The following abbreviations are used in hotel listings:

MAP (Modified American Plan) usually means room, breakfast, and dinner, unless the room rate has been quoted separately, and then it means only breakfast and dinner.

AP (American Plan) includes your room plus three meals.

CP (Continental Plan) includes room and a light breakfast.

EP (European Plan) means room only.

The Best of Jamaica & Barbados

Your aim in flying to Jamaica or Barbados is to relax and have a good time—not to waste precious vacation hours searching for the best deals and experiences. Take us along and we'll do the work for you. We've tested the best beaches, reviewed countless restaurants, inspected the hotels, sampled the best scuba diving, and taken the best hikes. We've found the best buys, the hottest nightclubs, and even the best places to get away from it all when you want to escape the crowds. Here's our very opinionated selection, compiled after years of traveling through these islands.

1 The Best Beaches

Both Jamaica and Barbados are known for the white, sandy beaches that put them on world tourist maps in the first place. This is not true of all islands in the Caribbean, many of which have only jagged coral outcroppings or beaches with black volcanic sand (which gets very hot in the noonday sun when only mad dogs and Englishmen run about). Best of all, the beaches on Jamaica and Barbados are open to the general public. So even though the top resorts naturally grabbed the prime coastal real estate, you can still enjoy their beaches, even if you have to walk across the resort's grounds to reach them.

- **Doctor's Cave Beach** (Montego Bay, Jamaica): This 5-mile stretch of white sand made "Mo Bay" a tourist destination. It's named for Dr. Alexander McCatty, who promoted the curative powers of seawater to skeptical Edwardians. Although he donated the beach to Montego Bay as a bathing resort in 1906, it wasn't until the '40s that it really caught on. Waters are placid and crystal clear, and there are changing rooms and a beach bar. This one is a family favorite. See Chapter 4.
- **Cornwall Beach** (Montego Bay, Jamaica): Although too packed with tourists for our tastes, this beach is covered in white sand that will make you think of soft sugar. It's deep enough to really sink your toes into. The water is clean and warm, and it's a place to take your family. The admission charge entitles you not only to swim and sunbathe, but to use the changing room. The beach is near the main tourist strip and close to the popular and larger Doctor's Cave Beach (see above). The "higglers"—as local vendors

are called—will seek you out and try to sell you everything from black coral jewelry to drugs. See Chapter 4.

- **Negril Beach** (Negril, Jamaica): On the island's west coast, this beach stretches for 7 miles along the sea—once the haunt of the Caribbean's most notorious pirates. In the background are some of the most hedonistic resorts in the Caribbean, mixed in with a few family favorites. Many strips of these golden sands are fine for families, although there are several nudist patches where guests bare all. The nude beach areas are sectioned off, even though some new oceanfront resorts have Peeping Tom views of these areas. See Chapter 5.

- **Booby Cay** (Negril, Jamaica): Although it's X-rated, the aptly named Booby Cay is the haunt of nude sunbathers and snorkelers, many of whom are from Hedonism II, Jamaica's answer to Club Med. Scenes from *Twenty Thousand Leagues Under the Sea* were filmed here. Once landed by motor launch or even kayak, bathers in the buff—mainly male/female couples—disperse to seek out their own little white sandy patch of private heaven. See Chapter 5.

- **Boston Beach** (Port Antonio, Jamaica): It's known not only for its white sands, but for its jerk pork stands. "Jerking" is the spicy, slow barbecue method of cooking pork, lobster, or chicken first created by the Maroons, escaped slaves who hid in Jamaica's rugged mountains. You can enjoy your unique beach barbecue while gazing out upon the incredibly clear waters of the bay. The beach has the biggest waves in Jamaica, and young men will rent you surfboards and even give you lessons. See Chapter 6.

- **Treasure Beach** (South Coast, Jamaica): Tired of fighting the crowds for your place in the sun? Head for Treasure Beach on Jamaica's dry, sunny, and isolated south coast, a real hideaway that's a secret among young Jamaicans. There are drawbacks here, and the undertow can be dangerous, so swimming is a bit tricky. These secluded sands are gray, and waves crash into the shore: It's one of the most dramatic beachscapes in Jamaica. Local residents you encounter often have *café au lait* complexions, a slight Scottish accent, blue eyes, and blondish hair—they're descended from Scottish seamen who wrecked offshore. See Chapter 5.

- **Crane Beach** (Barbados): This southern beach—one of the most photographed and fabled in the West Indies—has big Atlantic waves of incredibly blue waters rolling in, but lifeguards are standing by. The beach is filled with pink-tinged coral sand. If you dig into it with your fingers, it's like reaching into a bowl of sugar. Prince Andrew must have agreed; he built a vacation retreat nearby. The long-range ocean views are the most panoramic in Barbados, and water sports and chaises are available. In the unlikely event you tire of all this beautiful sand, you can retreat to the nearby Crane Beach Hotel, where guests have been flocking since 1867. See Chapter 11.

- **The Beaches of St. James** (Barbados): Whether it's called "the Platinum Coast" or "the Gold Coast," this fabled strip along the Caribbean Sea along the western side of Barbados is a beachcomber's paradise. It literally launched Barbados into world tourism. Against a backdrop of some of the most exclusive hotels in the West Indies, you can literally stroll for miles along this strip of white sandy beaches, taking in the natural beauty of the coastline and the clear blue sea. Local families come here to picnic on Sunday, roasting their breadfruit or flying fish over open fires, and fishers can be seen drying their nets. You'll find plenty of beach cricket games. Our favorite spots along the strip are Paradise Beach, Brighton Beach, and Brandon's Beach, a strip of white sandy beaches at Fresh Water Bay, directly south of Payne's Bay. See Chapter 11.

2 The Best Water Sports Outfitters

- **Negril Scuba Centre** (Negril, Jamaica; ☎ 809/957-4425, or 800/818-2963 in the U.S.): This is the best equipped dive facility in this popular resort area. It has one of the most professional staffs on the island, all certified instructors, and they will take you for dives into a bay once frequented by some of the most notorious pirates—male and female—in the West Indies. See Chapter 5.
- **Buccaneer Scuba Center** (Port Royal, Jamaica; ☎ 809/924-8148): Based at Morgan's Harbour Hotel and Beach Club, this operator is unique in the Caribbean. It offers the widest range of dive sites in Jamaica, including the *Texas Wreck*, an American naval ship that sank in 1944. Other sites include South East Cays, a reef that runs alongside the south of Jamaica, and Sandra's Buoy, one of the largest reefs and filled with marine life, including coral growth. You can spot turtles, dolphins, and rays. See Chapter 7.
- **The Dive Shop** (Barbados; ☎ 809/426-9947): Offering the best scuba diving on the island, the staff of qualified instructors will take you to intriguing dive sites where 50 varieties of fish are found. Off Sandy Beach are found sea fans, corals, gorgonias, and dozens of rainbow-hued reef fish. Asta Reef, with a drop of 80 feet, has coral, sea fans, and reef fish galore as well. See Chapter 11.

3 The Best Golf Courses

Jamaica has far greater golf courses than Barbados. An official PGA golf destination, it has some of the most challenging courses in the West Indies, with a dozen championship links.

- **Wyndham Rose Hall Resort** (Montego Bay, Jamaica; ☎ 809/953-2650, or 800/822-4200 in the U.S.): Wyndham has been called one of the top five courses in the world—a bit of an exaggeration perhaps, but it's an unusual and challenging seaside and mountain course built on the shores of the Caribbean. The 10th fairway abuts the family burial grounds of the Barretts of Wimpole Street, and the 14th passes the vacation home of singer Johnny Cash. The 300-foot-high 13th tee offers a rare panoramic view of the sea and the roof of the hotel, and the 15th green is next to a 40-foot waterfall, once featured in a James Bond movie. See Chapter 4.
- **Tryall Golf, Tennis & Beach Club** (Montego Bay, Jamaica; ☎ 809/956-5660, or 800/238-5290 in the U.S.): Jamaica's finest course, Tryall is the site of the annual Johnnie Walker World Championship. A par-17, 6,680-yard course, it crosses hills and dales on what was once land growing sugarcane. Some ruins, including an old waterwheel, remain. Wind direction can change suddenly, making the course more intriguing. One golfer confessed he's played the course 50 times, and "each game was different." See Chapter 4.
- **Half Moon Golf, Tennis & Beach Club** (Montego Bay, Jamaica; ☎ 809/953-2211, or 800/626-0592 in the U.S.): The island's second championship course was designed by Robert Trent Jones in 1961. Played by the likes of former U.S. President George Bush, the course has manicured and diversely shaped greens, but it's not as challenging as the one at Tryall. See Chapter 4.
- **Royal Westmoreland Golf & Country Club** (Barbados; ☎ 809/422-4653): The premier golf course on Barbados dates from 1994. On the west coast, near its twin Pemberton properties, Glitter Bay and Royal Pavilion, it is a private residential

The Caribbean Islands

FLORIDA

Miami

Straits of Florida

THE BAHAMAS

Havana

Cuba

Little Cayman

Grand Cayman — Cayman Brac

CAYMAN ISLANDS

Montego Bay

JAMAICA

Kingston

Haiti

Port-au-Prince

GREATER

Caribbean Sea

COLOMBIA

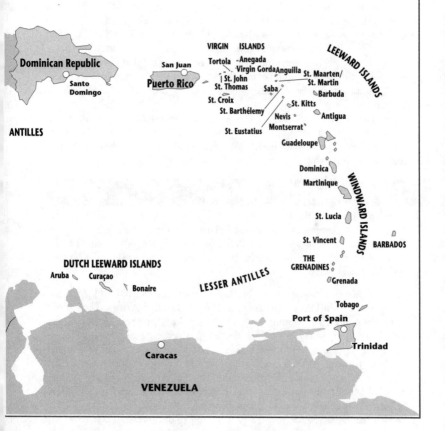

Atlantic

Ocean

TURKS AND CAICOS ISLANDS

Dominican Republic

Santo
Domingo

ANTILLES

San Juan

Puerto Rico

VIRGIN   ISLANDS

Tortola   -Anegada
          Virgin Gorda Anguilla
| St. John
St. Thomas   Saba
St. Croix
St. Barthélemy   Nevis
St. Eustatius   Montserrat

LEEWARD ISLANDS

St. Maarten/
St. Martin/
Barbuda
St. Kitts
Antigua

Guadeloupe

Dominica
Martinique

St. Lucia

St. Vincent

THE
GRENADINES

Grenada

WINDWARD ISLANDS

BARBADOS

DUTCH LEEWARD ISLANDS
Aruba   Curaçao
        Bonaire

LESSER ANTILLES

Tobago

Port of Spain

Trinidad

Caracas

VENEZUELA

community. The course can only be played by guests of certain hotels. Serious golfers will want to book into one of these hotels (a wide price range) to be granted the privilege of playing this course, designed by Robert Trent Jones, Jr. The $30 million, 27-hole course is spread across 500 acres, overlooking the western Gold Coast, the island's fabled beach strip. See Chapter 11.

4 The Best Tennis Facilities

- **Half Moon Golf, Tennis & Beach Club** (Montego Bay, Jamaica; ☎ 809/953-2211, or 800/626-0592 in the U.S.): Half Moon has Jamaica's best tennis—13 state-of-the-art courts, seven of which are lit for night games. Richard Russell, the head pro, a former Davis Cup/Wimbledon player, offers a clinic with a video playback. See Chapter 4.
- **Wyndham Rose Hall Resort** (Montego Bay, Jamaica; ☎ 809/953-2650, or 800/822-4200 in the U.S.): The Wyndham Rose Hall features six hard-surfaced courts, each lit for night games. Residents play for free, and nonguests are charged. There's also a resident pro on hand to offer lessons. See Chapter 4.
- **Tryall Golf, Tennis & Beach Club** (Montego Bay, Jamaica; ☎ 809/956-5660, or 800/822-4200 in the U.S.): Tryall is rivaled only by the Half Moon Club in Jamaica. It has nine hard-surface courts, three of which are lit for night games. Four pros on site will help improve your skills. See Chapter 4.
- **Ciboney Ocho Rios** (Ocho Rios, Jamaica; ☎ 809/974-1027, or 800/333-3333 in the U.S.): This Raddison franchise offers three clay surfaces and three hard-surface courts, all lit for nighttime play. There's a lot of emphasis here on tennis, including Pan-Caribbean competitions and even pan-parish tournaments. Twice-a-day clinics are sponsored, both for beginners and more advanced players. See Chapter 6.
- **Sandy Lane Hotel** (Barbados; ☎ 809/432-1311, or 800/225-5843 in the U.S.): Sandy Lane places more emphasis on tennis than any other resort on Barbados. It offers five courts with an open-door policy to nonresidents. Two of the five courts are lit for night games. See Chapters 10 and 11.

5 The Best Hiking

Jamaica has the best hiking possibilities in the Caribbean, but there are serious drawbacks; you should never undertake such an adventure on your own.

First, you could get hopelessly lost. Alone in some wilderness, you could be set upon, mugged, robbed, or even worse. Always venture into the interior of Jamaica with skilled guides (see below).

- **The Blue Mountains** (near Kingston, Jamaica): Jamaica has some of the greatest hiking in the West Indies, providing that it is an organized activity. The island's mountain peaks climb to some 7,400 feet, a rich, lush landscape of flora, fauna, and waterfalls, especially in the Blue Mountains which rise over Kingston. Canoe trips along rivers are also possible. The most popular ascent is to the Blue Mountain Peak, particularly at full moon. Hikers who depart from their campsite at 2am get to see the sun rise over the mountains. The best outfitter arranging tours of the Blue Mountains and canoe trips is **SENSE Adventurers Ltd.** (☎ 809/927-2097), operating out of Kingston. See Chapter 7.
- **The Green Hills** (Barbados): It's possible to explore Barbados' Green Hills, where the true beauty of the island can be discovered by treks and hillclimbing.

Contact **Highland Outdoor Tours** (☎ 809/438-8069) for outings on horseback or foot, traversing lands that were once some of the most productive sugar plantations in the British Empire. Some of the terrain, with its rolling windswept hills, is evocative of a balmy Scotland. See Chapter 11.

- **The Barbados National Trust** (St. Michael; ☎ 809/426-2421): This organization sponsors five-mile walks that take in the most panoramic and scenic views of Barbados. Walks are conducted throughout the year, but only on Sundays from 6:30am to 9:30pm and from 3:30 to 5:30pm. Special moonlight hikes are sometimes conducted. See Chapter 11.

6 The Best Natural Attractions

The most dramatic attractions in either Barbados or Jamaica weren't made by the island's settlers but by Mother Nature.

- **Somerset Falls** (Port Antonio, Jamaica): This sun-dappled spot is not as tourist-trodden as Dunn's River. The waters from Daniels River race down a deep gorge split through a rain forest. Flowering vines, waterfalls, and foaming cascades form the lush backdrop. You can swim in the deep rock pools. See Chapter 6.

- **Dunn's River Falls** (Ocho Rios, Jamaica): A favorite of cruise-ship passengers, these 600 feet of clear, cold mountain waters race over a series of stone steps. Visitors splash in the waters at the bottom of the falls or drop into the cool pools higher up between cascades of water. It's the best way to cool off on a hot day in Jamaica. Visitors hold hands climbing the falls and trust that the human chain won't have a weak link! See Chapter 6.

- **Welchman Hall Gully** (Barbados): This lush tropical rain forest is operated by the Barbados National Trust. Occasionally you'll spot a wild green monkey (though we can't give you any guarantees). What is guarenteed is that you'll see specimens of plants growing when the first English settlers arrived in 1627. These include tree fern, cacao, nutmeg, and clove. You can commune with nature and experience the island's most serene tranquility. See Chapter 11.

- **Harrison's Cave** (Barbados): This series of limestone caverns with a 40-foot waterfall and subterranean streams is viewed as one of the finest cave systems in the world and is the leading tourist attraction of Barbados. Visitors can view the caves aboard an electric tram and trailer. Bubbling streams, tumbling cascades, stalagmites rising from the floor, and deep pools are just part of the attraction. See Chapter 11.

7 The Most Intriguing Historical Sights

Most travelers heading for Jamaica or Barbados aren't really interested in history—at least not much beyond what they read in James Michener's *Caribbean*. For those who are, here are our top choices if you want to see the ruins of yesterday.

- **Fort Charles** (Port Royal, Jamaica; ☎ 809/922-0620): This is the only remaining fort of the six that used to guard this port from Henry Morgan and his buccaneers. In those days, Port Royal was known as "the wickedest city on earth." Built in 1656, the site was later strengthened with the addition of more than 100 cannons, capable of repulsing attacks by land or sea. In 1779 Lord Horatio Nelson commanded the fort. It has withstood earthquakes and hurricanes reasonably well. See Chapter 7.

- **St. Nicholas Abbey** (Barbados; ☎ **809/422-8725**): One of Barbados' most famous structures dates from the mid-17th century. In spite of its name, it was never an abbey. Its stone and wood architecture is the finest representation of the Jacobean style in Barbados. More than 200 acres of sugarcane is still cultivated here every year, keeping alive the old tradition. See Chapter 11.
- **Marriott's Sam Lord's Castle** (Barbados; ☎ **809/432-7350**, or 800/223-6388 in the U.S.): This may now be the most famous hotel in the southern Caribbean, but the Regency house was built by an infamous buccaneer, Sam Lord, who grew rich by deliberately wrecking ships. He became known as the "Regency Rascal." He placed lanterns imitating the lights of a safe harbor, and lured the ships to their doom. The great house of this pirate still stands, with all its antiques and beautiful art which can be viewed by the public. See Chapters 10 and 11.

8 The Best Offbeat Travel Experience

- **Jamaica's People to People:** Almost 700 Jamaican families are registered to spend a few hours with off-island visitors. Tell the Jamaican tourist board what your interests are—butterflies, reggae, Bible studies, sailing, whatever—and they'll pair you up with respectable Jamaicans who will, without fuss or bother, include you in the normal routine of their lives, such as eating at the table, going to the beach, or visiting Grandma. No overnight accommodations are included in the program, but there are no costs involved either. Of course, a small gift as a gesture of appreciation is always welcome. Many lasting friendships have formed as a result of this program. See "Meeting the Jamaicans" in Chapter 3.
- **Mountain Valley Rafting** (Montego Bay, Jamaica; ☎ **809/952-0527**): Some 10 miles south of Mo Bay, you can board a raft built of bamboo trunks for an adventure on the Great River, departing from Lethe Plantation. It's a close-up encounter with the interior of Jamaica and a connection with an old and passing way of life. After rafting, you can tour the plantation and enjoy a lunch like the rich plantation owners of yore did. See Chapter 4.
- **Black River Safaris** (South Coast, Jamaica; ☎ **809/965-2513**): The longest river in Jamaica is real Tarzan country, with mangrove trees and crocodiles in the wild. At the mouths of the Broad and Black Rivers, saltwater meets freshwater, and extensive red mangroves are formed with aerial roots of some 40 feet. Lots of wild things grow in these swamps. Birders look for ring-necked ducks, whistling ducks, herons, egrets, and even the blue-winged teal. See Chapter 5.
- **Rafting on the Rio Grande** (Port Antonio, Jamaica; ☎ **809/993-2778**): Until the late actor Errol Flynn discovered what fun it was, rafting on this river was simply a means of transporting bananas. Now it's the most amusing sport in Jamaica. Propelled by stout bamboo poles, you're guided down the river for 8 miles viewing a lush backdrop of coconut palms and banana plantations. You're even taken through the Tunnel of Love. See Chapter 6.

9 The Best Honeymoon Resorts

Many hotels in Jamaica or Barbados will help you get married, doing everything from arranging the flowers and the photographer to applying for the marriage license (see Chapter 3 for more information about Jamaica or Chapter 9 for Barbados). Regardless of where you decide to hold your wedding, both Jamaica and Barbados offer romantic destinations for post-wedding wind-downs and honeymoons.

- **Sandals** (Montego Bay, Negril, and Ocho Rios, Jamaica; ☎ **800/SANDALS** in the U.S.): These resorts for male/female couples pride themselve on providing an all-inclusive environment where food and drink are spread out in abundance and you never have to carry cash or tip. Enthusiastic members of the staff bring in heroic amounts of community spirit to whatever knot-tying rituals happen to be celebrated on-site. All of these resorts can provide a suitable setting, but the most favored ones are Sandals Royal Jamaican at Montego Bay and Sandals Dunn's River at Ocho Rios. See Chapters 4, 5, and 6.
- **Half Moon Golf, Tennis & Beach Club** (Montego Bay, Jamaica; ☎ **809/953-2211,** or 800/626-0592 in the U.S.): This resort offers honeymooners deluxe oceanview rooms fronting a near perfect crescent-shaped beach from which it takes its name. Better-heeled newlyweds opt for one of the large private "cottages," complete with their own swimming pool. Although there are plenty of nooks and crannies where you can retreat for romantic interludes, this is also the resort of choice for activity-oriented honeymooners, who in addition to making love are into aerobics, tennis, swimming, and most definitely golf. See Chapter 4.
- **Trident Villas & Hotel** (Port Antonio, Jamaica; ☎ **809/993-2602,** or 800/237-3237 in the U.S.): Here you can follow in the footsteps of that perpetual honeymooner, the late actor Errol Flynn. Poet Ella Wheeler Wilcox called Port Antonio "the most exquisite on earth," and if you're here there's no better hideaway than this posh hotel, enjoying a 14-acre setting on a rocky bluff at the edge of the Caribbean. White cottages and villas are staggered about the property to ensure maximum privacy. The main building has an English country house tradition with formal service, whereas the private accommodations allow you to retreat, listening only to the sound of the pounding surf, a large paddle fan, and pillow talk. See Chapter 6.
- **Jamaica Inn** (Ocho Rios, Jamaica; ☎ **809/974-2514,** or 800/837-4608 in the U.S.): At one of the great hotels of the island, the "White Suite" is secluded on the brink of a promontory—Winston Churchill slept here—and it's the preferred place in Ocho Rios for a honeymoon if you can afford it. Otherwise, there are plenty of other spacious and classic rooms in which to launch your married life. The resort opens onto a private cove with powdery champagne-colored sand. The inn is the best choice for those seeking a colonial aura with a certain degree of formality, as opposed to one of the more free-for-all Sandals properties where anything (well, almost) goes. See Chapter 6.
- **Ciboney Ocho Rios** (Ocho Rios, Jamaica; ☎ **809/974-1027,** or 800/333-3333 in the U.S.): The honeymoon villas at this stately, plantation-style spa and beach resort are set on lush hillside acreage and are perfect private retreats for newlyweds. Each has a private attendant and pool, and guests are pampered here and given complimentary massages, pedicures, and manicures. A private beach is reached by shuttle as the resort is not on the water. The resort is all inclusive and there's a range of sporting activities, such as tennis courts, but it's also a place where you can retreat and be alone with your newly acquired mate. See Chapter 6.
- **The Enchanted Garden** (Ocho Rios, Jamaica; ☎ **809/974-1400,** or 800/847-2535 in the U.S.): The island's most romantic retreat seems to have been designed just for honeymooners who want to return to Adam and Eve's Garden of Eden. Tropical plants and flowers are spread across some 20 acres of gardens, along with a series of waterfalls and streams. The rooms may be a bit small but 30 come with their own private plunge pool. A shuttle will transport you to the nearest beach. Some of the resort's drinking and dining choices evoke *Arabian Nights,* which should put you in a romantic mood. See Chapter 6.

- **Sandy Lane** (Barbados; ☎ **809/432-1311**, or 800/225-5843 in the U.S.): This is Barbados' poshest choice for a romantic interlude, as members of the fabled jet set of the 1970s can testify. A satisfying sense of ritual pervades this venerable British-inspired hotel, something that's attractive to honeymooners who want a degree of colonial formality at their post-wedding interlude instead of the wet T-shirt contests you'd find at a typical Sandals resort. The hotel is set on one of the island's best beaches, with acres of well-maintained grounds. Rooms have private balconies for having breakfast *à deux* or watching a romantic sunset. See Chapter 10.
- **Royal Pavilion** (Barbados; ☎ **809/422-4444**, or 800/283-8666 in the U.S., **800/567-5327** in Canada): Many consider the Royal Pavilion an even finer choice for a honeymoon than Sandy Lane. Your honeymoon breakfast or lunch can be served alfresco at your oceanfront suite. Children are discouraged, at least in the winter, so the resort becomes something of a couples-only retreat. There are plenty of activities to occupy your day, if you're so inclined, including tennis courts and water sports (golf available nearby), followed by supper club entertainment—and then it's off to bed. See Chapter 10.

10 The Best Family Vacations

Jamaica and Barbados—especially Jamaica—have some of the most family-oriented resorts in the Caribbean. Some resorts, especially in the winter, discourage children under 12, but the hotels below aggressively pursue the family market, and offer plenty of extra advantages for booking with them.

- **Vista Ambassador** (Montego Bay, Jamaica; ☎ **809/952-4703**, or 800/JAMAICA in the U.S.): At this all-inclusive family resort on 10 acres of tropical gardens, children under 12 stay free, and those 13–17 pay half price for everything including room, food, and drink. It's a five-minute walk to the beach. There's a special pool for children on-site, however. The various bedrooms can be adjusted to accommodate different family sizes; some of the villa suites contain two bedrooms for families wanting more privacy. See Chapter 4.
- **Boscobel Beach** (Ocho Rios, Jamaica; ☎ **809/974-3331**, or 800/859-7873 in the U.S.): The best family resort in the Caribbean goes out of its way to welcome and encourage visits by families, and offers the finest children's programs on the island, with a playground center, mini-zoo, and other activities. It also recognizes the single parent traveling with children, offering special rates. Not only that, but it provides special programs and rates for grandparents who'd like to travel with their grandchildren. There's even a "kids only" restaurant. See Chapter 6.
- **FDR (Franklyn D. Resort)** (Runaway Bay, Jamaica; ☎ **809/973-4591**,or 800/ 654-1FDR in the U.S.): The FDR doesn't rival Boscobel Beach in attracting the family trade, but it's a good runner-up. All meals and activities are included in one net price, and families are housed in Mediterranean-style villas on the grounds 17 miles west of Ocho Rios. A personal attendant does all the cooking, cleaning, and child-caring, and many programs are provided for the amusement of children in residence. The Kiddies' Centre features everything from computers to arts and crafts. There are dinners for tots as well. See Chapter 6.
- **Sandy Beach Hotel** (Barbados; ☎ **809/435-8000**): This is one of the island's most family-oriented resorts, allowing children under 12 to stay free in their parents' room. The resort contains only one- or two-bedroom suites, each with a fully equipped kitchenette and private balcony or patio. Bajan buffets are popular with

the entire family, and the resort reserves a play area for children, plus a wading pool. See Chapter 10.

- **Almond Beach Village** (Barbados; ☎ 809/422-4900, or 800/822-4200 in the U.S.): This all-inclusive resort, located on 30 acres of prime beachfront property 15 miles north of Bridgetown, maintains one of the best children's programs on the island. It offers a club just for children, with videos, Nintendo, a computer lab, books, and board games, plus two children's playgrounds, a kiddies' pool, an activity center, beach games, nature walks, water sports, treasure hunts, storytime, arts and crafts, and even evening entertainment. See Chapter 10.

11 The Best Places to Get Away from It All

There are plenty of tranquil retreats in Jamaica and even in overcrowded Barbados. Some are luxurious, some are rustic, but what they share in common is lack of crowds, tranquility, and quiet. To reach most of them, you'll have to arm yourself with a good map.

- **Good Hope** (Falmouth, Jamaica; ☎ 809/954-3289, or 800/OUTPOST in the U.S.): Montego Bay is hardly a place to escape from the tourist hordes, but this romantic 18th-century great house in the nearby mountains above Falmouth is just the sort of place where you can run away and hide. It is set on a 2,000-acre plantation with lush gardens. Our impresario, Chris Blackwell—who seems to specialize in sylvan retreats—also owns this choice property, which offers hiking along country trails, horseback riding, tennis, and swimming. The main house is furnished with antiques. In the evening after a family-style classic Jamaican dinner, you hear only the sounds of the night lulling you to sleep. See Chapter 4.
- **Treasure Beach Hotel** (South Coast, Jamaica; ☎ 809/965-2305): Lying on a lushly landscaped hillside above a sandy beach on Jamaica's unhurried south coast, this is a place where no one will ever find you. It hardly competes with the grand mega-resorts of Jamaica, such as those found in Ocho Rios, but Treasure Beach offers a return to the 1950s; tranquility and a laid-back attitude prevail. Bedrooms are in a series of outlying cottages, offering complete privacy. There's a freshwater pool, but most activities are those you organize yourself. It's cheap too. See Chapter 5.
- **Navy Island Marina Resort** (Port Antonio, Jamaica; ☎ 809/933-2667): Once owned by the late actor Errol Flynn, this resort and marina is Jamaica's only private island getaway. Part of Flynn's hedonism still prevails, especially at the clothing-optional beach called Trembly Knee Cove. Accommodations are in studio cottages or villas, and ceiling fans and trade winds recapture the romantic aura of Jamaica's past. See Chapter 6.
- **Strawberry Hill** (Blue Mountains, Jamaica; ☎ 809/944-8400, or 800/ OUTPOST in the U.S.): This highland retreat has been called "a home-away-from-home for five-star Robinson Crusoes." Lying 3,100 feet above the sea, it's our preferred retreat in all of East Jamaica. Set in a well-planted botanical garden, it is a cottage complex built on the site of a 17th-century great house. Multimillionaire Chris Blackwell is the owner, but he accepts paying guests at his lush, sylvan retreat. See Chapter 7.
- **Kingsley Club** (Barbados; ☎ 809/433-9422): On the hidden-away east coast of the island, this property opens onto the turbulent Atlantic Ocean and seems a world removed from Barbados' overbuilt west coast beach strip. Here you can return more to the laid-back life of Barbados of 30 years ago. It's just a simple,

nothing-fancy West Indian inn lying in the foothills of the little hamlet of Bathsheba. Its rooms are clean and comfortable, and the Bajan food is good, too. It's a very reasonable place to stay, although the beach is not suitable for swimming. Come here to beachcomb. See Chapter 10.

12   The Best All-Inclusive Resorts

It seems that every resort in Jamaica is going all-inclusive—that is, offering everything (or almost everything), certainly food and drink, for one net price. The trend is catching on in Barbados, too. Lavish buffets, evening entertainment, and fun and games in the sun characterize these resorts. The major drawback is that they are virtually fenced-in compounds, completely isolating guests and discouraging them from having a true experience with Jamaican or Barbadan life. But it is this very sense of retreat that many vacationers seek, especially those who don't want to face a lot of hidden extra costs at the end of their trips.

- **Sandals Montego Bay** (Montego Bay, Jamaica; ☎ **809/952-5510**, or 800/ SANDALS in the U.S.): This is a honeymoon haven in spite of the nearby airport and its zooming planes. This 19-acre all-inclusive resort—catering only to male/ female couples—is one of the most popular in the Caribbean. Everything's included, even those notorious toga parties. It's mainly for couples wanting to have a good time. Guests tend to be extroverted and gregarious, and they usually eat and drink their money's worth here. It is easily outclassed by some of the better resorts of Ocho Rios, but many prefer this Mo Bay location instead. See Chapter 4.
- **Grand Hotel Lido** (Negril, Jamaica; ☎ **809/957-4010**, or 800/859-7875 in the U.S.): This hedonistic resort is a class act. It's the grandest and most architecturally interesting along Negril's beach strip. Adjacent to the often raunchy Hedonism II, the Grand Lido is upscale and discreetly elegant. The smaller of its two beaches is reserved for nudists. Unlike many of Jamaica's resorts, it is not a male/female couples–only joint. It is open to singles or those of various sexual proclivities, and it entertains and treats them in a grand style, which is far superior to the typical Club Med in the Caribbean. The dining options are the best in Negril. See Chapter 5.
- **Ciboney Ocho Rios** (Ocho Rios, Jamaica; ☎ **809/974-1027**, or 800/333-3333 in the U.S.): This Raddison franchise is the leading all-inclusive resort in the Greater Ocho Rios area. Its accommodations are in one-, two-, or three-bedroom villas, each with its own pool and fully equipped kitchen. The dining choices are the best of any of the competing resorts, including one venue with a menu based on haute cuisine combined with the concept of healthy foods. It's not on the beach but there's a beauty spa and a health and fitness center. A private beach club nearby offers an array of water sports. See Chapter 6.
- **Couples Ocho Rios** (Ocho Rios, Jamaica; ☎ **809/975-4271**, or 800/268-7537 in the U.S.): "Any man and woman in love" are pampered and coddled during their stay at Couples. The resort offers its own private island where couples can bask in the buff. Couples is a far classier operation than either of the more mass-market Sandals resorts found in the Ocho Rios area. Accommodations are first class in either king-size or double beds, and the food is among the best in the area, with a choice of four restaurants featuring widely varied cuisine. See Chapter 6.
- **Almond Beach Club** (Barbados; ☎ **809/432-7840**, or 800/4-ALMOND in the U.S.): On the island's swanky west coast, The Almond Beach Club was established

in 1991 as the first all-inclusive resort on Barbados. Accommodations are in seven low-rise three-story buildings, and everything's included. To break the monotony of dining in one place every night, an eat-around option exists at neighboring hotels. Lively nightly entertainment is offered, followed by days spent enjoying a trio of freshwater swimming pools, a fitness center, fishing, windsurfing, kayaking, or even banana boating. See Chapter 10.

- **Almond Beach Village** (Barbados; ☎ **809/422-4900**, or 800/822-4200 in the U.S.): Set on 30 acres of prime beachfront property 15 miles north of the capital of Bridgetown, this is a companion resort to the also all-inclusive Almond Beach Club (see above). Rooms are spread among seven three- or four-story buildings. Best are the units lying along the beach with views of the Caribbean. The resort offers four different restaurants and five bars, including our favorite, Enid's, for a typically Bajan cuisine. Lively entertainment is presented, along with an array of sports, including a water sports kiosk and nine freshwater swimming pools. See Chapter 10.

13 The Best Restaurants

The debate over which restaurants serve the best food will rage as long as there are places to dine. Here are our favorites.

- **Norma at the Wharfhouse** (Montego Bay, Jamaica; ☎ **809/979-2745**): In a coral stone warehouse, this is Mo Bay's finest adventure in dining out. It's the domain of Norma Shirley, the foremost female restaurateur in Jamaica. With a view of Montego Bay glittering in the background, Ms. Shirley serves a nouvelle Jamaican cuisine that is without equal in the area. From Caribbean lobster steamed in Red Stripe beer (the island's local brew) to jerk chicken with flambéed mangoes, from chateaubriand larded with pâté in a peppercorn sauce to grilled deviled crab backs, Ms. Shirley sets a table that keeps them coming back for more. See Chapter 4.

- **Sugar Mill Restaurant** (Montego Bay, Jamaica; ☎ **809/953-2228**): In the Half Moon Club, this is the premier restaurant at any of the mega-resorts in the Mo Bay area. Chef Hans Schenk may be from Switzerland, but he pioneered a style of cookery using local ingredients that is innovative for the island. For example, he'll take a classic Dijon mustard and blend it with the island's local pick-me-up, Pickapeppa, creating unique taste sensations. His smoked north coast marlin is without equal, and he makes his own version of bouillabaisse à la Jamaican that is the island's finest. See Chapter 4.

- **Pork Pit** (Montego Bay, Jamaica; ☎ **809/952-1046**): It may look like a dump, but the Pork Pit is a classic, the best place to go on the Jamaica's north coast for the famous jerk pork or jerk chicken. A recipe said to have been handed down by the Maroons, who lived high in the mountains, the highly spiced meat is barbecued slowly over wood fires until crisp and brown. Its taste is unique, and will make you forget about any so-called barbecues you might have sampled elsewhere. Of course, only a Red Stripe beer would go with a meal such as this. See Chapter 4.

- **Evita's Italian Restaurant** (Ocho Rios, Jamaica; ☎ **809/974-2333**): Evita's reigns supreme in an area not noted for having topnotch independent eateries. Evita (actually Eva Myers) is a local culinary star, devoting at least half her menu to pastas. Her recipes are wide ranging, from the north to the south of Italy. Try her snapper stuffed with crabmeat or the lobster and scampi in a buttery white cream sauce—everything washed down with a good Italian vino. See Chapter 6.

- **Blue Mountain Inn** (near Kingston, Jamaica; ☎ 809/927-1700): The continental and Caribbean cuisine matches the elegant setting on the grounds of a coffee plantation from the 18th century, high on the slopes of Blue Mountain, which produces the world's best and most expensive coffee. Steaks and seafood dominate the repertoire, and the chef is never better than when preparing his lobster thermidor or his tender chateaubriand with a classic Béarnaise sauce. See Chapter 7.
- **Carambola** (Barbados; ☎ 809/432-0832): Standing on the upper edge of a seaside cliff, with one of the most dramatic and panoramic terraces in the Caribbean for dining, this is the island's most romantic dining spot, and serves some of the best food, a unique blend of Thai and continental cuisine among other influences and inspirations. See Chapter 10.
- **The Cliff** (Barbados; ☎ 809/432-1922): Opened in 1995, The Cliff quickly became one of the island's premier dining choices. It's an open-air restaurant blasted into a coralstone cliff and set on four levels. The menu, a combination of West Indian and international cookery, is of the highest level. The grilled snapper, drizzled in three types of coriander sauce, is just one of the innovative touches to this all-too-familiar dish. Sushi is presented when available, and the fresh local tuna is terrific. See Chapter 10.
- **Olives Bar & Bistro** (Barbados; ☎ 809/432-2112): Established in 1994, Olives Bar & Bistro occupies the site of the first two-story house ever built in Holetown. Its historic status, however, is not why savvy foodies flock here. The Mediterranean and Caribbean cuisine is unique on the island, celebrating its warm climes. In honor of its name, only olive oil is used to prepare the savory cuisine. One of the many stellar examples in the chef's repertoire is yellowfin tuna marinated and seared rare, then served on a bed of roast garlic mashed potatoes with grilled ratatouille. See Chapter 10.
- **The Orchid Room** (Barbados; ☎ 809/422-2335): In the Colony Club Hotel, this dining room blends a plantation house ambience with velvet-glove service. It's one of the most formal and elegant dining venues on the island, to be savored and reserved for that special evening. Sparkling chandeliers and period furnishings form the mere backdrop for this successful blend of a French and West Indian cuisine. Gallic flare is brought to the fresh and often home-grown local ingredients. A cold lettuce soup with peppercorns may not sound like much, but the chefs manage to bring out natural flavors in all their dishes. Their grilled dorado—laid on a purée of eggplant and potato and dressed with olive oil and lime—is worth crossing the island to sample. See Chapter 10.
- **Raffles** (Barbados; ☎ 809/432-6557): On the main street of Holetown, in a setting of weather-beaten buildings, this restaurant has been turned into one of the island's best by its young international owners. Although their repertoire is vast, they focus on some of the most authentic and best tasting dishes of the West Indies. Their food is spicy and has even been called "decadent," a reference to their rich and zesty flavors. Simple Bajan flatfish cakes take on a renewed elegance when created in the kitchen here. The changing array of local fish—including the most famous on Barbados, the flying fish so beloved of Hemingway—are always available. Ask for it blackened, grilled, or sautéed—it's always delectable in any of these presentations. See Chapter 10.

14 The Best Shopping Buys

Jamaica and Barbados aren't the serious shopping meccas of the Caribbean in the way that San Juan, St. Thomas, and St. Maarten are. But there are some good deals here, on both islands, especially in arts and crafts.

- **Art:** Its paintings may never rival that of Haitian artists when they are at their finest, but Jamaica is at least the "second best" center for art in the Caribbean. Prices are still reasonable, too, even when the artist has a certain renown. Although paintings are sold all over the island, the finest art is found in Kingston at either the **Frame Centre Gallery** or the **Mutual Life Gallery,** the two leading display showcases for the best of the island's artistic talent. See Chapter 7.

  In Barbados art is displayed at many sources, with quality work showing up at **Queen's Park Gallery** in Bridgetown. See Chapter 11.

- **Handcrafts:** If you see something you like, either in Barbados or Jamaica, you'd better purchase it on the spot, as it isn't likely to turn up again. Many Jamaicans produce unique creations, a one-time carving or a one-time straw basket, then vary their pattern if they make it again. Crafts come in many forms, ranging from alabaster carvings to wood carvings and weavings. Some wood carvings show extreme style and others are so hideous you wonder whey they were carved in the first place. Any outlet of **Things Jamaican,** including one in Montego Bay (see Chapter 4), displays a good assortment of Jamaican crafts, as does **Harmony Hall** outside Ocho Rios on the north coast (see Chapter 6). In Bridgetown, the capital of Barbados, **Articrafts** has the most impressive display of Bajan arts and crafts (see Chapter 11).

- **Fashions:** Many artisans in both Jamaica and Barbados produce quality resortwear. (On many other islands, the clothing is inferior and often tacky.) Both Jamaican and Bajan women are known as good seamstresses, and they often make quite passable copies based on the works of top designers and sell at a fraction of the original's price. Some of the best resort wear—for both men and women—is found at **Caribatik,** a famous outlet outside Falmouth (see Chapter 4). In Barbados **Colours of De Caribbean** has a very individualized display of tropical clothing (see Chapter 11).

- **Jewelry and Watches:** Sometimes watches at various outlets in Jamaica sell for 20% to 40% off Stateside prices. Major international brands are sold, but you must buy from a reliable dealer—not from vendors hustling so-called gold Rolex watches at laughably low prices. Prices of Seiko watches in Barbados are often priced 20% below Stateside prices.

  In jewelry, Jamaican gemstones include coral agate and black coral, and many fashionable pieces are made from these stones. Handmade necklaces are sold everywhere, even on the beach. Dozens of outlets in both Jamaica and Barbados, especially at shopping malls, sell a vast array of jewelry and watches, but you must shop carefully.

15 The Best Nightlife

Jamaica reggae and Bajan calypso are never better than when heard on their own turf. Yet there's a surprising lack of independent (nonhotel) nightclubs on these islands— that is, safe clubs to visit. (Many visitors don't want to take their chances traveling potholed and often dangerous roads at night.) So the diversions, especially live bands, come to the hotels instead. Nearly all major hotels feature entertainment in the evening, maybe even fire-eaters and limbo dancers.

But there are some nighttime diversions outside the hotels, including the following.

- **An Evening Cruise Aboard the** *Calico* (Montego Bay, Jamaica; ☎ 809/952-5860): This 55-foot gagg-rigged wooden ketch sails from the Montego Bay waterfront. From Wednesday through Saturday, there is no better or more romantic way to spend an evening at Mo Bay than by taking this cruise. From 5 to 7pm you sail into the sunset while enjoying drinks and the sound of reggae. See Chapter 4.

- **Baxters Road** (Barbados): This entire street in Bridgetown, the capital, is where Bajans go "caf crawling"—that is, hopping from bar to bar while listening to records, often the scratchy recorded voice of Billie Holiday. **Enid's** is the most famous café to check out during your nighttime crawl (think of it as similar to a pub crawl in London). The joint's jumping after 11pm, especially on a Friday or Saturday night. See Chapter 11.

- **Club Xanadu** (Barbados; ☎ 809/427-7821): In the Ocean View Hotel, the best musical revues on the island are presented, and they're written and choreographed by an American, David McCarthy. A buffet precedes the 9:30pm showing Thursdays and Fridays only. See Chapter 11.

- **1627 and All That** (Barbados; ☎ 809/428-1627): Combining entertainment and dancing, 1627 and All That is the most exciting choice on a Thursday night in Barbados. Sample a large buffet of Bajan food and then sit back to watch a historic and cultural presentation. See Chapter 11.

- **Plantation Restaurant and Garden Theatre** (Barbados; ☎ 809/428-5048): Here you'll find the best evening dinner theater and Caribbean cabaret on the island. You get lots of exotic costumes, plenty of reggae and calypso, and the inevitable limbo. Dinner and show are presented every Wednesday and Friday nights. See Chapter 11.

Getting to Know Jamaica **2**

Most visitors already have a mental picture of this English-speaking nation before they arrive: its boisterous culture of reggae and Rastafarianism, and its white sandy beaches, jungles, rivers, mountains, and clear waterfalls. Jamaica's art and cuisine are also remarkable.

Jamaica can be a tranquil and intriguing island, but there's no denying that it's plagued by crime and drugs. There is also palpable racial tension here. But many visitors are unaffected; they're escorted from the airport to their hotel grounds and venture out only on expensive organized tours. These vacationers are largely sheltered from the more unpredictable and sometimes dangerous side of Jamaica. Those who want to see "the real Jamaica," or at least to see the island in greater depth, should be prepared for some hassle. Vendors on the beaches and in the markets can be particularly aggressive.

Most Jamaicans, in spite of their hard times, have unrelenting good humor and genuinely welcome visitors to the island. Others, certainly a minority, harm the tourism business, so that many visitors vow never to return. Jamaica's appealing aspects have to be weighed against its poverty and problems, the legacy of traumatic political upheavals that have characterized the island in past decades, beginning in the 1970s.

So should you go? By all means, yes. Be prudent and cautious—just as if you were visiting New York, Miami, or Los Angeles. But Jamaica is worth it! The island has fine hotels and terrific food. It's well-geared to couples who come to tie the knot or celebrate their honeymoon. As for sports, Jamaica boasts the best golf courses in the West Indies, and its landscape affords visitors lot of activities that just aren't available on other islands, like rafting and serious hiking. The island also has some of the finest diving waters in the world.

This country lies 90 miles south of Cuba, with which it was chummy in the 1970s (when much of the world feared that Jamaica was going Communist). It's the third largest of the Caribbean islands, with some 4,400 square miles of predominantly green, lush land; a mountain ridge that climbs to 7,400 feet above sea level; and many beautiful white-sand beaches with clear blue sea.

1 The Natural Environment

Jamaica and the rest of the West Indian archipelago are summits of a submarine string of mountains, which in prehistoric times probably formed a land bridge between modern Mexico and Venezuela. Although not the area's largest island, Jamaica offers a diverse landscape.

Covering about 4,240 square miles, Jamaica is approximately the size of Connecticut. The island is some 146 miles long, with widths of 22 to 58 miles.

Millions of years ago, volcanoes thrust up from the ocean floor, forming mountains, ranging to 7,402 feet high, which are loftier than any along the eastern seaboard of North America. These mountains, located in an east-to-west line in central Jamaica, contain more than 120 rivers and many waterfalls as well as thermal springs. In the high mountains of the east, the landscape features semitropical rain forest and copses of mist-covered pines.

The mountains are bordered on the north and east by a narrow coastal plain fringed with beaches. The flat, arid southern coastline reminds visitors of African savannah or Indian plains, whereas the moist, fertile north coast slopes steeply from hills down to excellent beaches.

Much of Jamaica is underlain by limestone, dotted with dozens of caves that store large reservoirs of naturally filtered drinking water.

Almost everything grows in Jamaica, as proved by colonial British botanists who imported flowers and fruits from Asia, the Pacific, Africa, and Canada. The island contains unique kinds of orchids, ferns, bromeliads, and varieties of fruit, like the Bombay mango, that don't flourish elsewhere in the Western Hemisphere. Birds, insects, and other animals are also abundant.

Framing the capital of Kingston, the Blue Mountains dominate the eastern third of the island. This is the country's most panoramic area, and it's split through with a network of paths, trails, and bad roads—a paradise for hikers. From this region comes Blue Mountain coffee, the most expensive in the world.

Younger than the Blue Mountains, the John Crow Mountains rise at the northeastern end of the island. Only the most skilled mountain climbers or advanced hikers should attempt this rugged karst terrain. It rains here almost daily, creating a rain forest effect.

Jamaica's longest river is called Black River, and it's bordered by marshes, swamps, and mangroves where bird and animal life, including reptiles, flourish. Black River, which is also the name of a small port, is in the southwestern section, lying east of Savanna-La-Mer and reached along route A2.

2 The Regions in Brief

Montego Bay   The second-largest city in Jamaica, Montego Bay serves as the capital and main point of entry for the north coast. Known for glamour, the city contains the country's greatest density of resort hotels and some of its finest beaches and golf courses. Tourists come to "Mo Bay" for its duty-free shopping, good restaurants, late-night discos, museums, historic buildings, and tours of nearby rum distilleries.

Negril   Situated near Jamaica's relatively arid western tip, Negril enjoys a reputation as the nudist center of the West Indies, with a kind of gently provocative do-as-you-please attitude that appeals to hedonists. Its 7-mile beach is one of the longest uninterrupted stretches of sand in the Caribbean. Because of a boom in hotel construction, the Negril region is no longer the hippie hideaway it was during the 1960s and early '70s. The area has become big business and mainstream, competing aggressively for tourist dollars once headed almost exclusively to Montego Bay and Ocho Rios.

Mandeville & the Blue Mountains   Located in southcentral Jamaica, Mandeville is the country's highest-altitude town, and is built in a style strongly influenced by the English. A departure point for tours of the Blue Mountains, Mandeville was the first community in Jamaica to receive tourists on a large scale (Victorian English visitors looking for a cool mountain retreat). It is now the center of the island's noted coffee cultivation. A sense of slow-paced colonial charm remains a trademark of the town.

Ocho Rios   Set on a deep-water harbor easily able to accommodate cruise ships, Ocho Rios boasts a dense concentration of resort hotels and other vacation spots. A relative newcomer to the tourist trade, the community lures visitors with its north coast natural beauty and the aura of history left behind by Spanish colonists. The region's primary natural attractions include the steeply sloping terrain, which has challenged the architectural skill of Jamaica's most sophisticated hotel developers and provided the setting for panoramic public gardens and dramatic waterfalls.

Port Antonio   The hub of verdant eastern Jamaica, Port Antonio has retained a sense of glamour ever since financier J. P. Morgan and actors Bette Davis, Ginger Rogers, and Errol Flynn took their vacations—and their paramours—here many years ago. Frequently photographed for its Victorian/Caribbean architecture (with slightly rotted gingerbread) the town is refreshing and not frequented as extensively as Negril, Ocho Rios, and Montego Bay.

Kingston & Spanish Town   Located on the southeast coast, Kingston is Jamaica's capital, largest city, and principal port. Nearby are the remains of Port Royal, once an infamous lair of pirates and renegades, most of whom were unofficially pressed into service to the English Crown. Port Royal was superseded by Kingston after being destroyed by earthquakes in 1692 and again in 1907. Kingston is a cosmopolitan city with approximately 650,000 residents in its metropolitan area. It serves as the country's main economic, cultural, and government center. Residents proudly say it is the world's reggae capital as well. The city's northern district, called New Kingston, includes most of the capital's high-rises, showcase modern buildings, upscale hotels, and upscale private homes. There are also extensive poverty-stricken areas in Kingston, though, and it's not the safest place to be—it's certainly not a real tourist destination.

Twenty minutes by car west of Kingston is Spanish Town, the country's capital from 1534 to 1872. It was the second town built by Spanish colonists in Jamaica after Nueva Sevilla (now abandoned). The slow-paced village today contains the Cathedral of St. James (early 16th century)—one of the oldest Spanish churches in the West Indies—and memorials to English colonization.

3 Jamaica Today

A favorite of North American honeymooners, Jamaica is one of the most densely populated islands of the Caribbean and has a vivid sense of its own identity. Its history, long rooted in the plantation economy, has now given way to tourism, bringing prosperity to some but also causing social unrest. The turbulent and impassioned politics of Jamaica are the most volatile in the Caribbean.

Despite a regrettable increase in crime and harassment of tourists by vendors in such resorts as Ocho Rios, Jamaica remains one of the most successful black

Jamaica

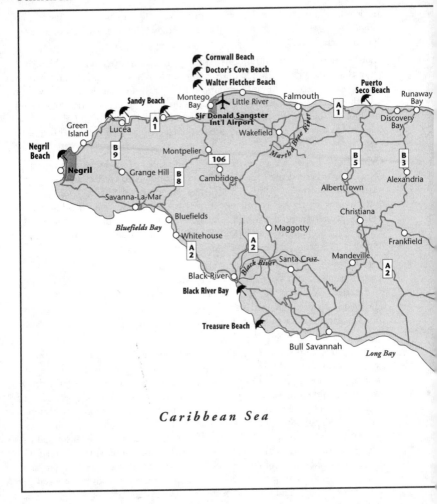

democracies in the world. Its people also share a sense of humor so keen and so strongly developed that it's probably helped them get through many hard times, political and economic.

The island is large enough to allow the more or less peaceful coexistence of all kinds of people within its beach-lined borders—including everything from expatriate English aristocrats to dyed-in-the-wool Rastafarians. Overall—and despite its long history of social unrest, political turmoil, unemployment, drugs, and increasing crime—it remains among the top three or four most interesting islands in the Caribbean to visit.

Agriculture and mining, the traditional ways that Jamaicans have earned money, have declined in relation to tourism. If anything, Jamaica approaches the millennium almost too heavily dependent on tourism. If the world economy grows shaky and its visitors diminish, Jamaica will be unduly affected.

Already Jamaica's economy is battered. Like that of the United States, its debt burden grows. Export earnings continue a downward spiral. With little money to

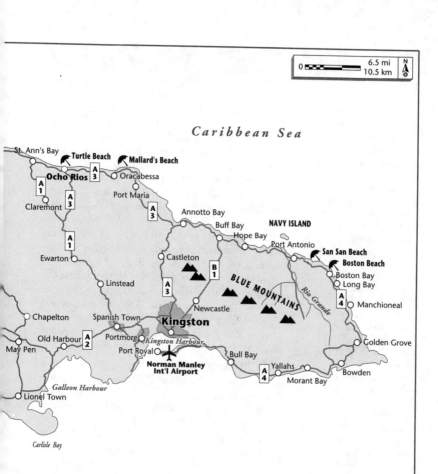

0   6.5 mi
         10.5 km

Caribbean Sea

St. Ann's Bay

Turtle Beach   **Mallard's Beach**

Ocho Rios   A 3   Oracabessa

A 1

A 3   Port Maria

Claremont

A 3

Annotto Bay

A 1   Buff Bay   **NAVY ISLAND**

Ewarton   Hope Bay

Castleton   Port Antonio

   San San Beach

B 1   **Boston Beach**

BLUE MOUNTAINS   Boston Bay

Linstead   A 3   *Rio Grande*   Long Bay

      Newcastle   A 4   Manchioneal

Chapelton   Spanish Town

Old Harbour   A 2   Portmore   **Kingston**

May Pen   Port Royal   *Kingston Harbour*   Golden Grove

            Norman Manley   Bull Bay

            Int'l Airport   Yallahs

Galleon Harbour   A 4   Bowden

Lionel Town   Morant Bay

Carlisle Bay

Airport ✈   Beach ⚑

keep them in state-of-the-art or even passable condition, its highways and city streets—especially those in Kingston—are potholed and pitted. Imported goods and food—often from Asia—undercut local farmers, making it tougher for them to eke out a living. And even though its soil is extremely fertile, the island has had severe summer droughts.

Fortunately, the mindless violence of the 1970s, when political differences were often settled by gunfire, has ended. Under then-Prime Minister Michael Manley, many of Jamaica's young doctors, educators, and other professionals left the country for careers in the United States or England. Under Manley's successor, Prime Minister Edward Seaga, some came back—they are known as "returnees"—and they've rekindled enterprises that had been allowed to decline under Manley. Nevertheless, as Jamaica nears the 21st century, it remains a troubled land, one of the most chaotic in the Caribbean.

But, as any Jamaican looking into an uncertain future will tell you: "We've come a long way, *mon*, but we've got a long way to go."

4 History 101

continues

IN THE BEGINNING   Jamaica has long been viewed as one of the most desirable islands of the West Indies, richer and more diverse, with better anchorages and more rainfall, than many of the sandier, smaller, and less dramatic islands that lie nearby. Attempts by outsiders to control Jamaica have influenced much of its history.

Jamaica was settled around 6000 B.C. by Stone-Age people about whom little is known. They were displaced around A.D. 600 by the Arawak, Indians who originated in northern South America (probably in the area of modern Guyana). Skillful fishers and crafters of pottery and bead items, they had copper-colored skin and lived in thatch-covered huts similar to those used in parts of Jamaica today. The Arawak made flint knives and spears tipped with sharks' teeth, but they never developed the bow and arrow. They lived mainly on a diet of fish and turtle steak. The Arawak were completely unprepared for the horrors brought by the Spanish conquest.

A CRUEL COLONY   In 1494, during his second voyage to the New World, Christopher Columbus visited Jamaica, and claimed the island for the Spanish monarchy. Although he quickly departed to search for gold and treasure elsewhere, he returned accidentally in 1503 and 1504, when he was stranded with a group of Spanish sailors for many months off Jamaica's northern coastline while they repaired their worm-eaten ships.

Beginning in 1509, Spaniards from the nearby colony of Santo Domingo established two settlements on Jamaica: one in the north (Nueva Sevilla, later abandoned) in modern St. Ann Parish and another in the south, San Jago de la Vega (St. James of the Plain), on the site of present-day Spanish Town. Pirates estimated the Arawak population in Jamaica at the time to be about 60,000.

In 1513 the first African slaves reached Jamaica, and in 1520 sugarcane cultivation was intro-duced. In the 1540s the Spanish Crown grudgingly offered the entire island to Columbus's family as a reward for his service to Spain. Columbus's de-scendants did nothing to develop the island's vast potential, however. Angered by the lack of immediate profit (abundantly available from gold and silver mines in Mexico and Peru), the Spanish colonists accomplished very little other than to wipe out the entire Arawak population. Forced into slavery, every last

Arawak was either executed or died of disease, over-work, or malnutrition.

RAISING THE UNION JACK   After 146 years as a badly and cruelly administered backwater of the Spanish Empire, Jamaica met with a change of fortune when a British armada arrived at Kingston Harbour in 1655. The fleet had sailed on orders from Oliver Cromwell, but it had failed in its mission to conquer the well-fortified Spanish colony of

- **1980s** High unemployment spreads, though tourism thrives.
- **1988** Hurricane Gilbert devastates Jamaica.
- **1989** Manley, now moderate, returns to power.
- **1992** P. J. Patterson becomes prime minister

Santo Domingo. Almost as an afterthought, it went on to Jamaica. Within a day, the Spaniards surrendered the whole island to the British, who allowed them to escape. Most of the Spaniards immigrated to nearby Cuba, although a handful remained secretly on the island's north coast.

Six months later, British colonists arrived, but many died from poisoning and disease. In 1657, Spaniards based in Cuba initiated a last-ditch effort to recapture Jamaica. Two of the fiercest and biggest battles in Jamaican history pitted the Spanish against the English. The defection from the Spanish by some Maroons (escaped slaves and their descendants living in the Jamaican mountains) led to the permanent exit in 1660 of Spanish troops from Jamaica. Humiliated, these soldiers escaped to Cuba in canoes.

In 1661 the British began to colonize Jamaica in earnest. They appointed a governor directly responsible to the Crown, with orders to create a governing council elected by the colonists. All children born of English subjects in Jamaica became free citizens of England. In two years the population of Jamaica grew to more than 4,000. Hostilities between England and Spain continued, with occasional skirmishes and richly successful raids by the English on Spanish colonies in Cuba and Central America.

The Maroons formed an important subculture in Jamaica. They lived independently in the mountainous interior, often murdering every white person who transgressed their boundaries. In the coastal areas, the population swelled with the importation of many slaves from Africa and the immigration of more than 1,000 settlers from Barbados. Additional settlers came from the ranks of semiautonomous bands of privateers, who with the full approval of the British Crown, plundered any ship or settlement belonging to nations hostile to England. Under Gov. Thomas Modyford, Britain initiated a policy of full protection of privateers at Port Royal, near Kingston. Modyford simultaneously encouraged cacao, coffee, and sugarcane cultivation, tended by an increasing number of slaves.

A few years later, Britain committed one of the most cynical, yet practical, acts in the history of Jamaica when it appointed the notorious privateer, Welsh-born Henry Morgan, as the island's lieutenant governor. Morgan's previous bloody but profitable exploits had included plundering Panama City and Porto Bello on the Isthmus of Panama, both laden with treasure from the mines of Peru waiting shipment to Spain. Despite the well-known torments and atrocities he had inflicted on non-English colonists throughout the Caribbean, Morgan was buried with honors in 1688 at Port Royal. By then more than 17,000 persons lived in Jamaica. Port Royal reveled in its reputation as "the wickedest city on earth." It likely contained more houses of dubious repute than any other contemporary city in the Western Hemisphere.

EARTHQUAKES, FIRES & PROSPERITY   British interest in Jamaica grew as opportunities for adding profits and territory increased. In 1687, Sir Hans Sloane, physician to powerful aristocrats of Britain and namesake of London's Sloane Square, wrote two influential scholarly books on the geography, flora, fauna, and people of Jamaica. The volumes helped convince Britain to continue its investments in the island.

In 1690 a slave rebellion was crushed by the British, who executed its leaders. Some participants escaped to the mountains, where they joined the independent Maroons.

On June 7, 1692, just before noon, one of the most violent earthquakes in history struck the city of Port Royal. In less than 20 minutes the three shocks, ascending in intensity, caused the sea to recede and then rush back with terrible force, drowning the virtuous and wicked alike. Much of the city actually dropped into the sea. A handful of survivors attempted to rebuild parts of the city, but in 1704 a great fire destroyed every building except a stone-sided fort.

Although the centerpiece of Jamaica had disappeared, the countryside was becoming one of the world's great producers of sugar. This corresponded neatly with the increasing demand in England for sugar to sweeten the flood of tea imported from Asia. Within four years of the destruction of Port Royal, Jamaica contained more than 47,000 inhabitants. They were divided into three main classes—white property owners (planters, traders, and professionals, many of whom prospered), slaves from Africa and their descendants (the largest by far in number but with little power), and white indentured servants. This last group consisted mostly of impoverished Scots and Welsh, who had exchanged labor for transport to Jamaica. After a predetermined number of years, they could buy land and thus some degree of prosperity. Other inhabitants were criminals sent to Jamaica by English courts for 5 to 10 years as punishment. In 1693 the newly founded city of Kingston was laid out in a grid pattern on private property, at that time covered with trees and grassland.

In 1694 a French fleet led by Admiral Du Casse invaded the north shore of Jamaica, at Carlisle Bay. At the time France and Britain were at war in Europe as well, and the French plan was meant to divert English warships from Europe. Although the French were eventually driven back to their ships, they destroyed at least 50 sugar plantations and captured some 1,300 slaves. Six years later the French fleet was counterattacked by the English off the coast of Colombia, but after after five days of concentrated fighting, the battle ended in a draw. Back in Kingston, the captains responsible for the early withdrawal of the British fleet from the fighting were convicted of misconduct and shot.

POWER STRUGGLES   The struggle for control of Jamaica intensified over the next 50 years as the island became one of the most profitable outposts of the British Empire, despite hurricanes, pirate raids, and slave rebellions. For ease of government, it was divided into 13 parishes, whose boundaries remain today.

Most troublesome for the English were the Maroons, who escaped control by fleeing into the mountains and forests. In 1734, in one of many dramatic battles, the English captured the Maroon stronghold of Nanny Town, destroying its buildings and killing many of its inhabitants. The survivors committed suicide by jumping off a cliff, preferring death to enslavement. By 1739, however, both the English and the Maroons recognized the virtues of increased cooperation, and they signed a series of peace agreements. The Maroons were given tax-free land in different parts of the island. They were allowed to govern themselves and to be tried and punished by their own leaders, who could not, however, sentence a subject to death. Also very important, the Maroons agreed to capture all runaway slaves and return them to their masters, and to assist in suppressing any slave rebellion.

In 1741 the British navy used Jamaica as a base of operations for mostly unsuccessful military strikes against Spanish strongholds in Cartagena, Colombia, and on the Isthmus of Panama. Caused by harsh conditions, slave rebellions in 1746 and

1760 led to many deaths. The British ended both revolts, killing many, and sending most survivors to Honduras to work in swamps and sweltering timberlands.

By the time of the American Revolution, the population of Jamaica had reached almost 210,000, some 193,000 of whom were slaves. After 1776 some Loyalist residents of the United States moved to Jamaica. France, which sided with the Americans against the British, sent an opportunistic militia to the West Indies. It captured many British islands in the eastern Caribbean, and Jamaicans trembled with anticipation of a French invasion. Admiral Horatio Nelson, later famous for defeating Napoléon's French fleet at the Battle of Trafalgar, drilled the Jamaican garrisons to repel the expected attack. It never came, however.

Naval skirmishes among the British, Spanish, and French continued offshore, with Jamaica usually serving as the stronghold for British forces. In 1782, Admiral George Brydges Rodney defeated a huge French force off Dominica, killing more than half of the 6,000 men intended for an invasion of Jamaica. Rodney brought the captured French ships to the rebuilt Port Royal. Appreciative colonists voted to spend £3,000 to erect a statue in his honor, and the British government made him a peer.

In 1793, Britain tried to influence a rapidly disintegrating situation in nearby Haiti, a dependency of France. Although several Haitian cities were captured by English troops, an outbreak of disease and the fierce opposition of the noted leader Toussaint L'Ouverture (who later ruled all Haiti) soon ended the venture.

Also in 1793, some 5,000 British troops equipped with specially trained bloodhounds imported from Cuba fought another bloody war against the Maroons in the Jamaican highlands. The British sent the captured Maroons first to Canada, then to Sierra Leone, in West Africa. Those not involved were allowed to remain in Jamaica.

An official census in 1800 revealed a Jamaican population of 300,000 blacks and 20,000 whites. This disparity was not lost upon either the powers in London or the leaders of the increasingly politicized blacks.

Despite revolts by blacks and military expeditions to neighboring islands, Jamaica in 1803 exported the largest sugar crop in the country's history. In part the island's wealth resulted from acts of Parliament that imposed high tariffs on sugar imported into Britain from Cuba, Haiti, Martinique, Guadeloupe, and other areas. The Jamaican planters maintained one of the best-organized political machines in London, lobbying hard and spending great amounts of money to retain the trade barriers that kept sugar prices artificially high in England. Adding to the wealth was coffee; in 1814 the island exported a record crop.

After Nelson defeated Napoléon at Trafalgar in 1805, the huge sums expended by Jamaica to defend against French raiders decreased dramatically. At the same time, Jamaica's role as a depot for smuggling contraband British goods to Cuba and Spanish colonies of South America also diminished. Within 20 years the island's economy worsened considerably, signaling an end to a great era of Jamaican prosperity.

SLAVERY & PROSPERITY END   After the United States became independent in 1776, Britain imposed an embargo on U.S. products and cut off trade between North America's eastern seaboard and Jamaica, a condition that caused great hardship throughout the island.

Adding to Jamaica's woes was increasing popular sentiment in Britain against the slave trade. The importation of forced laborers from Africa was outlawed in 1807, and in 1838 slavery itself was made illegal in all British dependencies, including Jamaica. Parliament voted £20 million to compensate the slaveowners. Partly because of Jamaica's influence in Parliament, almost £6 million of that money was designated for the island's slaveowners. Freed blacks celebrated throughout Jamaica, with credit for the legislation going (rightly or wrongly) to Queen Victoria.

The problem now arose of finding workers for the labor-intensive sugar plantations. Planters offered blacks only low wages (about 9 pence a day) for the difficult labor, and in addition many former enslaved persons refused to work under any circumstances for their former owners. As a result, the large sugar industry declined.

The Jamaica Railway opened in 1845, having been built by inexpensive laborers from India. Any benefits the line might have offered the sugar planters, however, was quickly undercut by passage in 1847 of the Free Trade Act. Designed to encourage untaxed trade in the British Empire, the act removed the protection enjoyed by Jamaican sugar in Britain, placing it on even par with the plentiful, cheap sugar produced in other parts of the Caribbean.

Between 1850 and 1852 epidemics of Asian cholera and smallpox ripped through the island's overcrowded shantytowns, whose sanitation facilities were minimal. More than 32,000 people died from the maladies brought from other parts of the British Empire. At the same time, Jamaica suffered from an exodus of creative entrepreneurs, a lack of funds to run the government, and a continuing decline of the agricultural base. The island's work force vehemently protested low wages and competition from cheap labor brought in from British dependencies in India and China.

REVOLTS & REFORMS   As a result of the American Civil War fought between 1861 and 1865, many vital shipments formerly brought to Jamaica from North America were blocked or rendered very expensive. During this period, the lieutenant governor of the colony, at odds as usual with both planters and laborers, publicly described the colony as "in a state of degeneration." Labor unrest, attempts by blacks to overturn the government, and interference in Jamaican affairs by committees of English Baptists and London-based liberals plagued the planters. In 1866, Jamaican laborers mounted an extremely bloody revolt, which was put down by English troops. Many changes were initiated thereafter, however, including the recall of the very unpopular lieutenant governor of the island. Eventually, a more liberal form of government emerged, and island residents had a larger voice in Jamaican affairs. The police and judicial systems were reorganized into a fairer system directly responsible to the British Crown, rather than to local potentates who had often abused their power. Also, administrative divisions of the island's parishes were changed and their numbers reduced.

Meanwhile, telegraph communication with Europe was established in 1869, the Jamaica Railway was extended, and nickel coins, guaranteed by the Bank of England, were issued for the first time. The educational system was improved, great irrigation works were initiated, and the dependency became known for the enlightened application of British ways. Hurricanes seemed to demolish parts of the island at regular intervals, however, and the power struggle between British authorities in London and local administrators in Kingston went on.

British tourism to Jamaica began in the 1890s, and a quintet of hotels was built to house the administrators and investors who showed keen interest in developing the island's fertile land. A Lands Department was organized to sell government-held land to local farmers cheaply and on easy terms. The island's teachers were organized into unions, and the railroad was extended to Jamaica's northeast tip at Port Antonio. New bridges and improved roads also helped open the island. Frustrated by low sugar prices, Jamaican planters invested heavily in the production of bananas.

On January 14, 1907, another great earthquake shattered much of the city of Kingston, destroying or damaging just about every building. More than 800 lives were lost, and total damage was estimated at £2 million. It seemed to be a repeat of the earthquake that had shattered Port Royal 215 years earlier. Parliament and the

Impressions

Jamaica, an island then considered as one of the most unhealthy in the West Indies, or in the world.

—William Hickey, *Memoirs*, 1749–1809

Church of England sent massive funds to rebuild Kingston. The new street plan remains the basis for the city's layout today.

JAMAICA IN THE WORLD WARS   During World War I, Jamaica sent about 10,000 men to fight with British forces. They were eventually deployed in Palestine, where they battled heroically against the Ottoman Empire. Many ships used in peacetime to export Jamaican agricultural products were commandeered for use in European waters. Martial law was imposed on Jamaica, and local volunteers were organized to defend the island from attack. In 1915, 1916, and 1917 the war effort was complicated by hurricanes that devastated the island's banana crop. But some progress was made: In May 1917, Jamaican women were given the right to vote.

In 1936, George V died, and the British throne passed to his son, known as Edward VIII. The scandal that erupted regarding Edward's abdication and subsequent marriage to an American divorcée, Wallis Warfield Simpson, drew residents of Jamaica into the general consternation surrounding the affair. Within six months of the abdication, Edward's younger brother was crowned as George VI. News of events reached Jamaica via the island's first overseas telephone link, which in 1936 connected the island to England, Mexico, Cuba, Canada, and the United States.

In 1938, Alexander Bustamante organized Jamaica's first officially recognized labor union. At first imprisoned but later freed and knighted by the British, he is today regarded as a founder of modern Jamaica.

At the outbreak of World War II in 1939, Jamaica was placed under rigid control, and the governor set prices and censored the press, the telephones, the telegraph, and international mail. In 1940, the United States was granted the right to establish army and navy bases in British territories, including Jamaica, where two bases were quickly built. By 1943, many Jamaicans had moved to the United States to work in munitions factories. In the same year, bauxite, the raw material for making much-needed aluminum, was mined for the first time in St. Ann Parish. The next year a new constitution provided for universal adult suffrage.

In 1947, after the war, Jamaica served as the meeting place for discussions concerning the amalgamation of English-speaking lands of the Caribbean area into a single political unit. The countries sending representatives to the meetings included Barbados, Trinidad and Tobago, the Leeward Islands, the Windward Islands, British Guiana (now Guyana), and British Honduras (now Belize). The union never developed fully, however, mainly because of political infighting and local attachments.

FREEDOM ARRIVES   In 1950, newly formed Radio Jamaica Ltd. (RJR) provided an outlet for the ideologies rapidly being shaped in Jamaica.

In 1951 the worst hurricane in almost 100 years completely demolished Port Royal for the third time. No serious attempt was made thereafter to rebuild the city, which had played a vital part in developing Jamaica.

In 1952, Elizabeth II became the British monarch, an event much celebrated in Jamaica. A year later she paid a very successful state visit to the island on her way to Australia. Her sister, Princess Margaret, visited for a longer period in 1955 to celebrate the 300th anniversary of British influence in Jamaica. The island became known as a stylish place for a midwinter vacation in the British Empire. Meanwhile, cement production began, and quickly grew substantially.

In 1957, Jamaica attained full internal self-government under a system based on well-established English models. Lengthy celebrations marked the event. The same year, nearly 17,000 Jamaicans emigrated to England to find work because the island's economy was not growing as fast as the population. Concurrently, bauxite and alumina (processed bauxite) exports surged, and the government demanded and received a higher percentage of profits from the mining companies. With the advent of the intercontinental jet airliner, Jamaica's tourist industry also expanded at this time, and hotels were built to accommodate visitors from North America and Europe.

After the rise to power in 1959 of Fidel Castro, Jamaica cut many ties with Cuba, and established trade and cultural links with other islands, especially Puerto Rico. In 1959, Montego Bay airport was opened, and Kingston airport was expanded to handle the flood of visitors. Despite economic growth, however, large-scale emigration to Great Britain continued.

In 1961, Jamaica withdrew from the Federation of the West Indies, which had been formed in 1958, after Jamaicans voted to seek independence as a separate nation. The next year, on August 6, Jamaica achieved its independence, although still recognizing the British monarch as the formal head of state and maintaining other ties as a member of the Commonwealth of Nations. Sir Alexander Bustamante, head of the Jamaica Labour Party (JLP), became the country's first prime minister. Also in 1962, the Royal Hampshire Regiment—the last British troops in Jamaica—departed the island, thus ending the colonial era begun in 1655.

RECENT TIMES   In 1966, Haile Selassie I, emperor of Ethiopia, came to Jamaica on a three-day state visit. The stay sparked national interest in the emperor's life, and as a result there was a notable increase in Jamaican converts to Rastafarianism, a religion that venerates the late emperor, known earlier as Ras Tafari (see "Rastafarianism" later in this chapter). During the 1970s, the popularity of Rastafarian musician Bob Marley and other Jamaican reggae performers spread around the world, giving the country an important role on the international music stage.

In 1972, Michael Manley, a trade unionist who headed the left-wing People's National Party (PNP), was sworn in for the first of what would eventually be several terms as Jamaica's prime minister. For many historians, this marked the beginning of full-scale ideological battles for the heart and soul of the Jamaican people. Jamaicans argued vehemently over whether the young nation should embrace socialism and over its relationship with the United States. A noteworthy event of Manley's Democratic Socialism occurred in 1977, when Cuban President Fidel Castro paid a six-day official visit to Jamaica, which led to a perception in Washington that Jamaican politics was increasingly shifting leftward. Despite Manley's political prowess, the months leading up to the 1980 elections were particularly violent, with episodes of civil disobedience and numerous deaths on both sides. The elections were won by the moderate, free-enterprise JLP, led by relatively conservative Edward Seaga, who became prime minister. Shortly afterward, Jamaica broke diplomatic ties with Cuba. Seaga's mandate was solidified in the 1983 elections, which the PNP claimed were unfairly run. Seaga attempted to promote economic growth and cut inflation, but with little success. Unemployment rose, as did violent crime.

In September 1988, the island was devastated by Hurricane Gilbert, which destroyed some 100,000 homes.

A much more moderate Manley returned to power in 1989. This time he sought friendly ties with the United States.

In the early 1990s Jamaica continued to face daunting economic difficulties, as unemployment hovered near 18% of the work force. In Kingston there was gang violence, some reputedly tied to the country's main political parties. Tourism boomed, however, with some one million vacationers visiting the island each year. Manley retired in 1992 due to ill health and was succeeded by an associate, Percival J. Patterson, also a moderate. Patterson was confirmed in office when his PNP won 53 of 60 seats in the House of Representatives in elections in March 1993.

5 The Jamaican People & Their Culture

Jamaica's 2.5 million people form a spectrum of types that bespeak the island's heritage. About 75% of the people are classified as black African and about 15% as Afro-European, but there are also people of Chinese, Asian Indian, Middle Eastern, and European background.

Jamaicans are above all friendly, funny, opinionated, talented, and almost impossible to forget. Their sense of humor is dry and understated but robust and physical; one makes fun of oneself and others. It is also both subtle and direct. National pride is specific—beating the English at cricket, winning gold medals in the Olympics, or attaining world boxing titles. Individuals take pride in outstandingly bright and successful family members, a new house, a successful business, and the ability to survive, not easy in some urban slums.

To grow sugarcane, the English colonialists brought in African slaves. Most came from the west coast of Africa, notably the area of modern Ghana, and belonged to the Fanti and Ashanti ethnic groups. Others are descended from the Ibo and Yoruba people of present-day Nigeria. When the slaves were freed in 1838, most deserted the plantations and settled in the hills to cultivate small plots of land. They founded a peasantry that is still regarded as the backbone of Jamaica.

After slavery was abolished, the English brought in Chinese and later East Indians as indentured laborers for the plantations. When the English came, the Spaniards fled to neighboring islands, and their slaves escaped into the mountains and formed the independent groups called Maroons.

Jews are among the oldest residents of Jamaica. Some Jewish families have been here from the time of the earliest Spanish settlements. Although small in number (about 400), the Jewish community has been influential in government and commerce.

ART

Jamaica has produced many artists since the prehistoric Arawak first inscribed interiors of the island's caves with petroglyphs. Although its artistic production is less renowned than neighboring Haiti's, Jamaica nonetheless is considered a Caribbean art capital, with a vibrant tradition ranging from street art to formal canvases that receive acclaim in chic galleries of London and New York. Jamaican art tends to be

Impressions

We had, close to over our port now, the most beautiful island in the world. It is useless to deny it, and to declare you know a better island.

—H. M. Tomlinson, *The Sea and the Jungle,* 1912

less stylized than Haiti's, less uniform in its assumptions, and more broadly based on a wide array of differing philosophical traditions. The bulk of Jamaican artwork has been executed since 1940, when the yearning for independence and a sense of national destiny colored many aspects of the country's life. Whereas reggae, the national musical form, is strongly influenced by a subculture (the Rastafarians), Jamaican painting is much wider ranging and diverse.

The most easily accessible Jamaican artwork is "yard art," which rises from the concrete, litter, and poverty of the island's cities. Punctuated with solid blocks of vivid color, and sometimes interspersed with graffiti, these murals are often viewed as an authentic reflection of the Jamaican soul. Subjects include political satire, naïve (or intuitive) depictions of an artist's friends and family, idealized Jamaican landscapes, and kaleidoscopic visions of heaven and hell. Examples of yard art seem to increase, along with graffiti and political slogans, before each election. Predictably, however, a flood of uninspired wood carving, handcrafts, and banal painting has appeared in recent years because of worldwide commercial and sociological interest in yard art. *Caveat emptor:* buyer beware.

Much yard art is a legacy of a group of self-taught intuitive artists (sometimes known as "primitives") who rose to fame in the 19th century. Most famous was John Dunkley (b. 1881), a Kingston barber, whose spare time was devoted almost entirely to covering the walls, ceilings, and furniture of his shop with flowers, vines, trees, and abstract symbols that a psychologist might describe as Jungian. Although his painting was scorned by mainstream art critics during his lifetime, it survives as the most sought-after—and among the most expensive—artwork in the Caribbean today. Jamaican artists who followed Dunkley's lead include Mallica Reynolds, Gaston Tabois, Allan Zion, and Sydney McLaren.

Despite the artistic merits of these painters, it required the organizational efforts of Edna Manley, wife and mother of two of Jamaica's prime ministers and an acclaimed sculptor in her own right, to foster the development of Jamaican art. Beginning around 1940, she encouraged self-taught artists and organized art classes at the Institute of Jamaica, thereby inspiring islanders to view local artwork in a more respectful way.

Jamaican nationalists view as pivotal the day in 1939 when a group of about 40 highly politicized artists stormed the annual meeting of the Institute of Jamaica, then the island's most visible art museum. Demanding freedom from the domination of Jamaican art by European aesthetics, the nationalists insisted that the English-inspired portraits of the colonial age be replaced in galleries by works of Jamaica's artists. In response, Edna Manley and some volunteers started a series of informal art lessons, which in 1950 blossomed into the Jamaican School of Art and, several years later, the Cultural Training Centre. Based in Kingston, these two schools have trained many of Jamaica's established artists, dancers, and actors.

Today, Jamaica's leading painters include Carl Abrahams, whose recurrent theme is the Last Supper; Barrington Watson, known for a romanticized, charming view of the Jamaican people; Eugene Hyde, one of the country's first modern abstract artists; and English-born Jonathon Routh, whose illustrations of Queen Victoria during elaborate state visits to Jamaica—none of which really occurred—provoke laughter as far away as London. Also noteworthy are Christopher Gonzalez, who won a commission by the Jamaican government for a statue of reggae superstar Bob Marley; David Boxer, one of the first Jamaican surrealists; and Osmond Watson, known for his sharp-angled and absorbing depictions of the human face.

A discussion of Jamaican art would not be complete without mentioning the rich tradition of art left by the colonial English and wealthy planters. The earliest published illustrations of Jamaica include the Spillsbury prints, which show in subtle detail the harbors and fine Georgian buildings of 18th-century Jamaica. English-born Philip Wickstead painted portraits of the island's wealthiest families. George Robertson, following in the great tradition of English landscape painting exemplified by John Constable, depicted the lush forests and sugarcane fields of Jamaica during the peak of their commercial prosperity.

Other artists, some white and itinerant, captured the charm and sorrow of 19th-century Jamaica. Isaac Mendes Belisario, an English-born Jew whose family stemmed from Italy, set up a studio in Kingston and produced portraits of enslaved persons and sketches of carnivals and musical parades. Scottish-born Joseph Bartholomew Kidd executed finely detailed sketches of Kingston buildings and the homes of wealthy planters. Also noteworthy are statues erected by the British in honor of military heroes, among the finest in the Caribbean. A good example is the Rodney Memorial Statue, by John Bacon Sr., in the heart of Spanish Town.

More scandalous, and perhaps more famous, are the Jamaica-inspired works produced during the 18th century by William Hogarth, whose reputation as a satirist had already been assured by the publication and wide distribution of a series of engravings entitled *A Harlot's Progress.* Equally ribald was Hogarth's series entitled *The Sugar Planter, at Home and Abroad.* Savagely satirical, the engravings showed a grossly bloated planter alternately whipping forced laborers and hoarding gold, while surrounded by his mulatto children. In the same series, a better-behaved London incarnation of the planter is shown dressed in urban finery entertaining the peerage, manipulating votes in Parliament, and smiling benignly as lines of impoverished English housewives pay artificially inflated prices for his sugar. The release of this effective series was carefully timed to coincide with popular movements in Parliament to curtail price-fixing by Jamaica sugar barons.

ARCHITECTURE

The colonization of Jamaica occurred during a great period of British expansion. Much effort was expended in displaying the cultural allegiance of Jamaican planters to their native England, and one of the most obvious methods of doing so was to adapt the contemporary architectural motifs of Britain to the tropics. Partly because of a desire to protect their political prerogatives in Parliament, Jamaican planters returned to England frequently, maintaining their political links with Parliament, their investments, their social status, and an elevated price for sugar, which had made them rich. The obsession of Jamaican planters with contemporary English taste helped create an architectural elegance rivaled by only a handful of other English colonies, notably Pennsylvania, Massachusetts, and Barbados. Although the island style began with an allegiance to Georgian models, concessions were made to the heat, humidity, bugs, hurricanes, and earthquakes of the tropics. Later, after Jamaica became recognized as the leading outpost of English military power and agrarian skill in the West Indies, Jamaican architectural principles spread to other parts of the Caribbean.

Georgian-type design, manifest in Jamaica's port facilities, Customs houses, and civic buildings, was most graceful in the island's many great houses. Intended as centerpieces for enormous sugar plantations, these buildings include some of the finest examples of domestic architecture in the West Indies. Among common design elements are wide verandas on at least two sides, balustrades, intricate fretwork, sophisticated applications of contrasting types of lattice, deep and sometimes ornate fascia boards, and a prevalence of pineapple-shaped finials above cornices and rooflines (the pineapple was the sign of hospitality throughout the British Empire).

Individual houses varied with the personality of the architects and the wealth and taste of the owners. Unlike great houses in other English-speaking Caribbean islands, the first floors of Jamaican buildings were usually elevated by low stilts or pilings to allow air to circulate underneath. This prevented rot, cooled the ground floor, and helped keep rats, snakes, insects, and scorpions out of living quarters. Jamaican masonry and wood pilings are radically different from showplace buildings on St. Kitts, for example, where lower foundations were usually crafted from massive bulwarks of stone.

Not all of Jamaica's 18th-century buildings were designed along Georgian lines. Smaller, less pretentious houses were built in styles appropriate to the income of the owners and demands of the sites. Jamaican vernacular architectural style was developed by tenant farmers and indentured servants, many from Scotland, and by the children of freed slaves. These houses usually were positioned to take advantage of the prevailing trade winds, and typically were angled to prevent smoke from the kitchen from blowing into living quarters. Known for the pleasing proportions of their inner spaces, the buildings continue to surprise contemporary architectural critics by their appropriate placement and convenient interior traffic patterns.

Noteworthy on virtually all Jamaican houses is the technique of attaching porch roofs and verandas to the main body of the house. In the hurricane-prone area, an experienced carpenter would deliberately not interconnect the beams of a porch with the beams supporting the main roof of the house. Because of their tendency to be destroyed during hurricane-strength wind gusts, porch roofs were usually built as separate, loosely attached architectural adornments not considered vital to the building's main core. Roofs were covered with split mahogany shingles until the 1930s, when Canadian cedar shingles became readily available. In the English tradition, gardens were usually considered important adjuncts to the great house. Altogether, Jamaican houses were graceful reflections of the good life, with only one major drawback: Their easy destruction by fire.

Since the end of World War II, architecture in Jamaica has followed two distinct variations on colonial themes. Banks, civic buildings, and commercial structures have generally been inspired by the thick walls, small windows, and massive dignity of the island's 18th- and 19th-century English forts. Hotels and private dwellings, on the other hand, typically trace their inspiration to the island's great houses or to the unpretentious wooden cottages that still dot the landscape. Other commercial buildings were inspired by the International Style that swept over most of the industrialized world between 1945 and 1980.

Jamaica today boasts an important contingent of locally born architects trained in the United States or Canada. The dean of Jamaican architects, Vayden McMorris, whose practice began in the mid-1950s, is credited with nurturing Jamaica's young architects. McMorris designed such New Kingston towers as the Panjam Building, the Citibank Building, the Doyall Building, and the Victoria Mutual Building Society's head office.

Wilson Chong, a Jamaican of Chinese descent, is responsible for the design of one of Jamaica's most-visited buildings, the football (soccer) stadium. Viewed as a master of the shell-shaped concrete curve, Chong flourished in the 1960s. A dramatic but rarely visited Chong design is the grandstand of Marley Racetrack, whose triple cantilever is considered an engineering marvel. The racetrack, located some 23 miles west of Kingston, has not been operated for several years.

Another bright star among Jamaican architects is H. Denny Repol, whose firm designed about a dozen major hotels on the north shore. Repol also designed in the

1980s the administrative headquarters of the Jamaica Tourist Board (21 Dominica Drive, in Kingston), considered a model version of the "work-related open space." Another Repol commission is the Life of Jamaica Head Office Building, whose four floors of reinforced concrete shelter a sun-flooded atrium spanned with a bridge and thousands of verdant plants.

DANCE & DRAMA

A sense of drama and theatrics is innate to the Jamaican character, as shown in the easy laughter, irreverent humor, and loose-limbed style that are the island's pride and joy. In Kingston in particular, everyone is a star, if only for a moment, during one or another of any day's interpersonal exchanges.

The natural flair of Jamaicans has been channeled into many different drama and dance groups. One of the most visible is the National Dance Theatre Company (NDTC), whose goal is to assemble a body of dancers, actors, and singers to express and explore the Jamaican sense of stylized movement. Applauded by audiences around the world, the company offers abstract interpretations of the Jamaican experience, going far beyond the priorities of a purely folkloric dance troupe. Members are mostly volunteers (lawyers, secretaries, laborers, and nurses by day, highly motivated performers by night), and the troupe has usually refused to accept funds from the government. Among the troupe's most famous performers are cofounder and dancer Rex Nettleford, and Louise Bennett, pantomime artist and storyteller, and an early proponent of Jamaican patois as a literary language. Established in 1962, NDTC holds a season running from July to December, with most performances in August. It performs at several locations so you'll need to inquire about where to attend on a particular day.

Jamaica also supports dozens of smaller theater companies, dance troupes, pantomime artists, and raconteurs of folktales. Most performances are in Kingston, but a few are in high school auditoriums, town halls, and churches scattered throughout the island. Also noteworthy are nightclub singers and reggae bands that offer performance-related flair, plus the many street musicians who play on the sidewalks of downtown Montego Bay every weekend throughout much of the summer.

A local newspaper or a hotel receptionist can usually give you an idea of the drama and dance performances offered in the area.

LANGUAGE

The official language of Jamaica is English, but the unofficial language is a patois. Linguists and a handful of Jamaican novelists have recently transformed this oral language into written form, although for most Jamaicans it remains solely spoken—and richly nuanced. Experts say that more than 90% of its vocabulary is derived from English, with the remaining words largely borrowed from African languages. There are also words taken from Spanish, Arawak, French, Chinese, Portuguese, and East Indian languages.

Although pronounced similarly to standard English, the patois preserves many 17th- and 18th-century expressions in common use during the time of early British colonial settlement of Jamaica. This archaic and simplified structure, coupled with African accents and special intonation, can make the language difficult to understand. Some linguists consider it a separate language, whereas others view it as just an alternate form of English. Some of the most interesting anecdotes and fables in the Caribbean are usually told in the patois, so understanding its structure can add to your insight into Jamaican culture.

Proverbs and place-names express some of the vitality of Jamaican language. For "Mind you own business," there is "Cockroach no business in fowl-yard." For being corrupted by bad companions, "You lay wid dawg, you get wid fleas." And for the pretentious, "The higher monkey climb, the more him expose." Both British and biblical place-names abound in Jamaica. Examples include Somerset and Siloah, Highgate and Horeb. One also sees Arawak names like Linguanea, Spanish ones like Oracabessa, Scottish names like Rest-and-Be-Thankful, and entirely Jamaican names like Red Gal Ring.

A final note: The patois has been embellished and altered with the growth of Rastafarianism. Rastas have injected several grammatical concepts, one of the most apparent being the repeated use of "I"—a reminder of their reverence of Ras Tafar *i*. "I" is almost always substituted for the pronoun "me." It is also substituted for many prefixes or initial syllables. Thus, "all right," becomes "I're," "brethren" becomes "Idren," and "praises" becomes "Ises." The Rastafarian changes of Jamaica's patois are a recent phenomenon, and have not always been adopted by non-Rastas.

6 From Anansi to Rasta

Nothing shaped the modern culture of the Caribbean more than the arrival of slaves from various parts of Africa. They brought gods, beliefs, superstitions, and fears with them. Although later converted to Christianity, they kept their traditions vibrant in fairs and festivals. Jamaican cultural and social life revolved mostly around the church, which was instrumental in molding a sense of community. Storytellers helped maintain ties to the past for each new generation, since little was written down until the 20th century. Since the advent of television, however, Jamaicans rarely gather to hear stories of the old days.

FOLKLORE

The folklore and ancient oral traditions of Jamaicans have fascinated English colonizers as well as modern-day visitors searching for a pattern to the mysticism that sometimes seems to pervade the countryside. Oral tradition forms a powerful undercurrent in this devoutly religious island; many folk beliefs were brought from Africa by slaves during the 17th and 18th centuries. Despite the later impact of Christian missionaries, a strong belief in magic remains, as does a wide array of superstitions.

Some folk beliefs are expressed in music, notably in the lyrics of reggae. Others are expressed in rhythmic chanting, whose stresses and moods once accompanied both hard labor and dancing. Other beliefs can be found in fairy tales and in legends concerning the island's slaves and their owners. The telling of oral narrations is considered a highly nuanced art form. Repetition and an inspired use of patois are important features.

Healing arts make use of Jamaican tradition, especially in the "balm yard," a herb garden-cum-healing place where a mixture of religion and magic is applied by a doctor or "balmist" of either sex. Some medicines brewed, distilled, or fermented in the yard are derived from recipes handed down for many generations, and can be effective against ailments ranging from infertility to skin disease. A balm yard is usually encircled by a half-dozen thatch-covered huts, which house supplicants (patients). Bright red flags fly above each hut to chase away evil spirits. Ceremonies resembling revival meetings are held nightly, with a "mother" and a "father" urging the crowd to groan ecstatically and in unison. The threat of damnation in hellfire may be mentioned as punishment for anyone who doesn't groan loudly enough or believe fervently enough. Prayer and supplications to Jesus and various good and evil spirits will help relieve the sick of their ailments, it is believed.

The two most famous spirits of Jamaica are Obeah and the jumbie. Originating in the southern Caribbean, Obeah is a superstitious force that believers hold responsible for both good and evil. It is considered prudent not to tangle with this force, which might make trouble for you. Because of a long-established awareness of Obeah, and an unwillingness to tempt it with too positive an answer, a Jamaican is likely to answer "Not too bad" if asked about his or her health.

There is no agreement on the nature of a jumbie. It's been suggested that it is the spirit of a dead person that didn't go where it belonged. Some islanders, however, say that "they're the souls of live people, who live in the bodies of the dead." Jumbies are said to inhabit households and to possess equal capacities for good and evil. Most prominent are Mocko Jumbies, carnival stilt-walkers seen in parades.

One folk tradition that can while away hours of a Jamaican's time is reciting Anansi stories. Such narration is an authentic performing art, which celebrates the nuances of Jamaican patois as well as the cunning, or lack thereof, of the stories' protagonists. Partly reflecting the tellers, the richly funny stories can include repeated key phrases whose rhythms add dramatic effect. Some stories concern Anansi, the spider-man. Like ancient Greeks, Africans invested the spider with human characteristics and intelligence. Whereas the Greeks linked the spider with Arachne, who taught humans to weave and spin, Africans emphasized the wiles and craft of a poisonous and vaguely repulsive eight-legged animal. By the time the tradition reached Jamaica, the spider had become a spider-man, and had been given both a name (Anansi) and a distinctive personality.

A notorious trickster, with a distinctly Jamaican humor, Anansi manipulates those around him and eventually acquires whatever spoils happen to be available. In one well-known story, Anansi steals sheep from a nearby plantation; in another, he pilfers half of every other person's plantain. Among the funniest are episodes in which Anansi exposes the indiscretions of an Anglican priest. Anansi's traits include a lisp, a potent sense of greed, and a tendency to be wicked. The stories are sometimes funny, sometimes poignant, sometimes sexually suggestive. They often are parables, teaching a basic lesson about life. Each narrative has a well-defined and often charming ending, which tends to be followed by an explosion of laughter from the storyteller. Several collections of Anansi stories have been published.

A discussion on Jamaican folklore would be incomplete without citing the many tales involving notorious figures from Jamaica's history. Examples include the legend of the sexually insatiable Annie Palmer, the sadistic "white witch" of Rose Hall. Also popular are biographical narratives about Cudjoe, the Ashanti leader of the island's biggest revolt of enslaved persons, and the French Huguenot who was buried twice. The Huguenot was swallowed by an earthquake during the destruction of Port Royal in 1692, but within a few moments was spewed from the earth and lived for many happy years before dying a natural death and receiving a proper burial.

RELIGION

Religion is an important force in Jamaica; so is religious tolerance. The vast majority of Jamaicans are Christian, but there are communities of Jews, Hindus, and Muslims. The Church of God in Jamaica has the largest membership, about 400,000 in the 1980s. Other Christian groups with large memberships include the Baptist Union, Anglicans, Seventh-day Adventists, Pentecostals, Roman Catholics, and Methodists. There are also some Quakers, Moravians, and Christian Scientists.

However, the one religion in Jamaica that has sparked world interest is **Rastafarianism.**

Although relatively small in number (it had about 14,000 firm adherents in the early 1980s), Rastafarians have had much influence on Jamaican culture. Their identifying dreadlocks (long, sometimes braided, hair) can now be seen at virtually every level of Jamaican society.

To understand the origins of Rastafarianism, it's necessary to introduce Marcus Garvey. Born in 1887 in Jamaica's St. Ann Parish, Garvey did much to build black pride in the United States as well as in the West Indies. To combat the vast cultural upheavals wrought by slavery, Garvey founded the Universal Negro Improvement Association (UNIA) to raise the consciousness of blacks about a diaspora unmatched since the scattering of the Jews. Advocating a "back to Africa" kind of self-reliance, he aroused the loyalty of blacks and the hostility of whites. Garvey died in London in 1940, almost forgotten, but his body was later returned to Jamaica, where he received a hero's burial.

None of the power of Garvey, however, could match the later revival of African consciousness by the Rastafarians. Stressing the continuity of black African culture throughout history, Rastas believe in their direct spiritual descent from King Solomon's liaison with the queen of Sheba. Rastafarianism, according to some, is based on an intuitive interpretation of history and scripture—sometimes with broad brush strokes—with special emphasis on the reading of Old Testament prophecies. Rastafarians stress contemplation, meditation, a willingness to work inwardly to the "I" (inner divinity), and an abstractly political bent. Their assumptions are enhanced through sacramental rites of ganja (marijuana) smoking, Bible reading (with particular stress on references to Ethiopia), music, physical exercise, art, poetry, and cottage industries like handcrafts and broom making. Reggae music developed from Rasta circles and produced such international stars as the fervently religious Bob Marley. Jamaica's politicians, aware of the allure of Rastafarianism, often pay homage to its beliefs.

A male Rastafarian's beard is a sign of his pact with God (Jah or Jehovah), and his Bible is his source of knowledge. His dreadlocks are a symbol of his link with the Lion of Judah and Elect of God, the late Emperor of Ethiopia Haile Selassie, who while a prince was known as Ras Tafari (hence the religion's name.) During the emperor's 1966 visit to Jamaica, more than 100,000 visitors greeted his airplane in something approaching religious ecstasy. The visit almost completely eclipsed Queen Elizabeth's a few months earlier. Rastas believe Haile Selassie to be their personal savior.

7 Calypso, Reggae & Rap: The Rhythms of Jamaica

Swaying palms, silvery moonlight, and walks beside the murmuring ocean are not the only nighttime pleasures on the island—there's also a wide array of musical and social diversions.

Responding to the wishes of guests, almost every large and medium-sized hotel in Jamaica offers nighttime floor shows and reggae music. Music usually begins after the dinner hour, and might include the visual distractions of limbo dancers, fire-eaters, and other entertainment.

Many people visit Jamaica just to hear its authentic reggae. Reggae is now known around the world and recognized in the annual Grammy awards run by the U.S. music industry.

The roots of Jamaica's unique reggae music can be found in an early form of Jamaican music called **mento.** This music was brought to the island by African slaves, who played it to help forget their anguish. Mento is reminiscent of the rhythm and blues that in the mid-20th century swept across North America. It was usually accompanied by hip-rolling dances known as dubbing, with highly suggestive lyrics to match. Famous Jamaican mento groups reaching their prime in the 1950s included the Ticklers and the Pork Chops Rhumba Box Band of Montego Bay.

In the late 1950s, Jamaican musicians combined boogie-woogie with rhythm and blues to form a short-lived but vibrant music named **ska.** Jamaican artists in this form included Don Drummond, Roland Alphanso, Lloyd Knibbs, Theophilus Beckford, and Cluet Johnson. The five often played together during a vital chapter in Jamaica's musical history. It was the politicization of ska by Rastafarians that led to the creation of reggae.

CALYPSO

No analysis of Jamaican music would be complete without the inclusion of Jamaican-born musician, actor, and political activist Harry Belafonte. Recognizable to more North American and British listeners than any other Jamaican singer in the 1950s and early '60s, he became famous for his version of the island's unofficial anthem, "Jamaica Farewell," in which the singer leaves a little girl in Kingston Town. Although he worked in other musical forms, Belafonte is particularly known for his smooth and infectious calypsos. *Note:* Some purists point out that calypso is really a product of Trinidad, but it remains very popular in Jamaica (and Barbados).

REGGAE

Sometimes referred to as the heartbeat of Jamaica, reggae is the island's most distinctive musical form, as closely linked to Jamaica as soul is to Detroit, jazz to New Orleans, and blues to Chicago. The term reggae is best defined as "coming from the people." It is taken from a song written and performed in the late 1960s by Jamaica-born "Toots" Hibbert and the Maytals ("Do the Reggay"). With a beat some fans claim is narcotic, it has crossed political and racial lines and temporarily drained the hostilities of thousands of listeners, injecting a new kind of life into their pelvises, knees, fingertips, and buttocks. It has influenced the music of international stars like the Rolling Stones, Eric Clapton, Paul Simon, the B-52s, Stevie Wonder, Elton John, and Third World as well as lesser-known acts like Uhuru, Chicago's Blue Riddim Band, and rap groups. Most notably, it propelled onto the world scene a street-smart kid from Kingston named Bob Marley. Today, the recording studios of Kingston, sometimes called "the Nashville of the Third World," churn out hundreds of reggae albums every year, many snapped up by danceaholics in Los Angeles, Italy, and Japan.

Reggae's earliest roots lie in the African musical tradition of mento. Later, the rhythms and body movements of mento were combined with an improvised interpretation of the then-fashionable French quadrille to create the distinctive hip-rolling and lower-body contact known as **dubbing.** Lyrics became increasingly suggestive (some say salacious) and playful as the musical form gained confidence and a body of devoted adherents.

In the 1950s calypso entered Jamaica from the southern Caribbean, especially Trinidad, whereas rhythm and blues and rock 'n' roll were imported from the United States. Both melded with mento into a danceable mixture that drew islanders into beer and dance halls throughout Jamaica. This music led to the powerful but short-lived form called ska, made famous by the Skatalites, who peaked in the mid-1960s. When their leader and trombonist, Drummond, became a highly politicized convert to Rastafarianism, other musicians followed and altered their rhythms to reflect the

Ganja

Marijuana use is the island's biggest open secret, and you'll no doubt encounter it during your vacation. (To be honest, it's the big draw for some visitors.) Vendors seem to hawk it at random, often through the chain-link fences surrounding popular resorts.

Ganja is viewed with differing degrees of severity in Jamaican society, but it's still officially illegal. We should warn you that possession can lead to immediate imprisonment and/or deportation.

Marijuana and Jamaica have long endured a love/hate relationship. The plant was brought here by indentured servants from India in the mid-19th century. Revered by them as a medicinal and sacred plant, and referred to by the British as "Indian hemp," it quickly attracted the attention of the island's plantation owners because its use significantly reduced the productivity of those who ingested it. Legislation against its use quickly followed—not for moral or ethical reasons, but because it was bad for business.

During the 1930s, the slow rise of Rastafarianism (whose adherents believe marijuana use is an essential part of their religion) and the occasional use of marijuana by U.S. bohemians, artists, and jazz musicians led to a growing export of the plant to the United States. A massive increase in U.S. consumption occurred during the 1960s. Since the mid-1970s, after more stringent patrols were instituted along the U.S.–Mexico border, it is estimated that between 75% and 95% of all marijuana grown in Jamaica is consumed in the United States.

Cultivation of the crop, when conducted on the typical large scale, is as meticulous and thorough as that of any horticulturist raising a prize species of tomato or rose. Sold illegally by the quart, seeds must first be coaxed into seedlings in a greenhouse, then transplanted into fields at 2-foot intervals. Popular lore claims that the most prolific seedlings are raised in Jamaica's red, bauxite-rich soil and nurtured with all-organic fertilizers such as bat dung or goat droppings. As the plants mature, tattered scarecrows, loud reggae music, fluttering strips of reel-to-reel

African drumbeats known as kumina and burru. This fertile musical tradition, when fused with ripening political movements around 1968, became reggae.

Leading early reggae musicians included Anton Ellis and Delroy Wilson. Later, Bob Marley and (to a lesser degree) Jimmy Cliff propelled reggae to world prominence. Marley's band, the Wailers, included his Kingston friends Peter MacIntosh (later known as Peter Tosh), Junior Brathwaite, and Bunny Livingston (now known as Bunny Wailer). Since the death of Marley in 1981, other famous reggae musicians have included his son Ziggy Marley, Roy Parkes, Winston "Yellowman" Foster, and Roy Shirley. Among noteworthy bands are Third World and The Mighty Diamonds.

One of the most recent adaptations of reggae is **soca,** which is more upbeat and less politicized. Aficionados say that reggae makes you think, but soca makes you *dance.* The music is fun, infectious, and spontaneous—perfect for partying—and often imbued with the humor and wry attitudes of Jamaican urban dwellers. Soca's most visible artists include Byron Lee and the Dragonaires. A skillful entrepreneur and organizer, Lee is the force behind the growing annual Jamaica Carnival, which draws more than 15,000 foreign visitors.

recording tape, and slingshots manned by local laborers are used to fend off the birds that feed off the seeds.

Even more feared than natural predators, however, are the Jamaican police. The constables periodically raid fields and destroy the crop by burning it or spraying it with herbicide.

Marijuana plants reach maturity five to six months after transplanting, often with a height of about 9 1/2 feet. Stalks and stems are then pressed for hash oil; leaves are dried for smoking, baking into pastries, or use in herbal teas. Most seeds are saved for the next planting.

Various types of ganja can be grown in a single field, each identified by names like McConey, Cotton, Burr, Bush, Goat's Horn, Lamb's Breath, and Mad. Bush and Mad are considered the least potent of the crop, whereas the strongest are acknowledged to be Lamb's Breath, Cotton, and Burr. The last three are marketed in the United States under the name of sinsemilla (Spanish for "without seeds"). Rastafarians typically prefer specific types of marijuana, much the way a gastronome might prefer specific types of caviar or red wine. To each his own.

Smuggling of the dried and packaged final product is disconcertingly efficient. A small plane lands at any of the country's hundreds of outlaw airstrips, which are sometimes disguised immediately before and after use by huts and shacks, moved into place by crews of strong-armed men. The planes then wisk away the crop, much of it to Florida. Undoubtedly, in a country with chronically low wages and constant fear of unemployment, the temptation to accept bribes among government officials in both high and low positions runs high.

Now that we have told you all we know about ganja, we remind you again that marijuana is illegal in Jamaica despite its widespread presence and religious use by the Rastas. Above all, don't try to buy a bag and bring it home to the United States—drug-sniffing dogs are employed at the airports, and we don't want you to end your vacation in jail.

RAP

After 1965, the influx of Jamaican immigrants to the potboiling pressures of North America's ghettos had a profound (and sometimes profitable) influence on popular music. Such Jamaican-born stars as Clive Campbell, combining the Jamaican gift for the spoken word with reggae rhythms and high electronic amplification, developed the roots of what eventually became known as rap. Taking on a street-smart adaptation of rhyming couplets, some of which were influenced by Jamaica's rich appreciation of word games and speech patterns, he organized street parties where the music of his groups—Cool DJ Herc, Nigger Twins, and the Herculords—was broadcast to thousands of listeners from van-mounted amplifiers.

Designed to electrify rather than soothe, and reflecting the restlessness of a new generation of Jamaicans bored with the sometimes mind-numbing rhythms of reggae, popular Jamaican music became less awestruck by Rastafarian dogmas, less Afro-centric, and more focused on the urban experiences of ghetto life in New York. Music became harder, simpler, more urban, and more conscious of profit-searching market trends. Dubbed dancehall music, the sounds seemed inspired by the hard edge of survival-related facts of life ("girls, guns, drugs, and crime") on urban streets.

One of the major exponents of the new form is Super Cat (William Maragh), who wears his hair cut short ("bald-head") in deliberate contrast to the dreadlocks sported by the disciples of Marley. The sounds are hard and spare, the lyrics as brutal and cruel as the ghetto that inspires them. Super Cat's competitors include Kris Kross, an Atlanta-based rap duet who affect Jamaican accents and speech patterns, and Shabba Ranks, known for often blatant sexual references and unconcealed black machismo. Whereas Marley during the peak of his reggae appeal sold mainly to young whites, the new sounds appeal mostly to young black audiences who relate to the sense of raw danger evoked by dancehall music's rhythms and lyrics. During some of Shabba Ranks's concerts, audiences in Jamaica have shown their approval by firing gunshots into the air in a gesture known locally as a "salute of honor."

8 A Taste of Jamaica

A visit to Jamaica doesn't mean a diet of just local cuisine. The island's eating establishments employ some of the best chefs in the Caribbean, hailing from the United States and Europe, and they can prepare a sumptuous cuisine of elegant French, continental, and American dishes.

When dining in Jamaica, try some fish, which is often delectable, especially dolphin (the game fish, not the mammal), wahoo, yellowtail, grouper, and red snapper. These fish, when broiled with hot lime sauce as an accompaniment, may represent your most memorable island meals. With no claws and a tail full of sweet-tasting meat, Caribbean lobster is not to be confused with the Maine variety.

Elaborate buffets are often a feature at the major resorts. These buffets display a variety of dishes along with other more standard fare, and they are almost always reasonably priced. Entertainment is often a reggae band. Even if you are not staying at a particular hotel, you can call on any given night and make a reservation to partake of a buffet.

APPETIZERS & SOUPS

Except for soup, appetizers don't loom large in the Jamaican kitchen. The most popular appetizer is *stamp and go*, or saltfish cakes. *Solomon Gundy* is made with pickled shad, herring, and mackerel, and seasoned with onions, hot peppers, and pimiento berries. Many Jamaicans begin their meal by enjoying plantain and banana chips with their drinks.

The most famous soup, pepperpot, is an old Arawak recipe. It is often made with callaloo, okra, kale, pig's tail (or salt beef), coconut meat, yams, scallions, and hot peppers. Another favorite, ackee soup, is made from ackees (usually from a dozen ripe open pods), flavored with a shin of beef or a salted pig's tail. Pumpkin soup is seasoned with salted beef or a salted pig's tail. Red pea soup is also delicious (note that it's actually made with red beans).

Tea in Jamaica can mean any nonalcoholic drink, and fish tea, a legacy of plantation days, is made with fish heads or bony fish, along with green bananas, tomatoes, scallions, and hot pepper and other spices.

MAIN COURSES & SIDE DISHES

Because Jamaica is an island, there is great emphasis on seafood, but many other tasty dishes are also offered. Rock lobster is a regular dish on every menu, presented grilled, thermidor, cold, or hot. *Saltfish and ackee* is the national dish, a mixture of salt cod and a brightly colored vegetablelike fruit that tastes something like scrambled eggs. *Escovitch* (marinated fish) is usually fried and then simmered in vinegar with onions and peppers.

Among meat dishes, curried mutton and goat are popular, each highly seasoned and likely to affect your body temperature. Jerk pork is characteristic of rural areas, where it is coated in spices and barbecued slowly over wood fires until crisp and brown.

Apart from rice and peas (really red beans), usually served as a sort of risotto with added onions, spices, and salt pork, some vegetables may be new to you. They include *breadfruit,* originally brought here from the South Pacific (see box); *callaloo,* rather like spinach, used in pepperpot soup (not to be confused with the stew of the same name); *cho-cho,* served boiled and buttered or stuffed; and green bananas and plantains, fried or boiled and served with almost everything. Then there is pumpkin, which goes into a soup, as mentioned, or is served on the side, boiled and mashed with butter. Sweet potatoes are part of main courses, and there is also a sweet potato pudding made with sugar and coconut milk, flavored with cinnamon, nutmeg, and vanilla.

You'll also come across the intriguing *dip and fall back,* a salty stew with bananas and dumplings, and *rundown,* mackerel cooked in coconut milk and often eaten for breakfast. The really adventurous can try *manish water,* a soup made from goat offal and tripe said to increase virility. *Patties* (meat pies) are a staple snack; the best are sold in Montego Bay. Boiled corn, roast yams, roast saltfish, fried fish, soups, and fruits are available at roadside stands.

DRINKS

As mentioned above, "tea" is used in Jamaica to describe any nonalcoholic drink, a tradition dating back to plantation days. Fish tea (see "Appetizers," above) is often consumed as a refreshing pick-me-up, and is sometimes sold along the side of the road. *Skyjuice* is a favorite Jamaican treat for a hot afternoon. It's sold by street vendors, but beware: their carts are not always sanitary. It consists of shaved ice with sugar-laden fruit syrup and is offered in small plastic bags with a straw. Coconut water is refreshing and is safe to drink when a roadside vendor chops the top off a nut straight from a tree.

Rum punches are available everywhere, and the local beer is Red Stripe. The island produces many liqueurs, the most famous being *Tía Maria,* made from coffee beans. *Rumona* is another good one to bring back home with you. *Bellywash,* the local name for limeade, will supply the extra liquid you may need to counteract the tropical heat. Blue Mountain coffee is considered among the world's best coffees—it's also very expensive. Tea, cocoa, and milk are also usually available to round out a meal.

9 Recommended Books & Recordings

BOOKS

GENERAL *Catch a Fire, The Life of Bob Marley,* by Timothy White (Guernsey Press, 1983), chronicles the reggae musician's life and career, from poverty in Kingston's Trench Town to international fame. It's an insightful exploration of the historical, cultural, religious, and folkloric milieu that shaped Marley's spiritual and political beliefs, from which reggae emerged.

The Real Bob Marley Story, by Don Taylor (Barricade, 1995), is a memoir by the reggae star's manager. Taylor strays from the subject, often turning the Bob Marley story into the Don Taylor story, but there is much Marley lore here in spite of that. The most fascinating part concerns the attempt on Marley's life in the 1970s. Taylor was there and was seriously injured himself. Because the book is so poorly written, it is recommended only for the most diehard fans.

Tales of Old Jamaica, by Clinton V. Black (Longman Caribbean, reprinted 1991), brings together 10 of the most intriguing tales of the island's famous personalities, including Three-Fingered Jack (the terror of Jamaica) and the notorious Annie Palmer of Rose Hall.

Jamaican Folk Tales and Oral Histories, by Laura Tanna (Institute of Jamaica Publications, 1984), is a collection culled from the best Jamaican storytelling, such as spicy Anansi or Nancy stories and lore told with humor and style.

West Indian Folk-tales, retold by Philip Sherlock, illustrated by Joan Kiddell-Monroe (Oxford University Press, 1990), offers a colorful selection of West Indian myths and legends recounted with warmth and humor.

The Rebel Woman in the British West Indies During Slavery, by Lucille Mathurin, illustrated by Dennis Ranston (African Caribbean Publications, 1975), explores the variety of methods used to express resentment toward the institution of slavery. The quiet, subtle methods of protest—which today might be termed civil disobedience—are examined, as are violent armed rebellion.

The Cimaroons, by Robert Leeson (William Collins, 1978), is the story of slaves who refused to accept their status. Wherever the Cimaroons took off their chains, they fought stubbornly for their freedom. Their story does not appear in many history books, yet it is true and exciting.

X/Self, by Edward Kamau Brathwaite (Oxford University Press, 1987), one of the finest of the Caribbean poets, traces his African/Caribbean ancestry. In *X/Self,* the four landscapes—European, African, Amerindian, Maroon—meet and mingle in an extraordinarily rich, imaginative sequence of poems.

The How to be Jamaican Handbook, by Kim Robinson, Harclyde Walcott, and Trevor Fearon (Jamrite Publications, 1987), is a candid look at Jamaican characters and humorous aspects of island life. It is mandatory reading for anyone who wants to blend into Jamaican society.

Jamaica Talk, Three Hundred Years of the English Language in Jamaica, by Frederic G. Cassidy (Macmillan Caribbean, 1982), is a thorough study of English as spoken in Jamaica. It covers the language, both past and present, of Jamaicans of all ranks. Chapters deal with composition, pronunciation, grammar, and vocabulary.

Garvey's Children, The Legacy of Marcus Garvey, by Tony Sewall (Macmillan Caribbean, 1990), is a look at a great Jamaican's philosophy and opinions. It explores Garvey's insights into the condition of millions of blacks. It is said that Garvey linked the Caribbean, the United States, and Africa in a vision that saw all black people working together to determine their own destiny.

TRAVEL   *Tour Jamaica,* by Margaret Morris (Gleaner Company, 1988), describes an island of infinite variety with interesting and warmhearted people. Covering six regions, the book provides data on places of interest, local personalities, and historical and topical anecdotes. Featured are 19 recommended tours.

The Adventure Guide to Jamaica, by Steve Cohen (Hunter Publishing, 1988), leads you on a tour of unforgettable parts of the island few visitors know how to reach. The book emphasizes walking, cycling, river travel, and horseback touring; it also includes a guide to hundreds of roadside vendors.

Jamaica Guide, by Clinton V. Black (William Collins & Sangster, Jamaica, 1973), provides much information a visitor will find interesting, including a detailed introduction to the history of the people and country.

CUISINE   *The Jamaican Chef,* by Byron Murray and Patrick Lewin (Life Long Publishers, 1990), provides recipes for an array of sumptuous and mouthwatering dishes that get high marks from even the most critical gourmets.

Strange Fruit

Reading of Capt. James Cook's explorations of the South Pacific in the late 1700s, the English planters on Jamaica were intrigued by his accounts of the breadfruit tree, which grew in abundance on Tahiti. Seeing it as a possible source of cheap food for their slaves, they beseached King George III to sponsor an expedition to bring the trees to Jamaica.

The king put Capt. William Bligh in command of H.M.S. *Bounty* in 1787 and sent him to do just that. One of Bligh's lieutenants, a former shipmate named Fletcher Christian, became history's most famous mutineer when he overpowered Bligh, threw the breadfruit trees into the South Pacific Ocean, and disappeared into oblivion.

Bligh survived by sailing the ship's open longboat 3,000 miles to the East Indies, where he hitched a ride to England on a Dutch vessel. Later he was sent back to Tahiti to get more breadfruit. This time he succeeded—all for naught, as it turned out, for the slaves on Jamaica refused to eat the strange fruit of the new tree, preferring instead their old, familiar rice.

The descendants of those trees still grow in Jamaica. Their green, headsize fruit provides a meat which is vaguely reminiscent of the sweet potato.

Traditional Jamaican Cookery, by Norma Benghiat (Penguin, 1985), includes recipes never before written down, having been passed from generation to generation by word of mouth.

RECORDINGS

Legend (Best of Bob Marley). Marley has been referred to as a poet and prophet, and was the undisputed leader of reggae music. This collection of hits includes "Could You Be Loved," "Buffalo Soldier," and "One Love." *Legend* was released in 1984, and the album has outsold such megahits as Michael Jackson's *Thriller,* the Beatles' *Sgt. Pepper's Lonely Hearts Club Band,* and Pink Floyd's *Dark Side of the Moon.* Tuff Gong/Island Records, 422846210-2.

Liberation, by Bunny Wailer. When *Newsweek* selected the three most important musicians in the Third World, Bunny Wailer was one of them. He has controlled his artistic development to avoid compromising his vision. Shanachie Records, 43059.

Jahmekya, by Ziggy Marley and The Melody Makers. This album features "Kozmik," "Good Time," and "Drastic." Ziggy Marley is the son of Bob Marley. Virgin, 2-91626.

Toots in Memphis, by Toots and The Maytals, combines rhythm and blues and reggae. Included are "Freedom Train" and "Knock on Wood." Mango/Island Records, CCD-9818.

One Love, by Bunny Wailer, Bob Marley, and Peter Tosh (Three Greats). This compilation is the first chronological and definitive study of Bob Marley and the Wailers in their formative years. The music, the cornerstone of the ska era, includes previously unreleased alternate takes and rarely recorded Jamaican singers. Heartbeat Records, CDHB 111/112.

Yellowman Strikes Again, by Yellowman (who is considered one of the forerunners of rap music). Recorded live in Kingston. VP Records, VPCD-1078.

Earth Crisis, by Steel Pulse, produced and arranged by Jimmy Haynes and Steel Pulse. The album includes "Bodyguard" and "Throne of Gold." Elektra/Asylum, 960315-2.

Too Long In Slavery, by Culture. All songs were written and sung by J. Hill, K. Daley, and A. Walker. Virgin, CDFL9011.

Easy to Catch, by The ITALS, with lead vocals by Keith Porter, Ronnie Davis, and Lloyd Ricketts. Rhythm Safari/Priority, CDL 57159.

Jah Kingdom, by Burning Spear (known for his strongly political lyrics). Includes "World Power" and "Land of My Birth." Mango/Island Records, 162539915-2.

In Concert Best of Jimmy Cliff, by Jimmy Cliff. Produced by legendary producer Andrew Loog Oldham and Jimmy Cliff, this album features Ernest Ranglin on lead guitar and Earl "Baga" Walker on bass. Includes the classics "Many Rivers to Cross" and "The Harder They Come." Reprise, 2256-2.

Best Sellers, by Mikey Dread. All vocals are by Mikey Dread, Jamaica's number one DJ. Material ranges from 1979 to 1990. Rykodisc Records, 20178.

Planning a Trip to Jamaica

3

This chapter is devoted to the where, the when, and the how of your trip to Jamaica—what you need to do before leaving home. In addition to helping you decide when to take your vacation, we answer questions about what to take along, where to gather information, and what documents to obtain. We also cover alternative and specialty travel options, such as educational and wilderness travel.

Some of the information in this chapter applies to Barbados as well as to Jamaica, especially health, insurance, and tips for travelers with special needs. If you're going to Barbados, these sections are for you, too.

1 Visitor Information & Entry Requirements

VISITOR INFORMATION

Before you go, you can obtain information from the Jamaica Tourist Board (JTB) in the following U.S. cities. **Atlanta:** 300 W. Wienca Rd., Suite 100A, Atlanta, GA 30342 (☎ 770/452-7799); **Chicago:** 500 N. Michigan Ave., Suite 1030, Chicago, IL 60603 (☎ 312/527-4800); **Miami area:** 1320 S. Dixie Hwy., Suite 1101, Coral Gables, FL 33146 (☎ 305/665-0557); **Detroit area:** 26400 Lahser Rd., Lahser Center One, Suite 114A, Southfield, MI 48034 (☎ 313/948-9557); **Los Angeles:** 3440 Wilshire Blvd., Suite 1207, Los Angeles, CA 90010 (☎ 213/384-1123); and **New York:** 801 Second Ave., New York, NY 10017 (☎ 212/856-9727).

In Canada, obtain information in **Toronto:** 1 Eglinton Ave. East, Suite 616, Toronto, ON M4P 3A1 (☎ 416/482-7850). The JTB can also be reached via the toll-free telephone number 800/233-4582 in both the U.S. and Canada.

In **London** contact the tourist board at 1-2 Prince Consort Rd., London SW7 2BZ (☎ 0171/224-0505).

Once in Jamaica, you will find tourist board offices in **Kingston:** 2 St. Lucia Ave., Kingston (☎ 809/929-9200); **Montego Bay:** Cornwall Beach, St. James, Montego Bay (☎ 809/952-4425); **Negril:** Shop no. 20, Adrija Place, Negril, Westmoreland (☎ 809/957-4243); **Ocho Rios:** Ocean Village Shopping Centre, Ocho Rios, St. Anne (☎ 809/974-2582); **Port Antonio:** City Centre Plaza, Port Antonio (☎ 809/993-3051); and **Black River:** 2 High Street in Hendricks Building, Black River (☎ 809/956-2074).

You may also want to purchase U.S. State Department background bulletins. Contact the Superintendent of Documents, **U.S. Government Printing Office,** Washington, DC 20402 (☎ **202/512-1800**).

A good travel agent can also be a source of information. Make sure your agent is a member of the American Society of Travel Agents (ASTA). If you get poor service from an agent, you can write to the **ASTA Consumer Affairs Department,** 1101 King St., Alexandria, VA 22314, (☎ **703/706-0387**) for satisfaction.

Jamaica also maintains a 24-hour toll-free hotline that provides information about the island and its various events and activities. Call **809/991-9999** from the U.S. or Canada.

If you have Internet access, check out "The Unofficial Web Site on Jamaica" (**http://home.navisoft.com/xkcom/jam.htm**), the best all-around Jamaica site, with some good before-you-leave pointers, cultural tidbits, a patios primer, and plenty of humor. This is one of the few Jamaica Web pages that isn't either a blatant travel agent or resort ad, or just somebody's homepage with a few vacation pictures. "City.Net" (**http://www.city.net/countries/jamaica/**) also has pointers to several of the more official, and generally more staid, Jamaica sites on the Web. The Jamaica Tourist Board and the U.S. Government weigh in here with their ideas on travel and tourism to the island.

ENTRY REQUIREMENTS

DOCUMENTS   U.S. and Canadian residents do not need passports, but must have proof of citizenship (or permanent residency) and a return or ongoing ticket. A passport is the best bet, but an original birth certificate (or a certified copy), plus photo ID will suffice. A voter registration card is acceptable in some cases, but only if you have a notorized affadavit of citizenship, plus photo ID Always double-check with your airline, though: sometimes *they* won't accept a voter registration card.

Other visitors, including British citizens, need passports that are good for a maximum stay of six months.

Immigration cards are given to visitors at the airport arrivals desks. Hold on to it, as you will need to surrender the document to Jamaican Customs when you leave the country.

Document Protection   Before leaving home, make two copies of your most valuable documents, including the identification pages of your passport, your driver's license, or any other identity document; your airline ticket; and hotel vouchers. If you're taking prescribed medication, make copies of prescriptions.

VACCINATIONS   Vaccinations are not required to enter Jamaica if you're coming from the United States or Canada.

2 Money

The unit of currency in Jamaica is the Jamaican dollar, with the same symbol as the U.S. dollar, "$." There is no fixed rate of exchange for the Jamaican dollar. It is traded publicly and is subject to market fluctuations.

Visitors to Jamaica can pay for any goods in U.S. dollars. *But be careful!* Unless clearly stated, always insist on knowing whether a price is quoted in Jamaican or U.S. dollars.

In this guide, we quote most prices in U.S. dollars, denoted by "$." Any prices given in Jamaican dollars are indicated by "J$." Because Jamaican dollars tend to fluctuate widely, U.S.-dollar prices give a better indication of costs.

Many British travelers prefer to use U.S. dollars in Jamaica, especially if they also plan to visit Puerto Rico, the U.S. Virgin Islands, or the U.S. mainland.

Jamaican currency is issued in bank notes of J$1, J$2, J$5, J$10, J$20, J$50, and J$100. Coin denominations are 1¢, 5¢, 10¢, 20¢, 25¢, and 50¢. At press time (but subject to change), the exchange rate of Jamaican currency was about J$38 to U.S.$1 and J$54 to U.K.£1. When commissions are included, commercial banks and exchange bureaus will give a less favorable rate.

There is no limit to the amount of foreign currency you can bring in or out of Jamaica.

Before leaving your hotel, take along some small bills and coins. They will come in handy, since Jamaica is a tip-oriented society, and you'll find tips expected for any small service rendered.

TRAVELER'S CHECKS Although it's now possible to use ATM machines around the world to access your own bank account back home, some travelers still prefer the security of carrying traveler's checks so that they can obtain refunds if their checks are stolen.

Most large banks sell traveler's checks, charging fees averaging 1% to 2% of the value of the checks you buy, although some banks, in rare instances, have charged as much as 7%. If your bank wants more than a 2% commission, it sometimes pays to call the traveler's check issuers directly for the addresses of outlets where commissions will be lower. Issuers sometimes have agreements with groups to sell checks commission free. For example, American Automobile Association (AAA) offices sell American Express checks in several currencies without commission.

American Express (☎ 800/221-7282 in the U.S. and Canada) is one of the largest and most immediately recognized issuers of traveler's checks. No commission is charged to AAA members and to holders of certain types of American Express credit cards. For questions or problems that arise outside the U.S. or Canada, contact any of the company's many regional representatives.

Other issuers include **Citicorp** (☎ 800/645-6556 in the U.S. and Canada, or 813/623-1709, collect, from anywhere else in the world); **Thomas Cook** (☎ 800/223-7373 in the U.S. and Canada, or 609/987-7300, collect, from other parts of the world), which issues MasterCard traveler's checks; and **Interpayment Services** (☎ 800/221-2426 in the U.S. or Canada, or 212/858-8500, collect, from most other parts of the world), which sells Visa checks sponsored by Barclays Bank and/or Bank of America at selected branches around North America.

CREDIT & CHARGE CARDS Credit cards are widely used in Jamaica and Barbados. Visa and MasterCard are the major cards, although the American Express Card and, to a lesser extent, Diners Club, are also popular.

ATM NETWORKS Plus, Cirrus, and other networks connecting automated-teller machines operate in Jamaica and Barbados. For locations of Cirrus abroad, call **800/424-7787.** For Plus usage abroad, call **800/843-7587.** These are global information lines that will help you find local ATMs.

If your credit card has been programmed with a PIN number, it is likely that you can use your card at Caribbean ATMs to withdraw money as a cash advance on your credit card. (Discover can be used this way only within the U.S.)

These services exist in such places as Montego Bay and Bridgetown, but don't count on it in the remote villages. Before going, check to see if your PIN number must be reprogrammed for usage in Jamaica and Barbados.

The Jamaican Dollar, the U.S. Dollar & the U.K. Pound

The Jamaican dollar (J$) is freely traded, and its rate of exchange with the U.S. dollar, British pound, and other currencies varies. The chart below gives rounded U.S. dollar and British pound values for Jamaican prices. The chart's exchange rates of J$38 to U.S.$1 and J$54 to U.K.£1 were in effect as this edition was printed, but may be different when you visit the island. Check with a bank or currency trader for current exchange rates.

J$	U.S.$	U.K.£
5	0.13	0.09
10	0.26	0.19
25	0.65	0.46
50	1.30	0.93
75	1.95	1.39
100	2.60	1.85
200	5.20	3.70
300	7.80	5.55
400	10.40	7.40
500	13.00	9.25
750	19.50	13.88
1,000	26.00	18.50
5,000	130.00	92.50
10,000	260.00	185.00
25,000	650.00	462.50
50,000	1,300.00	925.00
75,000	1,950.00	1,387.50
100,000	2,600.00	1,850.00
200,000	5,200.00	3,700.00
300,000	7,800.00	5,550.00
400,000	10,400.00	7,400.00
500,000	13,000.00	9,250.00
1,000,000	26,000.00	18,500.00

MONEYGRAM   Running out of funds while on the road can be a disaster. Assuming you have friends or relatives who will advance you the money, a new service sponsored by American Express might be able to help you out of your jam.

Moneygram, 6200 S. Quebec St., P.O. Box 5118, Englewood, CO 80155-5118 (☎ **800/926-9400**), can transfer funds from one individual to another in less than 10 minutes between any of thousands of locations throughout the world. An American Express phone representative will give you the names of four or five offices near you; locations within the U.S are as diverse as a local pharmacy or convenience store in many small communities. The sender fills out a form, and pays the designated amount with cash or a credit card. AMEX service charges are $10 for the first $300 sent, with a sliding scale of commissions after that. Sending $5,000 costs about $200 worth of fees. Included in the transfer are a 10-word telex-style message, and a three-minute phone call to the recipient. Funds are transferred within 10 minutes,

What Things Cost in Jamaica	$ U.S.
Taxi from Kingston airport to city center	15.00
Local bus ride	0.30
Local telephone call	0.30
Double room at Tryall, Montego Bay (very expensive)	270.00
Double room at Reading Reef Club, Montego Bay (moderate)	125.00
Double room at Coral Cliff, Montego Bay (inexpensive)	59.00
Lunch for one at Town House, Montego Bay (moderate)	18.00
Lunch for one at Pork Pit, Montego Bay (inexpensive)	10.00
Dinner for one at Sugar Mill, Montego Bay (expensive)	35.00
Dinner for one at Reading Reef Club, Montego Bay (moderate)	20.00
Dinner for one at Pelican, Montego Bay (inexpensive)	10.00
Bottle of Red Stripe beer	1.30
Coca-Cola in a cafe	2.00
Cup of coffee in a cafe	3.00
Glass of wine in a restaurant	4.00
Roll of ASA 100 color film, 36 exposures	5.50
Admission to Rose Hall, Montego Bay	10.00
Movie ticket	3.20

and can be retrieved by the beneficiary at any of dozens of locations. Naturally, the beneficiary must present photo ID, and in some cases, a security code established by whomever provided the funds. Both Jamaica and Barbados are hooked into this program.

WHAT WILL IT COST?

You can live on $50 a day or $1,000 a day in Jamaica, depending on your budget and your taste. *Frommer's Jamaica & Barbados* documents a wide range of choices to suit all but the most rock-bottom of budgets. Most of the recommendations in this guide are at neither the highest nor lowest ends of the spectrum. Instead, they focus on moderately priced places, which in Jamaica can mean a steep price by some standards.

HOTEL PRICES   **Very expensive** Jamaican hotels in the winter high season (mid-December to mid-April) can command $250 to $400 and up for a double room without meals. Hotels classified in this book as **expensive** generally cost between $175 and $250 nightly for a double room in season. Hotels classified as **moderate** typically charge $110 to $175, and **inexpensive** hotels usually range below $110 per day. Each price applies to double occupancy. Because a single room typically is a double room rented to just one person, it costs only about 25% less than a double room.

Hotels that offer Modified American Plan (MAP) with breakfast and dinner add $35 to $60 a day to your tab; such plans usually cost less than purchasing the meals separately. MAP is often compulsory during the winter high season. From mid-April to mid-December, hotel prices are usually slashed by 20% to 60%. As a rule, breakfast then is extra, costing $6 to $10 for a continental breakfast and $8 to $20 for an American breakfast. We give the room rates in U.S. dollars.

RESTAURANT PRICES   Very expensive restaurants in Jamaica ask more than $40 a per person for a meal, excluding drinks and service charge. Expensive restaurants range in price from $30 to $40; moderate $20 to $30, and anything under $20 is considered inexpensive. Lunch in each restaurant category usually costs 30% to 40% less. Prices in our restaurant listings are given in U.S. dollars.

3 When to Go

With its fabled weather balmy all year, Jamaica is more and more a year-round destination. Nevertheless, it has a distinct **high season** running roughly from mid-December to mid-April. Hotels charge their highest prices during this peak winter period, when visitors fleeing from cold north winds crowd onto the island.

Reservations should be made two to three months in advance during the winter. At certain hotels it's almost impossible to book accommodations for the Christmas holidays and in February.

The off-season in Jamaica—roughly from mid-April to mid-December, with variance from hotel to hotel—amounts to a summer sale. In most cases, hotel rates are slashed a startling 20% to 60%. It's a bonanza for cost-conscious travelers, especially families who like to vacation together.

In the chapters ahead, we'll spell out in dollars the specific amounts hotels charge during the off-season, which offers several other benefits.

OFF-SEASON ADVANTAGES

Year-round resort facilities are often offered at reduced rates during the off-season. Some package-tour charges are as much as 20% lower, and individual excursion airfares are reduced from 5% to 10%. And airline seats and hotel rooms are much easier to come by.

Resort boutiques often feature summer sales, hoping to clear merchandise not sold in February to accommodate stock for the coming winter.

After the winter hordes have left, a less hurried way of life prevails on the island. You'll have a better chance to appreciate the food, culture, and local customs. Swimming pools and beaches are less crowded, sometimes not crowded at all. There's no waiting for a rental car (only to be told none are available), no long tee-up for golf, no queuing for tennis courts and water sports. You can often walk in unannounced at a top restaurant and find a seat for dinner that in winter would have required reservations far in advance. Also, when waiters are less hurried, they give better service.

The atmosphere is more cosmopolitan in the off-season than in the winter, mainly because of the influx of Europeans and Japanese. You'll no longer feel as if you're at a Canadian or American outpost. Also, the Jamaicans themselves travel in the off-season, and your holiday becomes more of a people-to-people experience.

Summer is also the time for family travel, not often possible during the winter season.

Finally, the very best of wintertime attractions remain undiminished—sea, sand, and surf, usually with lots of sunshine.

CLIMATE

Jamaica's large size and wide variation in altitude result in one of the most varied climates of any Caribbean island.

Along the seashore where most visitors congregate, the island is air-conditioned by the northeast trade winds, and temperature variations are surprisingly slight. Coastal readings average between 71° and 88° Fahrenheit all year. The Jamaican winter is usually like May in the United States or northern Europe, however, and there can be really chilly times, especially in the early morning and at night. Winter is generally the driest season, but can be wet in mountain areas; you can expect showers especially in northeast Jamaica.

Inland, Jamaica's average temperatures decrease by approximately 1°F for every 300 feet increase in elevation. Temperatures atop the highest of the Blue Mountains might descend to a chilling 50°F, although most visitors find that a light jacket, sweater, or evening wrap is suitable for even the coldest weather on the island. In some cases, a wrap is a good idea even on the beach because of nighttime breezes or strong drafts from a dining room's air conditioner.

Average yearly precipitation in Jamaica is more than 80 inches. Rainfall is heaviest along the eastern edge of the island's north coast, with Port Antonio receiving some of the most intense downpours. The island has two rainy seasons, May and October–November, although with the recent trend toward global warming, there have been less strict seasonal variations.

THE HURRICANE SEASON

The curse of Jamaican weather, the hurricane season officially lasts from June 1 to November 30. But there's no need for panic. Satellite weather forecasts generally give adequate warning so precautions can be taken.

If you're heading for Jamaica during the hurricane season, you can call your nearest branch of the National Weather Service, listed in the phone directory under U.S. Department of Commerce.

You can also obtain current weather information at a charge by calling **WeatherTrak.** For the telephone number for your destination's area, dial **900/370-8725;** a taped message gives you the three-digit access code for the area. The call costs 75¢ for the first minute and 50¢ for each additional minute.

And if your local cable television system carries it, don't forget **The Weather Channel.** Its team of meterologists keep close track of all Atlantic hurricanes.

HOLIDAYS

Jamaica observes the following public holidays: New Year's Day (January 1); Ash Wednesday; Good Friday; Easter Monday; National Labor Day (late May); Independence Day (a Monday in early August); National Heroes Day (third Monday in October); Christmas Day (December 25); and Boxing Day (December 26).

JAMAICA CALENDAR OF EVENTS

Jamaica offers a many events that could be the highlight of a visitor's stay on the island. There are a wide array of small-scale festivals, plus many major events, some of which are described below.

January
- **Jamaica Sprint Triathlon,** Negril. Hundreds participate in a three-part competition joining swimming, cycling, and running in one sweat-inducing endurance test. Contact the Jamaica Tourist Board or Swept Away Resort (☎ 809/957-4061). January 28.

March–April
- **The JAMI Awards,** at Kingston, annual Jamaica Music Industry Awards with a program of reggae, folk, gospel, jazz, and classical music, with guest performers. Contact Pulse Investments Ltd. at **809/968-1089.**

- **Spring Break,** at Negril, Montego Bay, and Ocho Rios, an annual program for students vacationing in Jamaica. Discounted rates at selected hotels, attractions, restaurants, and nightclubs. Featured are reggae concerts with live bands and beach volleyball competitions; entry to concerts is free with valid student ID Contact the Jamaica Tourist Board at **800/233-4JTB.**
- **Montego Bay Yacht Club's Easter Regatta.** An annual sailing event with several races staged along the north coast over a four-day period at Eastertime. Contact the Montego Bay Yacht Club (☎ **809/979-8262** or 809/979-8038).

June
- **Ocho Rios Jazz Festival** in both Ocho Rios and Montego Bay. International performers from Great Britain, Europe, Japan, and the United States and the Caribbean perform here along with Jamaican jazz artists. A series of jazz concerts are presented, along with jazz lunches, jazz teas, jazz feasts on the river, and even jazz barbecues. Contact the Jamaica Tourist Board office worldwide at **800/233-4JTB.** June 11–18.

July
- **National Dance Theatre Company,** Kingston. A midsummer, month-long dance festival featuring the musical and dance traditions of the Caribbean, along with expositions of island art. Contact the Jamaica Tourist Board (☎ **809/926-6129**) for a specific schedule. Mid-July through August.
- ✪ **Reggae Sunsplash,** at the Dover Raceway. An annual and internationally famous reggae festival, featuring top local and international reggae performers. Contact SYNERGY Productions at **809/942-9670,** or the Jamaica Tourist Board at **800/233-4JTB.** July 12–15.

August
- **Royal Jamaican Yacht Club's Annual Independence Regatta,** Kingston Harbour. Presided over by Jamaica's governor general, the regatta features races for all sizes of oceangoing craft, at the country's most historic harbor. Contact RJYC (☎ **809/924-8685**). Early August.
- **Reggae Summerfest,** at Catherine Hall, Montego Bay, an annual five-day music festival featuring international singers and top local talent. Contact Summerfest Productions at **809/952-8592** or the Jamaica Tourist Board at **800/233-4JTB.** August 8–12.
- **National Pushcart Derby,** Kaiser Sports Club, Discovery Bay. Assembled onto one sloping landscape are the finest motorless handcarts in Jamaica, crafted and steered by the flower of Jamaican youth (lads aged 10 to 18), usually cheered on by members of their extended families. Call **809/973-2221** for information. Mid-August.

September
- **Miss Jamaica World Beauty Pageant,** National Arena, Kingston. Here is proof that Jamaica is beautiful. Contact the Spartan Health Club (☎ **809/927-7575**). End of September.

October
- ✪ **Port Antonio International Marlin Tournament.** One of the oldest and most prestigious sportfishing events in the Caribbean, with participants from Europe and North America. Contact the Jamaica Tourist Board at **800/233-4582.** Third week in October.

December
- **Johnnie Walker World Championship of Golf,** Tryall Golf, Tennis & Beach Club, Montego Bay. A relatively new international golf contest, it offers what is to date the largest purse ($2.7 million) in the golfing world. Contact the Jamaica Tourist Board at **800/233-4582.** December 14–17.

4 The Active Vacation Planner

The principal activities of Jamaica are swimming and sunning, but there's a lot more going on than that.

If sports are important to you, you may want to learn more about the offerings of particular parts of Jamaica before deciding on a resort. Sports are so dispersed, and Jamaica so large, that it isn't much fun to undertake a long day's excursion just to play golf, for example. The cost of most activities is generally the same throughout the island.

Below is a summary to get you going and help you choose the destination that's right for you.

BEACHES

Many visitors want to do nothing more sporting than lie on the beach. For specific recommendations, refer to the regional chapters that follow and Section 1 of Chapter 1. On the whole, the best beaches are the 7-mile stretch of sand at Negril, with many sections reserved for nudists (see Chapter 5); Walter Fletcher Beach at Montego Bay, with especially tranquil waters (see Chapter 4); the unfortunately crowded Doctor's Cave Beach, also at Montego Bay, with water sports and changing rooms (see Chapter 4); and San San Beach, at Port Antonio on the north coast, with clean white sand, plenty of water sports, and a favorite picnic area (see Chapter 6).

BIRDING

Victor Emanuel Nature Tours (☎ 800/328-8368) offers weeklong birding trips to Jamaica, costing $1,250 per person. Jamaica is home to some 30 species of birds found nowhere else in the world. Trips are conducted by a Jamaican ornithologist. Visits are to the Blue Mountains (north of Kingston, the capital) and to the ponds and lagoons of Mandeville in the southwest.

DEEP-SEA FISHING

The waters off north Jamaica are world-renowned for game fish, including dolphin, kingfish, wahoo, blue and white marlin, sailfish, tarpon, Allison tuna, barracuda, and bonito. **The Jamaica International Fishing Tournament** and the **Port Antonio International Marlin Tournament** run concurrently at Port Antonio, usually every October. Most major hotels from Port Antonio to Montego Bay offer deep-sea fishing, and there are many charter boats. See Chapters 4 and 6.

GOLF

Jamaica has the best golf courses in the West Indies, with Montego Bay alone sporting four championship links. Those at **Wyndham Rose Hall Resort** (☎ 809/953-2650) are ranked as one of the top five golf courses in the world, according to an expert assessment. It is an unusual and challenging seaside and mountain course, built on the shores of the Caribbean.

Jamaica's Favorite Sport

In the early 1960s, at the end of British control of Jamaica, a handful of English authors concluded that one of the most reassuring signs of Jamaica's preparedness for independence was the island's enthusiasm for the rules and sportsmanship of cricket.

Since independence, cricket has continued to fascinate Jamaicans, some of whom yearn for the fame conferred on such legendary Jamaican-born stars as the quiet and ever-modest George Headley, who reached a peak during the 1930s. Headley's fame in Jamaica is like that of Babe Ruth in the United States. Michael Holding is a more contemporary cricket star. He was born in the Panama Canal Zone, of a Barbadian father and a Jamaican mother.

Cricket originated in England during the 16th century, and has since been uniquely associated with the British Empire. British governors in Jamaica and throughout the Empire encouraged the game as an adjunct of colonial policy, hoping to imbue the occupied territories with a taste for English sportsmanship and British culture. During the Edwardian Age, cricket games between such British dependencies as Trinidad, Barbados, Jamaica, New Zealand, and South Africa became a symbol of an empire on which the sun never set. The intricacies connected with game strategies have spurred debate in pubs throughout the Commonwealth for generations.

Aging cricket stars stood an excellent chance of good careers in law or civic administration, with a handful of players eventually being knighted; Learie Constantine of Trinidad became the first black member of the British House of Lords. Encouraged by social pressure as well as by the sheer excitement of the action, Jamaicans learned the game quickly and well, and today cricket is one of the country's most enduring passions.

Jamaica's leading cricket field is Kingston's 12,000-seat Sabina Park. Some of the best cricket in the Caribbean is played there, amid picnicking families, groups of boisterous friends, ample quantities of Jamaican rum and Red Stripe beer, and waves of noise cascading from cement-sided bleachers.

The excellent course at **Tryall Golf, Tennis & Beach Club** (☎ 809/956-5660) is the site of the Jamaica Classic Annual, first played in January 1988, and the Johnnie Walker Tournament. The Mazda Champions Tournament was played here from 1985 to 1987.

The **Half Moon** (☎ 809/953-2560) at Rose Hall features a championship course designed by Robert Trent Jones. The **Ironshore Golf & Country Club** (☎ 809/953-2800) is another well-known 18-hole golf course with a 72 par. See Chapter 4 for details about these Montego Bay courses.

On the north shore, there's **Super Club's Runaway Golf Club** (☎ 809/973-2561) at Runaway Bay and **Sandals Golf & Country Club** (☎ 809/974-0119) at Ocho Rios. See Chapter 6.

In Mandeville, **Manchester Country Club,** Brumalia Road (☎ 809/962-2403), is Jamaica's oldest golf course but with only nine greens. Beautiful vistas unfold from 2,201 feet above sea level. See Chapter 7.

HIKING

Unlike many of its neighboring islands, Jamaica offers landscapes that include mountain peaks of up to 7,400 feet. The flora, fauna, waterfalls, and panoramas of those peaks have attracted increasing numbers of hikers and hillclimbers, each determined to experience the natural beauty of the island firsthand.

One outfit that caters to these needs is the **Jamaica Alternative Tourism Camping and Hiking Association,** whose membership includes at least three separate tour operators well versed in Jamaica's ecological wonders. Foremost among these is **SENSE Adventures Ltd.,** based in Kingston (☎ **809/927-2097;** fax 809/929-6967), whose owner, Peter Bentley, offers individually designed, island-wide driving and hiking tours of Jamaica, including the Blue Mountains and canoe trips along its rivers. His organization's crew of Jamaican guides can accompany participants on expeditions ranging from one to several days. Each tour can be completely customized, based upon the interests of the participants, and groups are limited to no more than 6–8 people.

Most of these expeditions use the Maya Lodge, a rustic but clean and comfortable 15-acre base from which all tours depart for explorations of the mountain regions to the north and east. The site contains a cafe which offers good Jamaican and vegetarian fare, and of course, Blue Mountain coffee. Also available are laundry facilities, five simply built cabins, a simple hostel, and ample space for campsites. Most important, a team of trained guides is on hand for guided exploration of the Blue Mountains. The cost for one of these guides is between $35 and $100 a day, depending on the guide's level of expertise, plus tips, food, and accommodation for the guide. Camping gear can be rented. Many participants opt for all-inclusive packages priced at $55 to $90 U.S. per person per day, depending on the number of participants. Other luxury accommodations, scattered throughout the Blue Mountains and the rest of Jamaica, are also available for daily or weekly rentals, at a cost ranging from $100–$300 per day.

HORSEBACK RIDING

The best riding is on the north shore. Jamaica's most complete equestrian center is **Chukka Cove Farm and Resort** (☎ **809/972-2506**), at Richmond Llandovery, less than 4 miles east of Runaway Bay (see Chapter 6). The best ride here is a 3-hour jaunt to the sea, where you can unpack your horse and swim in the surf. See Chapter 6.

Another good program is offered at the **Rocky Point Riding Stables** (☎ **809/953-2286**), Half Moon Club, Rose Hall, Montego Bay, which is housed in probably the most beautiful barn and stables in Jamaica (see Chapter 4).

SCUBA DIVING

Diving is sometimes offered as part of all-inclusive packages by the island's major hotels. There are also well-maintained facilities independent of the hotels.

Jamaica boasts some of the finest waters for diving in the world, with depths averaging 35 to 95 feet. Visibility is usually 60 to 120 feet. Most diving is on coral reefs, which are protected as underwater parks. Fish, shells, coral, and sponges are plentiful on them. Experienced divers can also see wrecks, hedges, caves, dropoffs, and tunnels.

Near Montego Bay, **Seaworld** (☎ **809/953-2180**), at the Trelawny Beach Hotel in Falmouth, offers scuba-diving excursions to offshore coral reefs considered among the most spectacular in the Caribbean. There are also PAIC-certified dive guides, one dive boat, and all necessary equipment for either inexperienced or certified divers. See Chapter 4.

Outside Kingston, the **Buccaneer Scuba Club,** Morgan's Harbour, Port Royal (☎ **809/924-8148**), is one of Jamaica's leading dive and water sports operators. It offers a wide range of dive sites to accommodate various diver's tastes—from the incredible *Texas Wreck* to the unspoiled beauty of the Turtle Reef. See Chapter 7.

Negril is a hotbed of diving. **Negril Scuba Centre** (☎ 809/957-4425 or 800/ 818-2963), in the Negril Beach Club Hotel, Norman Manley Boulevard, is the area's most modern, best-equipped scuba facility. Also highly recommended is **Sundivers, Inc.,** a PADI-approved five-star dive shop located on the premises of the Poinciana Beach Hotel (☎ 809/957-4069), on Norman Manley Boulevard, near Sandals Negril. See Chapter 5.

TENNIS

All-Jamaica Hardcourt Championships are played in August at the **Manchester Country Club,** Brumalia Road, P.O. Box 17, Mandeville (☎ 809/962-2403). The courts are open for general play during the rest of the year. See Chapter 7.

Ciboney Ocho Rios, Main St., Ocho Rios (☎ 809/974-1036), focuses more on tennis than any other resort in the area. It offers three clay surface and three hard-surface courts, all lit for nighttime play. Residents play free either day or night, but non-residents must call and make arrangements with the manager. See Chapter 6.

In Montego Bay, you'll find excellent tennis facilities at **Wyndham Rose Hall Resort,** at Rose Hall (☎ 809/952-2650); **Half Moon Golf, Tennis & Beach Club** (☎ 809/953-2211); and **Tryall Golf, Tennis & Beach Club,** St. James (☎ 809/ 956-5660). See Chapter 4.

5 Health & Insurance

Traveling to Jamaica should not adversely affect your health. Finding a good doctor in Jamaica is no real problem, and all of them speak English. The following health and insurance information generally also applies to Barbados.

STAYING HEALTHY

Before leaving home, you can obtain a list of English-speaking doctors from the **International Association Medical Assistance to Travelers** (IAMAT), in the United States at 417 Centre St., Lewiston, NY 14092 (☎ 716/754-4883); in Canada, at 40 Regal Rd., Guelph, ON N1K 1B5 (☎ 519/836-0102).

HEALTH PROBLEMS   If you have a chronic medical condition, always talk to your doctor before leaving home. For problems like epilepsy, a heart condition, diabetes, or an allergy, wear a **Medic Alert identification tag.** For a lifetime membership, the cost is a well-spent $35 if steel, $45 if silver-plated, and $60 if gold-plated. In addition there's a $15 annual fee. Contact **Medic Alert Foundation,** P.O. Box 1009, Turlock, CA 95381-1009 (☎ 800/432-5378). Medic Alert's 24-hour hotline enables a foreign doctor to obtain your medical records.

Although tap water in Jamaica or Barbados is considered safe, it's better to drink bottled mineral water. Avoid iced drinks; stick to beer, hot tea, or bottled soft drinks.

Many visitors suffer from diarrhea, even if they follow precautions. It usually passes quickly without medication, if you moderate your eating habits and drink only bottled mineral water until you recover. If symptoms persist, consult a doctor.

The Jamaican sun can be brutal, especially if you've come from a winter climate and haven't been exposed to a strong sun in some time. Limit your time on the beach the first day. If you do overexpose yourself, stay out of the sun until you recover. If your exposure is followed by fever or chills, a headache, nausea, or dizziness, see a doctor.

Mosquitoes are a nuisance. One of the biggest menaces is the "no-see-ums," which appear mainly in the early evening. Even if you can't see these tiny insects, you sure can "feel-um," as many Jamaicans or Bajans will agree. Screens can't keep these critters out, so you'll need to carry your favorite bug repellent.

Malaria-carrying mosquitoes in the Caribbean are confined largely to Haiti and the Dominican Republic, less so in Jamaica or Barbados. If you're going into the "wilds" of Jamaica, consult your doctor for anti-malarial medication at least eight weeks before you leave.

MEDICINES   Take along an adequate supply of any prescription medications you require. Also, for safety's sake, bring along a written doctor's prescription that uses the generic name of the medicine—not the brand name.

You may want to bring such over-the-counter items as first-aid cream, insect repellent, aspirin, and band-aids.

INSURANCE

Before purchasing insurance, check your current homeowner's, automobile, and medical insurance policies, and reread the membership contracts of automobile and travel clubs and credit cards.

Many credit-card companies insure their users in case of travel accidents when they pay for the travel with their card. Sometimes fraternal organizations have policies that protect members in case of sickness or accidents abroad.

Many homeowner's insurance policies cover theft of luggage during foreign travel and loss of such documents as a passport or an airline ticket. Coverage is usually limited to about $500. To submit a claim, you'll need police reports or a statement from a local medical authority that you did in fact suffer a loss or experience an illness. Some policies provide cash advances or arrange for immediate funds transfers.

If you need additional insurance, check with the following companies:

Access America, 6600 W. Broad St., P.O. Box 11188, Richmond, VA 23230 (☎ 800/284-8300), offers travel insurance and 24-hour emergency travel, medical, and legal assistance for the traveler. One call to their hotline center, staffed by multilingual coordinators, connects travelers to a worldwide network of professionals able to offer specialized help in reaching the nearest physician, hospital, or legal advisor, and in obtaining emergency cash or the replacement of lost travel documents. Varying coverage levels are available.

Mutual of Omaha (Tele-Trip), Mutual of Omaha Plaza, Omaha, NE 68175 (☎ 800/228-9792). This company offers insurance packages priced from $113 for a three-week trip. Included in the packages are travel-assistance services, and financial protection against trip cancellation, trip interruption, flight and baggage delays, accident-related medical costs, accidental death and/or dismemberment, and medical evacuation coverages. Application for insurance can be taken over the phone for major credit card holders.

Travel Guard International, 1145 Clark St., Stevens Point, WI 54481 (☎ 800/826-1300 outside Wisconsin, 715/345-0505 in Wisconsin), offers a comprehensive seven-day policy that covers lost luggage, emergency assistance, accidental death, trip cancellation, and medical coverage abroad. The cost of the package is $62, but there are restrictions that you should understand before you accept the coverage.

Travelers Insurance PAK, Travel Insured International Inc., P.O. Box 280568, East Hartford, CT 06128 (☎ 800/243-3174 or 860/528-7663), offers illness and accident coverage costing from $10 for 6 to 10 days. For lost or damaged luggage, $500 worth of coverage costs $20 for 6 to 10 days. You can also purchase trip cancellation insurance for $5.50 per $100 of coverage to a limit of $10,000 per person.

Wallach and Co., 107 W. Federal St., P.O. Box 480, Middleburg, VA 22117-0480 (☎ 540/687-3166 or 800/237-6615), offers coverage for between 10 and 120 days at $3 per day; this policy includes accident and sickness coverage to the tune of $100,000. Medical evacuation is also included, along with a $25,000 accidental death and dismemberment compensation.

6   Tips for Travelers with Special Needs

FOR TRAVELERS WITH DISABILITIES

Hotels rarely give much publicity to the facilities, if any, they offer the disabled, so it's always wise to contact the hotel directly, in advance. Tourist offices usually have little data about such matters.

You can obtain a free copy of "Air Transportation of Handicapped Persons," published by the U.S. Department of Transportation. Write for Free Advisory Circular No. AC12032, Distribution Unit, **U.S. Department of Transportation,** Publications Division, 3341Q 75 Ave., Landover, MD 20785 (☎ 301/322-4961; fax 301/386-5394). Only written requests are accepted.

You may also want to consider joining a tour specifically designed for disabled visitors. For names and addresses of such tour operators, contact the **Society for the Advancement of Travel for the Handicapped** (SATH), 347 Fifth Ave., Suite 610, New York, NY (☎ 212/447-7284; fax 212/725-8253). Yearly membership costs $45 for adults or $25 for senior citizens and students. Send a stamped, self-addressed envelope. SATH will also provide you with hotel/resort accessibility for Caribbean destinations.

The **Information Center for Individuals with Disabilities,** 29 Stanhope St., 4th Floor, Boston, MA 02116, (☎ 617/450-9888 or 800/462-5015 in Mass.) is another good source. It has lists of travel agents who specialize in tours for the disabled, and provides travel tip fact sheets for Caribbean destinations.

For the blind or visually impaired, the best source is the **American Foundation for the Blind,** 11 Penn Plaza, Suite 300 New York N.Y. 10001 (☎ 212/502-7600 or 800/232-5463 to order information kits and supplies). It acts as a referral source for travelers and can offer advice on various requirements for the transport and border formalities for seeing-eye dogs.

One of the best organizations serving the needs of the disabled (wheelchairs and walkers) is **Flying Wheels Travel,** 143 W. Bridge St. (P.O. Box 382), Owatonna, MN 55060 (☎ 507/451-5005 or 800/535-6790). It offers customized, all-inclusive vacation packages in the Caribbean.

For a $25 annual fee, consider joining **Mobility International USA,** P.O. Box 10767, Eugene, OR 97440 (☎ 503/343-1284 (TDD); fax 503/343-6812). It answers questions on various destinations and also offers discounts on its programs, videos, and publications. Their quarterly newsletter, "Over the Rainbow" provides information on Caribbean hotel chains, accessibility, and transportation.

Finally, a bimonthly publication, **Handicapped Travel Newsletter,** keeps you current on worldwide, accessible sights for the disabled. To order an annual subscription for $10, call **903/677-1260.**

TIPS FOR BRITISH TRAVELERS

The **Royal Association for Disability and Rehabilitation** (RADAR), Unit 12, City Forum, 250 City Rd., London, EC1V 8AF (☎ 0171/250-3222), publishes holiday "fact packs"—three in all—which sell for £2 each or all three for £5. The first one provides general information, including planning and booking a holiday, insurance, finances, and useful organization and holiday providers. The second outlines transportation available when going abroad and equipment for rent. The third deals with specialized accommodations.

FOR GAY & LESBIAN TRAVELERS

Jamaica and Barbados have repressive laws to contend with. Homosexuality is illegal in Barbados, and there is often a lack of tolerance here in spite of the large number of gay residents and visitors. Jamaica is the most homophobic island in the Caribbean, with harsh anti-gay laws, even though there is a large local gay population. One local advised that it's not smart for a white gay man to wander the streets of Jamaica at night.

Many all-inclusive resorts, notably the famous Sandals of Jamaica, have discriminatory policies. Although Sandals started off welcoming "any two people in love," they quickly switched to allowing only male/female couples. Gays are definitely excluded from their love nests. However, not all all-inclusives practice such blatant discrimination. Hedonism II, a rival of Sandals in Negril, is a "couples-only" resort, but any combination will do here. The Grand Hotel Lido, a more upscale all-inclusive in Negril, will welcome whatever combination shows up (even singles, for that matter).

To learn about gay and lesbian travel in the Caribbean, you can secure publications or else join data-dispensing organizations before you go. Men can order *Spartacus,* the international gay guide ($32.95), or *Odysseus 1996, The International Gay Travel Planner,* a guide to international gay accommodations ($25). Both lesbians and gay men might way to pick up a copy of *Gay Travel A to Z* ($16), which specializes in general information, as well as listings of bars, hotels, restaurants, and places of interest for gay travelers throughout the world. These books and others are available from **Giovanni's Room,** 1145 Pine St., Philadelphia, PA 19107 (☎ **215-923-2960**).

Our World, 1104 North Nova Rd., Suite 251, Daytona Beach, FL 32117 (☎ **904/441-5367**), is a magazine devoted to options and bargains for gay and lesbian travel worldwide. It costs $35 for 10 issues. ***Out and About,*** 8 West 19th St., Suite 401, New York, NY 10011 (☎ **800/929-2268**), has been hailed for its "straight" reporting about gay travel. It profiles the best gay or gay-friendly hotels, gyms, clubs, and other places, with coverage of destinations throughout the world. Its cost is $49 a year for 10 information-packed issues. It aims for the more upscale gay male traveler, and has been praised by everybody from *Travel & Leisure* to *The New York Times.* Both of these publications are also available at most gay and lesbian bookstores.

The **International Gay Travel Association** (IGTA), P.O. Box 4974, Key West, FL 33041 (☎ **305/292-0217** or voice mailbox 800/448-8550), encourages gay and lesbian travel worldwide. With around 1,200 member agencies, it specializes in networking, providing the information travelers would need for an individual traveler to link up with the appropriate gay-friendly service organization or tour specialist. It offers quarterly newsletters, marketing mailings, and a membership directory that is updated four times a year. Travel agents who are IGTA members will be tied into this organization's vast information resources.

FOR SENIORS

For information before you go, obtain a copy of "101 Tips for the Mature Traveler," available from **Grand Circle Travel,** 347 Congress St., Suite 3A, Boston, MA 02210

(☎ **617/350-7500** or 800/221-2610); this travel agency also offers escorted tours and cruises for seniors.

SAGA International Holidays, 222 Berkeley St., Boston, MA 02115 (☎ **800/ 343-0273**), is known for its all-inclusive tours and cruises for seniors, preferably 60 years old or older. Insurance is included in the net price of their tours, except for cruises.

Information is also available from the **National Council of Senior Citizens,** 1331 F St. NW, Washington, DC 20004 (☎ **202/347-8800**). A nonprofit organization, the council charges $12 per person/couple for which you receive a newsletter 11 times a year, part of which is devoted to travel tips. Discounts on hotels and auto rentals are provided.

Mature Outlook, P.O. Box 10448, Des Moines, IA 50306 (☎ **800/336-6330**), is a membership program for people over 50 years of age. Members are offered discounts at ITC-member hotels and will receive a bimonthly magazine. The annual membership fee of $14.95 entitles its members to coupons for discounts at Sears & Roebuck Co. Savings are also offered on selected car rentals and restaurants.

Golden Companions has been successful in helping travelers 45-plus find compatible companions since 1987. It is the only travel companion network to offer personal voicebox mail service enabling members to connect instantly 24 hours a day. Membership services also include free mail exchange, the bimonthly newsletter *Golden Gateways,* get-togethers, and tours. Annual membership is $85, and newsletter-only subscriptions are $17.95 for 12 months or $26.95 for 24 months. For a free brochure, write Golden Companions, P.O. Box 5249, Reno, NV 89513 (☎ **702/324-2227;** fax 702/324-223). A sample newsletter is $2.

Elderhostel, 75 Federal St., Boston, MA 02110-1941 (☎ **617/426-7788**), maintains an array of postretirement study programs, several of which are in the Caribbean, primarily in Jamaica and the Bahamas. Programs do vary throughout the year, but some, like the one offered at Hofstra University's Marine Laboratory in St. Anne's Bay, Jamaica, is usually scheduled several times during the year. Participants in this $1,065, 11-day, all-inclusive (except airfare) program study marine biology including snorkeling in the morning course. The afternoon course includes hiking and bus trips to natural history sites, and in the evening, guest lecturers present local cultural histories. Most courses last two or three weeks and are a good value, considering that hotel accommodations in student dormitories or modest inns, all meals, tuition, and activities are included. Courses involve no homework, are ungraded, and center mostly on the liberal arts. Participants must be age 55 or older. However, if two members go as a couple, only one member needs to be 55 or over. Write for their free newsletter and a list of upcoming courses and destinations.

FOR FAMILIES

Jamaica and Barbados are two of the top family vacation destinations in the Caribbean. The smallest toddlers can spend blissful hours on sandy beaches and in the shallow sea water or in swimming pools constructed with them in mind. There's no end to the fascinating pursuits offered for older children, ranging from boat rides to shell collecting to horseback riding, hiking, and disco dancing. Some children are old enough to learn to snorkel and to explore an underwater wonderland. Skills such as swimming and windsurfing are taught, and there are a variety of activities unique to the islands.

Most resort hotels will advise about fun for all ages, and many have play directors and supervised activities for various youthful age groups. See "The Best Family Vacations" in Chapter 1 for our top picks.

Family Travel Times is published quarterly by TWYCH, **Travel With Your Children,** and includes a weekly call-in service for subscribers. Subscriptions cost $40 a year and can be ordered by writing to TWYCH, 40 Fifth Ave., New York, NY 10011 (☎ 212/477-5524). TWYCH also publishes a nitty-gritty information guide called *Cruising with Children,* which sells for $22 and is discounted to subscribers to the newsletter. An information packet describing TWYCH's publications and including a recent sample issue is available by sending $3.50 to the above address.

7 Getting There

BY PLANE

There are two **international airports** in Jamaica—Donald Sangster outside Montego Bay and Norman Manley outside Kingston. That means you can fly directly to the resorts areas via Montego Bay without having to go to Kingston.

The most popular routings to Jamaica are from New York or Miami, and several airlines make connections through those cities convenient and easy. Remember to reconfirm all flights, going and returning, no later than 72 hours before departure.

Flying time from Miami is 1¼ hours; from Los Angeles, 5½ hours; from Atlanta, 2½ hours; from Dallas, 3 hours; from Chicago and New York, 3½ hours; and from Toronto, 4 hours.

MAJOR AIRLINES   One of the most popular services to Jamaica, partly because of its dozens of connections to other parts of its vast North American network, is provided by **American Airlines** (☎ 800/433-7300). Passengers in the U.S. Northeast can opt for American's nonstop flight departing from New York's Kennedy International Airport every morning. It touches down first in Montego Bay, then it continues on to Kingston. On its return to New York, it usually departs from Montego Bay, touches down in Kingston for additional passengers, then continues nonstop back to Kennedy.

American Airlines passengers from other parts of North America usually will connect at Miami, where at least four daily flights depart throughout the day and evening for both Kingston and Montego Bay.

Air Jamaica (☎ 800/523-5585), the national carrier, operates a number of weekly flights between the island and New York, Philadelphia, Baltimore, Atlanta, and Orlando, most of which stop at both Montego Bay and Kingston. Even more frequent are the flights Air Jamaica operates to Miami. Two fly nonstop to Kingston; the other four stop at both Montego Bay and Kingston. Through its reservations network, the airline offers connecting service within Jamaica to small airports, including Port Antonio, Boscobel (near Ocho Rios), Negril, and Tinson Pen (a small airport on the outskirts of Kingston).

Continental Airlines (☎ 800/231-0856) offers nonstop service from its hub at Newark, New Jersey, to Montego Bay. Considered a key contributor to the revitalization of Newark International Airport, Continental offers Jamaica-bound flights that depart late enough each morning to allow convenient connections from Boston, Hartford, Washington, D.C., Pittsburgh, and Detroit.

Canadians who prefer to fly their national carrier, **Air Canada** (☎ 800/363-5440 in the U.S. or 800/268-7240 in Canada), can depart for Jamaica either from Toronto or Montreal. Flights from Toronto leave four to seven times a week, depending on the season, touching down at both Montego Bay and Kingston. Flights from Montreal's Mirabel airport depart twice a week (usually on Saturday and Sunday) for Montego Bay. Montreal-based travelers bound for Kingston transfer in either

Toronto or Montego Bay, depending on the schedule. Connections on Air Canada link both Toronto and Montreal to virtually every other airport in Canada.

Travelers based in Britain usually opt for one of the flights operated by the country's premier airline, **British Airways** (☎ **800/247-9297**). Aircraft fly three times a week nonstop between London's Gatwick and Montego Bay, touching down briefly in Kingston before continuing back to London. **Air Jamaica** (see above) also began flying to London in 1996.

REGULAR AIRFARES   Airlines compete fiercely with one another for the patronage of sun-seeking vacationers. American and its competitors usually match dollar-for-dollar each other's fares to Jamaica.

The least expensive regular fares are for **Advance Purchase Excursion** (APEX) tickets, whose definitions and restrictions come in a wide array. For example, at press time, American Airline's least expensive fare from New York to Montego Bay requires a seven-day advance purchase and a stopover in Jamaica of between 3 and 30 days. Fares from New York to either Kingston or Montego Bay for travel on weekdays (Monday through Thursday) ranged from $363 to $383, whereas fares for travel on weekends (Friday, Saturday, or Sunday) ranged from $408 to $431, depending on the season, plus taxes.

Meeting the Jamaicans

The Jamaica Tourist Board operates a **Meet-the-People program** in Kingston and the island's five major resort cities and towns. Through the program, visitors can meet Jamaican families who volunteer to host them free for a few hours or even a whole day.

More than 650 families are registered in the project with the tourist board, which keeps a list of their interests and hobbies. All you need do is give the board a rough idea of your interests, and they will arrange for you to spend the day with a similar family. You go along with whatever the family does, sharing their life, eating at their table, accompanying them to a dinner party. You may end up at a beach barbecue, afternoon tea with neighbors, or just sitting and expounding theories, arguing, and talking far into the night. The program does not include overnight accommodation.

If you have a particular interest—birds, butterflies, music, ham radio, stamp collecting, or spelunking in Jamaica's many caves—the tourist board will find you a fellow enthusiast. Lasting friendships have developed because of this unique opportunity to meet people.

Although the service is entirely free, your hostess will certainly enjoy receiving flowers or a similar token of appreciation after your visit.

In Jamaica, apply at any of the local tourist board offices (see "Visitor Information" earlier in this chapter).

Another program is offered by **World Learning,** founded in 1932 as The U.S. Experiment in International Living, Kipling Road, P.O. Box 676, Brattleboro, VT 05302-0676 (☎ **802/257-7751** or 800/336-1616). Their College Semester Abroad program in Jamaica focuses on women and development, and life and culture in Jamaica. Participants become one of the family, taking part in its daily activities, while studying in the region. The program includes field work and an independent study project.

Airlines generally charge different fares according to season. **Peak season,** which means winter in Jamaica, is most expensive; **basic season,** during the summer months, offers the least expensive fares. **Shoulder season** refers to the spring and fall months in between.

Some airlines (including American) offer special rates at a number of Jamaica's most interesting hotels, but only if you pay for them at the same time you buy your airline ticket. Most hotels participating in American's program are recommended separately in this guidebook, and the savings of simultaneous air and hotel bookings can at times be substantial.

PROMOTIONAL FARES   It's important to watch your local newspaper for special promotional fares, which come and go with frequency and carry stringent requirements like advance purchase, minimum stay, and cancellation penalties. Any promotion could make the price of airfare to Jamaica even lower, depending on market conditions. Land arrangements (prebooking of hotel rooms) are often tied to promotional fares.

OTHER GOOD-VALUE CHOICES   Proceed with caution through the following grab bag of suggestions. "Good value" keeps changing in the airline industry. It's hard to keep up, even if you're a travel agent. Fares, especially to Jamaica, change all the time—the lowest fare one day can change overnight as a new promotional fare is introduced.

Bucket Shops (Consolidators)   Consolidators resell blocks of tickets consigned by major carriers. They exist in many shapes and forms. In its purest sense, a bucket shop acts as a clearinghouse for blocks of tickets that airlines discount and consign during normally slow periods of air travel. In the case of Jamaica, that usually means from mid-April to mid-December.

Tickets are sometimes—but not always—discounted from 20% to 35%. Terms of payment can vary, from 45 days prior to departure to the last minute. Discounted tickets can also be purchased through regular travel agents, who usually mark up the ticket 8% to 10%, maybe more, thereby greatly reducing your discount. A survey conducted of flyers who use consolidator tickets voiced only one major complaint: The ticket doesn't qualify you for an advance seat assignment, and you are therefore likely to be assigned a poor seat on the plane at the last minute.

Many people who book consolidator tickets report no savings at all, as the airlines will sometimes match the consolidator ticket by announcing a promotional fare. The situation is a bit tricky and calls for some careful investigation on your part to determine just how much you might save.

Although air-ticket discounters are widespread within the transatlantic market, they are rare within the highly competitive Caribbean. One of the few exceptions is **TFI Tours International,** 34 W. 32nd St., 12th floor, New York, NY 10001 (☎ **212/ 736-1140** in New York State or 800/745-8000 elsewhere in the U.S.). TFI offers tickets on both TWA and American Airlines from New York to such islands as St. Thomas, St. Croix, Puerto Rico, Jamaica, St. Maarten, and the Dominican Republic at prices that usually averaged around 10% less than those offered by the airlines to anyone who phoned them directly. Depending on inventory, tickets require no advance purchase, but are usually nonrefundable, or carry penalties for changes in plans or itineraries.

Charter Flights   Charter flights allow you to travel at rates cheaper than on regularly scheduled flights. Many of the major carriers offer charter flights at rates that are sometimes 30% (or more) off the regular airfare.

There are some drawbacks to charter flights that you need to consider. Advance booking, for example, of up to 45 days or more may be required, and there are hefty cancellation penalties, although you can take out insurance against emergency cancellations (see "Insurance," above). Also, you must depart and return on your scheduled dates or you will lose your money. It will not help to telephone the airline and tell them you're in Jamaica with malaria! If you're not on the plane, you can kiss your money goodbye.

Since charter flights are so complicated, it's best to go to a good travel agent and ask him or her to explain the problems and advantages. Sometimes charters require ground arrangements, such as the prebooking of hotel rooms.

Rebators   To confuse the situation even more, in the past few years rebators have begun to compete in the low-cost airfare market. Rebators are outfits that pass along to the passenger part of their commission, although many assess a fee for their services. And although they are not the same as travel agents, they sometimes offer roughly similar services. Some rebators sell discounted travel tickets, and also offer discounted land arrangements, including hotels and car rentals. Most rebators offer discounts averaging anywhere from 10% to 25%, plus a $25 handling charge.

Rebators include **Travel Avenue,** 10 S. Riverside Plaza, Suite 1404, Chicago, IL 60606 (☎ **312/876-1116** or 800/333-3335), and **The Smart Traveller,** 3111 SW 27th Ave., P.O. Box 33010, Miami, FL 33133 (☎ **305/448-3338** or 800/ 448-3338). This agency also discounts hotel or condo packages and cruises. Both of these companies can arrange air travel to Jamaica or Barbados.

Travel Clubs   Another possibility for low-cost air travel is the travel club, which supplies an unsold inventory of tickets offering discounts in the range of 20% to 60%.

After you pay an annual fee, you are given a hotline number to call to learn of available discounts. Many discounts become available several days in advance of actual departure, sometimes as long as a week, and sometimes as much as a month. It all depends. Of course, you're limited to what's available, so you have to be fairly flexible.

Some of the best of these clubs include:

Moment's Notice, 7301 New Utrecht Ave., Brooklyn, New York 11228 (☎ **718/ 234-6295**), charges $25 per year for membership, which allows spur-of-the-moment participation in dozens of tours. Each is geared for impulse purchases and last-minute getaways, and each features discounted air and land packages to all Caribbean islands, which sometimes represent substantial savings over what you'd have paid through more conventional channels. Members can call the hotline to learn what options are available. Most of the company's best-valued tours depart from New Jersey's Newark airport.

Sears Discount Travel Club, 3033 S. Parker Rd., Suite 900, Aurora, CO 80014 (☎ **800/433-9383** in the U.S.), offers members a catalog (issued four times a year), maps, discounts at select hotels, and a limited guarantee that equivalent packages will not be undersold by any other travel organization. Membership costs $49. It also offers a 5% rebate on the value of all airline tickets, tours, hotel accommodations, and car rentals that are purchased through them. To collect this rebate, participants are required to fill out some forms and photocopy their receipts and itineraries. For Travel Membership, call **800/255-1487.**

Encore Travel Club, 4501 Forbes Blvd., Lanham, MD 20706 (☎ **800/ 638-8976**), charges $49.95 a year for membership in a club that offers 50% discounts at well-recognized hotels around the country. It also offers substantial discounts on airfare, cruises, and car rentals through its volume-purchase plans. Membership includes a travel package outlining the company's many services, and use of a toll-free phone number for advice and information.

BY CRUISE SHIP

If you'd like to sail to Jamaica, in a home with an ocean view, a cruise ship might be for you. It's slow and easy, and it's no longer only for the enjoyment of the rich. Cruises today appeal to middle-income travelers who have no more than one or two weeks to spend in the Caribbean. Some 300 passenger ships ply the Caribbean all year, and in January and February the number increases by 100 or so. You might want to pick up a copy of *Frommer's Caribbean Cruises* for more detailed information, or consult a good travel agent.

Vacations to Go, 1502 Augusta Dr., Suite 415, Houston, TX 77057 (☎ **800/ 338-4962** in the U.S.), provides catalogs and information on discount cruises through the Atlantic, the Caribbean, and the Mediterranean. Annual membership costs $5.95 per family.

8 Package Tours

Economy and convenience are the chief advantages of a package tour—cost of transportation (usually airfare), a hotel room, food (sometimes), and sightseeing (sometimes) are combined, neatly tied up with a single price tag. There are extras, of course, but in general you'll know in advance the rough cost of your vacation, and can budget accordingly. The disadvantage is that you may find yourself in a hotel room you dislike, yet are virtually trapped there because you've already paid for it.

Choosing the right package can be a problem. It's best to go to a travel agent and see what's currently offered.

Packages are available because tour operators can mass-book hotels and make other volume purchases. You typically must pay the cost of the total package in advance. Transfers between your hotel and the airport are often included. (This can be a considerable break, because an airport can be a $40-or-more taxi ride from your resort.) Many packages carry options, including low-cost car rentals. Nearly all tour packages are based on double occupancy.

To save time comparing the price and value of all the package tours out there, consider calling **TourScan Inc.,** P.O. Box 2367, Darien, CT 06820 (☎ **203/ 655-8091** or 800/962-2080). Every season, the company gathers and computerizes the contents of about 200 brochures containing 10,000 different vacations in the Caribbean, the Bahamas, and Bermuda. TourScan selects the best value at each hotel and condo. Two catalogs are printed each year. Each lists a broad-based choice of hotels on most of the islands of the Caribbean, in all price ranges. (The scope of the islands and resort hotels is amazing.) Write to TourScan for their catalogs ($4 each; the price is credited to any TourScan vacation).

One of the cheapest arrangements any traveler could make to Jamaica might be arranged through the tour operators at one of the Caribbean's airlines. Most prominent among these is the tour desk at **American Airlines** (☎ **800/433-7300**). Holding an impressive array of vacant hotel rooms in inventory, American often sells Caribbean hotel bookings at prices substantially lower than similar rooms booked by an individual traveler. The packages are available only to passengers who simultaneously purchase transit to the Caribbean on American Airlines.

It's best to remain flexible in your departure and return dates, because greater savings might be available to those willing to shift preferred dates slightly to take advantage of an unsold block of nights at a hotel. For details and more information, ask for the tour desk at American Airlines. (Many hotels they might offer are reviewed in this guidebook.) The telephone representative can sometimes also arrange a discounted rental car for however many days you specify.

Other leading tour operators to the Caribbean include:

Caribbean Concepts, 575 Underhill Blvd., Syosset, NY 11791 (☎ **516/ 496-9800** or 800/423-4433), which offers air-and-land packages to the islands, some including hotel, resort, apartment, villa, or condo rentals. Car rentals and local sightseeing can also be arranged.

Consider also **Delta's Dream Vacations** (☎ **800/872-7786**), which offers customized trips to Jamaica or Barbados lasting from 2 to 20 days, including airfare, accommodations, and transfers. Tickets are refundable, and you can cancel for any reason.

Clothing-optional tours are arranged through **Caribbean Travel Naturally,** 1900 Land O'Lakes Boulevard, Suite 113, Lutz, FL 33549 (☎ **809/491-6882**) to nudist resorts in Jamaica, as well as French St. Martin, Antigua, and the Dominican Republic.

If you're seeking just general independent packages, consider:

Renaissance Vacations, 2655 LeJeune Rd., Suite 400, Coral Gables, FL 33134 (☎ **800/874-0027** in the U.S.), offers all-inclusive deals to Ocho Rios. **Horizon Tours,** 1010 Vermont Ave. NW, Suite 202, Washington, DC 20005 (☎ **202/ 393-8390** or 800/395-0025 in the U.S.; fax 202/393-1547), specializes in all-inclusive upscale resorts on both Jamaica and Barbados. **Apple Vacations East** (☎ **800/727-3400**) offers some 40 resorts in Jamaica, ranging from Ocho Rios to Negril, from European-plan resorts to all-inclusives.

Finally, advertising more packages to the Caribbean than any other agency is **Liberty Travel** (☎ **800/216-9776**), with offices in many states.

FOR BRITISH TRAVELERS

Caribbean Connection, Concorde House, Forest Street, Chester CH1 1QR (☎ **01244/341131**), offers all-inclusive packages (airfare and hotel) to the Caribbean and customizes tours for independent travel. It publishes two catalogs of Caribbean offerings, one featuring more than 160 properties on all the major islands, and a 50-page catalog of luxury all-inclusive properties.

Other Caribbean specialists operating out of England include **Kuoni Travel,** Kuoni House, Dorking, Surrey RH5 4AZ (☎ **01306/740-888**). **Caribtours,** 161 Fulham Rd., London SW3 6SN (☎ **0171/581-3517**), a small, very knowledgeable specialist, tailoring itineraries to meet your demanding travel requirements.

9 Getting Around

BY RENTAL CAR

Jamaica is big enough—and public transportation is unreliable enough—that a car is a necessity if you plan to do much independent sightseeing. Unfortunately, prices of car rentals in Jamaica have skyrocketed, and it is now one of the most expensive rental scenes in the Caribbean.

Subject to many variations depending on road conditions, driving time from Montego Bay to Negril (about 52 miles) is 1 1/2 hours; from Montego Bay to Ocho Rios (67 miles), 1 1/2 hours; from Ocho Rios to Port Antonio (66 miles), 2 1/2 hours; from Ocho Rios to Kingston (54 miles), 2 hours; from Kingston to Mandeville (61 miles), 1 1/2 hours; and from Kingston to Port Antonio (61 miles), 2 hours.

Since accident claims may be difficult to resolve, and since billing irregularities can occur up even in the best of companies, it's best to stick to branches of U.S.-based rental outfits. **Avis** (☎ **800/331-1212**) maintains offices at the international airports in both Montego Bay (☎ 809/952-4543) and Kingston (☎ 809/924-8013). At press time, the least expensive car required a two-day advance booking and costs $420 per week for a Toyota Starlet with manual transmission and no air-conditioning plus 15% tax with unlimited mileage. The company's collision damage waiver (CDW) is another $15 per day. If you choose not to accept it, you'll be responsible for up to the full value of damage to the car. (Your own insurance policy may cover you, at least in part. Check the precise wording of the policy.)

Budget is represented in Jamaica by Sun Tours Car Rental (☎ **809/952-5185** for reservations and information, or call 809/952-3838 at the Montego Bay airport). Renters must be at least 25 years old with a valid driver's license. Cars such as the Suzuki Alto rented for $288 and up per week at press time, with unlimited mileage, plus 15% government tax. A daily collision damage waiver of $15 is mandatory. In the event of an accident, renters are still responsible for the first $1,000, plus tax, worth of damage to a rented car. A security deposit of the above amount is therefore required for a rental agreement to be completed.

Hertz (☎ **800/654-3001**) operates branches at the international airports in both Montego Bay (☎ 809/979-0438) and Kingston (☎ 809/924-8028). Most of its vehicles rented for $300 to $400 per week (plus 15% tax) with unlimited mileage when we went to press. A collision damage waiver costs $15 extra per day, and reduces (but does not eliminate) the customer's responsibility for accident damage to the car. (Without the waiver, you'll be liable for up to $3,000 worth of damage, depending on where you rent it; with the waiver, the amount of your liability is reduced to between $750 and $1,000.)

At most companies, you'll be required to leave an imprint of a valid credit card before you can drive away in a rental car. In rare instances, an exception might be made that allows you to leave a substantial cash deposit of around $1,000 instead. You'll also face a sometimes rigorous background check of your credit record and employment history.

DRIVING RULES   *Driving in Jamaica is on the left side of the road,* not on the right side as in the United States, Canada, and Europe. You should exercise more than usual caution because of the unfamiliar terrain and be especially cautious at night. Don't drink and drive. Speed limits in towns are 30 m.p.h., and outside towns, 50 m.p.h. Gas is measured by the imperial gallon (a British unit of measurement that is 25% more than a U.S. gallon); most stations don't accept credit cards. Your valid driver's license from home is acceptable for short-term visits to Jamaica.

ROAD MAPS   The major highways of Jamaica tend to be well-marked and easily discernible because of their end-destination, which is often adequately signposted. More complicated are secondary roads, urban streets, and feeder roads, whose markings sometimes are infuriatingly unclear. Recognizing this problem, the Jamaica Tourist Board has issued one of the best maps of the island available anywhere, the "Discover Jamaica" road map. Conforming to international cartographical standards, it contains a detailed overview of the entire island, as well as blowups of the Kingston, Montego Bay, Negril, Mandeville, Spanish Town, Port Antonio, and Ocho Rios areas. The map includes a very useful street index to Kingston. A copy of the map is usually available from any branch of the Jamaica Tourist Board, or from car-rental agencies. It's best to obtain one before your visit (see "Information," above), as local branches might be out of stock.

Road Mileage Chart

	Black River	Falmouth	Kingston	Mande-ville	Montego Bay	Negril	Ocho Rios	Port Antonio	St. Anne's Bay
Black River	0	62	107	43	46	49	94	156	87
Falmouth	62	0	91	53	23	75	44	110	37
Kingston	107	91	0	61	119	153	54	61	59
Mandeville	43	53	61	0	70	92	72	117	62
Montego Bay	46	23	119	70	0	52	67	133	60
Negril	49	75	153	92	52	0	117	181	110
Ocho Rios	94	44	54	72	67	117	0	66	7
Port Antonio	156	110	61	117	133	181	66	0	73
St. Anne's Bay	87	37	59	62	60	110	7	73	0

AUTO BREAKDOWNS   In case of breakdowns, telephone your car-rental agency for assistance. The staff will contact the nearest garage with which it has an affiliation, and a tow truck or mechanic will be dispatched to help you.

BY TAXI & BUS

Taxis in Kingston don't have meters, so agree on a price before you get in the car. In Kingston and the rest of the island, special taxis and buses for visitors are operated by JUTA (Jamaica Union of Travellers Association) and have the union's emblem on the side of the vehicle. All prices are controlled, and any local JUTA office will supply a list of rates. JUTA drivers do nearly all the ground transfers, and some offer sightseeing tours. We've found them pleasant, knowledgeable, and good drivers. There are many companies offering sightseeing tours of the island. Most cabs are old vehicles made in the United States.

BY MOTORBIKE & SCOOTER

Motorbikes and scooters can be rented in Montego Bay. You'll need a valid driver's license. **Montego Honda/Bike Rentals,** 21 Gloucester Ave. (☎ **809/952-4984**), rents Hondas for $35 a day, plus a $300 deposit. Scooters also cost $35 per day. Mountain bikes are available as well. Deposits are refundable if the vehicles are returned in good shape. Hours are 7:30am to 5pm daily.

FAST FACTS: Jamaica

American Express   The representative is Stewart's Travel Service, 9 Celio Ave., Kingston 10 (☎ 809/929-3077). Open Monday through Friday from 9am to 5pm. There is a branch office in Montego Bay at 32 Market St. (☎ **809/952-2586**). Open Monday through Friday from 9am to 5pm and Saturday 9am to noon.

Airports   See "Getting To Jamaica" and "Getting Around Jamaica" in this chapter.

Bookstores   The island's best is **Sangster's,** whose head office is at 20 Constant Spring Rd., The Mall Plaza, Kingston (☎ 809/926-2271). Open Monday through Friday from 10am to 6pm, Saturday 10am to noon. A branch is at 2 St. James St.,

Montego Bay (☎ **809/952-0319**). Open Monday through Saturday from 8:30am to 4:30pm.

Business Hours   Banks are open Monday through Friday from 9am to 5pm. Store hours vary widely, but as a general rule most business establishments open at 8:30am and close at 4:30 or 5pm Monday through Friday. Some shops are open on Saturday until noon.

Car Rentals   See "Getting Around," earlier in this chapter.

Climate   See "When to Go," earlier in this chapter.

Currency   See "Money," earlier in this chapter.

Currency Exchange   There are Bank of Jamaica exchange bureaus at both international airports (near Montego Bay and Kingston), at cruise-ship piers, and in most hotels.

Dentist   Hotels keep a list of nearby dentists.

Doctor   See "Hospitals," below. Many major resorts have doctors on call. If you need any particular medicine or treatment, bring evidence, such as a letter from your own doctor.

Documents Required   See "Visitor Information & Entry Requirements," earlier in this chapter.

Driving Rules   See "Getting Around," earlier in this chapter.

Drugstores   In Montego Bay, try **McKenzie's Drug Store,** 16 Strand St. (☎ **809/925-2467**); in Ocho Rios, **Great House Pharmacy,** Brown's Plaza (☎ **809/974-2352**); and in Kingston, **Moodie's Pharmacy,** New Kingston Shopping Centre (☎ **809/926-4174**). Prescriptions are accepted by local pharmacies only if issued by a Jamaican doctor.

Electricity   Most places have the standard electrical voltage of 110, as in the U.S. However, some establishments operate on 220 volts, 50 cycles. If your hotel is on a different current from your U.S.-made appliance, ask for a transformer and adapter.

Embassies and Consulates   The **U.S. Embassy** is at Jamaica Mutual Life Centre, 2 Oxford Rd., Kingston 5 (☎ **809/929-4850**). Open Monday through Friday from 8am to noon and 1 to 4:30pm. The **Canada High Commission** is at Mutual Security Bank Building, 30-36 Knutsford Blvd., Kingston 5 (☎ **809/926-1500**). The **Canadian Consulate** is at 29 Gloucester Ave., Montego Bay (☎ **809/952-6198**). Both Canadian offices are open Monday through Friday from 8am to noon and 1 to 4:30pm. The **United Kingdom High Commission** is at 26 Trafalgar Rd., Kingston 10 (☎ **809/926-9050**). Open Monday through Friday from 8:30am to 1pm and 2 to 4:30pm.

Emergencies   For police and air rescue, dial 119; to report a fire or call an ambulance, dial 110.

Eyeglasses   One reliable optician is **Broadbent,** 1 Duke St., Kingston (☎ **809/922-4721**). Open Monday through Friday from 8:30am to 4:30pm. For north shore resorts, ask your hotel for the nearest practitioner.

Holidays   See "When to Go," earlier in this chapter.

Hospitals   In Kingston, **University Hospital** is at Mona (☎ **809/927-1620**); in Montego Bay, **Cornwall Regional Hospital** is at Mount Salem (☎ **809/952-5100**); and in Port Antonio, **Port Antonio General Hospital** is at Naylor's Hill (☎ **809/993-2646**).

Information   See "Visitor Information & Entry Requirements," earlier in this chapter.

Mail   Instead of going to a post office, you can, in most cases, give mail to personnel at your hotel's reception desk. Most hotels sell postage stamps. A hotel worker will give your mail to a postperson at the time of mail pickup or include them in the hotel mail when a staff member goes to the post office. Parcels can often be mailed by a hotel worker. Allow about one week for an airmail postcard or letter to reach the North American mainland. Increases in postal charges can be implemented at any time, so find out the current rate before depositing mail. Call **809/922-5420 in Kingston** for any problems or questions about mail in Jamaica. If you want to be sure of delivery, consider employing a courier service like DHL or Federal Express.

Maps   See "Getting Around," earlier in this chapter.

Newspapers and Magazines   Jamaica supports three daily newspapers (*Daily Gleaner, The Jamaica Record,* and *Daily Star*), several weekly periodicals, and a handful of other publications. U.S. newsmagazines, such as *Time* and *Newsweek*, as well as occasional copies of *The Miami Herald,* are available at most newsstands.

Nudity   Nude sunbathing and swimming are allowed at a number of hotels, clubs, and beaches (especially in Negril), but only where signs state that swimsuits are optional. Elsewhere, law enforcers will not even allow topless sunbathing.

Police   Dial 119.

Radio & TV   Jamaica is served by two major radio broadcasters, both of which are instantly recognizable to thousands of island residents. Radio Jamaica (RJR) is the more popular of the two, partly because of its musical mix of reggae, rock 'n' roll, and talk show material of everyday interest to Jamaicans. The broadcaster is owned by the Jamaican government, its employees, and members of the Jamaican community. RJR's two islandwide services are known as Supreme Sound and FAME FM. The second broadcaster is Jamaica Broadcasting Corporation (JBC), run by a board appointed by the government. JBC also operates the island's only television station (JBC-TV, established in 1963), which transmits from at least two different points on the island.

The availability of Jamaican radio and TV stations does not prevent many island residents from tuning in TV and radio programming from the U.S. mainland, South America, and other Caribbean islands. Many of Jamaica's better hotels offer Cable News Network (CNN) and other satellite broadcasts. Hotels also offer in-house video movies transmitted from a central point in the establishment.

Safety   You can get into a lot of trouble in Jamaica or you can have a carefree vacation—much depends on what you do and where you go. Major hotels have security guards to protect the grounds. Under no circumstances should you accept an invitation to see "the real Jamaica" from some stranger you meet on the beach. Exercise caution when traveling around the country. Safeguard your valuables and never leave them unattended on a beach. Likewise, never leave luggage or other valuables in a car's passenger compartment or trunk. For the latest advisories, call the **U.S. State Department (☎ 202/647-5225).**

Taxes   The government imposes a 12% room tax, per room, per night. You will also be charged a J$400 (U.S.$10.40) departure tax at the airport, payable in either Jamaica or U.S. dollars.

Taxis   See "Getting Around," earlier in this chapter.

Telephone, Telex & Fax   All overseas telephone calls are subject to a government tax of 15%. Most calls can be made from the privacy of your hotel room or, in some budget or moderate hotels, from the lobby. Even the island's smallest hotels maintain their own fax machines. For telexes, and in case your hotel isn't equipped with suitable phone or fax equipment, contact the local branch of **Jamintel,** the country's telecommunications operators. In Kingston, its address is 15 North St. (☎ **809/922-6031**).

Time   In the winter, Jamaica is on eastern standard time. When the United States is on daylight saving time, however, it's 6am in Miami and 5am in Kingston, because Jamaica does not switch to DST.

Tipping   Tipping is customary in Jamaica. Typically, 10% or 15% is expected in hotels and restaurants on occasions when you would normally tip. Most places add a service charge to the bill. Tipping is not allowed in the all-inclusive hotels.

Useful Telephone Numbers   Ambulance, 110; fire, 110; police, 119; time, 117; toll operator and telephone assistance on local and intra-island calls, 112; overseas calls operator, 113; and **Post and Telegraph Department, ☎ 809/922-9430.**

Water   It's usually safe to drink tap water islandwide, as it is filtered and chlorinated; however, it's prudent to drink bottled water, if available.

Weather   See "When to Go," earlier in this chapter.

Weddings   Some of the all-inclusive Jamaican hotel chains are more involved with weddings than others, mainly **Sandals (☎ 800/SANDALS**), which have helped tie the knot for many couples.

In high season, some Jamaican resorts witness several weddings a day. Many of the larger Jamaican resorts can arrange for an officiant, a photographer, and even the wedding cake and champagne. Some resorts will even throw in your wedding with the cost of your honeymoon at the hotel. Both the Jamaican Tourist Board and your hotel, perhaps one of the many Sandals resorts in Jamaica, will assist you with the paperwork.

The bride and groom must reside on Jamaica for 24 hours before the ceremony. Bring birth certificates and affidavits saying you've never been married before, or, if you've been divorced, bring copies of your divorce papers; in the case of widows and widowers, a copy of the deceased spouses' death certificate. The cost of the formalities and the ceremony ranges from $50 to $200, depending on how much legwork you want to do yourself. You may apply in person at The **Ministry of National Security and Justice,** 12 Ocean Blvd., Kingston, Jamaica (☎ **809/922-0080**).

10 Tips on Accommodations

Because of the island's size and diversity, Jamaica offers a wider array of accommodations than anywhere else in the Caribbean. Part of your vacation's success depends on your understanding of the various available options.

Accommodations can range from intimate inns, with no more than six or seven rooms (and the very visible on-site presence of the owner/manager), to giant mega-hotels with an enviable array of services and such facilities as tennis compounds, therapeutic spas, and golf courses.

Jamaica Accommodations

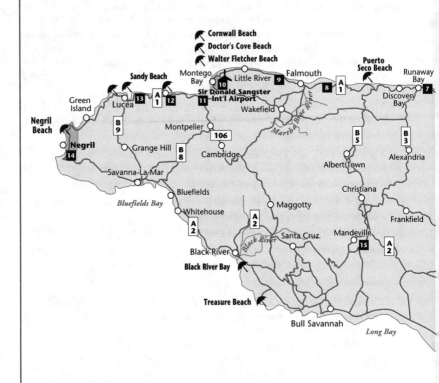

Blue Harbour **3**
Boscobel Beach **4**
Charela Inn **14**
Ciboney Ocho Rios **6**
Coral Cliff **10**
Couples Ocho Rios **5**
Doctor's Cave Beach
    Hotel **10**
Eaton Hall Beach Hotel **7**
Enchanted
    Garden, The **6**
Fantasy Resort **10**

FDR (Franklin D. Resort) **7**
Fern Hill Club **2**
Goblin Hill Villas
    at San San **2**
Good Hope **8**
Grand Hotel Lido **14**
Half Moon Club **9**
Hedonism II **14**
Hibiscus Lodge Hotel **6**
Holiday Inn **9**
Hotel Astra **15**
Hotel Four Seasons **1**

Indies Hotel **1**
Jack Tar Village **10**
Jamaica Grande
    Renaissance Resort **6**
Jamaica Inn **6**
Jamaica, Jamaica **7**
Jamaica Palace Hotel **2**
Jamaica Pegasus **1**
Mandeville Hotel **15**
Navy Island Marina Resort **2**
Negril Beach Club Hotel **14**
Negril Cabins **14**

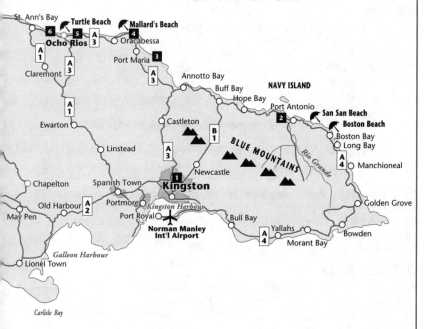

Negril Gardens 14
Negril Inn 14
Negril Tree House 14
Ocean View Guest
  House 10
Plantation Inn 6
Poinciana Beach Resort 14
Reading Reef Club 11
Round Hill Hotel &
  Villas 12
Royal Court Hotel 10

Runaway H.E.A.R.T.
  Country Club 7
Sandals Dunn's River 6
Sandals Inn, The 10
Sandals Montego Bay 10
Sandals Negril 14
Sandals Ocho Rios 6
Sandals Royal Jamaican 10
Sans Souci Lido 14
Seacastles 9
Sea Garden Beach
  Resort 10

Seasplash Resort 14
Swept Away 14
Terra Nova Hotel 1
Trident Villas & Hotel 2
Tryall Golf, Tennis &
  Beach Club 13
Vista Ambassador 10
Wexford Court Hotel 10
Winged Victory Hotel 10
Windham Kingston Hotel 1
Windham Rose Hall
  Resort 9

One increasingly popular option is the **all-inclusive resort.** Well-publicized, solidly financed, and boasting a wealth of facilities, these tend to be large resorts where all your drinking, dining, and sporting diversions are offered *within the hotel compound* as part of one all-inclusive price. Although they tend to limit your exposure to local life, they are undeniably convenient; they usually operate as self-sufficient planets with few incentives to travel beyond the fences that surround them. For carefree vacations, however, they're hard to beat, especially since your total cost will be made explicitly clear before you ever leave home.

An equally attractive option might be a **European-style hotel,** one designed on European principles. Jamaica offers many of these, a few of which are considered the finest in the Caribbean. There, on any given day, you'll be given an option of dining either within the hotel or at any of the small and charming restaurants that flourish nearby. Although you'll have to arrange evening transportation between your hotel and these independent restaurants, a battalion of taxis is almost always available throughout the evening to carry you there and back.

Other options include renting a **self-catering villa or apartment,** where you can save money by making your own meals in your own kitchen.

Also noteworthy are Jamaica's simple but decent **guesthouses,** where low costs combine with a maximum exposure to local life. Unfortunately, these sometimes tend to lie far from beaches and offer almost none of the diversions and activities that vacationers seem to crave, and will probably not appeal to clients who insist on problem-free luxury.

Regardless of what you select, be assured that every choice has its own style, flavor, and methods of operating. Any will contribute richly to your understanding of the kaleidoscopic tapestry that is Jamaica.

HOTELS & RESORTS

There is no rigid classification of Jamaican hotels. The word "deluxe" is often used— or misused—when "first class" might be a more appropriate term. First class itself often isn't apt. We've presented fairly detailed descriptions of the properties mentioned in this book, so you'll get an idea of what to expect once you're there. Even in deluxe and first-class properties, however, don't expect top-rate service and efficiency. "Things," as they are called in Jamaica, don't seem to work as well in the tropics as they do in certain fancy resorts of California or Europe. When you go to turn on the shower, sometimes you get water and sometimes you don't. You may even experience island power failures.

Facilities often determine the choice of a hotel. For example, if golf is your passion, you may want to book into a hotel resort such as Tryall outside Montego Bay. If scuba diving is your goal, then head, say, for Negril. Regardless of your particular interest, there is probably a hotel catering to you.

One of the most common hotel and resort rates is **MAP,** meaning Modified American Plan. MAP usually includes room, breakfast, and dinner, unless the room rate has been quoted separately, and then it covers only breakfast and dinner. **CP** means Continental Plan—room and a light breakfast. **EP** is European Plan, room only. **AP,** American Plan, is the most expensive rate, because it includes room plus three meals a day. Nevertheless, you can save money by booking the AP rate. See "Tips on Dining Out," below, for some advice on making your choice.

GUESTHOUSES

An entirely different type of accommodation is the guesthouse, where most of the Jamaicans themselves stay when they travel. In Jamaica, the term "guesthouse" can

---

🄰 Family-Friendly Hotels

Boscobel Beach *(see p. 133)*   The best place on the island for families with children is outside Ocho Rios. There's a children's center and a mini-zoo, and special deals exist for single parents. There's also a special program for grandpartents and their grandchildren.

FDR (Franklyn D. Resort) *(see p. 129)*   At Runaway Bay, this all-inclusive resort caters to families and features a Kiddies' Centre. There's even a disco for tots. Special children's meals are served.

Wyndham Rose Hall *(see page 87)*   This hotel outside Montego Bay offers a "Kids Klub," with an array of supervised activities that's included in the rate. Of the the pools, one is suited for small children. There's also a thin crescent of beach, and baby-sitting can be arranged.

---

mean anything. Sometimes so-called guesthouses resemble simple motels built around swimming pools. Others are made up of small individual cottages with kitchenettes, constructed around a main building often containing a bar and a restaurant serving local food. Some are surprisingly comfortable, often with private baths and a swimming pool. You may or may not have air-conditioning. The rooms are sometimes cooled by ceiling fans, or breezes entering through open windows at night.

The guesthouse can't be topped for value. You can usually go to a big beach resort to enjoy its seaside facilities for only a small charge. Although bereft of frills, the guesthouses we've recommended are clean and safe for families or single women. On the other hand, the least expensive are not places where you'd want to spend much time, because of their simple furnishings, diversions, and amenities.

HOME EXCHANGES

House swapping keeps costs low if you don't mind a stranger living in your mainland home or apartment, and sometimes the exchange includes use of the family car.

Many home-exchange directories are published, but there's no guarantee that you'll find a house or apartment in the area you're seeking.

The Invented City, 41 Sutter St., Suite 1090, San Francisco, CA 94104 (☎ **415/ 252-1141** or 800/788-CITY; fax 415/252-1171), is an international home-exchange agency. Home-exchange listings are published three times a year, in February, May, and November. A membership fee of $50 allows you to list your home, and you can also give your preferred times of travel, and member-written description of one's home-exchange offer.

Intervac U.S., P.O. Box 590504, San Francisco, CA 94119 (☎ **415/435-3497** or 800/756-HOME in the U.S.; fax 415/435-7440), is part of the largest worldwide home-exchange network. It publishes four catalogs a year, containing more than 9,400 homes in more than 36 countries. Members contact each other directly. Exchanges usually include cars and homes and are on the honor system. The $65 cost, plus postage, includes the purchase of three of the company's catalogs (which will be mailed to you), plus the inclusion of your own listing in whichever one of the three catalogs you select. If you want to publish a photograph of your home, it costs $11 extra. Hospitality and rentals are also available.

Vacation Exchange Club, P.O. Box 650, Key West, FL 33041 (☎ **305/ 294-1448** or 800/638-3841), will send you five directories a year for $70. You're listed in one of the directories.

11 Renting Your Own Condo, Cottage, or Villa

Particularly if you're going as a family or group of friends, a housekeeping holiday can be one of the least expensive ways to vacation in Jamaica. Self-catering accommodations are now available at many locations.

The more upscale villas have a staff, or at least a maid who comes in a few days a week, and they also provide the essentials for home life, including bed linen and cooking paraphernalia. Condos usually come with a reception desk and are often comparable to life in a suite in a big resort hotel. Nearly all condo complexes provide swimming pools (some more than one).

Some private apartments in Jamaica are rented, either with or without maid service. This is more of a no-frills option than the villas and condos. The apartments may not be in buildings with swimming pools, and they may not maintain a front desk to help you. Cottages are the most freewheeling way to live in the four major categories of vacation homes. Most are fairly simple, many ideally opening onto a beach, although others may be clustered around a communal swimming pool. Many contain no more than a simple bedroom with a small kitchen and bath. In the peak winter season, reservations should be made at least five or six months in advance.

Travel experts agree that savings, especially for a family of three to six people, or two or three couples, can range from 50% to 60% of what a hotel would cost. If there are only two in your party, these savings don't apply.

The savings will be on the rent, not on the groceries, which are sometimes 35% to 60% more costly than on the U.S. mainland. Grocery tabs reflect the fact that much foodstuff must be imported. Even so, preparing your own food will be a lot cheaper than dining around, as most restaurants, even the so-called inexpensive places, are likely to be more expensive than what is considered cheap in your hometown.

Villas of Distinction, P.O. Box 55, Armonk, NY 10504 (☎ **914/273-3331** or 800/289-0900), is one of the best booking agencies offering "complete vacations," including airfare, rental car, and domestic help. Some private villas offer two to five bedrooms, and almost every villa features a swimming pool. Islands on which you can rent villas include Barbados and Jamaica, among others.

At Home Abroad, Suite 6-H, 405 E. 56th St., New York, NY 10022 (☎ **212/421-9165**), has a roster of private homes for rent in the Caribbean, often with maid service included. All the Barbados and Jamaican villas have cooks and maids.

Caribbean Connection Plus Ltd., P.O. Box 261, Trumbull, CT 06611 (☎ **203/261-8603;** fax 203/261-8295), offers many apartments and villas in the Caribbean. This is one of the few reservations services whose staff has actually been on the islands and seen the various properties. Hence, the staff can talk to people from experience and not from a computer screen.

Hideaways International, 767 Islington St., P.O. Box 4433, Portsmouth, NH 03801-4433 (☎ **603/430-4433** or 800/843-4433; fax 603/430-4444), provides a 144-page guide with illustrations of its accommodations in the Caribbean so you'll get some idea of what you're renting. Most of its villas, which can hold up to three couples or a large family of about 10, come with maid service. You can also ask this travel club about discounts on plane fares and car rentals.

VHR, Worldwide, 235 Kensington Ave., Norwood, NJ 07648 (☎ **201/767-9393** or 800/633-3284 in the U.S. and Canada), offers the most comprehensive portfolio of luxury villas, condominiums, resort suites, and apartments for rent not only in the Caribbean, but also in the Bahamas, Mexico, and the United States, including complete packages with airfare and car rentals. The company's more than 4,000 homes and suite resorts are hand-picked by the staff, and accommodations are generally less expensive than comparable hotel rooms.

Heart of the Caribbean Ltd., 17485 Peinbrook Dr., Brookfield, WI 53045 (☎ 414/783-5303), is a villa wholesale company offering travelers a wide range of private villas and condos on several islands. Accommodations range from one to six bedrooms, and the establishment offers modest villas and condos, as well as palatial estates. Homes have complete kitchens.

Rent-a-Home International, 7200 34th Ave. NW, Seattle, WA 98117 (☎ 206/789-9377; fax 206/789-9379), maintains an inventory of several thousand properties, specializing in condos and villas with weekly rates ranging from $700 to $30,000. It arranges weekly or longer bookings. For their color catalog including prices, descriptions and pictures, send $15, which will be applied to your rental.

Sometimes local tourist offices will also advise you on vacation-home rentals if you write or call them directly.

12 Tips on Dining Out

The bad news is that dining in Jamaica is generally more expensive than in either the United States or Canada. Restaurant prices are in tune with Europe rather than America. Virtually everything must be imported, except the fish or Caribbean lobster that is caught locally, and some fruits and vegetables. Service is automatically added to most restaurant tabs, usually 10% to 15%. Even so, if service has been good, it's customary to tip extra.

To save money, many visitors prefer the Modified American Plan (MAP), which includes room, breakfast, and one main meal per day, nearly always dinner. You can then have lunch somewhere else, or if your hotel has a beach, order a light à la carte lunch at the hotel, the cost of which is added to your bill. The American Plan (AP), on the other hand, includes all three meals per day. Drinks, including wine, are usually extra.

If you want to eat your main meals outside the hotel, book a Continental Plan (CP), which includes only breakfast. To go one step further, choose the European Plan (EP), which includes no meals.

Before booking a hotel, it's wise to have a clear understanding of what is included in the various meal plans offered.

In the summer, only the most sophisticated and posh establishments require men to wear jackets. Always check the policy of the restaurant or hotel before going to a particular establishment or dining room. Check also to see if reservations are required. In the winter, you may find all the tables gone at some of the more famous places. At all places, wear a cover-up if you're lunching; don't enter a restaurant attired in a bikini.

To save money, stick to regional food whenever possible. For a main dish, that usually means Caribbean lobster or fish (see "A Taste of Jamaica" in Chapter 2). Don't eat too much red meat; it's probably flown in and may have been waiting on the island long before you arrived on the beach.

Frankly, it's difficult for first-time visitors driving rented cars to navigate the unsatisfactory Jamaican roads at night looking for a special little restaurant. The restaurant's food may be good, but getting there can be dangerous, because roads are narrow and not well lit. To complicate matters for Americans, Canadians, and Europeans, Jamaicans drive on the left side of the road, as in Great Britain. If you

Jamaica Dining

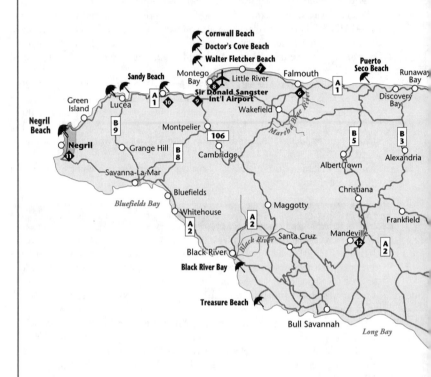

Almond Tree
   Restaurant **5**
Blue Mountain Inn **1**
Cafe au Lait/Mirage
   Cottages **11**
Calabash Restaurant **8**
Casanova, The **4**
Cascade Room **8**
Castles, The **4**
Chelsea Jerk Centre **1**
Chicken Lavish **11**

Cosmo's Seafood
   Restaurant & Bar **11**
Devonshire Restaurant /
   The Grogg Shoppe **4**
Dock "On the Bay" **5**
El Dorado Room **1**
Evita's Italian Restaurant **5**
Fern Hill Club **2**
Georgian House **8**
Glistening Waters
   Inn & Marina **6**

Hot Pot, The **1**
Indies Pub and Grill **1**
Jade Garden **1**
Julia's **8**
Le Vendome **11**
Little Pub Restaurant **5**
Mandeville Hotel **12**
Marguerite's Seafood
   by the Sea **8**
Margueritaville Sports
   Bar & Grill **8**

78

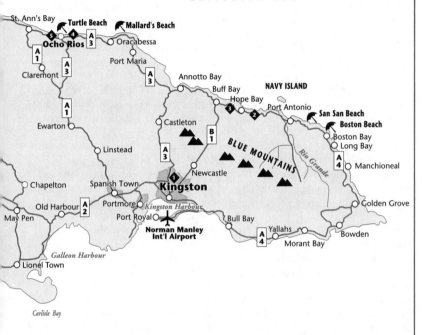

Caribbean Sea

St. Ann's Bay
Turtle Beach **Mallard's Beach**
Ocho Rios Oracabessa
Claremont
Port Maria
Annotto Bay
Buff Bay
NAVY ISLAND
Hope Bay
Port Antonio
San San Beach
Boston Beach
Ewarton
Castleton
Boston Bay
Long Bay
BLUE MOUNTAINS
Rio Grande
Linstead
Manchioneal
Chapelton
Spanish Town
Newcastle
Kingston
Golden Grove
Old Harbour
Portmore
Kingston Harbour
May Pen
Port Royal
Bull Bay
Yallahs
Bowden
Norman Manley Int'l Airport
Morant Bay
Galleon Harbour
Lionel Town
Carlisle Bay

Airport ✈ Beach ⚑

Mariners Inn and
   Restaurant 🔶
Native Restaurant, The 🔶
Negril Tree House 🔶
Norma at the
   Wharfhouse 🔶
Paradise Yard 🔶
Parkway Restaurant 🔶
Pier 1 🔶
Plantation Inn
   Restaurant 🔶

Pork Pit 🔶
Port Royal
   Restaurant, The 🔶
Rafter's Restaurant 🔶
Reading Reef Club
   Restaurant 🔶
Restaurant Ambrosia 🔶
Restaurant Tan-Ya /
   Calico Jack's 🔶
Richmond Hill Inn 🔶
Rick's Cafe 🔶

Round Hill Dining Room 🔶
Ruins Restaurant, Gift
   Shop & Boutique 🔶
Sugar Mill Restaurant 🔶
Taste Jamaica Ltd. 🔶
Town House 🔶
Trident Hotel
   Restaurant 🔶
Yachtsman's Wharf 🔶

go out for dinner, consider taking a taxi; all taxi drivers know the badly marked roads well. Once at the restaurant, you can arrange for the taxi to pick you up at an agreed on time or else have the restaurant call the taxi when you are ready to leave. Some restaurants, such as the first-class establishments in Montego Bay, will arrange to have a minivan pick you up and return you to your hotel if you call in advance.

13 Tips on Shopping

If your shopping tastes run toward the electronic, you might discover an occasional bargain in audio equipment in the marketplaces of Jamaica, as well as a scattering of wristwatches, discounted gold chains, and a small appliance or two. Much more appealing, however, are the thousands of handcrafted items whose inspiration seems to spring from the creative depths of the Jamaican soul.

The arts are not a new tradition in Jamaica. During the 1700s, Jamaican wig holders, combs, boxes, and art objects were considered charming decorative objects as far away as London. Today, the tradition of arts and handcrafts continues to flourish, with a far greater array of purchasable possibilities.

In Jamaica, as everywhere else, the distinction between what is art and what is considered merely a craft is often a matter of personal preference. However varied your artistic background and tastes may be, an estimated 50,000 artisans labor long and hard to produce thousands of paintings, wood carvings, textiles, and whatnots, any of which might serve as an evocative reminder of your Jamaican holiday. It is estimated that there are at least 500 wood-carving stands set beside the road between Montego Bay and Ocho Rios, and many dozens of others scattered throughout the rest of Jamaica as well.

Usually chiseled from either mahogany or a very hard tropical wood known as *lignum vitae*, **wood carvings** run the gamut from the execrably horrible to the delicately delightful, with many works of power and vision in between. Frequently, pieces have been carved with such crude tools as antique iron chisels, and (sometimes) nothing more than a graduated set of pocketknives and nails. Also available are all sizes of **baskets** woven from palm fronds or the straw of an island plant known as the *jipijapa*, calabash (gourds) etched with illustrations of hummingbirds and vines, and hammocks woven into designs handed down from the time of the Arawak Indians.

Although many of Jamaica's crafts are distributed by entrepreneurial middlepeople, it always (at least for us) gives a purchase an especially subjective memory when the purchase is made directly from the hands which crafted it.

The island's inventory of wood carvings and weavings is supplemented by establishments selling **leather goods** (sandals and shoes are often a good buy), locally made jewelry fashioned from gold, silver, onyx, and bone, and garments (especially casual wear and sportswear) whose light textures nicely complement the heat of the tropics. Also noteworthy are the many handbags woven from straw or palm fronds, which are sometimes rendered more ornate through colorful embroideries applied by any of the island's "straw ladies."

Many people head home with several bottles of the heady **spices** whose seasonings flavor the best of Jamaica's dishes. Vacuum-sealed plastic containers filled with **Blue Mountain coffee** are enviable gifts for loved ones after your return home, as well as any of the bottles of specialty rums whose flavors (orange, coconut, and coffee, among others) can evoke the heat of Jamaica even during a snow-blanketed northern winter.

Especially noteworthy are the handful of **art galleries** that stock the paintings of local artists. Jamaica's impressive inventory of painters have been well-documented in art galleries throughout Europe and North America. You'll probably find dozens of paintings for sale. Some critics say the island's most valuable export, after aluminum, is its art. These paintings range from the banal and uninspired to richly evocative portrayals of universal themes. If the painting speaks to you, consider buying it. Before investing in a major purchase, however, we suggest you consult with an expert at one of the island's better-known galleries, where paintings can easily cost several thousand dollars. Lesser works, or works by as-yet unknown artists, are sometimes available for as little as $15 each on sidewalks throughout the country.

Polite and good-natured **bargaining** is usually expected, especially in the informal markets. In fact, if you bargain with goodwill and humor, you might get some pleasant insights into the interpersonal dynamics that are part of the island's daily life. And you should get a discount of around 15% to 20%. In more formal environments, bargaining often will simply not work. The aura projected by the owner or salesperson will quickly communicate the degree to which bargaining is welcomed.

Although shopping possibilities abound in virtually every tourist resort, every serious shopper should visit an outlet of the government-funded **Things Jamaican.** The quality of inventory varies widely from outlet to outlet, but they all offer a sampling under one roof of some of the best products of the island. (Addresses of Things Jamaican are listed under the "Shopping" section of this guide.)

4

Montego Bay

Montego Bay made its first appearance on the world's tourism stage in the 1940s when wealthy travelers discovered the warm, spring-fed waters of Doctor's Cave Beach. Now Jamaica's second largest community, the town of Mo Bay—as the locals call it—lies on the northwest coast of the island. In spite of its large influx of visitors, Montego Bay retains its own identity. A thriving business and commercial center, it functions as the main market town for most of western Jamaica. It supports cruise-ship piers and a growing industrial center at the free port.

Montego Bay is served by its own airport, Donald Sangster International, so vacationers coming to Jamaica have little need to visit Kingston, the island's capital, unless they want to see its cultural and historical attractions. Otherwise, you will find everything in Mo Bay, the most cosmopolitan of Jamaica's resorts.

Some 23 miles east of Montego Bay, the small 18th-century port town of Falmouth is one of the most interesting morning or afternoon excursions from Mo Bay. (Ocho Rios and Runaway Bay are other good choices; they're covered in Chapter 6.) Falmouth is not really a tourist town. It derives most of its income from farming and fishing; more than any resort town, it is the "real" Jamaica. We'll take you there at the end of this chapter.

1 Where to Stay

The Montego Bay region boasts a superb selection of hotels, ranging from very expensive world-class establishments to notable bargains. There is also an amazing selection of all-inclusive resorts.

VERY EXPENSIVE

✪ Half Moon Golf, Tennis & Beach Club

8 miles east of Montego Bay along A1 (P.O. Box 80), Rose Hall, Montego Bay, Jamaica, W.I. ☎ **809/953-2211** or 800/626-0592. Fax 809/953-2731. 341 units. A/C TEL. Winter $265–$480 double, $530 suite or villa; off-season $190–$270 double, $300–$500 suite or villa. MAP $66 extra per person per day. AE, DC, MC, V.

Located about about halfway between Montego Bay's city center and the international airport, the Half Moon Club is considered one of the 300 best hotels in the world. It boasts an incredible array of sports facilities, including any water sports your heart desires.

What's Special About Montego Bay

Beaches
- Cornwall Beach, Jamaica's finest underwater marine park and fun complex, a long stretch of white sandy beach with water sports galore.
- Doctor's Cave Beach, a 5-mile stretch of sugary sand that launched Mo Bay as a resort in the 1940s. Unfortunately it's become Jamaica's worst-kept secret.
- Walter Fletcher Beach, one of the premier beaches of Jamaica. Its tranquil waters and lifeguard service make it a family favorite.

Memorable Sights & Experiences
- The Hilton High Day Tour, a scenic drive through historic north-coast plantation areas with a Jamaican lunch of roast suckling pig and rum punch.
- An Evening on the Great River, a fishing canoe ride up the river where a torchlit path leads to a re-created Arawak village.
- Martha Brae's Rafters Village, reached by driving east beyond Falmouth. A river ride on a raised dais lashed atop bamboo logs.

Historic Homes
- Rose Hall, east of Montego Bay, subject of at least a dozen Gothic novels, former abode of Annie Palmer, the "White Witch of Rose Hall."
- Greenwood, east of Montego Bay near Falmouth, 19th-century Georgian-style building and former home of the famous Barrett family of England.

Especially for Kids
- Jamaica Safari Village, east of Montego Bay near Falmouth, film set for the James Bond thriller *Live and Let Die,* and known for its crocodile ponds and petting zoo.

Attracting such distinguished guests as former U.S. President George Bush or Queen Elizabeth II, the resort complex consists of spacious hotel rooms, suites, and private four- to six-bedroom villas scattered over 400 acres of rich and fertile landscape. Each accommodation is comfortably furnished in an English colonial-Caribbean motif, and many of the villas have private swimming pools. Much made-in-Jamaica reproduction furniture is used, including some mahogany four-poster beds. The landscaping here is arranged to provide maximum privacy from the rest of the resort.

Dining/Entertainment: The Sugar Mill Restaurant has a personal touch; it's set beside a working water wheel from a bygone sugar estate (see "Where to Dine," below). Connected to the resort's main building, the Seagrape Terrace (named after the 80-year-old sea grape trees that push up from the pavement that surrounds them) is also a choice place to dine, with meals served outdoors by a uniformed staff. Il Giardino offers a savory Italian cuisine. The resort has nightly entertainment from a resident band, plus folklore and musical shows.

Services: Laundry, baby-sitters, room service (7am to midnight), massage; lessons in golf, tennis, and various water sports.

Facilities: Shopping village (with a pharmacy, Jamaican restaurant, Japanese restaurant, English-style pub, and boutiques), beauty salon, sauna, fitness center; facilities for ocean swimming, sailing, windsurfing, snorkeling, scuba diving, deep-sea fishing; 39 freshwater pools; horseback riding; four lighted squash courts, 13 tennis courts (seven floodlit at night), and an 18-hole Robert Trent Jones–designed golf course (see "Hitting the Beach, Hitting the Links & Other Outdoor Activities" later in this chapter).

Montego Bay

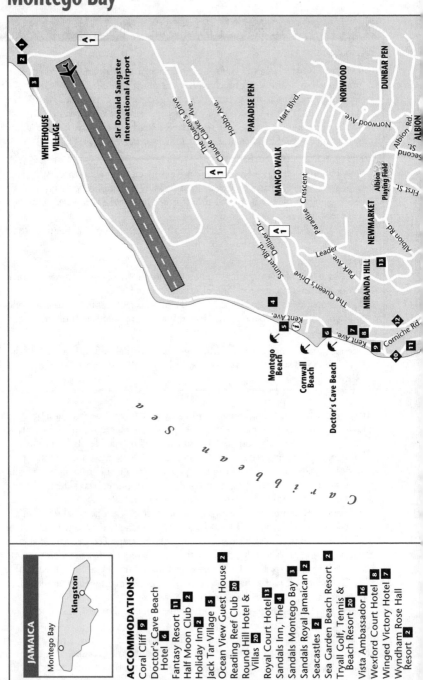

ACCOMMODATIONS

Coral Cliff 9
Doctor's Cave Beach Hotel 6
Fantasy Resort 11
Half Moon Club 2
Holiday Inn 2
Jack Tar Village 5
Ocean View Guest House 2
Reading Reef Club 20
Round Hill Hotel & Villas 20
Royal Court Hotel 13
Sandals Inn, The 4
Sandals Montego Bay 3
Sandals Royal Jamaican 2
Seacastles 2
Sea Garden Beach Resort 2
Tryall Golf, Tennis & Beach Resort 20
Vista Ambassador 16
Wexford Court Hotel 8
Winged Victory Hotel 7
Wyndham Rose Hall Resort 2

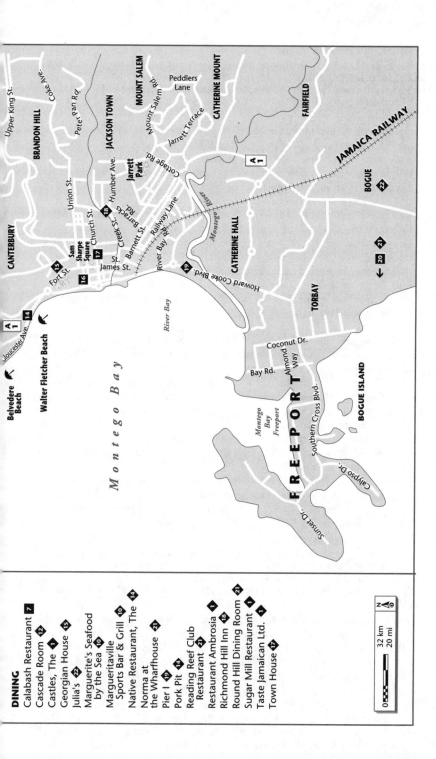

○ Round Hill Hotel & Villas

8 miles west of the town center along A1 (P.O. Box 64), Montego Bay, Jamaica, W.I. ☎ **809/ 952-5150,** or 800/972-2159 in the U.S. Fax 809/952-2505. 36 rms, 27 villas. A/C TEL. Winter $300–$380 double, $470–$690 villa suite; off-season $190–$250 double, $280–$400 villa suite. Additional person $50 extra. MAP $65 per person extra in winter, $60 in summer. AE, DC, MC, V.

Opened in 1953 and now a Caribbean legend, Round Hill is one of the most distinguished hotels in the West Indies. It stands on a lushly landscaped 98-acre peninsula, once part of Lord Monson's sugar plantation, which slopes gracefully down to a sheltered cove whose edges house the elegant reception area and social center. The list of celebrities and luminaries who have made this their Jamaican home includes the Kennedys, Sir Noël Coward, and Cole Porter. Today a "new Round Hill" attracts such visitors as Kim Basinger, Geraldo Rivera, Michael Douglas, and Ralph Lauren. In the past, black tie prevailed for dinner, but many evenings now are designated as informal, except Saturday, when black tie or a jacket and tie for men is required.

Surrounded by tropical gardens, Round Hill accommodates some 200 guests, who enjoy its private beach, vistas of Jamaica's north shore and the mountains, and the sense of colonial elegance. Full spa facilities and all kinds of water sports keep you as active as you'd like to be.

Deluxe hotel accommodations are in a richly appointed seaside building known as The Pineapple House. Each suite opens onto views of the water and beach. Privately owned villas dot the hillside and all are available for rental when the owners are not in residence. Each contains two, three, or four individual suites with a private living area and/or patio; 19 of the villas offer their own swimming pools.

Dining/Entertainment: At a little sandy bay is an intimate straw hut and an open terrace where guests congregate for informal luncheons. Jamaican and continental dishes are served on a candlelit terrace beneath a giant banyan tree or in the roofed-over Georgian colonial room overlooking the sea. The entertainment is varied.

Services: Laundry, baby-sitting, valet service, in-villa breakfast preparation, room service (10am to 9:30pm).

Facilities: Swimming pool, lighted tennis courts, windsurfing, glass-bottom-boat rides, sailing, scuba diving, snorkeling, paddleboats, rubber-sided inflatable boats, waterskiing; walking and jogging trail; full spa regime, private, low key, and personally geared to the guest, with classes ranging from yoga to aerobics.

○ Tryall Golf, Tennis & Beach Club

12 miles west of the town center along A1 (P.O. Box 1206), St. James, Montego Bay, Jamaica, W.I. ☎ **809/956-5660,** or 800/238-5290 in the U.S. Fax 809/956-5673. 47 rms, 45 villas. A/C TEL. Winter $270–$490 double, $507–$1,592 villa; off-season $160–$260 double, $365– $750 villa. Additional person $70 extra in winter, $55 off-season. MAP $66 extra per person. AE, DC, MC, V.

Occupying more acreage than any hotel in Jamaica, this stylish and upscale resort sits on the site of a 2,200-acre former sugar plantation. It doesn't have the fine beach that Half Moon does, nor the house party atmosphere of Trident at Port Antonio (see Chapter 6), but it's a formidable challenger, nevertheless. One of the grand Jamaican resorts, and famous for its world-class golf course and tennis facilities, Tryall lies along a 1 1/2-mile seafront and is centered on a 155-year-old Georgian-style great house.

Accommodations are either in modern wings built near the great house, or in luxurious villas scattered on the surrounding grounds. Bedrooms are decorated in cool pastels with a kind of English colonial restraint. All have ceiling fans and air-conditioning, along with picture windows framing sea and mountain views. The resort's villas are set amid lush foliage and designed for privacy. Each villa comes with a full-time staff, including a cook, maid, launderer, and gardener. All have private swimming pools.

Dining/Entertainment: The more formal of the resort's eating areas is in the great house, where antiques and quality reproductions evoke the grandeur and power of the plantation era. Less formal meals are served in a beachside cafe. A resident band plays everything from reggae to slow-dance music every night during dinner. Corresponding with the pervasive English tradition, afternoon tea is served in the great house.

Services: Laundry service, room service, baby-sitting, massage; lessons in golf, tennis, and water sports.

Facilities: The pride of this elegant property is its championship 18-hole golf course, site of many world-class golf competitions, and nine Laykold tennis courts (see Section 3 of this chapter, below). There's also a 2-mile jogging trail. The unique design of the large great house swimming pool includes a swim-up bar. Available water sports include windsurfing, scuba, snorkeling, deep-sea fishing, paddleboats, and glass-bottom boats.

EXPENSIVE

Seacastles

11 miles east of Montego Bay along A1 (P.O. Box 1), Rose Hall, Montego Bay, St. James, Jamaica, W.I. ☎ **809/953-3250** or (for reservations) 305/667-8860. Fax 809/953-3062. 198 suites. A/C TEL. Winter $150–$234 suite for two; $291–$330 suite for four; $390 suite for six. Off-season $102–$186 suite for two; $246–$282 suite for four; $342 suite for six. Additional person $24 extra. MAP $42 per person extra. AE, DC, MC, V.

One of the most architecturally dramatic hotels in the region was built on grassy and isolated seafront acreage in 1991, on what had once been sugarcane fields. Its development included at least 50% participation by the Jamaican government, which helped to market many of the units as privately owned condominiums. The result was an airy, widely separated compound of postmodern buildings vaguely influenced by Newport, Rhode Island. The resort contains only suites, each with kitchen or kitchenette, and each scattered among a half-dozen imposing outbuildings ringed with greenery and capped with cedar-shingled roofs. Lawns slope down to the beach, past gracefully designed arbors, gazebos, bars, and water-sports kiosks.

Dining/Entertainment: The main restaurant, Castles Restaurant, is a second-floor enclave overlooking the graceful symmetry of the swimming pool. Less formal meals and drinks are offered in the Clifftop Bar.

Services: Laundry, baby-sitting, recreation staff.

Facilities: Freshwater pool, water sports, tour desk.

Wyndham Rose Hall Resort

9 miles east of Sangster airport off A1 (P.O. Box 999), Rose Hall, Montego Bay, Jamaica, W.I. ☎ **809/953-2650,** or 800/822-4200 in the U.S. Fax 809/953-2617. 452 rms, 19 suites. A/C TV TEL. Winter $165–$205 double, from $400 suite; off-season $115–$145 double, from $300 suite. MAP $48.40 extra per person per day. AE, DC, MC, V.

Wyndham Rose Hall is at the bottom of a rolling 30-acre site along the north-coast highway, past the hamlet of Little River. On a former sugar plantation that once covered 7,000 acres, the hotel abuts the 200-year-old home of the legendary "White Witch of Rose Hall," now a historic site (see "What to See & Do" later in this chapter). Although it's popular for conventions, the hotel also caters to families, and children are considered an important part of the clientele. The seven-story H-shaped structure features numerous rooms with sea views and standard furnishings. Most units contain two queen-size beds, and all have a private balcony. What's missing here is a lack of Jamaican style and ambience (the locals say it "lacks soul, mon"). However, it is miles ahead of its nearby rival, the relatively drab Holiday Inn.

Dining/Entertainment: There are three restaurants and a busy staff of social organizers. It's never more than a short walk to one of the many bars scattered around the hotel property.

Services: Baby-sitting, room service, laundry facilities, massage.

Facilities: Three pools (wading, swimming, diving), thin strip of sandy beach, complimentary sailboats, a top-rated golf course (see Section 4 of this chapter), lighted tennis complex, fitness center.

MODERATE

⑤ Doctor's Cave Beach Hotel

Gloucester Avenue (in the town center, across from Doctor's Cave Beach; P.O. Box 94), Montego Bay, Jamaica, W.I. ☎ **809/952-4355.** Fax 809/952-5204. 78 rms, 12 suites. A/C TEL. Winter $130–$140 double, $160 suite (with kitchenette) for two; off-season $105–$115 double, $140 suite for two. Additional person $30 extra. MAP $35–$55 per person extra. AE, DC, MC, V.

In the bustle of the town's commercial zone, this three-story hotel features its own gardens, a swimming pool, a Jacuzzi, and a small gymnasium with sauna, all set on four acres of tropical gardens. Rooms are simply but comfortably furnished.

The hotel's two restaurants include the Coconut Grove, whose outdoor terrace is floodlit at night, and the less formal Greenhouse. In the Cascade Bar, which contains a waterfall tumbling down a stone-built wall, you can listen to a piano duo during cocktail hours.

Fantasy Resort

Gloucester Avenue (in the town center, near Doctor's Cave Beach; P.O. Box 161), Montego Bay, Jamaica, W.I. ☎ **809/952-4150.** Fax 809/952-0020. 119 rms. A/C. Winter $121 double; off-season $88 double. MAP $33 extra per person per day. Children under 12 stay free in their parents' room. AE, MC, V.

This angular blue-and-white building—at nine stories, one of the town's tallest structures—is a very reasonably priced resort. In spite of the urban location, you'll think you're in the Jamaican countryside if you turn your back to the busy boulevard outside and look only at the cliffs beyond. Although some of Fantasy's accommodations face the sea and Montego Bay's busy main street, the majority look onto an inner courtyard built around a swimming pool. Each contains a private balcony and comfortably unpretentious furniture. Facilities at the hotel include a freshwater pool, two tennis courts, a piano bar, an exercise room, a Jacuzzi, and nightly entertainment.

⑤ Reading Reef Club

A 15-minute drive west of the town center along A1, at the bottom of Long Hill Road (P.O. Box 225), Reading, Montego Bay, Jamaica, W.I. ☎ **809/952-5909,** or 800/315-0379 in the U.S., 800/424-5500 in Canada. Fax 809/952-7217. 30 rms, 4 suites. A/C TEL. Winter $125–$165 double; $250 two-bedroom suite, $325 three-bedroom suite. Off-season $100–$125 double; $200 two-bedroom suite, $250 three-bedroom suite. MAP $35 per person extra. AE, MC, V.

This pocket of posh was created by an American, JoAnne Rowe, a former fashion designer whose hobby is cooking. This hotel reflects her sense of style and flair for cuisine. Lying on 2¹/₂ acres, Reading Reef opened in 1986 on a 350-foot sandy beach where people relax in comfort, not bothered by beach vendors. The four-building complex overlooks reefs praised for their aquatic life by Jacques Cousteau.

The accommodations, which include two- and three-bedroom suites, open onto a sea view. All contain spacious private baths, ceiling fans, and air-conditioning. A light Caribbean motif is reflected in the design of the bedrooms. The luxury rooms have minibars, and the two- or three-bedroom suites offer kitchenettes.

Dining/Entertainment: See "Where to Dine," below, for the hotel's restaurant. There is also a bar lounge and a beachside luncheon barbecue specializing in Jamaican (jerk) sausages, English sausages, and Tex-Mex food.

Services: Laundry, valet, drivers for island tours.

Facilities: Freshwater swimming pool, boutique, private beach, free water sports (including snorkeling on Reading Reef, windsurfing, sailing in a 12-foot sailboat), massage salon, beauty salon.

Wexford Court Hotel

Gloucester Avenue (in the town center near Doctor's Cave Beach; P.O. Box 108), Montego Bay, Jamaica, W.I. ☎ **809/952-2854** or 800/237-3421. Fax 809/952-3637. 61 rms, 6 one-bedroom apts (all with kitchenette). A/C TV TEL. Winter $120–$125 double, $130 apt; off-season $90–$95 double, $100 apt. MAP $30 per person per day extra. AE, DC, MC, V.

Wexford Court, on the main road about 10 minutes from the center of Mo Bay, is a small hotel with a tiny pool and a patio where calypso is enjoyed in season. The hotel is owned and operated by Godfrey G. Dyer, who has led an interesting life as police officer, detective, and taxi entrepreneur. Stay here for reasons of economy, not for style. The rooms are air-conditioned, and some contain living/dining areas and kitchenettes. All back-to-basics rooms feature patios shaded by gables and Swiss chalet–style roofs.

The Wexford Grill includes a good selection of Jamaican dishes, such as chicken deep-fried with honey. Guests can enjoy drinks in a bar nearby.

Winged Victory Hotel

5 Queen's Dr. (in Miranda Hill district, near central Montego Bay), Montego Bay, Jamaica, W.I. ☎ **809/952-3892.** Fax 809/952-5986. 16 rms, 8 suites. A/C. Winter $90–$110 double, $175–$225 suite; off-season $70–$90 double, $110–$150 suite. MAP $35 extra per person per day. AE, MC, V.

Tall and modern, Winged Victory delays revealing its true beauty until you pass through its comfortable public rooms into a Mediterranean-style courtyard in back. There, urn-shaped balustrades enclose a terraced garden, a pool, fringes of plants, trees, flowering shrubs, and a veranda looking over the faraway crescent of Montego Bay. The veranda's best feature is the Calabash Restaurant. The dignified owner, Roma Chin Sue, added hotel rooms to her already well-known restaurant in 1985. All but five contain a private balcony or veranda, along with an attractively eclectic decor that is part Chinese, part colonial, and part Iberian.

INEXPENSIVE

Ⓢ Coral Cliff

165 Gloucester Ave. (1 mile west of town center, near junction of Corniche Rd.; P.O. Box 253), Montego Bay, Jamaica, W.I. ☎ **809/952-4130.** Fax 809/952-6532. 32 rms. A/C TEL. Winter $59–$66 double, $65–$68 triple; off-season $53–$64 double, $62–$68 triple. MC, V.

For value received, Coral Cliff may be your best all-around bet in Montego Bay. The hotel grew from a colonial-style building that was once the private home of Harry M. Doubleday of the famous publishing family. It is located only 2 minutes from Doctor's Cave Beach. The Coral Cliff also offers its own swimming pool. Many of the light, airy, and often spacious bedrooms open onto a balcony with a view of the sea. Rates are modest for what you get.

The hotel's breeze-swept restaurant is appropriately called Verandah Terrace, and it overlooks the bay. The food is good, too, and includes dishes such as lobster thermidor and pan-fried snapper.

Ocean View Guest House

26 Sunset Blvd. ($^{1}/_{2}$ mile west of Sangster airport; P.O. Box 210), Montego Bay, Jamaica, W.I. ☎ **809/952-2662.** 12 rms. A/C. Winter $40.50–$54.50 triple; off-season $31.50 double, $40.50 triple. No credit cards.

Originally established in the 1960s, when the grandparents of the present owners began to rent extra rooms in their private home, this super bargain is $^{1}/_{2}$ mile from the airport and the same distance from a public beach. Buses, marked Montego Bay, pass Ocean View's door for the ride into town. The simple and uncomplicated bedrooms are supplemented with a small library and TV room (satellite reception is available). All rooms are air-conditioned and equipped with fans, and most open onto a veranda or the spacious front porch. It's quietest at the back. Stay here only for reasons of economy, certainly not for state-of-the-art maintenance or service.

Dinner is offered for guests only; reservations must be made by 2pm. The large and extremely reasonable menu features such fare as T-bone steak, pork chops, roast chicken, and fresh fish.

⑤ Royal Court Hotel

Sewell Avenue (on a hillside above A1, near Paradise Avenue; P.O. Box 195), Montego Bay, Jamaica, W.I. ☎ **809/952-4531.** Fax 809/952-4532. 20 rms, 3 suites. A/C TEL. Winter $90 double, $135 suite; off-season $70 double, $95 suite. AE, MC, V.

This reasonable accommodation overlooking Montego Bay offers rooms furnished with bright, tasteful colors, and all have patios. The larger units contain fully equipped kitchenettes. Meals are served in the Pool Bar and Eatery. A Jamaican buffet is served around the swimming pool on Sunday evenings. Free transportation is provided to town, the beach, and the tennis club. Royal Court is clean and attractive, has a charming atmosphere, and is good value. New amenities and facilities include massage, gym, steam room, Jacuzzi, TV room, conference room, and a doctor on the premises.

ALL-INCLUSIVE RESORTS

Jack Tar Village

Gloucester Avenue (2 miles north of the town center, near Cornwall Beach; P.O. Box 144), Montego Bay, Jamaica, W.I. ☎ **809/952-4340,** or 800/999-9182 in the U.S. Fax 809/952-6633. 128 rms. A/C TV TEL. Winter $360 double or triple; off-season $230 double, $330 triple. Children 2–12 $100 year-round. Rates include all meals, drinks, activities, taxes, service (and airport transfers in winter). AE, MC, V.

Called simply the "Village," this four-story resort offers all-inclusive package deals that include unlimited beer, wine, and liquor, and all services and facilities mentioned below. It is one of the smallest resorts in the Jack Tar chain, which adds some intimacy to its bustling all-inclusive format. Each modern but bland bedroom has a private balcony opening directly to Montego Bay, so many guests practically live in their swimsuits here. One guest said the Jack Tar appeals to "beach buffs on a budget," although the Sandals Inn next door offers superior quality for about the same price.

Dining/Entertainment: Lunch is served beachside or in the main dining room, and there is nightly entertainment. The food, although plentiful, will not give your palate new taste sensations.

Services: Reggae dance lessons, massage.

Facilities: A freshwater pool serves as the resort's focal point. Tennis clinic and tennis courts (for daytime play), sauna, windsurfing, waterskiing, snorkeling, sailing.

The Sandals Inn

Kent Avenue (in the town center, directly north of Cornwall Beach; P.O. Box 412), Montego Bay, Jamaica, W.I. ☎ **809/952-4140** or 800/SANDALS. Fax 809/952-6913. 52 rms. A/C TV TEL. Winter 3-night package $1,130–$1,270 double; off-season 3-night package $1,080–$1,220 double. Rates include all meals, snacks, drinks, sports and entertainment activities, airport transfers, taxes, and services. AE, MC, V.

For mixed-sex couples only, The Sandals Inn is built around a large pool and patio, with a beach a short walk across a busy highway. A transformation of an older hotel, this is the least expensive but also the least glamorous, spacious, and attractive of the five Sandals all-inclusive resorts scattered across Jamaica. The relative lack of plushness, however, is compensated by the nearby attractions of downtown Montego Bay, by the relatively low cost, and by guests here being allowed day use of the facilities at the other, more upscale Sandals resorts of Montego Bay (free transportation is provided).

Thirty-eight of the rooms open onto the swimming pool. All the accommodations contain king-size beds along with such amenities as hair dryers and clock radios. There is now "environmentally friendly" linen service, which means your sheets and towels aren't changed unless you request it.

Dining/Entertainment: Food is served in bountiful portions in the resort's only dining room, snack service is provided anytime, and there is nightly entertainment.

Services: Free round-trip airport transfers, 24-hour room service.

Facilities: Recreational and sports program, exercise room, saunas, Jacuzzi, tennis courts, swimming pool, room safes.

Sandals Montego Bay

Kent Avenue (5-minute taxi ride northeast of Sangster airport, in Whitehouse Village district; P.O. Box 100), Montego Bay, Jamaica, W.I. ☎ **809/952-5510** or 800/SANDALS. Fax 809/952-0816. 211 rms, 32 suites. A/C TV TEL. Winter 3-night package $1,350–$1,610 double; $1,740–$3,030 suite for two. Off-season 3-night package $1,320–$1,540 double; $1,690–$2,940 suite for two. Rates include all meals, drinks, activities, service, taxes, and airport transfers. AE, MC, V.

Located near the airport with its zooming planes, this honeymoon haven may have the highest occupancy rate of all resorts in the Caribbean. The 19-acre site is a male/female couples–only, all-inclusive resort—everything is covered in the price.

In contrast to its somewhat more laid-back nearby counterpart, the Sandals Royal Jamaican (see below), this resort offers many different fun-in-the-sun participatory activities for a clientele and staff that tend to be extroverted and gregarious. The Playmakers, as staff members are called, like to keep everybody amused and the joint jumping.

Accommodations are either in villas spread along 1,700 feet of white sandy beach or in the main house, where all bedrooms face the sea and contain private balconies. All units are well-furnished, with king-size beds, hair dryers, and radios. Try to avoid a room over the dining room; as well as being noisy, these rooms also lack balconies.

Reserve as far ahead as possible.

Dining/Entertainment: Dinner is by candlelight on an al fresco terrace bordering the sea. There are also two specialty restaurants. Offering Jamaican food and "white glove" service, Oleander Deck has the finest dining in the Sandals chain. Tokyo Joe's has Asian food. Those who haven't tired themselves out can head for the late-night disco, which often has rum-and-reggae nights.

Services: Free shuttle bus to the resort's twin, Sandals Royal Caribbean (see below), whose facilities are open without charge to residents here.

Facilities: Waterskiing, snorkeling, sailing, scuba diving with PADI or NAUI certification programs, windsurfing, paddleboats, glass-bottom boat, two freshwater pools, Jacuzzis, lighted tennis courts, fitness center.

Sandals Royal Jamaican

Mahoe Bay (4 miles east of town center along A1; P.O. Box 167), Montego Bay, Jamaica, W.I. ☎ **809/953-2231** or 800/SANDALS. Fax 809/953-2788. 176 rms, 14 suites. A/C TV TEL. Winter 3-night package $1,400–$1,600 double; $1,750–$1,970 suite for two. Off-season 3-night package $1,570–$1,840 double; $1,990–$2,210 suite for two. Rates include all meals, snacks, drinks, activities, service, taxes, and airport transfers. AE, MC, V.

This all-inclusive, male/female couples–only resort is a reincarnation of the once-prestigious Montego Bay Hotel, which was constructed in the Jamaican colonial style and patronized by Queen Elizabeth and Prince Philip. Some of the British colonial atmosphere overlay remains, as reflected by a formal tea in the afternoon, but there are modern touches as well, such as a private island reached by boat where clothing is optional. The building sits beside its own private beach, which frankly isn't as good as the one at Sandals Montego Bay (see above).

The spacious rooms come in a wide range, from standard through superior to deluxe. Even higher in price are the deluxe beachfront accommodations or a junior suite. Amenities include hair dryers and radios. Prices at this resort are similar to those at Sandals Montego Bay (see above), which offers a nearly identical list of all-inclusive drinking, dining, and sports facilities.

Dining/Entertainment: Regency Suite and Deck is the Jamaican-inspired main dining room. Specialty restaurants include Bali Hai, an Indonesian restaurant built on the previously mentioned offshore island, and the Courtyard Grill, with such specialties as grilled sirloin, grilled snapper, and smoked marlin. There are four different bars, plus food and drink available throughout the day. Live music from a local reggae band is presented.

Services: Free shuttle bus to the resort's twin Sandals (Montego Bay), whose facilities are available without charge to guests here. If you're not married to your companion by the time you arrive here, management can arrange for the wedding before you leave. Laundry, massage.

Facilities: Scuba, windsurfing, sailing, three tennis courts, swimming pool.

Sea Garden Beach Resort

Kent Avenue (1¹⁄₂ miles east of Montego Bay along A1), Montego Bay, Jamaica, W.I. ☎ **809/952-4780,** or 800/545-9001 in the U.S. Fax 809/952-7543. 97 rms. A/C TEL. Winter 3-night package $780–$840 double per person. Off-season 3-night package $660–$720 double per person. Rates include all meals, snacks, drinks, activities, service, taxes, and airport transfers. AE, MC, V.

The Sea Garden stands near some of Montego Bay's most popular public beaches. Designed in a British colonial style with neo-Victorian gingerbread, tall columns, and white lattices, it is airy, comfortable, and stylish. The accommodations lie in sprawling motel-like units built around the pool in back. Each unit contains a private balcony or patio and simple mahogany furniture. Frankly, a rejuvenation of the rooms is in order (we even think the lackluster Jack Tar has an edge at present), so cost should be your sole consideration in deciding to stay here. Prices depend on whether your room has a sea- or garden view.

Dining/Entertainment: The dining room, with a high arched ceiling, opens onto a flagstone-covered courtyard and offers international meals. There are three bars. A resident band plays nightly.

Services: Free transportation to and from the airport, baby-sitting, laundry. The service leaves much to be desired even in laid-back Jamaica.

Facilities: Two lighted tennis courts; water sports such as sailing, snorkeling, and windsurfing; tour desk for excursions.

Vista Ambassador

Gloucester Avenue (adjacent to the Montego Bay Craft Market; P.O. Box 262), Montego Bay, Jamaica, W.I. ☎ **809/952-4703,** or 800/JAMAICA in the U.S. Fax 809/952-6810. 116 units. A/C TEL. Winter 5-night package $2,000–$2,500 double; from $2,060 villa suite for two. Off-season 5-night package $1,730–$1,930 double; $2,060 villa suite for two. Children 1–12 (one per adult) sharing parents' room are free; children 13–17 are charged 50% of the adult rate. Rates include all meals, drinks, and airport transfers. AE, MC, V.

Set on 10 acres of tropical gardens, this hotel was once known as Lifestyles but was transformed in 1995 into the first all-inclusive family resort spa on Jamaica. Although it stands on a hillside with no beach of its own (it does have a swimming pool), it lies a 5-minute walk from the white sands of Walter Fletcher Beach.

Contemporary tropical furnishings decorate the bedrooms, whose bed configurations can be adjusted to accommodate various family sizes. There are standard and deluxe rooms as well as junior, one-bedroom, and two-bedroom villa suites. Each is equipped with a cable TV, safe, radio, clock, and ironing board. Each suite also has a private terrace with a Jacuzzi and wet bar.

Dining/Entertainment: The Island Verandah offers breakfast and casual dining, whereas the Blue Horizon is more elegant, featuring à la carte selections at dinner. Three conveniently located lounges are Dolphins, a pool and juice bar; Expressions, a karaoke bar; and Rhapsody, a piano lounge.

Facilities: Spa and gym (with sauna, steam room, Jacuzzi, wet rooms, and many spa services, including massages, facials, body scrubs, and herbal wraps), adult swimming pool and children's pool, tennis court, private beach club.

2 Where to Dine

The Montego Bay area offers some of the finest—and most expensive—dining on Jamaica. But if you're watching your wallet and don't have a delicate stomach, some intriguing food is sold right on the street. For example, on Kent Avenue you might try jerk pork. Seasoned spareribs are also grilled over charcoal fires and sold with extra-hot sauce. Naturally, it goes down better with a Red Stripe beer. Cooked shrimp are also sold on the streets of Mo Bay; they don't look it, but they're very hotly spiced, so be warned. If you're cooking your own meals, you might also want to buy fresh lobster or the catch of the day from Mo Bay fishers.

EXPENSIVE

Georgian House

2 Orange St. ☎ **809/952-0632.** Reservations recommended. Main courses $13–$33. AE, MC, V. Mon–Sat noon–3pm; daily 6–11:30pm. When you make reservations, ask for the restaurant's round-trip transportation provided to and from most hotels. INTERNATIONAL.

Georgian House brings grand cuisine and an elegant setting, complete with an art gallery, to the heart of town. It's said that an English gentleman constructed the 18th-century buildings for his mistress. You can select either the upstairs room, which is more formal, or the garden terrace with fountains, statues, lanterns, and cut-stone exterior.

You might begin with a typically Jamaican appetizer such as ackee and bacon, then follow with pan-barbecued shrimp (you peel the shrimp yourself, but are given a scented fingerbowl). Baked spiny lobster is another specialty, but ask that it not be overcooked. Continental dishes such as tournedos Rossini are also prepared with flair.

For dessert, the temptations include English plum pudding with coconut sauce. The international cuisine is complemented by a fine wine list.

Julia's

Julia's Estate, Bogue Hill. ☎ **809/952-1772.** Reservations required. Fixed-price dinner $33. AE, DC, MC, V. Daily 5:30–10:30pm. When you make your reservation, you can ask for a van to come to pick you up at your hotel. ITALIAN.

The winding jungle road you take to reach Julia's is part of the before-dinner entertainment. After a jolting ride to a site high above the city and its bay, you pass through a walled-in park that long ago was the site of a private home built in 1940 for the duke of Sutherland. Today the building at the land's focal point is a long, low-slung modern house whose fresh decor encompasses sweeping views.

Raimondo and Julia Meglio, drawing on the cuisine of their native Italy, prepare chicken cacciatore, breaded milanese cutlet with tomato sauce and mozzarella cheese, filet of fresh fish with lime juice and butter, and 18 different kinds of pasta. Lobster, veal, and shrimp are regularly featured. Although competently prepared with fresh ingredients whenever possible, the food has trouble competing with the view.

○ Norma at the Wharfhouse

Reading Road (a 15-minute drive west of the town center along A1). ☎ **809/979-2745.** Reservations recommended. Main courses $26–$32. MC, V. Thurs–Sun noon–3:30pm; Tues–Sun 6:30–10pm. NOUVELLE JAMAICAN.

Set within a coral-stone warehouse whose two-foot-thick walls are bound together with molasses and lime, this is the finest restaurant in Montego Bay, a favorite of many of Jamaica's visiting celebrities. Originally built in 1780, it was restored by Millicent Rogers, heiress of the Standard Oil fortune, and now serves as the north shore domain of Norma Shirley, one of Jamaica's foremost restaurateurs. You can request a table either on the large pier built on stilts over the coral reef (from whence a view of Montego Bay glitters in the distance), or within an elegantly formal early 19th-century dining room illuminated only by flickering candles. Before- or after-dinner drinks are served either in the restaurant or within the Wharf Rat, an informal bar in a separate building much favored by local clients. Service is impeccable, and the food is of the quality you hope to find in Jamaica but so rarely do.

Menu specialties include grilled deviled crab backs, smoked marlin with papaya sauce, chicken breast with callaloo, nuggets of lobster in a mild curry sauce, chateaubriand larded with pâté in a peppercorn sauce, roast Cornish game hen stuffed with callaloo and glazed with tangerine marmalade, and filet of snapper marinated in Cajun spices and lime sauce. Dessert might be a rum-and-raisin cheesecake or a piña colada mousse. Each of these dishes is individually prepared and filled with flavor.

Richmond Hill Inn

45 Union St. (a 4-minute taxi ride uphill/east from the town's main square). ☎ **809/952-3859.** Reservations recommended. Main courses $35. AE, MC, V. Daily 7–10am and 5–10pm. INTERNATIONAL/CONTINENTAL.

This plantation-style house was originally built in 1806 by members of the Dewar's whisky distillery, who also happened to be distantly related to Annie Palmer, the "White Witch of Rose Hall." Today, it's run by an Austrian mother-daughter team, who prepare well-flavored food for an appreciative clientele. Lunches are simple affairs featuring club sandwiches, salads, and, if anyone asks for it, a lobster platter. Dinners are more substantial, and include a shrimp-and-lobster cocktail, an excellent house salad, different preparations of dolphin, breaded breast of chicken, surf-and-turf, wiener schnitzel, filet mignon, and a choice of dessert cakes.

Many of the dishes are relatively standard international fare, but others, especially the lobster, are worth the trek up the hill. The price of a dinner main course seems steep, but it includes soup, salad, garlic bread, and dessert. Usually, a pianist performs six days a week during the dinner hour.

✪ Round Hill Dining Room

In the Round Hill Hotel and Villas, on A1, 8 miles west of the center of Montego Bay. ☎ **809/952-5150.** Reservations required. Main courses $18–$49. AE, DC, MC, V. Daily 12:30–2:30pm and 7–9:30pm. INTERNATIONAL.

The most prestigious dining room in Montego Bay, this place has attracted its share of renowned personalities. To reach the dining room, you'll have to pass through the resort's open-air reception area and proceed through a garden. Many visitors opt for a drink in the large and high-ceilinged bar area before moving on to their dinner, which is served either on a terrace perched above the surf or (during inclement weather) under an open-sided breezeway.

Although many dishes are classic, others innovatively reflect the flavors of Jamaica. For example, the shrimp in pasta Caribe is sautéed with chopped herbs, cream, and wine, while the rasta pasta is tossed with vegetables and basil. Caribbean veal is stuffed with spicy crab meat and seared, and the catch of the day is served jerked, broiled, or steamed with butter, herbs, and ginger. Calypso chicken is slowly roasted with aromatic herbs, chunks of tomatoes, and served with natural *jus.* You can also order more classic dishes, including rack of lamb and prime rib of beef, along with a medallion of lobster sautéed with cream and served over fettuccine. Afternoon tea and sandwiches are served daily at 4pm.

✪ Sugar Mill Restaurant

At the Half Moon Club, Half Moon Golf Course, Rose Hall (8 miles east of Montego Bay on A1). ☎ **809/953-2228.** Reservations required. Main courses $15–$40; lunches from $8. AE, MC, V. Daily 11am–2:30pm and 7–10pm. When you reserve, ask to be picked up by the restaurant's minivan. INTERNATIONAL/CARIBBEAN.

After a drive through rolling landscape, you arrive at the stone ruins of what used to be a waterwheel for a sugar plantation. In the comfortable, breeze-filled building, Sugar Mill guests dine on an open terrace by candlelight, with a view of a pond, the waterwheel, and plenty of greenery.

Although he came from Switzerland, it was with Caribbean produce that chef Hans Schenk blossomed as a culinary artist. He has entertained everybody from the British royal family to former King Farouk of Egypt. Lunch can be a relatively simple affair, perhaps an ackee burger with bacon, preceded by Mama's pumpkin soup and followed with homemade rum-and-raisin ice cream. At dinner, smoked north-coast marlin is a specialty. You might follow with pork chops stuffed with mango chutney, or an exotic array of fresh fish. Schenk makes the most elegant Jamaican bouillabaisse on the island, or refined jerk versions of pork, fish, or chicken. Should you prefer something less exotic, he also prepares today's catch, either broiled or meunière, with considerable flair. On any given day you can ask the waiter what's cooking in the curry pot. Chances are, it will be a Jamaican specialty such as delicately spiced and full-flavored goat served with island chutney. Top off your meal with a cup of Blue Mountain coffee.

Taste Jamaica Ltd.

In the Half Moon Plaza (about 8 miles east of Montego Bay). ☎ **809/953-9688.** Main courses $17.50–$23. AE, DC, MC, V. Daily 9am–noon, 12:30–3pm, and 7:30–10pm. CARIBBEAN/INTERNATIONAL.

This restaurant is the focal point of an upscale shopping complex that opened in 1994. Set on the main coastal road, it caters to the culinary needs of about

45 upscale villas, administered by the Half Moon Club Hotel. It's usually filled with an appealing mix of local residents, sunseeking expatriates, and passing motorists.

You get authentic island flavor here. With a Caribbean-marketplace theme, the restaurant displays fresh fish, meats, tropical fruits, and freshly baked baguettes and pastries. Choices include fish escovitch, several kinds of pasta, chicken fricassée, curried conch, mango roast pork, and jerked fish or chicken. The most expensive main course allows you to select virtually everything available that day at "the market." There's also a deli section for sandwiches and a host of take-away dishes. An on-site pastry chef prepares a comforting array of French and Antillean pastries, so don't overlook this place as an option for a midmorning coffee break.

MODERATE

Calabash Restaurant

In the Winged Victory Hotel, 5 Queen's Dr. ☎ **809/952-3892.** Reservations recommended. Main courses $6–$35. AE, MC, V. Daily noon–2:30pm and 6–10pm. INTERNATIONAL/ JAMAICAN.

Perched on the hillside road in Montego Bay 500 feet above the distant sea, this well-established restaurant has amused and entertained Peter O'Toole, Francis Ford Coppola, and Roger Moore. It was originally built as a private villa by a doctor in the 1920s. More than 25 years ago, owner Roma Chin Sue turned its Mediterranean-style courtyard and its elegantly simple eagle's-nest patio into a well-managed restaurant.

The seafood, Jamaican classics, and international favorites include curried goat, lobster dishes, and the house specialty of mixed seafood en coquille (served with a cheese-and-brandy sauce). There's a Jamaican Christmas cake offered year-round. Flavors are blended beautifully, and there is real cooking flair here. Over the years dishes have been consistently pleasing, and savvy locals keep returning.

Cascade Room

At the Pelican, Gloucester Avenue (in the town center, near Doctor's Cave Beach). ☎ **809/ 952-3171.** Reservations recommended. Main courses $15–$25. AE, DC, MC, V. Daily 7am– 10pm. Ask for free minivan pickup when you reserve. SEAFOOD/JAMAICAN.

With an intimate setting and relaxing atmosphere, Cascade Room is one of Montego Bay's best seafood restaurants. Rushing waterfalls and cool tropical foliage blend with the natural cedar of the interior to make dining an enjoyable experience. Excellent service combines with the finest seafood, such as lobster thermidor, shrimp stuffed with crabmeat, filet of red snapper, and ackee and codfish. On our latest rounds, we found the seafood here better prepared than that at the more highly touted Marguerite's Seafood by the Sea (see below), although this place lacks the terrace setting overlooking the sea. Cascade is a family favorite. All main dishes include access to the salad bar and homemade bread. There is bar service and an adequate choice of wines.

The Castles

Seacastles, Rose Hall (along A1 east of Montego Bay, toward Falmouth). ☎ **809/953-3250.** Reservations recommended. Main courses $16.50–$26. AE, DC, MC, V. Daily 6–10pm. INTERNATIONAL.

One of the most elegant restaurants between Montego Bay and Falmouth is The Castles, in Seacastles (see "Where to Stay," earlier in this chapter). Its chefs range the globe in their search for dishes such as gazpacho from Spain and spicy spaghetti in meat sauce from Italy as an appetizer; beef consommé julienne is the chef's specialty appetizer. In a formal setting, open to the breezes, guests peruse a menu that is usually divided among seafood selections, such as a delicious lobster thermidor, or main dishes and roasts, perhaps tenderloin of pork with honey and thyme, or a savory roast prime rib of beef. Every night there is a selection of Italian dishes, ranging from veal parmigiana to chicken with peppers, although these tend to vary in quality. Carrot cake is the pastry chef's prized dessert.

Marguerite's Seafood by the Sea/Margueritavilla Sports Bar & Grill

Gloucester Avenue. ☎ **809/952-4777.** Reservations recommended at Marguerite's Seafood by the Sea. Main courses in restaurant $18–$30. Platters, sandwiches, snacks in sports bar $5–$10. AE, DC, MC, V. Restaurant daily 4–11pm; sports bar daily 7am–2am. INTERNATIONAL/SEAFOOD.

Across from the Coral Cliff Hotel, this two-in-one restaurant specializes in seafood served on a breeze-swept terrace overlooking the sea. There's also an air-conditioned lounge with an adjoining "Secret Garden." At a flambé grill the chef specializes in exhibition cookery. The menu is devoted mainly to seafood, including fresh fish; the cooks also turn out a number of innovative pastas but rather standard meat dishes. The changing dessert list is homemade, and a reasonable selection of wines is served.

The sports bar and grill features a 110-foot Hydroslide, live music, satellite TV, watersports, a sundeck, a CD jukebox, and a display kitchen offering a straightforward, unfussy menu of seafood, sandwiches, pasta, pizza, salads, and snacks. Naturally, Marguerite's bartenders specialize in margaritas.

Pier 1

Howard Cooke Boulevard. ☎ **809/92-2452.** Reservations not necessary. Main courses $15–$25. AE, MC, V. Mon–Fri 9:30am–11pm, Sat 1pm–midnight, Sun 4pm–midnight. If you call, the Russells can arrange to have you picked up in a minivan at most hotels. SEAFOOD.

Pier 1, one of the major dining and entertainment hubs of Mo Bay, was built on a landfill in the bay. It is operated by the Russell family whose Jamaican food is some of the best in the area (although the staff can be rude at times). Fishers bring fresh lobster right to this desirable waterfront setting. The chef prepares the spiny creatures in a number of ways, including Créole style or curried. You might begin with a typically Jamaican soup such as conch chowder or red pea (actually red bean). At lunch their hamburgers are the juiciest in town, or you might find their quarter-decker steak sandwich with mushrooms equally tempting. The chef also prepares such famous island dishes as jerk pork or chicken, and Jamaican red snapper. The jerk dishes here are done better at The Pork Pit (see below). You might also like a slice of moist rum cake to finish. You can drink or dine on the ground floor, open to the sea breezes, but most guests seem to prefer the more formal second floor.

✪ Reading Reef Club Restaurant

Coastal Road (at the bottom of Long Hill Road, 4 miles west of the town center along A1). ☎ **809/952-5909.** Reservations required. Main courses $5–$24; pastas $10–$11. AE, DC, MC, V. Daily 7am–3pm and 7–10pm. ITALIAN/CONTINENTAL/CARIBBEAN.

There are those—Lady Sarah Churchill among them—who claim that the food served at this second-floor terrace overlooking the bay is among the finest, perhaps *the* finest, in Montego Bay. Like the hotel itself (see "Where to Stay," earlier in this chapter), Reading Reef Club's menu is the creative statement of American JoAnne Rowe, who has a passion for cooking and menu planning, a skill perfected while entertaining prominent people in Montego Bay at private dinner parties. Today her cook specializes in seafood, Italian, continental, and Caribbean recipes, such as perfectly prepared scampi, along with imaginative pasta dishes such as spaghetti with fresh ginger, garlic, and parmesan. Her food is excellent, including a catch of the day, perhaps snapper, yellowtail, kingfish, or dolphin. She also imports quality New York sirloin steaks, but whenever possible likes to use local produce. Dinner might begin with a variety of Jamaican soups, such as pepperpot or pumpkin, and the restaurant is known for its lime pie. Lunches are low-profile, with a more limited menu.

Restaurant Ambrosia

Across from the Wyndham Rose Hall Resort, Rose Hall (9 miles east of Sangster airport along A1). ☎ **809/953-2650.** Reservations recommended. Main courses $13–$29. AE, MC, V. Daily 6:30–10pm. MEDITERRANEAN.

Ambrosia's cedar-shingled design and its trio of steeply pointed roofs give the impression of a neocolonial country club. Once you enter the courtyard, complete with a set of cannons, you find yourself in one of the loveliest restaurants in the area. You'll enjoy a sweeping view over the rolling lawns leading past the hotel and down to the sea, interrupted only by buff-colored Doric columns.

The cooks turn out a predictable array of good pasta and seafood dishes. Many of the flavors are evocative of the Mediterranean, especially the shrimp scampi and other seafood dishes. They also expertly handle a herb-crusted rack of lamb.

Town House

16 Church St. ☎ **809/952-2660.** Reservations recommended. Main courses $14–$30. AE, DC, MC, V. Mon–Sat 11:30am–3:30pm; daily 6–10:30pm. Ask for free limousine transportation when you reserve. JAMAICAN/INTERNATIONAL.

Set in a lovely old red-brick house built in 1765, Town House restaurant has been recommended by *Gourmet* magazine, among others. You find the bar and restaurant at the back of the house in what used to be the cellars, now air-conditioned with tables set around the walls. Old ship lanterns give a warm light, and the owner's personal art collection adorns the walls. Outdoor dining is also available on the popular terrace overlooking the floodlit 18th-century parish church. At lunch it is a cool oasis for the noonday shopper, but nighttime is when this delightful, owner-operated restaurant comes into its own.

On offer is a wide and good selection of main courses. Everybody talks favorably of red snapper *en papillotte* (baked in a paper bag). You might also try Jamaican stuffed lobster. We're fond of the chef's large rack of barbecued spareribs with the owner's special Tennessee sauce. Their pasta and steak dishes are also good, especially the homemade fettuccini with whole shrimp and the perfectly aged New York strip steak. Soups, which are increasingly ignored in many restaurants, are a specialty here. The pepperpot or pumpkin is a delectable opening to a meal.

INEXPENSIVE

The Native Restaurant

Gloucester Avenue. ☎ **809/979-2769.** Reservations recommended. Main courses $9–26. AE, MC, V. Tues–Sun 11:30am–10pm. JAMAICAN.

This restaurant won so many fans during its prior location on Queens Drive that it moved down the hill to the more convenient Gloucester Avenue, where it continues as a self-termed "sis and bro" act, turning out dishes that Jamaican foodies love. Visitors have also discovered it.

You begin with a tropical drink while selecting one of the international wines to go with your dinner. You know you're getting island flavor when faced with such appetizers as jerk reggae chicken, ackee and saltfish (an acquired taste), or perhaps smoked marlin. This can be followed by our favorite dish here, steamed fish. The cook will also serve you jerk or fried chicken, each filled with flavor. Lobster with garlic butter, although costing more, is hardly equaled by the curried shrimp. Perhaps the most tropical offering is "goat in a boat"—that is, a pineapple shell. It's too fruity for our tastes, but you may like it. Although fresh desserts are prepared daily, you may choose instead just a Jamaican Blue Mountain coffee to round the meal off nicely.

The Pelican

At the Pelican, Gloucester Avenue (in the heart of the main hotel strip near Doctor's Cave Beach). ☎ **809/952-3171.** Reservations recommended. Main courses $5–$23. AE, DC, MC, V. Daily 7am–11pm. Ask for free van pickup. JAMAICAN.

A Montego Bay landmark, the Pelican has been serving good food at reasonable prices for more than a quarter of a century. It shares the same space with the Cascade Room (see "Where to Dine, Moderate") but is much more informal. It's ideal for families, as it keeps long hours, breakfast flowing into lunch and lunch into dinner. Many diners come here at lunch for one of the well-stuffed sandwiches, or they order juicy burgers and barbecue chicken. You can also select from a wide array of Jamaican dishes, including stew peas and rice, curried goat or lobster, Caribbean fish, and fried chicken. A "meatless menu" includes such dishes as a vegetable plate or vegetable chili. Steak and seafood are also available, and the soda fountain serves old-fashioned sundaes with real whipped cream, making it a kiddies' favorite.

✪ Pork Pit

Gloucester Avenue (near Cornwall Beach). ☎ **809/952-1046.** Main course (1 pound of jerk pork) $7.80–$8.40. No credit cards. Daily 11am–11:30pm. JAMAICAN.

The Pork Pit, an open-air gazebo right in the heart of Montego Bay, is the best place to go for the famous Jamaican jerk pork and jerk chicken. In fact, many beach buffs come over here for a big lunch at reasonable prices. Picnic tables encircle the building, and everything is open-air and informal. The menu also includes steamed roast fish. A half-pound of jerk meat, served with a baked yam or baked potato and a bottle of Red Stripe, makes a sufficient meal.

Shakey's Pizza Restaurant

2A Gloucester Ave. (across from Doctor's Cave Beach). ☎ **809/952-2665.** Reservations not accepted. Breakfast from $2.35–$5.20; pizzas, burgers, platters, and pastas $3.90–$7.80. AE, MC, V. Daily 7:30am–11pm. AMERICAN.

Strewn with hanging plants and decorated in a style suitable to the tropics, this establishment is radically different from the Shakey's Pizza parlors you might have visited in North America. It requires a climb to the second floor of its premises, where a self-service counter allows diners to buy food to take away or to enjoy on the premises. There's also an airy, lattice-ringed bar area on the second floor, and a wide, colonial-style balcony looking out over the pedestrian traffic of Gloucester Avenue. There, a staff will take table orders for food and bottles of Red Stripe beer or a wide choice of rum-based drinks. In addition to breakfast (available anytime during open hours) menu choices include small, medium, and large pizzas, burgers, submarine sandwiches, and platters of deep-fried chicken.

3 Hitting the Beach, Hitting the Links & Other Outdoor Activities

BEACHES

Cornwall Beach (☎ 809/952-3463) is Jamaica's finest underwater marine park and fun complex, a long stretch of white sand beach with dressing cabanas. Water sports such as scuba diving and snorkeling are available. Admission to the beach is $1 per adult, 50¢ for children, for the entire day. A bar and cafeteria offer refreshment. Hours are 9am to 5pm daily.

> ### ⭐ Frommer's Favorite Montego Bay Experiences
>
> **Rafting on the Martha Brae.** It isn't quite as exciting as rafting on the Rio Grande near Port Antonio, but it's fun nonetheless. Lasting about an hour, the tour takes you on a raised dais on bamboo logs. The scenery drifts by.
>
> **Visiting Jamaica's Great Houses.** Rose Hall, the island's most famous home, has been the subject of a dozen Gothic novels. Greenwood has links with the family of poet Elizabeth Barrett Browning (*Sonnets from the Portuguese* [1850]).
>
> **Day and Evening Cruises.** Scenic bay cruises aboard a ketch such as *Calico* and a fishing canoe trip upriver to a re-created Arawak village are among the top sightseeing choices.

   Doctor's Cave Beach (☎ 809/952-2566), on Gloucester Avenue, across from the Montego Bay Club, helped launch Mo Bay as a resort in the 1940s. Operated by the Jamaican government, the area is more or less enclosed with a fence, and contains a stage for occasional reggae concerts, beach bars, T-shirt kiosks, and water sports facilities. Dressing rooms, chairs, umbrellas, and rafts are available every day from 8:30am to 5pm. Admission to the beach is $1 for adults, half price for children.
   Walter Fletcher Beach (☎ 809/952-2044) is one of the premier beaches of Jamaica. Near Pelican Grill in the heart of Mo Bay, it is noted for its tranquil waters, which makes it a particular favorite for families with children. There are facilities for snorkeling and waterskiing as well. Changing rooms are available, as is lifeguard service. You can have lunch here in a restaurant. The beach is open daily from 9am to 5pm. Admission is $1 for adults, half price for children.
   Frankly, you may want to skip all these public beaches entirely and head instead for the **Rose Hall Beach Club** (☎ 809/953-2323), lying on the main road 11 miles east of Montego Bay. Far better equipped than any of the public beaches, it is positioned on a half mile of secure, secluded white sandy beach with crystal-clear water. The club offers a full restaurant, two beach bars, a covered pavilion, an open-air dance area, showers, restrooms, and changing facilities, plus beach volleyball courts, various beach games, and a full water sports activities proram. There is also live entertainment. Admission fees are $8 for adults and $5 for children. The club is open daily from 10am to 6pm.

DEEP-SEA FISHING

Seaworld Resorts, Ltd., whose main office lies near the Cariblue Hotel, at Rose Hall Main Road, just east of Montego Bay (☎ 809/953-2180), operates flying-bridge cruisers, with deck lines and outriggers, for fishing expeditions. A half-day fishing trip costs $330 for up to four participants.

GOLF

With four championship courses, Montego Bay helps make Jamaica the best place to play in the West Indies.
   Wyndham Rose Hall Resort (☎ 809/953-2650), at Rose Hall, features one of the top five golf courses in the world, according to an expert assessment. It is an unusual and challenging seaside and mountain course, built on the shores of the Caribbean. The eighth hole skirts the ocean, then doglegs onto a promontory with a green thrust 200 yards into the sea. The back nine is the most scenic and in-teresting, rising into steep slopes and deep ravines on Mount Zion. The 10th fair-way abuts the family burial grounds of the Barretts of Wimpole Street, and the 14th

passes the vacation home of U.S. country music singer Johnny Cash. At an elevation of 300 feet, the 13th tee offers a rare panoramic view of the sea and the roof of the hotel, and the 15th green is next to a 40-foot-high waterfall, featured in a James Bond movie. A fully stocked pro shop, a clubhouse, and a professional staff are among the amenities. Nonresidents of the Wyndham pay $50 for 18 holes and $30 for nine holes. Guests at the Wyndham are charged $40 for 18 holes, $25 for 9 holes. For cart rentals, 18 holes costs $33, and the use of a caddy—which is mandatory—is another $12 for 18 holes.

The excellent course of **Tryall Golf, Tennis & Beach Club** (☎ **809/956-5660**), 12 miles from Hanover town, is the site of the Jamaica Classic Annual, first played in January 1988, and the Johnnie Walker Tournament. The Mazda Champions Tournament was played here from 1985 to 1987. For 18 holes, guests of Tryall pay $40 in the spring, summer, and fall, and $60 in winter. Nonresidents of Tryall pay $75 from mid-April to mid-December and $125 in the winter.

The **Half Moon** (☎ **809/953-2560**), at Rose Hall, features a championship course, designed by Robert Trent Jones, which opened in 1961. The course has manicured and diversely shaped greens. For 18 holes nonresidents pay $85 year round; hotel guests receive a 50% discount. Carts in any season cost $25 for 18 holes, and caddies (mandatory in any season) are hired for $12.

The **Ironshore Golf & Country Club** (☎ **809/953-2800**), Ironshore, St. James, is another well-known 18-hole golf course with a 72 par, which is privately owned. It is, however, open to all golfers who show up. In the winter, greens fees for 18 holes are $51.75, dropping in the summer to $34.50.

HORSEBACK RIDING

A good equestrian program is offered at the **Rocky Point Riding Stables** (☎ **809/953-2286**), Half Moon Club, Rose Hall. Housed in what are probably the most beautiful barn and stables in Jamaica (built in the colonial Caribbean style in 1992), it offers around 30 horses and a polite and friendly staff. A 90-minute beach or mountain ride costs $50, while a 2¹/₂-hour combination ride (including treks along hillsides, forest trails, beaches, and ending with a saltwater swim) goes for $70.

RIVER RAFTING

Rafting on the Martha Brae is an exciting adventure. To reach the starting point, drive east to Falmouth and turn approximately 3 miles inland to **Martha Brae's Rafters Village** (☎ **809/952-0889**). The rafts are similar to those on the Rio Grande, near Port Antonio (see Chapter 6), and cost about $36 per raft, with two riders allowed on a raft, plus a small child if accompanied by an adult. The 1-hour trips operate daily from 8:30am to 4:30pm. You sit on a raised dais on bamboo logs. The rafters supplement their incomes by selling carved gourds. Along the way you can stop and order cool drinks or beer along the banks of the river. There is a bar, a restaurant, and a souvenir shop in the village. Later you get a souvenir rafting certificate.

Mountain Valley Rafting offers rafting excursions on the Great River. These excursions depart from the Lethe Plantation, about 10 miles south of Montego Bay. Rafts are available for $35 for up to two participants as part of trips that last about an hour, and which operate daily from 8:30am to 4:30pm. Rafts are composed of bamboo trunks with a raised dais for sitting upon. In some cases, a small child can accompany two adults on the same raft, although due caution should be exercised if you choose to do this. Ask about pickup by taxi at the end of the rafting run to return you to your rented car. Another option is available for residents of local hotels who want to be picked up by van at their hotels: For $40 per person, a half-day experience will include transportation to and from your hotel, an hour's rafting, lunch, a garden tour of the Lethe property, and a taste of Jamaican liqueur. These tours are operated by Mountain Valley, 31 Gloucester Ave. (☎ 809/952-0527).

SCUBA DIVING

Seaworld (☎ 809/953-2180), at the Trelawny Beach Hotel in Falmouth, offers scuba-diving excursions to offshore coral reefs considered among the most spectacular in the Caribbean. There are also PAIC-certified dive guides, one dive boat, and all necessary equipment for either inexperienced or certified divers. Guests of the Trelawny benefit from free introductory lessons and a free daily dive; nonresidents are charged $35 per dive. Transportation is provided to all dive sites. Night dives costing $50 are also offered. PAIC certification costs $330 for a 4-day course. Trelawny Beach also offers free snorkeling, waterskiing, Sunfish sailing, windsurfing, and glass-bottom-boat rides to hotel guests; for others, various fees are charged.

TENNIS

The best courts in the area are at **Half Moon Golf, Tennis, & Beach Club** (☎ 809/953-2211). Its 13 state-of-the-art courts, seven of which are lit for night games, attract tennis players from around the world. Richard Russell, the head pro, a former Davis Cup–Wimbledon player, offers a clinic with a video playback. Lessons from him cost $25 per half hour, $45 per hour. Residents play free throughout the day or night. The pro shop is open daily from 7am to 8pm, accepting reservations for court times. If you want to play after those hours, you switch on the lights yourself. If you're a nonresident, you must purchase a day pass at the front desk, giving you access to the tennis courts, the gym, the sauna, Jacuzzi, pools, and the beach, costing $40 per person.

Next best are at **Tryall Golf, Tennis & Beach Club,** St. James (☎ 809/956-5660), which offers nine hard-surface courts—three lit for night play—near its great house. Costs to residents is free for day games, whereas nonresidents pay $25 per hour. All players are assessed $12 per hour for nighttime illumination. Four pros on site provide lessons, costing from $17 to $25 per half hour, or $25 to $40 per hour, depending on the rank of the pro.

Wyndham Rose Hall Resort, Rose Hall (☎ 809/952-2650), offers six hard-surface courts, each lit for night play, set near the east wing of the hotel on the side facing Falmouth. As a courtesy, nonresidents are invited to play for free, an invitation likely to be withdrawn when hotel guests want to take to the courts, especially in the winter months. A resident pro on site charges $45 per hour for lessons, or $25 for 30 minutes.

4 What to See & Do

If you ever feel like deserting Montego Bay's sandy beaches, there are several notable sights and activities in the area.

VISITING WITH THE ANIMALS

Jamaica Safari Village

Outside Falmouth. ☎ 809/954-3065 for reservations. Walking tours $6.50 adults, $3 children. Daily 9am–5pm.

Did you know that a 750-pound adult crocodile can move at 40 miles per hour? Ever hear the crocodile love call? You will learn all this and more during continual conducted walking tours through a petting zoo, a crocodile breeding center, and snake house. Safari Village served as a film set for the James Bond thriller *Live and Let Die.*

The White Witch of Rose Hall

Annie Mary Paterson, a beautiful bride of only 17, arrived at the Rose Hall great house near Montego Bay on March 28, 1820, to take up residence with her new husband, John Palmer. The house was said to affect her badly from the moment she entered it.

When John Palmer found out she was having an affair with a young slave, he is said to have beaten her with a riding whip. John Palmer died that night, and before long rumors were swirling that his young wife had poisoned his wine.

With her husband buried, Annie Palmer began a reign of terror at Rose Hall. Fearing her slave lover might blackmail her, she watched from the back of a black horse while he was securely tied, gagged, and flogged to death. Legend says that she then began to drift into liaison after liaison with one slave after another. But she was fickle: When her lovers bored her, she had them killed.

Her servants called her the *"Obeah* (voodoo) woman," the daughter of the devil, and "the White Witch of Rose Hall."

Although some scholars claim that they can produce no evidence of this legendary figure's cruelty or even of her debauchery, her story has been the subject of countless paperback Gothic novels.

When Ms. Palmer was found strangled in her bed in 1833, few speculated who her murderer might have been. Her household servants just wanted her buried as soon as possible in the deepest hole they could dig.

A boating tour of the environmentally balanced 50-acre lake, conducted by trained tour guides, costs $15 per adult, $7.50 for children.

Rocklands Wildlife Station

Anchovy. ☎ **809/952-2009.** Admission $6.25. Daily 2:30–5pm. To reach it from Montego Bay, head 1¹/₂ miles west of town. At Reading, turn inland for 2¹/₄ miles along LongHill.

Otherwise called Rocklands Bird Sanctuary, this was established by Lisa Salmon, known as the "Bird Lady of Anchovy." It attracts nature lovers and birdwatchers. It's a unique experience to have a Jamaican doctor bird perch on your finger to drink syrup, to hand-feed millet to small doves and finches, and to watch dozens of other birds flying in for their evening meal. (Don't take children ages five and under, as they tend to worry the birds. Smoking and playing radios are forbidden.)

THE GREAT HOUSES

Occupied by plantation owners, the great houses of Jamaica were always built on high ground so they overlooked the plantation itself and could see the next house in the distance. It was the custom of the owners to offer hospitality to travelers crossing the island by road. They were spotted by a lookout, who noted the rising dust. Bed and food were then made ready for the traveler's arrival.

✪ Rose Hall

Rose Hall Highway. (9 miles east of Montego Bay). ☎ **809/953-2323.** Admission $15 adults, $10 children. Daily 9am–6pm.

Charging a very steep admission, the most famous great house in Jamaica is the legendary Rose Hall. The house was built about two centuries ago by a John Palmer, but it was his grandnephew's wife, Annie Palmer, who was immortalized in H. G. deLisser's famous book as the *White Witch of Rosehall* (see box). Long in ruins, the house has now been restored and is open to the public. Annie's Pub on the ground floor offers libation and other refreshments.

Greenwood
Highway A1 (14 miles east of Montego Bay and 7 miles west of Falmouth). ☎ **809/953-1077.** Admission $10 adults, $5 children. Daily 9am–6pm.

Greenwood is even more interesting to some house tourers than Rose Hall (see above). Erected on a hillside perch in the early 19th century, the Georgian-style building was the residence between 1780 and 1800 of Richard Barrett, of the Elizabeth Barrett Browning family. On display is the original library of the Barrett family, with rare books dating from 1697, along with oil paintings of the Barrett family, china made by Wedgwood for the family, and a rare exhibition of musical instruments in working order, plus a fine collection of antique furniture. The house today is privately owned but open to the public.

CRUISES
Day and evening cruises are offered aboard the *Calico,* a 55-foot gaff-rigged wooden ketch, sailing from Margueritaville on the Montego Bay waterfront. You can be transported to and from your hotel for either cruise. The day voyage, departing at 10am and returning at 3pm, provides a day of sailing, sunning, and snorkeling (with equipment supplied), plus a Jamaican buffet lunch served on the beach, all to the sound of reggae and other music. The cruise costs $50 per person and is offered Tuesday through Sunday. On the *Calico's* evening voyage, which costs $25 per person and is offered from 5 to 7pm Wednesday through Saturday, cocktails and wine are served as you sail through sunset. For information and reservations, call Capt. Bryan Langford, **North Coast Cruises Ltd.** (☎ 809/952-5860). A three-day notice is recommended.

ORGANIZED ACTIVITIES & EVENTS
The **Croydon Plantation,** Catadupa, St. James (☎ 809/979-8267), a 45-minute ride from Montego Bay, can be visited on a half-day tour from Montego Bay (or Negril) on Tuesday, Wednesday, and Friday. Included in the $55 price are round-trip transportation from your hotel, a tour of the plantation, a tasting of varieties of pineapple and tropical fruits in season, plus a barbecue chicken lunch. Most hotel tour desks can arrange this tour.

A picnic to Miskito Cove Beach could be the highlight of your visit here. Hotel tour desks book the **Miskito Cove Beach Picnic** (☎ 809/952-5164), which leaves at 10am, returning at 4pm, with pickups at Tryall and Round Hill. For $55 per person, you can enjoy an open Jamaican bar, buffet lunch, calypso band, a glass-bottom-boat ride, a raft ride with a calypso singer on board, and water sports including snorkeling with a guide and equipment provided, Sunfish sailing with trained captains, jetskiing, and windsurfing. The picnics are offered on Sunday, Tuesday, and Thursday.

For a plantation tour, go on a **Hilton High Day Tour;** their office is at 11 Delisser Drive (☎ 809/952-3343). Round-trip transportation on a scenic drive through historic plantation areas is included. Your day starts with a continental breakfast served at the old plantation house on a patio overlooking the fields and hills. You can roam around the 100 acres and visit St. Leonards or the German village of Seaford Town nearby. Calypso music is played throughout the day, and a Jamaican lunch of roast suckling pig with chicken or fish, 12 Jamaican vegetables, and rum punch is served at 1pm. Dressmakers are on hand to create custom-tailored Jamaican fashions. The charge for the day is $50 per person for the plantation tour, breakfast, lunch, and transportation. There's an additional charge of $10 for 30 minutes of horseback riding. Tour days are Tuesday, Wednesday, Friday, and Sunday.

5 Shopping

For many visitors, Montego Bay is their introduction to shopping Jamaica-style. After surviving the ordeal, some visitors may vow never to go shopping again. Literally hundreds of Jamaicans pour into town hoping to peddle something, often something they made, to visitors who are mainly cruise-ship passengers.

Since their selling a craft may determine whether they can feed their family that night, there is often a feverish attempt to peddle goods to overseas visitors, all of whom are viewed as rich. Therefore, prepare yourself for some aggressive selling when you venture into the shopping centers.

Pandemonium greets many an unwary shopper, who must also be prepared for some fierce haggling. Every vendor asks too much for an item at first, which gives them the leeway to "negotiate" until the price reaches a more realistic level.

The main shopping areas are at **Montego Freeport,** within easy walking distance of the pier, **City Centre** (where most of the nonhotel in-bond shops are), and **Holiday Village Shopping Centre.**

ARTS & CRAFTS

The **Old Fort Craft Park,** a shopping complex with 180 vendors (all licensed by the Jamaica Tourist Board), fronts Howard Cooke Boulevard up from Gloucester Avenue in the heart of Montego Bay on the site of Fort Montego. A market with a varied assortment of handcrafts, it is ideal browsing not only for that little souvenir of Jamaica but for some more serious purchases as well. You'll see a selection of wall hangings, handwoven straw items, and hand-carved wood sculpture, and you can even get your hair braided if that is your desire. Vendors can be powerfully aggressive trying to get you to buy something, so be prepared for major hassle. If you want some item, also be prepared for some serious negotiation. Persistent bargaining on your part will lead to substantial discounts. Fort Montego, now long gone, was constructed by the British in the mid-18th century as part of their defense of "fortress Jamaica." But it never saw much action, except for firing its cannons every year to salute the monarch's birthday.

At the **Crafts Market** near Harbour Street in downtown Montego Bay you can find the best selection of handmade souvenirs of Jamaica, including straw hats and bags, wooden platters, straw baskets, musical instruments, beads, carved objects, and toys. That *jipijapa* hat is important if you're going to be out in the island sun.

Ambiente Art Gallery
9 Fort St. ☎ **809/952-7919.**

A 100-year-old clapboard-sided cottage set close to the road houses this gallery. Austrian-born owner Maria Hitchins is considered one of the doyennes of the Montego Bay art scene. She has personally encouraged and developed scores of local artists toward prominence, yet many of her good paintings sell for under $300. Open Monday to Friday from 9am to 6pm, Saturday from 10am to 3pm.

Blue Mountain Gems Workshop
At the Holiday Village Shopping Centre. ☎ **809/953-2338.**

Here you can take a tour of the workshops to see the process from raw stone to the finished product you can buy later. Wooden jewelry, local carvings, and one-of-a-kind ceramic figurines are also sold. Open Monday to Friday from 9am to 5pm, Saturday from 9am to 4pm.

Neville Budhai Paintings
Budhai's Art Gallery, Reading Main Road (5 miles east of Montego Bay), Reading. ☎ **809/ 979-2568.** Take bus no. 11 from Mo Bay.

This is the art center of a distinguished artist, Neville Budhai, president and cofounder of the Western Jamaica Society of Fine Arts. He has a distinct style, and captures the special flavor of the island and its people in his works. The artist may sometimes be seen sketching or painting in Montego Bay or along the highways of rural Jamaica. Open daily from 8:30am to early evening.

Things Jamaican Ltd.
44 Fort St. ☎ **809/952-5605.**

Affiliated with the government and set up to encourage the development of Jamaican arts and crafts, Things Jamaican is a showcase for the talents of the artisans of this island nation. Displayed are a wealth of Jamaican products, even food and drink, including rums and liqueurs, along with jerk seasoning and such jellies as orange pepper. Look for Busha Browne's fine Jamaican sauces, especially their spicy chutneys such as banana or their planters spicy piquant sauce or their spicy tomato (called *love apple*) sauce, which is not to be confused with catsup. These recipes are prepared and bottled by the Busha Browne Company in Jamaica just as they were 100 years ago. Many items for sale are carved from wood, including not only sculpture but salad bowls and trays. You'll also find large hand-woven Jamaican baskets and women's handbags made of bark (in Jamaica, these are known unflatteringly as "old lady bags").

Look also for reproductions of the Port Royal collection, named for the wicked city buried by an earthquake and tidal wave in 1692 (see Chapter 7). After resting in a sleepy underwater grave for 275 years, beautiful pewter items were recovered and are living again in reproductions (except the new items are leadless). Impressions were made, and molds were created to reproduce them. They include rat-tail spoons, a spoon with the heads of the monarchs William and Mary, Splay-footed Lion Rampant spoons, and spoons with Pied-de-Biche handles. Many items were reproduced faithfully, right down to the pit marks and scratches. To complement this pewter assortment, Things Jamaican created the Port Royal Bristol-Delft Ceramic Collection, based on original pieces of ceramics found in the underwater digs. Open Monday to Friday from 9am to 5pm, Saturday from 9am to 4pm.

DUTY-FREE SHOPPING

In Montego Bay, you can purchase good duty-free items, including Swiss watches, Irish crystal, French perfumes, English china, Danish silverware, Portuguese linens, Italian handbags, Scottish cashmeres, Indian silks, and liquors and liqueurs. Appleton's overproof, special, and punch rums are an excellent value. The best liqueurs are Tía Maria (coffee flavored) and Rumona (rum flavored). Khus Khus is the local perfume. Jamaican arts and crafts are available throughout the resort and at the Crafts Market (see below).

Golden Nugget
8 St. James Shopping Centre, Gloucester Avenue. ☎ **809/952-7707.**

The Golden Nugget is a duty-free shop with an impressive collection of watches for both women and men, and a fine assortment of jewelry, especially gold chains. Set within the manicured confines of one of Montego Bay's most modern shopping compounds, it is run by India-born Sheila Mulchandani. Open Monday to Saturday from 9am to 6pm, Sunday by appointment only.

FASHION

Jolie Madame Fashions
30 City Centre Building. ☎ **809/952-3126.**

Its racks of clothing for women and girls might contain an appropriately cool garment for a romantic dinner or a lunch beside the swimming pool, or something to wear as a cover-up at the beach. Many garments range from $50–$200. Norma McLeod, the establishment's overseer, designer, coordinator, and founder, is always on hand to arrange custom-made garments. Open Monday to Saturday from 9am to 6pm.

Klass Kraft Leather Sandals
44 Fort St. ☎ **809/952-5782.**

Next door to Things Jamaican, this store offers sandals and leather accessories made on location by a team of Jamaican craftspeople. All sandals cost less than $30. Open Monday to Friday from 9am to 5pm, Saturday from 10am to 3pm.

6 Montego Bay After Dark

There's a lot more to Montego Bay evenings than just discos. But most of the entertainment is based at the various hotels, which has spelled doom for local nightclubs trying to attract tourists.

Pier 1, Howard Cooke Boulevard (☎ **809/952-2452**), already previewed for its Jamaican cookery (see "Where to Dine," earlier in the chapter), might also be your entertainment choice for a night on the town. Friday night sees disco action from 10pm to 5am when a $2.60 cover charge is assessed.

The **Cricket Club** at the Wyndham Rose Hall (☎ **809/953-2650**) is more than just a sports bar. It's a place where people go to meet and mingle with an international crowd. Televised sports, karaoke sing-alongs, tournament darts, and backgammon are all part of the fun. Drinks begin at $3, and the club is open daily from 7pm to 1am. There's no cover charge.

Every Sunday, Tuesday, and Thursday, there's an **Evening on the Great River,** during which you ride in a fishing canoe up the river 10 miles west of Montego Bay. A torchlit path leads to a re-created Arawak village, where you eat, drink as much as you like at the open bar, and watch a floor show. The Country Store offers jackass rope (tobacco by the yard), nutmeg, cinnamon, brown sugar, and all sorts of country items for sale. You're picked up at your hotel no later than 7pm and returned by midnight. The cost, with transportation, is $55 per person. Children under 12 go for half price. The operator is Great River Productions, 42 Gloucester Ave., Reading, St. James (☎ **809/952-5047**).

7 A Side Trip to Falmouth

A port on the north coast about 23 miles east of Montego Bay, Falmouth is an interesting but ramshackle town. There is talk about fixing it up for visitors, but no one seems to have done that yet. If you leave your car at Water Square, you can explore the town in about an hour or so.

The present Courthouse was reconstructed from the early 19th-century building, and fishers still congregate on Seaboard Street. You'll pass the Customs Office and a parish church dating from the closing years of the 18th century. Later, you can go on a shopping expedition outside of town to Caribatik Island Fabrics (see below).

A SPECIAL SHOPPING EXPEDITION FOR BATIKS

Two miles east of Falmouth on the north-coast road is **Caribatik Island Fabrics,** at Rock Wharf on the Luminous Lagoon (☎ 809/954-3314). This is the private living and work domain of Keith Chandler, who established the place with his late wife, Muriel, in 1970. Today the batiks whose forerunners were created by Muriel Chandler are viewed as stylish garments by chic boutiques in the States.

In the shop there is a full range of fabrics, scarves, garments, and wall hangings, some patterned after such themes as Jamaica's "doctor bird" and various endangered animal species of the world. Muriel's Gallery continues to sell a selection of her original batik paintings. Either Keith or a member of the staff will be glad to describe the intricate process of batiking during their open hours: 9am to 4pm Tuesday through Saturday. They are closed in September.

WHERE TO STAY

✪ Good Hope

5 miles south of Falmouth (P.O. Box 50), Falmouth, Jamaica, W.I. ☎ **809/954-3289** or 800/ OUTPOST. Fax 809/954-3289. 10 rms. Winter $150–$250 double; off-season $100–$175 double. AE, MC, V.

Set on 2,000 acres, this estate was first granted to a Col. Thomas Williams in 1742, and the great house was built in 1755. It was the center for growing sugarcane and coconuts, and crops are still grown here, the land irrigated by the Martha Brae River, which meanders through the property. Renovated to its original Georgian style, Good Hope offers four bedrooms in the great house, one in the "Counting House," and five in the "Coach House." The Coach House can be rented as a self-contained villa for a family or group of friends, as it has a full kitchen, living and dining room, and balcony. Staff will be provided to prepare meals at the Coach House, if guests prefer to dine in rather than at the hotel's restaurant. The great house has been extensively restored and refurbished. Bedrooms have elegant furnishings and four-poster beds.

Dining/Entertainment: The formal dining room offers very Jamaican, plantation-style cooking, yet with a continental flair. Another more informal dining area is on the large terrace behind the pool. Outside guests who call for a reservation can also dine here. Lunch is served daily from noon to 3pm and dinner from 6:30 to 9:30pm.

Facilities: Swimming pool, tennis courts, bird sanctuary, riding stables; guests can also enjoy facilities of the Half Moon Club.

WHERE TO DINE

Glistening Waters Inn and Marina

On A1 (between Falmouth and Trelawny Beach Hotel, 28 miles east of Montego Bay). ☎ **809/ 954-3229.** Reservations not necessary. Main courses $8.50–$11.50. AE, MC, V. Daily 11am– 2:30pm and 6–9:30pm. SEAFOOD.

Montego Bay residents often make the drive out here just to sample the almost-forgotten ambience of another era. The furniture at Glistening Waters evokes a stage set for *The Night of the Iguana*. Menu items may include local fish, such as snapper or kingfish, served with bammy (a form of cassava bread). Other specialties are three different lobster dishes, three different preparations of shrimp, three different conch viands, fried rice, and pork served as chops or in a stew. The cookery is just what your mama would make had she come from Jamaica.

Many guests look forward to coming here because the waters of the lagoon contain a rare type of phosphorescent microbe, which, when the waters are agitated, glow in the dark. Ask about night boat cruises, which cost $3 per person for diners. Departures are nightly at about 6:40pm.

Negril, the South Coast & Mandeville

5

Situated on the arid western tip of Jamaica, Negril has had a reputation for bacchanalia, hedonism, marijuana smoking, and nude bathing since hippies discovered its sunny shores during the late 1960s. The resort became more mainstream in the early 1990s as the big-money capitalists of Kingston and North America built several new megaresorts, most of them managed by Jamaica's SuperClubs. Not all of the old reputation has disappeared, however, for some resorts here reserve stretches of their beach for nude bathers, and illegal ganja is peddled openly.

Whether clothed or unclothed, visitors are drawn here to Negril's 7-mile stretch of white sand and some of the best scuba diving in Jamaica. Opening onto a tranquil lagoon protected from the Caribbean by a coral reef, this great beach is set against a backdrop of sea grape and coconut palms. Local authorities mandate that no building can be taller than the highest palm tree, resulting in an ecologically conscious setting, with the resorts blending gracefully into the flat and sandy landscape.

While Negril gets the crowds, the South Coast of Jamaica has only recently begun to attract large numbers of tourists. Arawak once lived in sylvan simplicity along these shores before their civilization was destroyed. Early Spanish settlers came here searching for gold. Today's traveler comes looking for the untrammelled sands of its secluded beaches. Fishers still sell their catch at colorful local markets, and the prices, as they say here, are "the way they used to be" in Jamaica.

Most visitors to the south head east from Negril through Savanna-La-Mar to the high-country, English-style town of Mandeville, then on to a boat tour up the Black River, home of freshwater crocodiles. Those with more time continue southeast along the coast to Treasure Beach before heading up to Mandeville. On the South Coast, the best center for overnighting is either the town of Black River or the village of Treasure Beach.

Mandeville, about midway between Negril and Kingston, lies in the interior of the island at 2,000 feet above sea level. A large North American contingent employed in the bauxite industry lives here. Although dating from 1814, Mandeville was developed in the late 19th century as a retreat for English visitors attracted to the town's pleasant climate. The temperature in summer averages 70°F, and in winter, a comfortably cool 60°F, which also helped make Mandeville the center of the Jamaican coffee industry during an earlier era.

What's Special About Negril, the South Coast & Mandeville

Beaches
- Negril's 7 miles of white sand, the focal point of some of Jamaica's newest resort developments and onshore nudist locales. An anything-goes attitude prevails.
- Booby Cay, a small island off the coast of Negril across from Rutland Point. Popular with nude sunbathers.
- Treasure Beach, a beachcomber's paradise, tucked away on the secluded south coast. Savvy locals—many descended from Scottish seamen wrecked off their coast—consider it the "in" place. Swimming is tricky because of the undertow, and the sand is gray, but it's secluded and comfortable, and dramatic waves crash into the shore.

Great Towns/Villages
- Negril, 52 miles southwest of Montego Bay, Jamaica's informal and laid-back resort, with its white sandy beach protected by offshore coral reefs.
- Mandeville, 70 miles southeast of Montego Bay, an old British colonial inland town set among lush vegetation and misty mountains.

A Historic Home
- Marshall's Pen, Mandeville, an old coffee plantation once owned by the island's governor—an antique-filled great house.

Memorable Sights & Experiences
- The Milk River Mineral Baths, 9 miles south of the Kingston-Mandeville Highway, boasting the world's most radioactive mineral waters.
- A boat tour up the Black River—once a major logging conduit and still home to freshwater crocodiles.
- Hedonism II, Negril, an all-inclusive resort that's been called a "love poem to Mother Nature"—where you just might find yourself playing in a 3am nude volleyball game in the pool.
- Sunset at Rick's Cafe, Negril, an island tradition with reggae musicians, jugglers, and fire-eaters entertaining on 50-foot cliffs as the setting sun disappears.
- Marshall's Pen Cattle Estate and Nature Reserve, near Mandeville, featuring 89 of Jamaica's 256 species of birds.

Film Locations
- Booby Cay, across from Rutland Point, offshore from Negril, setting for the South Seas scenes in the Walt Disney movie *20,000 Leagues Under the Sea.*

Fortunes were also made in pimiento (allspice). The town contains the oldest golf course on Jamaica, and one of its major attractions is Marshall's Pen, an 18th-century great house on a 300-acre cattle farm.

Partly because of its Victorian gingerbread architecture, Mandeville has been called the most English town in Jamaica. Today it accepts its role as the sleepiest of the larger Jamaican cities—a fact that contributes significantly to its charm.

1 Introducing Negril

Long before the hippies established Negril's reputation for debauchery in the 1960s, it was noted for the buccaneer Calico Jack, famous for his carousings with the infamous women pirates Ann Bonney and Mary Read (see the box "Ann Bonney & Her Dirty Dog," later in this section).

Negril

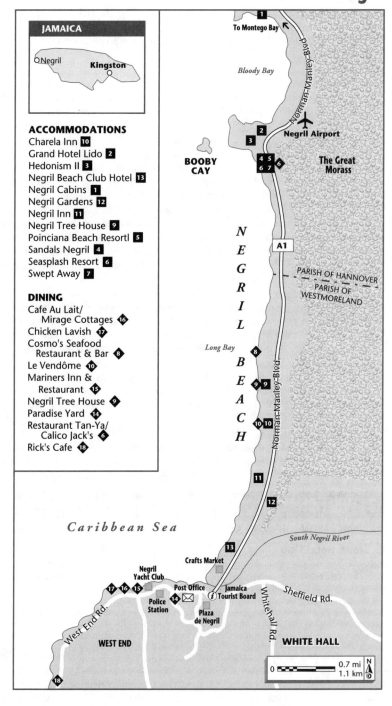

JAMAICA

Negril · Kingston

ACCOMMODATIONS
Charela Inn **10**
Grand Hotel Lido **2**
Hedonism II **3**
Negril Beach Club Hotel **13**
Negril Cabins **1**
Negril Gardens **12**
Negril Inn **11**
Negril Tree House **9**
Poinciana Beach Resortl **5**
Sandals Negril **4**
Seasplash Resort **6**
Swept Away **7**

DINING
Cafe Au Lait/
  Mirage Cottages **16**
Chicken Lavish **17**
Cosmo's Seafood
  Restaurant & Bar **8**
Le Vendôme **10**
Mariners Inn &
  Restaurant **15**
Negril Tree House **9**
Paradise Yard **14**
Restaurant Tan-Ya/
  Calico Jack's **6**
Rick's Cafe **18**

To Montego Bay

Bloody Bay

Negril Airport

BOOBY CAY

The Great Morass

N E G R I L   B E A C H

A1

PARISH OF HANNOVER
PARISH OF WESTMORELAND

Long Bay

Caribbean Sea

South Negril River

Crafts Market

Negril Yacht Club

Post Office

Police Station

Jamaica Tourist Board

Plaza de Negril

Sheffield Rd.

Whitehall Rd.

West End Rd.

WEST END

WHITE HALL

0   0.7 mi
      1.1 km

N

When the laid-back young Americans and Canadians arrived in the late '60s, Negril was a sleepy village with no electricity or telephones. The youngsters rented modest digs in little houses on the West End, where local people extended their hospitality. The sunsets were beautiful and free, and the ganja was cheap and readily available.

But those days are gone. Negril today is a tourist mecca. Visitors flock to its beaches, which lie along three well-protected bays—Long Bay, Negril Harbour (or Bloody Bay), and Orange Bay. This new Negril, with all-inclusive resorts such as Hedonism II and Sandals Negril, draws a better-heeled—if not always less rowdy—crowd, including hundreds of European visitors.

There are really two Negrils. The West End is the site of many little eateries with names like Chicken Lavish, and of modest cottages that still receive visitors. The other Negril is on the east end, along the road from Montego Bay. The best hotels, such as Negril Gardens, line the panoramic beachfront one after the other.

The actual town of Negril may have power and phones these days, but it has little of interest to travelers. The only building of any historical note in the area is **Negril Lighthouse,** at the westerly tip of Jamaica. Built in 1894, it offers a chance to climb some 100 steps for a view of Negril Point, the bay, and the sea inlet. An automatic light flashes every 2 seconds throughout the night. You can still see the old kerosene lamps used until the 1940s, when they were replaced by gas lamps.

Chances are, however, your main concern will be staking out your own favorite spot along Negril's 7-mile beach. You don't need to get up for anything; somebody will be along to serve you. Perhaps it'll be the banana lady, with a basket of fruit perched on her head. Maybe the ice cream man will set up a stand right under a coconut palm. Surely the beer lady will find you as she strolls along the beach, a carton of Red Stripe on her head and a bucket of ice in her hand. And just like in the old days, hordes of young men peddling illegal ganja will seek you out.

At some point you'll want to leave the beach long enough to explore Booby Key (or Cay), a tiny islet off the Negril Coast. It was featured in the Walt Disney film *20,000 Leagues Under the Sea.*

Negril is 50 miles (about a 2-hour drive) southwest of Montego Bay international airport along a winding road, past ruins of sugar estates and great houses. (Most of the resorts here will arrange to pick you up and provide your transfer from the Montego Bay airport.) It's 150 miles (about a 4-hour drive) west of Kingston.

2 Where to Stay

ALL-INCLUSIVE RESORTS

✪ Grand Hotel Lido

Bloody Bay (at the east end of the beach strip near Rutland Point; P.O. Box 88), Negril, Jamaica, W.I. ☎ **809/957-4010,** or 800/859-7875 in the U.S., 800/553-4320 in Canada. Fax 809/957-4317. 182 junior suites, 18 one-bedroom suites. A/C MINIBAR TV TEL. 3-night package in winter, $2,520 suite for two. 3-night package in the off-season $1,080 suite for two. Rates include all meals, snacks, drinks, entertainment, sports, activities, taxes, service charges, and airport transfers. AE, MC, V.

The grandest and most architecturally stylish hotel in its chain, Grand Hotel Lido is set on flat and lushly landscaped land adjacent to Hedonism II (see below), on the outer fringes of Negril. It is much more subdued and not as raunchy as its neighbor, although the smaller of the resort's two beaches is reserved for nudists, who, according to most accounts, seem to give the best cocktail parties, enjoy the most uninhibited humor, and make the greatest number of repeat visits to the resort. The most upscale and discreetly elegant of the string of resorts known as Jamaica's SuperClubs, it opened in 1989 to richly deserved fanfare.

Accommodations are more stylish than those at any other hotel in Negril. Each spacious unit contains a stereo system, and has either a patio or balcony crafted from massive timbers (almost all of these overlook the sands of a fine beach). Only adults are welcome, but unlike many other all-inclusive resorts, especially Club Med, there is no resistance here to renting a room to a single occupant.

Dining/Entertainment: In addition to the cavernous and airy main dining room is a trio of restaurants, one devoted to nouvelle cuisine, another to continental food, and the third to Italian pasta. Guests also enjoy an all-night disco, the piano bar, and the dozens of pool tables and dart boards of no fewer than nine bars. Obtaining a drink here (included in the tariff) is never a problem, for even after the resort's quartet of restaurants closes, there are three different dining enclaves that remain open through the night. These are tucked into corners of the resort, each with a bubbling Jacuzzi nearby, perhaps with a canopy overhead of allamander blossoms.

Services: Laundry, 24-hour room service, tour desk, instructors to teach tennis and sailing, concierge.

Facilities: Four tennis courts, two swimming pools, Jacuzzis, gym/sauna/health club, two fine beaches lined with chaises longues, and one of the most glamorous yachts in the West Indies, the MY *Zein*, offered in 1956 by Aristotle Onassis to Rainier III and Grace of Monaco as a wedding present.

Hedonism II

Norman Manley Boulevard (on Negril's main road, about 2 miles east of the town center; P.O. Box 25), Negril, Jamaica, W.I. ☎ **809/957-4200,** or 800/859-7873 in the U.S. Fax 809/ 957-4289. 280 rms. A/C. 3-night package in winter $535–$605 per person double occupancy. 3-night package in off-season $517–$586 per person double occupancy. Rates include all meals, drinks, activities, taxes, service charges, and airport transfers. AE, DC, MC, V.

Devoted to the pursuit of pleasure, Hedonism II packs the works into a package deal, including all the sports facilities you could want, all the booze you can drink, and all the late-night partying you can handle. There is no tender of any sort, and tipping is not permitted. Of all the members of its chain, this is the most raucous. It's something of a meat market, deliberately inviting its mainly single guests to get "wicked and wild" for a week. Understandably, the resort is closed to the public, and guests must be at least 18 years old (most are Americans). The hotel will find roommates for single guests and charge them the double occupancy rate. The rooms are stacked in two-story clusters dotted around a sloping 22-acre site.

Only nude bathers are allowed on one side of the beach here (guests facetiously call the other side "The Prude"). Among the few limits here: volleyball is the only sport played in the nude. The resort also maintains a secluded beach on nearby Booby Cay, where guests are taken twice a week for picnics.

Dining/Entertainment: Nightly entertainment is presented, along with a live band, a high-powered and high-energy disco with a stage for the occasional live performer, and a piano bar. Buffets are staged, and the cuisine is international. There is also a nude-only bar and grill, although one guest told us that when she dines, she likes to keep her mind on the cuisine, not on someone else's anatomy.

Services: Massage.

Facilities: Sailing, snorkeling, waterskiing, scuba diving, windsurfing, glass-bottom boat, Jacuzzi, swimming pool, six lighted tournament-class tennis courts, two badminton courts, basketball court, two indoor squash courts, volleyball, table tennis, Nautilus and free-weight gyms, aerobics, indoor game room.

Ann Bonney & Her Dirty Dog

It was at Bloody Bay, off the coast of Negril, that one of the most notorious pirates of all time, Calico Jack Rackham, was finally captured in 1720. His is a name that will live in infamy, along with Blackbeard's. He was captured with his lover Ann (also Anne) Bonney, the most notorious female pirate of all time. (The bay isn't called bloody, however, because of these pirates. Whalers used to disembowel their catch here, turning the waters red with blood.)

After tracking her husband, a penniless ne'er-do-well sailor named James Bonney, to a brothel in the Virgin Islands, Ann slit his throat. However, she soon fell for Captain Jack Rackham, who was known as "Calico Jack." Some say he came by his nickname because of the colorful shirts he wore; others claim it was because of his undershorts.

Until he met this lady pirate, Calico Jack hadn't done so well as a pirate, but she inspired him to greatness. In a short time, they became the scourge of the West Indies. No vessel sailing the Caribbean Sea was too large or too small for them to attack and rob. Ann is said to have fought alongside the men, and, according to reports, was a much tougher customer than Calico Jack himself. With her cutlass and marlinspike, she was usually the first to board a captured vessel. Sometimes they teamed up with the Caribbean's second most notorious female pirate, Mary Read, whose exploits don't quite match up to Ann's.

It was late in October, off the Negril coast, when Calico Jack and all the pirates were getting drunk on rum, that a British Navy sloop attacked. Calico Jack ran and hid, but Ann fought bravely, according to reports. She flailed away with battle-ax and cutlass.

Calico Jack and the other captured pirates were sentenced to be hanged. Ann, however, pleaded with "Milord" that she was pregnant. Since British law did not allow the killing of unborn children, she got off though her comrades were sentenced to death. Her final advice to Calico Jack: "If you'd fought like a man, you wouldn't be hanged like the dirty dog you are." So much for a lover's parting words. Ann's father in Ireland purchased her release and she opened a gaming house in St. Thomas and prospered until the end.

Negril Inn

Norman Manley Boulevard (on the main road, about 3 miles east of the town center), Negril, Jamaica, W.I. ☎ **809/957-4209,** or 800/NEGRIL-N in the U.S. Fax 809/957-4365. 46 rms. A/C. Winter $280 double, $390 triple; off-season $220 double, $270 triple. Rates include all meals, drinks, activities, taxes, service charges, and airport transfers. AE, MC, V.

Located in the heart of the 7-mile beach stretch, with comfortable lounge chairs spread on the sands, this inn is one of the smallest all-inclusive resorts in Negril. Because of its size, there aren't as many facilities and the atmosphere is more low-tech, more low-key, and less energy-charged than that at its larger competitors such as Hedonism II.

Negril Inn is not confined to couples only. The resort offers very simply furnished guest rooms, with private balconies, spread through a series of two-story structures in a garden setting of flowering hibiscus, coffee rose, and night jasmine. Children are not accepted in the winter. Offering a host of activities, day and night, the resort employs a helpful staff.

Dining/Entertainment: Included in the package are all meals, all alcoholic drinks (except champagne), and nightly entertainment (including a disco). Good-quality meals are offered in the resort's only restaurant, though there are bars in the disco and beside the pool.

Services: Filtered water, laundry, room service (for breakfast only).

Facilities: Windsurfing, waterskiing, scuba diving, snorkeling, hydrosliding, aqua bikes, glass-bottom boat, two lighted tennis courts, piano room, Universal weight room, freshwater pool.

Poinciana Beach Resort

Norman Manley Boulevard (on the main road into Negril, 5 miles east of town; P.O. Box 44), Negril, Jamaica, W.I. ☎ **809/957-4256,** or 800/468-6728 in the U.S. Fax 809/957-4229. 90 rms, 6 studios, 12 suites, 22 villas. A/C TV. Winter $396 double; $404 studio for two; $560 suite for two; $416–$430 villa for two. Off-season $330 double; $338 studio for two; $414 suite for two; $348–$360 villa for two. Rates are per person and all-inclusive. AE, MC, V.

Set on six acres of land, this hotel and villa vacation resort attracts a mix of couples, singles, and families, with a variety of accommodations and an extensive sports program. It is a mixture of both contemporary and colonial design, with tile floors, rattan and wood furnishings, and private balconies and ocean views. Located right on Seven Mile Beach, it opened in the 1980s with just two private accommodations and has grown considerably. Superior rooms consist of one bedroom and bath and a private balcony or patio, and suites are furnished with a kitchenette and a large wraparound balcony. Some suites offer Jacuzzi-type tubs. Villas consist of one or two bedrooms, a living/dining area with kitchenette, and private balcony or patio.

Dining/Entertainment: A poolside restaurant, The Captain's Table, serves three meals daily, with both Jamaican dishes and international specialties. Other dining choices include The Paradise Plum, with many innovative recipes, and the Starlight Terrace, with fresh pastas and grilled selections served under the stars. The Upper Deck Cafe serves after-dinner snacks, and at the Beach Bar, a lively native band entertains five evenings a week during happy hour. Other evening entertainment is often staged, including a reggae/soca barbecue night on Saturdays.

Services: Beauty salon, baby-sitting, children's program, massage.

Facilities: Two freshwater swimming pools, heated Jacuzzi, lawn and table tennis, 24-hour exercise gyms, water sports including windsurfing, snorkeling, kayaks, glass-bottom-boat rides, Sunfish and Hobie Cat sailing, scuba diving.

Sandals Negril

Rutland Point (on the main road, a short drive east of the town center and near Grand Lido; P.O. Box 12), Negril, Jamaica, W.I. ☎ **809/957-4216,** or 800/SANDALS in the U.S. and Canada. Fax 809/957-4338. 187 rms, 16 suites. A/C TV TEL. 3-night package in winter $1,580–$1,940 double; $2,140–$2,360 suite. 3-night package in off-season $1,500–$2,360 double; $2,020–$2,200 suite. Rates include all meals, snacks, drinks, activities, taxes, service charges, and airport transfers. AE, DC, MC, V.

This couples-only resort, occupying some 13 acres of prime beachfront land, is part of the ever-expanding empire of the enterprising Gordon "Butch" Stewart, who pioneered similar operations in Montego Bay. The word "Sandals" in Jamaica has come to stand for a "no problem, mon" vacation. If you're the wildest of raunchy and randy party types, you'd be better off at Hedonism. Life is hardly subdued at Sandals, but it is tamer.

The developers linked two older hotels, forming a unified whole. The crowd is usually convivial, decidedly informal, and often young. Its beach-oriented clientele likes the lazy lifestyle here. The resort offers well-furnished bedrooms and very little incentive to ever leave the property. There are five divisions of accommodations, rated standard, superior, and deluxe, plus deluxe beachfront rooms and 16 one-bedroom suites. Rooms are casually furnished in a tropical motif, with hair dryers and radios. For a balcony and sea view, you have to pay the top rates.

Dining/Entertainment: Rates include all meals, even snacks, and unlimited drinks day or night at one of four bars (two swim-up pool bars add a special feature). Coconut Cove is the main dining room, but guests can also elect to eat at one of the specialty rooms, including Sundowner, offering white-glove service and Jamaican cuisine, and the 4 C's, with low-calorie health food served beside the beach. Kimono offers a Japanese cuisine. Nightly entertainment, including theme parties, is also included.

Services: Laundry, massage.

Facilities: Two freshwater swimming pools, lighted tennis courts, scuba diving, snorkeling, Sunfish sailing, windsurfing, canoeing, glass-bottom boat, fitness center with saunas and Universal exercise equipment.

✪ Swept Away

Norman Manley Boulevard, Long Bay (on the main road into Negril, 3¹/₂ miles east of the town center; P.O. Box 77), Negril, Jamaica, W.I. ☎ **809/957-4040,** or 800/545-7937 in the U.S. and Canada. Fax 809/957-4060. 134 units. A/C TEL. 3-night package in winter $1,500–$1,620 per couple. 3-night package in off-season $1,380–$1,500 per couple. Rates include meals, drinks, activities, taxes, service, and airport transfers. AE, MC, V.

Opened in 1990, Swept Away is one of the best-equipped hotels in Negril—it's certainly the one most conscious of sports, emotional relaxation, and physical and mental fitness. It caters to male/female couples eager for an ambience with all possible diversions available but absolutely no organized schedule and no pressure. As a staff member told us in private, "We get the health and fitness nuts, and Sandals or Hedonism get the sex-crazed." The resort occupies 20 flat and sandy acres straddling the highway leading in from Montego Bay; the grounds are beautifully landscaped.

The spacious, airy accommodations (called "veranda suites" because of their large private balconies with comfortable chaise longues) are in 26 two-story villas clustered together into a tropical village accented with flowering shrubs and vines. Your room will be only a few steps from the 7-mile expanse of Negril's beachfront. Each accommodation contains a ceiling fan, a king-size bed, and sea views (unless yours is obscured by verdant vegetation).

Dining/Entertainment: The resort's social center is its international restaurant, Feathers, which lies inland, across the road from the sea. There's also an informal beachfront restaurant, and four bars scattered throughout the property, including a healthy veggie bar.

Services: Laundry service, room service (continental breakfast only), tour desk for arranging visits to other parts of Jamaica.

Facilities: Racquetball, squash, and 10 lighted tennis courts; fully equipped gym, aerobics, yoga, massage, steam, sauna, whirlpool; billiards; bicycles; beachside swimming pool; scuba diving, windsurfing, reef snorkeling.

OTHER ACCOMMODATIONS
EXPENSIVE

Seasplash Resort

Norman Manley Boulevard (on the main beach strip, directly south of Poinciana Beach Hotel), Negril, Jamaica, W.I. ☎ **809/957-4041,** or 800/526-2422 in the U.S. Fax 809/957-4049. 15 suites. A/C TV TEL. Winter $240 suite for two; $240 suite for three; $260 suite for four. Off-season $135 suite for two; $155 suite for three; $175 suite for four. Full board $57 per person extra. AE, MC, V.

Partly because of Seasplash's small size, guests enjoy a sense of intimacy and personal contact with the staff. In contrast to the nearby megaresorts, it occupies only a small landscaped sliver of beachfront land planted with tropical greenery. Seasplash contains only suites, each named after a local island flower or flowering tree, and each is spaciously proportioned and decorated in a Caribbean motif of wicker furniture and fresh pastel colors. The units are all the same size, and contain kitchenettes, balcony or patio, large closets, either king-size or twin beds, and a decor much like that of a private vacation home. Those on the upper floor have higher ceilings and an enhanced feeling of space.

Dining/Entertainment: The resort contains two different restaurants, Calico Jack's (a simple lunchtime *bohío*) and the more elaborate Tan-Ya (see "Where to Dine," below).

Services: Baby-sitting, laundry, room service.

Facilities: Small gym, Jacuzzi, swimming pool with a thatch-covered, gazebo-style bar, immediate access to the beach.

MODERATE

Charela Inn

Norman Manley Boulevard (on the main beach strip, north of the Negril Inn; P.O. Box 33), Negril, Jamaica, W.I. ☎ **809/957-4277.** Fax 809/957-4414. 39 rms. A/C. Winter $140–$170 double; off-season $96–$113 double. MAP $35 extra per person per day. 5-night minimum stay in winter. MC, V.

A seafront inn reminiscent of a Spanish hacienda, Charela sits on three acres of landscaped grounds. The building encloses an inner courtyard with a tropical garden and a round freshwater swimming pool opening onto one of the widest sandy beaches in Negril (250 feet). The inn attracts a loyal following of visitors seeking a home away from home.

The dining room, Le Vendôme (see "Where to Dine," below) features open arches facing both the sea and the gardens, and offers an à la carte Jamaican and French menu and a five-course table d'hôte, changed daily for the sake of half-board residents. Sunsets are toasted on open terraces facing the sea. Simplicity and a quiet kind of elegance are the keynotes here. Sunset cruises, lasting 3 1/2 hours, are offered, along with Sunfish, windsurfing, and kayaking. On Thursday and Saturday nights live entertainment is presented.

Negril Beach Club Hotel

Norman Manley Boulevard (on the main beach strip, north of Negril Crafts Market; P.O. Box 7), Negril, Jamaica, W.I. ☎ **809/957-4220,** or 800/526-2422 in the U.S. and Canada. Fax 809/957-4364. 47 rms, 6 suites. A/C. Winter $100 double, $167 suite for one; $224 suite for two. Off-season $67 double, $167 suite for two. MAP $30 extra per person per day. AE, MC, V.

This casual, informal place, where topless bathing is the order of the day, has many admirers, although it is far too laid-back and too basically furnished and maintained for demanding travelers who want to be pampered. The resort is designed around a series of white stucco cottages with exterior stairways and terraces. The entire complex is clustered like a horseshoe around a rectangular garden whose end abuts a sandy beach just north of Negril. The accommodations range from simply furnished units to one-bedroom suites with kitchens. The rooms each offer private bath or shower; the less expensive units don't include balconies. Because some units are held by time-share investors, a number of the accommodations are not always available for rentals.

The Seething Cauldron Restaurant on the beach serves barbecue, seafood, and such Jamaican specialties as roast suckling pig and ackee and codfish. There's ample parking on the premises and easy access to a full range of sporting facilities including snorkeling, a pool, volleyball, table tennis, and windsurfing. Other activities can be organized nearby, and beach barbecues and buffet breakfasts are ample and frequent.

Negril Gardens Hotel

Norman Manley Boulevard (on the main beach strip; P.O. Box 58), Negril, Jamaica, W.I. ☎ **809/957-4408,** or 800/752-6824 in the U.S., 800/567-5327 in Canada. Fax 809/957-4374. 65 rms. A/C TV. Winter $125–$135 double. Off-season $105–$120 double. Additional person $30 extra. MAP $40 extra per person per day. Two children stay free in parents' room. AE, MC, V.

Attracting a young international clientele, Negril Gardens rests amid tropical verdure on the famous 7-mile stretch of beach. The two-story villas, each accented with Chippendale-style crosshatch balconies, are well-furnished. Rooms open onto a front veranda or a balcony with either a beach or a garden view. The units on the garden side are less expensive, and many guests prefer this location because it's the site of a beautiful swimming pool with pool bar and a tennis court.

Directly on the beach is a Tahitian-style bar where you can observe the ever-changing scene night and day. Right behind it stands an al fresco restaurant serving some of the best food in Negril. Nonguests are invited to dine here, and Jamaican cookery is offered along with a scattering of international dishes. Memorable dishes include various versions of conch, lobster, and other seafood, plus curried goat and stew peas or chicken fricassée. Dinner is served from 7 to 10pm nightly.

Negril Tree House

Norman Manley Boulevard (on the main beach strip, north of the Charela Inn; P.O. Box 29), Negril, Jamaica, W.I. ☎ **809/957-4287,** or 800/NEGRIL-1 in the U.S. or Canada. Fax 809/957-4386. 55 units, 12 suites. Winter $115–$145 double; $245–$325 family suite for up to four. Off-season $85–$115 double; $145–$285 family suite for up to four. AE, MC, V.

The Negril Tree House is a desirable little escapist retreat with an ideal beachfront location. Scattered across the property in 11 octagonal buildings are the comfortably furnished units, including 12 suites, each with tile bath and air-conditioning or ceiling fans. Suites, as an added bonus, also provide kitchenettes and TVs. This rather rustic resort features a number of water sports, including parasailing, snorkeling, and jetskiing. Tree House also has a swimming pool and Jacuzzi.

INEXPENSIVE

☻ Negril Cabins

Rockland Point (on the easternmost edge of Negril, beside the main road leading in from Montego Bay), Negril, Jamaica, W.I. ☎ **809/957-4350.** Fax 809/957-4381. 50 cabins. TV TEL. Winter $120–$132 cabin for two, $155–$162 cabin for three; off-season $92–$109 cabin for two, $122–$139 cabin for three. MC, V.

Except for the palms and the Caribbean vegetation, you might imagine yourself at a log-cabin complex in the Maine woods. In many ways, this is Negril's best bargain, suitable for budget-conscious Robinson Crusoes eager to get away from it all. Standing in a forest across the road from a beach called Bloody Bay, Negril Cabins consists of small cottages, none more than two stories high, rising on stilts. Each timber cottage includes a balcony patio, and some are air-conditioned. The hotel's nine-acre garden is planted with royal palms, bull thatch, and a rare variety of mango tree (its fruit is called simply "number eight"). The bar and restaurant serve tropical punch—a medley of fresh Jamaican fruits—and flavorful but unpretentious Jamaican meals. A children's program is also available, and live entertainment is offered on some nights.

3 Where to Dine

Although many visitors in Negril eat at their hotels, there are several other atmospheric and intriguing dining possibilities.

EXPENSIVE

Rick's Cafe

West End Road (near Negril Lighthouse). ☎ **809/957-4335.** Reservations recommended for dinner. Main courses $14–$28. No credit cards. Daily 2–10pm. SEAFOOD/STEAK.

At sundown, everybody in Negril seems to head toward the lighthouse and Rick's Cafe—whether or not they want a meal. Of course, the name was inspired by the old watering hole of Bogie's *Casablanca;* the "Rick" in this case is owner Carl Newman. This is said to be the most glorious spot in Negril for watching the sun set, and after a few fresh-fruit daiquiris (pineapple, banana, or papaya), you'll not argue with that assessment. Dress is casual.

There are several Stateside specialties, including imported steaks along with a complete menu of Cajun-style blackened dishes. The fish, always fresh, includes red snapper, lobster, and grouper, and you might begin with a Jamaican fish chowder. The food is rather standard fare and expensive for what you get, but that hardly keeps the crowds away. You can buy plastic bar tokens at the door, for use instead of money, à la Club Med.

MODERATE

Café Au Lait/Mirage Cottages

Lighthouse Road, West End (on the beach strip, east of the police station, 1 1/2 miles from Negril center). ☎ **809/957-4471.** Main courses $8.50–$28.50. MC, V. Daily 8am–11pm. FRENCH/JAMAICAN.

Daniel and Sylvia Grizzle, a Jamaican/French couple, prepare the cuisine and direct the smooth operation of this place. Like the owners' marriage, the food is a successful blend of French mainland flair and Jamaican style and zest. The conch fritters or Jamaican patties are appropriately spicy to get you going. You can also order jerk pork here along with other spicy pork dishes. There are pizzas too, but you'll find better pies elsewhere. The fish, lobster, and shrimp dishes, however, are truly superb and well-flavored—not overly cooked either. The wine list leans to France, of course. If you like really sweet desserts, you may be attracted to the coconut pie and sweet potato pudding.

The property flanks two sides of the road on 4 1/2 acres of tropical garden. On the land side are two two-bedroom cottages, ideal for four to six people. On the sea side, where high cliffs dominate the coastline, is a one-bedroom cottage, a duplex, and four large studio rooms with big balconies and views of the coast. All accommodations offer private baths and ceiling fans. The studios are air-conditioned. Winter rates are $95 to $110 for two. Off-season tariffs range from $55 to $66 for two. There are sunning areas, three access ladders to the sea, and a gazebo for relaxing in the shade.

Le Vendôme

In the Charela Inn, on the main beach strip north of the Negril Inn. ☎ **809/957-4277.** Reservations required for Sat dinner. Continental breakfast $4.50, English breakfast $8.50; main courses $10–$29; five-course fixed-price menu $22.50–$29.50. MC, V. Daily 7:30–10am, 12:30–2:30pm, and 7–10pm. JAMAICAN/FRENCH.

Three and a half miles from Negril center, Le Vendôme enjoys a good reputation for its food. Nonresidents are invited to sample the cuisine that is a combination of—

in the words of the owners, Daniel and Sylvia Grizzle—a "dash of Jamaican spices" with a "pinch of French flair." The wine and champagne are imported from France. You dine on a terra-cotta terrace with a view of the palm-studded beach. You may want to order a homemade pâté, or perhaps a vegetable salad to begin with. You can follow with such dishes as baked snapper, duckling à l'orange, or a seafood platter. You will have eaten better versions of these dishes at many other places, yet the food is quite satisfying here, and there's rarely an unhappy customer. Entertainment ranging from calypso to soca to reggae is often presented.

INEXPENSIVE

Chicken Lavish

West End Road (east of the police station). ☎ **809/957-4410.** Main courses $4.50–$12.50. MC, V. Daily 10am–10pm. JAMAICAN.

Chicken Lavish, whose name we love, is the best of the lot of the low-budget eateries lining this West End beach strip. Just show up on the doorstep and see what's cooking. Curried goat is a specialty, as is fresh fried fish. Fresh Caribbean lobster is prepared to perfection here, as is the red snapper caught in local waters. But the main reason we've recommended the place is because of the namesake: Ask the chef to make his special Jamaican chicken. He'll tell you, and you may agree, that it's the best on the island. Come dressed as you would to clean up your backyard on a hot August day.

Cosmo's Seafood Restaurant & Bar

Norman Manley Boulevard (on the main beach strip near A1). ☎ **809/957-4330.** Main courses $4–$13. MC, V. Daily 9am–10pm. SEAFOOD.

One of the best places to go for local seafood is centered around a Polynesian thatched bohío open to the sea and bordering the beachfront. This is the domain of Cosmo Brown, who entertains locals as well as visitors. He's known in these parts for his conch soup, and you can order that or conch in a number of other ways, including steamed or curried. He's also known for his savory kettle of curried goat. You can order freshly caught shellfish or finfish, depending on what turned up in the catch. It's a rustic place, and prices are among the most reasonable in Negril. Cosmo's cooking is right on target, and he doesn't ask a lot for it either.

Mariners Inn and Restaurant

West End Road (east of the police station**).** ☎ **809/957-4348.** Reservations not accepted. Pizzas $3.10–$7.80; main courses $3.10–$7.80. AE, MC, V. Daily 8am–3pm and 6–10pm. JAMAICAN/AMERICAN.

Many guests escaping from their all-inclusive dining rooms head here for some authentic Jamaican flavor. The bar is shaped like a boat, and there's an adjoining restaurant, entered through a tropical garden that eventually slopes down to the beach. As you drink or dine, the breezes waft in, adding to one of the most laid-back and relaxed dining experiences in Negril. The one appetizer is a bacon-wrapped banana—not everybody's favorite way to begin a meal—but the food picks up considerably after that. The chef knows how to use curry effectively in the lobster and chicken dishs, and even the goat. The coq au vin has never been to France, so you're better off sticking to such dishes as pan-fried snapper or fried chicken. Pizzas and main courses cost the same.

Negril Tree House

In the Negril Tree House, Norman Manley Boulevard (on the main beach strip). ☎ **809/957-4287.** Main courses $7–$23. AE, MC, V. Daily 7am–11pm. JAMAICAN.

This informal beachfront eatery takes its name from a mamee tree that grows through the main building of the Negril Tree House Resort (see "Where to Stay," above). Dining is on the second floor, but guests can come early and have a drink in the beachfront bar. This is a lively spot both day and night. At lunch you can ask for a homemade soup, perhaps pepperpot, or a sandwich, or else more elaborate fare, such as a typically Jamaican dish of escovitched (marinated) fish. Some of the produce comes from the owner's farm in the country.

At night, Gail Y. Jackson, the host, brings out her full repertoire of dishes to amuse guests, including a lobster spaghetti worth a detour. You might begin with a callaloo quiche and later follow with roast chicken (a specialty) or conch steak. Try the Tía Maria parfait for dessert. You can dine both inside and out.

Paradise Yard

Gas Station Road (in the town center near the police station). ☎ **809/957-4006.** Main courses $3.90–$11.45. MC, V. Daily 8am–10pm. JAMAICAN.

Located on the verdant flatlands of downtown Negril, a 10-minute walk from the beach, simple but welcoming Paradise Yard is the undisputed domain of Jamaican-born chef and owner Lorraine Washington. Meals, served either on the terrace or in an airy and comfortable interior decorated with roughly textured boards and pink tiles, might include the house specialty, "Rasta Pasta." This is red-and-green "dreadlocks pasta," chosen in honor of the colors of the Jamaican flag, with tomatoes, pepper, and ackee. Among other specialties are a succulent version of pasta with lobster, curried chicken (either mild or fiery), many preparations of lobster and chicken, Mexican enchiladas, Jamaican escovitched fish, and some of the best pumpkin soup in Jamaica. Lorraine is a natural-born cook, and her meals are lustily flavored.

Restaurant Tan-Ya/Calico Jack's

In Seasplash Resort, Norman Manley Boulevard (on the main beach strip). ☎ **809/957-4041.** Reservations recommended. Lunch sandwiches and salads $5–$7; lunch platters $6.50–$7.50; dinner main courses $6–$26. AE, MC, V. Daily 11am–3pm and 6:30–10pm. JAMAICAN/ INTERNATIONAL.

Set within the thick white walls of the Sunsplash Resort (see "Where to Stay," above), Tan-Ya and Calico Jack's provide well-prepared food amid the charm of a small, family-run resort. Informal lunchtime fare is served at Calico Jack's, whose tables are in an enlarged gazebo, near a bar and the resort's swimming pool. The resort's gastronomic showcase, however, is Tan-Ya. Specialties there include lemon-flavored shrimp, snapper with herb butter, smoked Jamaican lobster with a fruit salsa, and deviled crab backs sautéed in butter. On many nights these dishes are filled with flavor and well-prepared; on some occasions we've found them to be slightly off the mark.

4 Scuba Diving

You're likely to spend most of your time on Negril's beach, and most resorts provide plenty of water sports toys to keep their guests busy. Offshore, the reefs protecting Negril offer some of Jamaica's top scuba diving.

If your resort doesn't have its own diving operation, the most modern, best-equipped diving facility here is **Negril Scuba Centre,** in the Negril Beach Club Hotel, Norman Manley Boulevard (☎ **809/957-4425** or 800/818-2963). A professional staff of internationally certified scuba instructors and divemasters teach and guide divers to several of Negril's colorful and exciting coral reefs. Beginner's dive lessons are offered daily as well as multiple-dive packages for certified divers.

Full scuba certifications and specialty courses are also available. A resort course, designed for first-time divers with basic swimming abilities, includes all instruction, equipment, a lecture on water and diving safety, and one open-water dive. It begins at 10am daily and ends at 2pm; its price is $75. A one-tank dive costs $30 per dive plus $20 for equipment rental (not necessary if you bring your own gear). More economical is a two-tank dive that includes lunch. It costs $55, plus $20 for the optional rental of equipment. The organization is PADI-registered, and accepts all recognized certification cards.

Another highly recommended operator is **Sundivers, Inc.,** a PADI-approved five-star dive shop located on the premises of the Poinciana Beach Hotel (☎ 809/957-4069), on Norman Manley Boulevard, near Sandals Negril. They are open daily from 8am to 5pm and offer a 4-day certification course for $330; a resort course for beginners costs $75; and a one-tank dive for already-certified divers costs $35, plus $10 for renting the necessary equipment.

5 Negril After Dark

Evenings in Negril really begin before dark, when everyone heads to Rick's Cafe for sundowner cocktails or a few Red Stripes (see "Where to Dine," above).

All the resorts have bars. Most offer evening entertainment for their guests, and some welcome nonguests as well.

One of the more charming of these is the **Seasplash Resort,** on Norman Manley Boulevard (☎ 809/957-4041), whose bar is located amid allamander vines, midway between a swimming pool and the edge of the sea. Sheltered from the sun with a teepee-shaped roof of palm leaves and thatch, it offers a tempting array of tropical drinks. These include such foamy concoctions as Calico Jack's rum punch or a white sands, either of which sells for around $3. The bar is open daily from 9am to 11pm.

6 A Side Trip to the South Coast

Think of this as undiscovered Jamaica. The arid South Coast is just beginning to attract more foreign visitors every year; they're drawn by Jamaica's sunniest climate.

Columbus discovered the Arawak living here when he circumnavigated Jamaica in 1494. When not repelling French pirates, five generations of Spaniards raised cattle on ranches on the broad savannahs of St. Elizabeth.

Local adventures are plentiful on the South Coast. Among the most popular is South Coast Safaris' boat tour up the Black River—once a major logging conduit and still home to freshwater crocodiles. Another favorite is the trip to the Y. S. Falls, where seven spectacular cascades tumble over rocks in the foothills of the Santa Cruz Mountains, just north of the town of Middle Quarters, famed for its spicy, freshwater shrimp.

EXPLORING THE SOUTH COAST

To reach the South Coast, head east from Negril, following the signposts to Savanna-La-Mar. This is known as Sheffield Road, and the highway isn't particularly good until it broadens into the A2 at Savanna. After passing through the village of Bluefields, continue southeast to the small town of **Black River** opening onto Black River Bay.

After leaving Black River, where you can find hotels and restaurants (see "Where to Stay," below), you can continue north along A2 to Mandeville or else go directly southeast to **Treasure Beach.**

The A2 north takes you to **Middle Quarters,** a village on the plains of the Great Morass, through which the Black River runs. Day visitors often stop here and order a local delicacy, pepper shrimp.

Just north of the town of Middle Quarters is **Y. S. Falls,** where seven waterfalls form crystal pools. Guests take a jitney and go through grazing lands and a horse paddock on the way to the falls where they cool off in the waters and often enjoy a picnic lunch.

After Middle Quarters, the road cuts east toward Mandeville along **Bamboo Avenue,** a scenic drive along 2 miles of highway covered with bamboo. Here you will see a working plantation, Holland Estate, growing sugarcane, citrus, papaya, and mango.

If you've decided to take the southern coast route to Treasure Beach, follow the signs to **Treasure Beach** directly southeast of Black River. Treasures here are seashells in many shapes and sizes. This is the site of the Treasure Beach Hotel (see "Where to Stay," below).

To the east of Treasure Beach is **Lovers' Leap** in Southfield, a cliff plunging hundreds of feet into the sea. Two slave lovers reportedly jumped to their deaths here rather than be sold off to different masters.

THE BLACK RIVER

The longest stream in Jamaica, the Black River has mangrove trees, crocodiles, and the insectivorous bladderwort, plus hundreds of different species of bird. You can indeed go on a safari to this wilderness. The best tours are operated by **South Coast Safaris** in Mandeville (☎ 809/965-2513 for reservations). The cost is $15, and children under 12 go for half price. Tours last $1^{1}/_{2}$ hours and cover 10 miles (5 miles upstream, 5 miles back). Daily tours are at 9am, 2pm, and 4pm.

WHERE TO STAY

Treasure Beach Hotel

Treasure Beach (on the coast, midway between Black River and Pedro Cross; P.O. Box 5), Black River, St. Elizabeth, Jamaica, W.I. ☎ **809/965-2305.** Fax 809/965-2544. 16 rms, 4 suites. A/C TEL. Winter $90–$130 double, $130 suite; off-season $80–$90 double, $103 suite. MAP $25 per person extra. AE, MC, V.

Set on a steep but lushly landscaped hillside above a sandy beach with an active surf, this white-sided hotel was built in the mid-1970s and renovated about a decade later. Although its staff is young and inexperienced, this is the largest and most elaborate hotel on Jamaica's South Coast. Its centerpiece is a long and airy rattan-furnished bar whose windows look down the hillside to the beach and the hotel's 11 acres that flank it. Bedrooms lie within a series of outlying cottages, each of which contains between two and six accommodations. Each unit has a ceiling fan and veranda or patio, and—in some cases—a TV.

Amenities include two freshwater pools, a loosely organized array of such activities as volleyball and horseshoes, and a simple restaurant with slow and casual service that's open for lunch and dinner.

Invercauld Great House & Hotel

High Street (on the harborfront, a few blocks west of Black River's commercial center), Black River, St. Elizabeth, Jamaica, W.I. ☎ **809/965-2750.** Fax 809/965-2751. 18 rms, 2 suites. A/C TV TEL. Year-round $50–$61 double, $72–$76 suite. AE, MC, V.

In 1889, when Black River's port was one of the most important in Jamaica, a Scottish merchant imported most of the materials for the construction of this white-sided manor house. Today, the renovated and much-enlarged house functions as a hotel.

Only a handful of rooms are within the original high-ceilinged house; most lie within a cement outbuilding that was added in 1991. Rooms are clean, stripped down, and simple, usually with mahogany furniture made by local craftspeople. On the premises is a cement patio and a swimming pool, a tennis court, and a conservatively dignified restaurant with white tiles and white walls. It's open daily for lunch and dinner.

WHERE TO DINE

Bridge House Inn

14 Crane Rd. (on the eastern outskirts of Black River, on the opposite side of the town's only bridge from the commercial center), Black River. ☎ **809/965-2361.** Full meals $6–$18.20. V. Daily 6am–noon, 11am–3pm, and 6–11:30pm. JAMAICAN.

This is the simple, uncomplicated, and very Jamaican restaurant that is contained within one of the town's two hotels. The structure that houses it was built in the early 1980s, a cement-sided beachfront motif within a grove of coconut palms and sea grapes. On the premises are 14 bedrooms, each with ceiling fan and simple furniture, but no TV and no telephone. Most clients appreciate this place, however, for its restaurant. Patrons include a cross-section of the region, including the occasional conference of librarians or nurses. Menu items—everything is home style—include complete dinners (fish, chicken, curried goat, oxtail, stewed beef, or lobster), served politely and efficiently by a staff of hardworking waiters. A separate bar area off to the side dispenses drinks. Main dishes include soup and vegetables.

7 Mandeville

The "English Town" of Mandeville lies on a plateau more than 2,000 feet above sea level in the tropical highlands. The commercial part of town is small, surrounded by a sprawling residential area that has a large North American expatriate population, mostly involved with the bauxite-mining industry.

Mandeville is the sort of place where you can become well-acquainted with the people and feel like part of the community in very short order. Much cooler than the coastal resorts, it's a comfortable base from which to explore the entire country.

Shopping here is a pleasure, whether in the old center or in one of the modern complexes, such as Grove Court. The central market teems with life, particularly on weekends when country folk bus into town for a visit. The town has several interesting old buildings. The square-towered church built in 1820 has fine stained glass, and gravestones in the little churchyard tell an interesting story of past inhabitants of Mandeville. The Court House was built in 1816, a fine old Georgian stone-and-wood building with a pillared portico reached by a steep, sweeping double staircase. Another key attraction is Marshall's Pen, one of Mandeville's great houses.

WHERE TO STAY & DINE

Hotel Astra

62 Ward Ave. (1 mile west of town center, along the A2 from Kingston), Mandeville, Jamaica, W.I. ☎ **809/962-3265.** 20 rms, 2 suites. TV TEL. Year-round $65 double; $150 suite. Rates include continental breakfast. AE, MC, V.

Our top choice for a stay in the Mandeville area is the family-run Hotel Astra, operated by Diana McIntyre-Pike. Known to her family and friends as Thunderbird, she is always coming to the rescue of guests. Diana happily picks up people in her car and takes them around to see the sights, plus organizes introductions to people of the island. The rather spartan accommodations are mainly in two buildings reached along open walkways.

Dining/Entertainment: The Country Style Restaurant, entered from the front desk area, offers excellent meals. Lunch or dinner is a choice of a homemade soup such as red pea or pumpkin, followed by local fish and chicken specialties. The kitchen is under the personal control of Diana, who is always collecting awards in Jamaican culinary competitions. Someone is on hand to explain to you the niceties of any particular Jamaican dish. A complete meal costs $10 to $20, with some more expensive items such as lobster. Dinner is served daily from 6 to 9:30pm.

Services: Laundry; baby-sitting; natural health program, including physical therapy and therapeutic massages.

Facilities: Tennis and golf at Manchester Country Club, horses provided for cross-country treks.

Mandeville Hotel

4 Hotel St. (a short walk from the police station; P.O. Box 78), Mandeville, Jamaica, W.I. ☎ 809/962-2138. Fax 809/962-0700. 47 rms, 9 suites. TV TEL. Year-round $65–$125 double; from $95 suite. AE, MC, V.

The richly ornate hotel in the heart of Mandeville was first established around the turn of the century, and for a while housed part of the British military garrison. In the 1970s, the original structure was replaced with this modern peach-colored substitute. Today, you'll find a large outdoor bar and spacious lounge. There are attractive gardens with many fine old trees and beautiful plants.

Dining/Entertainment: Popular with local businesspeople, the coffee shop by the pool is a quick, appetizing luncheon stop offering a wide selection of sandwiches, plus milk shakes, tea, and coffee. In the restaurant, an à la carte menu offers Jamaican pepperpot soup, lobster thermidor, fresh snapper, and kingfish. Potatoes and vegetables in season are included in the main-dish prices. There is no pretention to the food at all. It's homemade and basic, almost like that served in the house of a typical Jamaican family. From the restaurant's dining room, you'll have a view of the hotel's pool and the green hills of central Jamaica.

Services: Golf and tennis can be played at the nearby Manchester Country Club. Horseback riding can also be arranged.

WHAT TO SEE & DO

One of the largest and driest **caves** on the island is at Oxford, about 9 miles northwest of Mandeville. Signs direct you to it after you leave Mile Gully, a village dominated by **St. George's Church,** which is some 175 years old.

Interesting attractions include **Marshall's Pen,** a coffee plantation home some 200 years old and filled with antique furniture. The great house is a history lesson in itself, as it was once owned by the earl of Balcarres, the island's governor. The 300 acres have been in the hands of the Sutton family since 1939; they breed many Jamaican and red poll cattle. They also have a large collection of seashells, some fine Arawak artifacts, and a large general stamp collection. This is very much a private home and should be treated as such. Guided tours can be arranged; a contribution of $10 is requested. For information or an appointment to see the house, get in touch with Robert L. Sutton, P.O. Box 58, Mandeville, Jamaica, W.I. (☎ 809/963-8569).

At **Marshall's Pen cattle estate and nature reserve,** near Mandeville, 89 of Jamaica's 256 species of birds (including 25 endemic species and many North American winter migrants) can be seen. Groups can arrange guided birding tours of the scenic property *in advance,* for early morning or evening (to see nocturnal birds) or to go to other outstanding birding spots in Jamaica, at negotiated rates. For further information, contact Robert L. Sutton, P.O. Box 58, Mandeville

(☎ **809/963-8569**). Sutton is co-author of *Birds of Jamaica,* a photographic field guide published by Cambridge University Press.

Milk River Mineral Bath, Milk River, Clarendon (☎ **809/924-9544;** fax 809/ 986-4962), lies 9 miles south of the Kingston-Mandeville highway. It boasts the world's most radioactive mineral waters, recommended for the treatment of arthritis, rheumatism, lumbago, neuralgia, sciatica, and liver disorders. The mineral-laden waters are available to guests of the Milk River Mineral Spa & Hotel, Milk River, Clarendon, Jamaica, W.I. Casual visitors can also take the enclosed baths or paddle around the mineral-water swimming pool. The water, at approximately body temperature (90°F), is channeled into small tubs 6 feet square by 3 feet deep, each enclosed in a changing cubicle. The cost of a bath is $1.05 for adults and 65¢ for children, and baths last usually about 30 minutes. It isn't good to remain too long in these warm waters. The restaurant offers fine Jamaican cuisine, health drinks, and special diets in a relaxed, old-world atmosphere. Nearby Milk River affords boating and fishing. Some guests check into the adjacent hotel, where there are 25 rooms (17 with bath); all are air-conditioned and offer TVs and phones. About six of the rooms lie within a century-old great house that was converted into a hotel in the 1930s. The remainder lie within a simple "new" wing that also contains the restaurant. Rates are $60 for rooms with bath, $56 double for rooms without bath, including breakfast and dinner. American Express, MasterCard, and Visa cards are accepted.

The nine-hole **Manchester Country Club,** Brumalia Road (☎ **809/962-2403**), is Jamaica's oldest golf course. Beautiful vistas unfold from 2,201 feet above sea level. Greens fees cost $12.50, and caddy fees are $4 for 18 holes. The course has a clubhouse and restaurant. The All-Jamaica Hardcourt Championships are played on the tennis courts here in August. The courts are open for general play during the rest of the year, at a cost of $2 per person per game.

The North Coast Resorts: Runaway Bay, Ocho Rios & Port Antonio

6

Situated on Jamaica's northeast coast, the resort areas of Runaway Bay, Ocho Rios, and Port Antonio helped to launch large-scale tourism in Jamaica. Known for its abundant rainfall, verdant landscapes, rolling hills, and jagged estuaries, this region was once the preferred hangout for Noël Coward, Errol Flynn, and a host of British and American literati. Ian Fleming, creator of the James Bond spy thrillers, lived at Goldeneye, near Ocho Rios.

Starting from Montego Bay and heading east, you first reach Discovery Bay, whose name refers to the belief that Columbus first landed here in 1494. Finding no water, Columbus is said to have named it Puerto Seco (Dry Harbor). Puerto Seco Beach today is a popular stretch of sand, with a few places where you can get lunch or a drink.

Just beyond Discovery Bay is Runaway Bay, with some of the best-known resort hotels along the north coast. There is no real town of Runaway Bay; it is mainly a beachfront strip of hotels and sandy shores. Much of the resort takes up space once occupied by Cardiff Hall, a sprawling plantation owned by one of Jamaica's first English settlers.

From Runaway Bay, continue east along the A3, bypassing the sleepy hamlet of St. Anne's Bay, and you'll reach Ocho Rios. Today this is the north coast's major tourist destination, although it's not up there with Montego Bay.

Although Ocho Rios is considered the cruise-ship capital of Jamaica, with as many as a half-dozen major vessels anchored offshore at any one time, it is not a port at the mouth of eight rivers, as its Spanish name ("Eight Rivers") might suggest. It was once the lair of pirate John Davis, who remains famous for his plundering of French and Spanish vessels on the nearby seas. One of his best known exploits was the sacking and burning of St. Augustine, Florida. The long-ago village that contained Davis and other scoundrels has been enveloped by a massive development of resort hotels (many all-inclusive). Ocho Rios is fine for a lazy beach vacation, but it's definitely not for anyone seeking a remote hideaway for an undisturbed holiday.

The culmination of a tourist trend that began in the 1950s, Ocho Rios lies in the nerve center of tourism to Jamaica. You might see calypso and reggae bands greeting cruise-ship passengers, who are then herded onto buses and shuttled off to Dunn's River Falls.

What's Special About the North Coast

Beaches
- San San Beach, voted by the U.S. Navy men as one of the best beaches in the world.
- Mallards Beach, the busiest and best beach in Ocho Rios, a white sandy strip that's a favorite with the cruise-ship crowd.
- Turtle Beach, next door to Mallards, considered the ideal place for swimming by the locals of Ocho Rios.
- Puerto Seco Beach, Discovery Bay, west of Ocho Rios. A beach of white sand, site of Columbus's Jamaican landing in 1494.
- Boston Beach, Port Antonio, known not only for its white sands, but for the peppery jerk pork and chicken you can order here.

Memorable Sights & Experiences
- Rafting on the Rio Grande, Port Antonio, the granddaddy of river-rafting excursions. This 8-mile-long swift green waterway was made famous by Errol Flynn.
- Somerset Falls, 8 miles west of Port Antonio, where the waters of Daniels River pour down a deep gorge through a rain forest with waterfalls and foaming cascades.
- Jamaican Night on the White River, east of Ocho Rios, promises—and delivers—romance and adventure up the torchlit river before a picnic supper on its banks.
- Dunn's River Falls, Ocho Rios, where visitors climb with a guide to the top of a 600-foot cascade whose waters are among the most photographed in the Caribbean.
- Athenry Gardens and the Cave of Nonsuch, 20 miles from Port Antonio, a world of stalagmites and stalactites. You'll see fossilized marine life and Arawak artifacts along with exotic gardens.
- Fern Gully, outside Ocho Rios, a botanist's fantasy with a rain forest, hardwood trees, and varieties of wild ferns.

A Literary Landmark
- Firefly, outside Port Maria, where Sir Noël Coward entertained the rich and famous for 23 years in a modest house with a panoramic view that inspired his song, "A Room with a View."

Historic Homes
- Harmony Hall, 4 miles east of Ocho Rios, a 19th-century great house and former pimiento estate, now a sales outlet for Jamaican painting and arts and crafts.
- Prospect Plantation, $4^1/2$ miles east of Ocho Rios, a working plantation where horseback riding is possible. Notables ranging from Sir Winston Churchill to Charlie Chaplin have planted exotic trees here.

There they take a sometimes precarious trek across wooded limestone cliffs whose broad waterfalls are among the most frequently photographed sights in Jamaica. To the discomfiture of many visitors, souvenir vendors assail you at almost every point.

From Ocho Rios, drive east along highway A4/A3, which will take you through some sleepy fishing villages, including Port Maria, until you reach Port Antonio. Since it's situated on the coast just north of the Blue Mountains, Port Antonio is surrounded by some of the most rugged and beautiful scenery in Jamaica.

Many visitors prefer to visit the mountains and highlands from a base here, rather than starting out in Kingston, thus avoiding the capital's crime and urban sprawl.

Although Port Antonio was the cradle of Jamaican tourist development, it has been eclipsed by other areas such as Montego Bay, Ocho Rios, and Negril. It remains a preferred hideaway, however, for a chic and elegant crowd that still vacations in its handful of posh hotels. The tourist flow to Port Antonio began in the 1890s, when cruise-ship passengers started to arrive for rest and relaxation. Perched above twin harbors, the estuary was pronounced by the poet Ella Wheeler as "the most exquisite harbor on earth."

1 Runaway Bay

Runaway Bay used to be just a western satellite of Ocho Rios. However, with the opening of some large resorts, plus a colony of smaller hotels, it's now become a destination in its own right.

This part of Jamaica's north coast has several distinctions: It was the first part of the island seen by Columbus, the site of the first Spanish settlement on the island, and the point of departure of the last Spaniards to leave Jamaica following their defeat by the British. Columbus landed at Discovery Bay on his second voyage of exploration in 1494, and in 1509 Spaniards established a settlement called Sevilla Nueva (New Seville) near what is now St. Anne's Bay, about 10 miles east of the present Runaway Bay village. Sevilla Nueva was later abandoned, the inhabitants moving to the southern part of the island.

In 1655 an English fleet sailed into Kingston Harbour and defeated the Spanish garrison there. However, a guerrilla war broke out on the island between the Spanish and English in which the English prevailed. The remnants of the Spanish army embarked for Cuba in 1660 from a small fishing village on the north coast. Some believe that this "running away" from Jamaica gave the name Runaway Bay to the village. However, later historians believe that the name possibly came from the traffic in runaway slaves from the north-coast plantations to Cuba.

WHERE TO STAY & DINE

Runaway Bay offers several unusual accommodations as well as all-inclusive resorts and notable bargains.

VERY EXPENSIVE

Chukka Cove Farm and Resort

4 miles east of Runaway Bay off A1 (P.O. Box 160), Richmond Llandovery, Ocho Rios, Jamaica, W.I. ☎ **809/974-2239.** Fax 809/974-5568. 6 villas. A/C MINIBAR TEL. Winter $2,000 villa per week; off-season $1,500 villa per week. No credit cards.

Known for its horse-riding tours (see "Outdoor Activities," below), Chukka Cove is also an ideal center for horse lovers who'd like to live on the grounds. Located 4 miles east of Runaway Bay, it is frequented by Capt. Mark Phillips, former husband of Britain's Princess Anne. On the estate's acreage lie six two-bedroom villas, each suitable for four guests, with a veranda, plank floors, and an architectural plan vaguely reminiscent of 18th-century models. A pampering staff will prepare meals in your villa. Rates can be prorated for shorter stays. Snorkeling is also included. Taxis are necessary to get east to Ocho Rios or west to Montego Bay.

EXPENSIVE

FDR (Franklyn D. Resort)

Main Road (on A1, the main seaside highway, 17 miles west of Ocho Rios; P.O. Box 201), Runaway Bay, St. Anne, Jamaica, W.I. ☎ **809/973-4591** or 800/654-1FDR. Fax 809/973-3071.

76 suites. A/C TV TEL. Winter $280 per person; off-season $266 per person. Children under 16 stay free. Rates include meals, bar drinks, beer, cigarettes, sports, and entertainment. AE, DC, MC, V.

The all-inclusive FDR resort is geared to families with children. Named after its Jamaican-born owner and developer (Franklyn Dance Rance), the resort is scattered over six acres of flat, sandy land dotted with flowering shrubs and trees. Each Mediterranean-inspired building has a terra-cotta roof and a loggia or outdoor terrace. Slabs of Spanish marble sheath the bathrooms, and each unit has a kitchenette. You can have your meals prepared by the personal attendant (they call her a "Girl Friday") who's assigned to each unit for cooking, cleaning, child-care, and miscellaneous services.

Although neither its narrow beach nor its modest swimming pools are Jamaica's most desirable, many visitors appreciate the spacious units and the wholehearted concern of the resort for making sure the guests' children are entertained and well cared for.

Dining/Entertainment: Two restaurants on the property serve free wine with lunch and dinner, a piano bar provides music every evening, and a handful of bars keeps the drinks flowing whenever you are ready for them. Live music is provided nightly.

Services: Free baby-sitting every day between 8am and 5pm, after which the sitter can be engaged privately for $3 an hour. There's a children's supervisor in attendance at a "Kiddies' Centre" with a computer center, a kiddies' disco, and even kiddies' dinners. Adults appreciate the Centre's scuba lessons, picnics, photography lessons, arts and crafts lessons, and donkey rides.

Facilities: Water sports, lighted tennis courts, satellite-TV room, disco, exercise gym, free use of bicycles, free transport to Dunn's River Falls and Ocho Rios shopping.

Jamaica, Jamaica

16 miles west of Ocho Rios along A1 (P.O. Box 58), Runaway Bay, Jamaica, W.I. ☎ **809/973-2436,** or 800/859-7873 in the U.S. Fax 809/973-2352. 234 rms, 4 suites. A/C TEL. 3-night package in winter $675–$725 per person. 3-night package in off-season $555–$625 per person. For suite add $50 per person per day. Rates are all-inclusive. Children under 16 not accepted. AE, MC, V.

This resort has known several identities before this stylish incarnation. It now operates on a price plan including three meals a day, all drinks, and a galaxy of other benefits. Inside the lobby is the best re-creation of the South Seas in Jamaica, with hanging wicker chairs and totemic columns. Each room provides a view of a well-landscaped courtyard, with a private balcony overlooking the sea. Windows are angled toward the light.

Near the wide sandy beach is a mini-jungle with dangling hammocks, and nearby is a swimming pool. The beachside sports center presents a complete list of sports-related activities. There's even a nearby nude beach.

Dining/Entertainment: Live music emanates from a stylish terrace every evening at 7pm, and a nightclub offers live shows five nights a week at 10pm. You dine either in the beachside restaurant or in the more formal Italian restaurant, Martino's.

Services: Reggae exercise classes held twice daily.

Facilities: Gym with Nautilus equipment, swimming pool, sports-activities center (featuring scuba, windsurfing, horseback riding, golf school), 18-hole championship golf course.

MODERATE

⑤ Eaton Hall Beach Hotel

2 blocks east of the town's main square (P.O. Box 112), Runaway Bay, St. Anne, Jamaica, W.I.
☎ **809/973-3503** or 800/972-2158. Fax 809/973-2432. 52 rms. A/C. Winter $214–$254
double; off-season $180–$196 double. Rates include three meals a day, taxes, tips, and use of
facilities and services mentioned below. Children under 12 not accepted. AE, DC, MC, V.

An original plantation great house has been restored and turned into this small hotel, full of charm and character. The brick foundation walls are probably those of an
English fort dating from the 17th or 18th century. A subterranean passage, now
bricked up, leads from the living room to the coral cliffs behind the house. The property is a successful coordination of old blended with new. Some of the bedrooms of
the great house open onto an arched portico, and four units in the main house front
the sea. On each side of the hall are bedroom wings with ocean views. Rooms are
furnished with tropical designs and older mahogany pieces; carved mahogany four-
poster beds are found in some of the rooms. Three-bedroom villas have verandas extending over a rocky ledge with the water 6 feet below. Some rooms have phones.

Dining/Entertainment: Nightly entertainment, a floor show, and a Jamaican
buffet once each week are also part of the all-inclusive plan. There is one dining room
that offers American, Jamaican, and a few continental items, plus there is one bar.

Services: Safety-deposit box, laundry (small charge).

Facilities: Sunfish sailing, snorkeling, scuba orientation, scuba diving, daytime
tennis, swimming pool.

⑤ Runaway H.E.A.R.T. Country Club

On the main road (A1) opposite the public beach (P.O. Box 98), Runaway Bay, St. Anne, Jamaica, W.I. ☎ **809/973-2671.** Fax 809/973-2693. 20 rms. A/C TV TEL. Winter $112 double;
off-season $100 double. 5-day/4-night MAP package $509 per person. AE, MC, V.

Called "the best-kept secret in Jamaica," Runaway H.E.A.R.T. wins practically hands
down as the bargain of the north coast. One of Jamaica's few training and service
institutions, the club and its adjacent academy are operated by the government to
provide training for young Jamaicans interested in the hotel trade. It's well run with
a professional staff, intermixed with trainees, who are helpful and eager to please, and
offer the finest service of any hotel in the area.

The rooms are bright and airy and contain either a king-size bed, a double bed,
or twin beds. Accommodations open onto private balconies with views of well-
manicured tropical gardens or vistas of the bay and golf course.

All package rates include round-trip airport transfers, unlimited golf greens fees,
and use of a chaise longue at the pool or at a private beach, which is reached by a
free beach shuttle.

Dining/Entertainment: Guests enjoy having a drink in the piano bar (ever had
a cucumber daiquiri?) before heading for the dining room, the Cardiff Hall Restaurant, which serves a combination of Jamaican and continental dishes. Nonresidents
can also enjoy dinner, served nightly from 7 to 10pm. The academy has won awards
for some of its dishes, including "go-go banana chicken" and curried codfish.

Services: Laundry.

Facilities: Swimming pool, golf course.

INEXPENSIVE

Club Ambiance Jamaica

Runaway Bay, Jamaica, W.I. ☎ **809/973-4606** or 800/523-6504. Fax 809/973-2067. 77 rms,
5 suites. A/C TV TEL. Winter $85 per person double, $115 per person suite; off-season $75 per

person double, $105 per person suite. Rates include meals and drinks (but not water sports). AE, MC, V.

Refurbished in 1995, this is one of the most basic of the all-inclusives, catering to the family trade, often European travelers on a budget. The hotel is laid-back and casual. Lying at the west end of Runaway Bay, we recommended it primarily for economy—not for its somewhat bleak two-story appearance (instead of gardens in front, you get a sprawling parking lot). The shoreline near the hotel is rocky, and a small crescent of sand won't win the beach sweepstakes. Units are reasonably comfortable and clean, although hardly style-setters. Regional art decorates the walls, and the furniture is often upholstered wicker. Accommodations come with either double or king-size beds, with balconies opening onto views of the water.

A standard Jamaican cuisine is served in the Renaissance Dining Room and in La Café Coffee Shop. Later you can work off the calories in the Safari Disco. Other amenities include an exercise room and an outdoor swimming pool. Sometimes this sleepy place wakes up with theme nights and cultural shows including beach parties and a live band.

GOLF & HORSEBACK RIDING

Super Club's Runaway Golf Club (☎ 809/973-2561), charges no admission for residents who stay at any of Jamaica's affiliated "Super Clubs." For nonresidents, the price is $51 for 18 holes in the summer, rising to $56 in the winter.

Jamaica's most complete equestrian center is **Chukka Cove Farm and Resort** (☎ 809/972-2506), at Richmond Llandovery, less than 4 miles east of Runaway Bay (see "Where to Stay," above). The best ride here is a 3-hour jaunt to the sea, where you can unpack your horse and swim in the surf. Refreshments are served as part of the $50 charge. A 6-hour beach ride, complete with picnic lunch, goes for $100. Polo lessons are also available, costing $45 for 30 minutes.

A MUSEUM NOT TO MISS

Columbus Park Musuem

Queens Highway, Discovery Bay (about 8 miles west of Runaway Bay, off A1). ☎ **809/973-2135.** Admission free. Daily 9am–5pm.

This is a large, open area between the main coast road and the sea at Discovery Bay. You just pull off the road and then walk among the fantastic collection of exhibits, which range from a canoe made of a solid piece of cottonwood (in the same way the Arawak did it more than five centuries ago), to a stone cross, a monument originally placed on the Barrett estate at Retreat by Edward Barrett, brother of poet Elizabeth Barrett Browning. You'll see a tally, used to count bananas carried on men's heads from plantation to ship, as well as a planter's strongbox with a weighted lead base to prevent its theft. Also among the exhibits are 18th-century cannons, a Spanish water cooler and calcifier, a fish pot made from bamboo, a corn husker, and a waterwheel of the type used on the sugar estates in the mid-19th century for all motive power. You can follow the history of sugar since its introduction in 1495 by Columbus, who brought canes from Gomera in the Canary Islands. Also, see how Khus Khus, a Jamaican perfume, is made from the roots of a plant and how black dye is extracted from logwood. Pimiento trees, from which allspice is produced, dominate the park. There is a large mural by Eugene S. Hyde, depicting the first landing by Columbus at Puerto Bueno (Discovery Bay) on May 4, 1494.

2 Ocho Rios

A 2-hour drive east of Montego Bay or west of Port Antonio, Ocho Rios was once a small banana and fishing port, but tourism long ago became its leading industry. Now Jamaica's cruise-ship capital, the bay is dominated on one side by a bauxite-loading terminal and on the other by a range of hotels with sandy beaches fringed by palm trees.

Ocho Rios and neighboring Port Antonio have long been associated with celebrities, the two most famous writers being Sir Noël Coward, who invited the world to his Jamaican doorstep, and Ian Fleming, who created James Bond while writing here (see "What to See and Do," earlier in this chapter, for details about their local homes, Firefly and Goldeneye, respectively).

It is commonly assumed among Spanish-speakers that Ocho Rios was named for eight rivers, its Spanish meaning, but the islanders disagree. In 1657 British troops chased off a Spanish expeditionary force that had launched a raid from Cuba. The battle was near Dunn's River Falls, now the resort's most important attraction. Seeing the rapids, the Spanish called the district *los chorreros.* That battle between the Spanish and the British forces was so named. The British and the Jamaicans weren't too good with Spanish names back then, so *los chorreros* was corrupted into "ocho rios."

Ocho Rios has its own unique flavor, offering the usual range of sports and a major fishing tournament every fall in addition to a wide variety of accommodations including all-inclusive resorts, couples-only complexes, elegant retreats (some with spas), and inns of character holding to what is left of the area's former colonial culture.

Frankly, unless you are a passenger, you may want to stay away from the major attractions on cruise-ship days. Even the duty-free shopping markets are overrun then, and the street hustlers become more strident in promoting their crafts, often junk souvenirs. Dunn's River Falls becomes almost impossible to visit at these times.

WHERE TO STAY

Some of the accommodations in and around Ocho Rios include the best in all Jamaica.

ALL-INCLUSIVE RESORTS

Boscobel Beach

10 miles east of the town center along A3 (P.O. Box 63), Ocho Rios, Jamaica, W.I. ☎ **809/974-3331** or 800/859-7873. Fax 809/975-7370. 196 rms, 11 suites. A/C TV TEL. Winter $1,560–$1,690 double; $1,630–$2,110 suite for two. Off-season $1,140–$1,630 double; from $1,560 suite for two. One child under 14 per paying adult stays free in parents' room; second child under 14 $50 extra. Rates are for all-inclusive 3-day package. AE, MC, V.

The name Boscobel is old Spanish for "beautiful gardens by the sea"—it's that and more. Set on 14¹/₂ acres of prime seafront property, this once was one of Hugh Hefner's Playboy Clubs, and there was no sexier resort in all of Jamaica back then. But, with changing times, the playboys and their bunnies have long faded to make way for family fun in the sun. This is the most aggressively promoted family resort in the Caribbean. Dan Quayle, Marilyn, and the kids can show up here and not feel threatened.

✪ Frommer's Favorite North Coast Experiences

Rafting on the Rio Grande. Errol Flynn invented the number one tourist attraction of Port Antonio when he spotted bamboo craft ferrying bananas down to the port for shipping. Visitors today follow in the footsteps of this Hollywood legend, following the course of the river as it flows into the Caribbean Sea at St. Margaret's Bay.

Splashing Through Dunn's River Falls. At Ocho Rios, visitors take the famous steps along cascading waterfalls as they splash down the mountainside. It's called a "Get Wet Climbing Tour."

Visiting the Home of Sir Noël Coward. At Firefly, Coward's home 20 miles east of Ocho Rios, memorabilia ranges from his Hawaiian-print shirts to the two grand pianos on which he composed some of his memorable songs.

Children are encouraged and welcomed, with a big program set aside for them, including a children's center, a mini-zoo, and other activities. Boscobel offers special rates for single parents traveling with children and features a unique program for grandparents and their grandchildren. Naturally, baby-sitting can be arranged, too. But adults with no children are also given plenty of incentive to visit, including lots of sports facilities.

All the well-furnished and attractively decorated rooms are equipped with TVs, radios, and refrigerators. Some feature large balconies and sunken bathtubs. A series of 44 lanai rooms (these are smaller) open right onto the beach.

Dining/Entertainment: Dinner is offered in an open-air dining room (a special children's meal is served earlier). There are also five bars on the property, including one at the beach that serves snacks throughout the day. A disco opens at 11pm. Live local entertainment is a nightly feature.

Services: Transfers to and from the airport, transfers to the golf course, baby-sitting, laundry.

Facilities: Children's facilities (see above), four tennis courts lighted for night play, fully equipped gym, exercise classes, aerobics, two Jacuzzis, reggae dance classes, windsurfing, sailing, waterskiing, scuba diving, and golf nearby.

✪ Ciboney Ocho Rios

Main Street (1¹/₂ miles southeast of Ocho Rios along A3; P.O. Box 728), Ocho Rios, St. Anne, Jamaica, W.I. ☎ **809/974-1027,** or 800/333-3333 in the U.S. and Canada. Fax 809/974-5838. 36 rms, 162 one-bedroom suites, 16 junior villa suites, 26 two-bedroom villas, 14 honeymoon villas. A/C MINIBAR TV TEL. $600 double; $690 junior villa suite; $720 one-bedroom villa suite; $800 honeymoon villa; $720 two-bedroom villa for four. Rates per person all inclusive for 3-night package. No children under 16. AE, DC, MC, V.

Opened in late 1990, this all-inclusive resort is a Radisson-hotel franchise owned by Colony Hotels, one of the big tourist conglomerates of Jamaica. It stands on 45 acres of steeply sloping private estate dotted with red-tile villas and a great house in the hills overlooking the Caribbean Sea. Across from a gate near the entrance to the resort are the white sands of a private beach.

All but a handful of Ciboney's accommodations are contained in one-, two-, or three-bedroom villas, each of which offers a private or semiprivate pool, fully equipped kitchen, and shaded terrace. Each villa is enhanced by a personal attendant for service, cooking private meals, and cleaning. Honeymoon villas have their own Jacuzzis. Thirty-six of the accommodations are traditional double rooms on the third

Ocho Rios

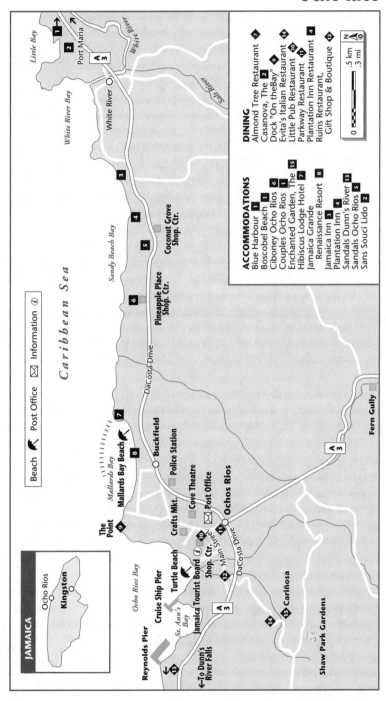

Caribbean Sea

Beach 🏖 Post Office 📮 Information ⓘ

JAMAICA
Ocho Rios
Kingston

DINING
1 Almond Tree Restaurant
2 Casanova, The
9 Dock "On theBay"
14 Evita's Italian Restaurant
10 Little Pub Restaurant
11 Parkway Restaurant
4 Plantation Inn Restaurant
12 Ruins Restaurant,
Gift Shop & Boutique

ACCOMMODATIONS
1 Blue Harbour
1 Boscobel Beach
6 Ciboney Ocho Rios
1 Couples Ocho Rios
15 Enchanted Garden, The
7 Hibiscus Lodge Hotel
Jamaica Grande
8 Renaissance Resort
3 Jamaica Inn
4 Plantation Inn
13 Sandals Dunn's River
5 Sandals Ocho Rios
2 Sans Souci Lido

N
.5 km
.3 mi
0

Little Bay
Port Maria
White River
White River Bay
A 3
White River
Salt River
Sandy Beach Bay
Coconut Grove Shop. Ctr.
Pineapple Place Shop. Ctr.
DaCosta Drive
Buckfield
Police Station
Cove Theatre
Post Office
Ochos Rios
Main Street
DaCosta Drive
A 3
Fern Gully
Mallards Bay
Mallards Bay Beach
The Point
Crafts Mkt.
Jamaica Tourist Board
Shop. Ctr.
Turtle Beach
Cruise Ship Pier
St. Ann's Bay
Ocho Rios Bay
Reynolds Pier
←To Dunn's River Falls
Cariñosa
Shaw Park Gardens

135

floor of the resort's social headquarters, the great house. Regardless of location, accommodations are high-ceilinged, airy, and decorated in Caribbean colors of aquamarine, turquoise, mauve, and peach.

Dining/Entertainment: The Manor Restaurant & Bar offers both indoor and outdoor patio dining for dinners and entertainment, with classic Jamaican food. The Marketplace Restaurant has a contemporary menu of both American and Jamaican froods, and Alfresco Casa Nina, in a seaside setting, highlights Italian cuisine. Orchids is a restaurant developed in collaboration with the Culinary Institute of America, with a menu based on haute cuisine combined with the concept of healthy foods. Finally, late-night entertainment and dancing are featured at Nicole.

Services: Laundry, dry cleaning, massage.

Facilities: European-inspired beauty spa with its own health-and-fitness center, six lighted tennis courts (see "Beaches, Golf, Fishing & Tennis," below), beach club offering an array of water sports, two swimming pools with swim-up bars (plus 90 other semiprivate swimming pools on the grounds), spa with 20 Jacuzzis, and a golf course nearby.

Couples Ocho Rios

Tower Isle, along the A3 (P.O. Box 330), Ocho Rios, Jamaica, W.I. ☎ **809/975-4271** or 800/268-7537. Fax 809/975-4439. 161 rms, 11 suites. A/C TEL. Winter $1,450–$1,970 per couple. Off-season $1,310–$1,760 per couple. Rates for 3 nights include all meals, drinks, cigarettes, activities, and airport transfers. No one 17 or under allowed. AE, MC, V.

Don't come here alone or with your children—you won't get in! The management defines couples as "any man and woman in love." Everything is in pairs, even the chairs by the moon-drenched beach. Some couples slip away from the resort, which is an 18-minute drive from town, to Couples' private island to bask in the buff. In general this is a classier operation than either the Dunn's River or Ocho Rios versions of the more mass-market Sandals (see below).

Once you've paid the initial fee, you're free to use all the facilities—even the cigarettes and whiskey are included in the one tab. You're fed three meals a day (breakfasts are bountiful), including all the wine you want. And tips aren't permitted.

The bedrooms contain either a king-size bed or two doubles and pleasantly traditional furnishings. Each features a patio, fronting the sea or the mountains. The hotel usually accepts bookings for a minimum of any 3 nights of the week, but most guests book in here on weekly terms. A 4-day stay is required at certain peak periods such as over the Christmas holidays.

Dining/Entertainment: Dinners are five courses, and afterward there is dancing on the terrace every evening, with entertainment. Guests have a choice of four restaurants.

Services: Laundry, breakfast-only room service.

Facilities: Five tennis courts (three lighted), Nautilus gym, water sports activities (scuba, snorkeling, windsurfing, sailing, waterskiing).

✪ The Enchanted Garden

Eden Bower Road (P.O. Box 284), Ocho Rios, Jamaica, W.I. ☎ **809/974-1400**, or 800/847-2535 in the U.S. Fax 809/974-5823. 58 rms, 55 suites. A/C TV TEL. Winter $300–$380 double; $430–$500 suite for two. Off-season $250–$300 double; $380–$460 suite for two. Rates include meals, snacks, bar drinks, and house wines at lunch and dinner; aerobics, yoga, and meditation classes; all nonmotorized water sports; entertainment; daily shuttle to private beach club; taxes; and round-trip transfers to airport at Montego Bay. AE, DC, MC, V. Follow directional signs along Main Road, south of Main Street.

The most verdant Jamaican resort opened in 1991 on land that was formerly a private spring-fed botanical garden on a secluded hilltop high above the commercial center of town. Owned and developed by former Prime Minister Edward Seaga, the land includes 20 acres of rare botanical specimens, a serpentine mass of nature trails, and 14 cascading waterfalls much beloved by such former visitors as Mick Jagger. The resort's lobby is a pink-with-white gingerbread tower accented with marble floors, big windows, and enormous potted palms. Bisected by the Turtle River, whose 14 waterfalls are highlighted with garden paths and spotlights, the place is one of the most spectacular in Jamaica, of particular interest to botanists and birdwatchers.

Bedrooms contain sturdy rattan furniture. They are within eight different low-rise buildings set amid the resort's landscaping. Each has a private patio or balcony, and some contain kitchens.

Dining/Entertainment: Five restaurants incorporate some of the most lavish East Indian decor in the Caribbean. They include L'Eau Mirage (continental food), the Sultan's Table (Middle Eastern cuisine), and The Temples (Far Eastern food), where a fabric-covered rondavel rises above a kitchen where the cooking processes provide part of the meal's drama. The Pasta Bar is designed like a tree house amid the verdant leaves of a tropical forest. Guests may also dine at the Seaquarium, offering a cold buffet in a setting surrounded by tropical fish. A Beach Club is within a minivan ride of the hotel. Annabella's nightclub provides a variety of after-dinner entertainment amid a decor like something out of the *Arabian Nights.*

Services: Daily transportation to Beach Club; free shuttle for shopping.

Facilities: Spa, beauty salon, swimming pool, two lighted tennis courts, walk-in aviary featuring hundreds of exotic birds (feeding time around 4pm), fitness center. There's also a Seaquarium with 15 aquaria for marine-life exotica.

Jamaica Grande Renaissance Resort

Main Street (P.O. Box 100), Ocho Rios, St. Anne, Jamaica, W.I. ☎ **809/974-2201,** or 800/ HOTELS-1 in the U.S. and Canada. Fax 809/974-2289. 705 rms, 15 suites. A/C TV TEL. Winter $360–$380 double; $580–$850 suite. Off-season $300–$320 double; $440–$800 suite. Rates include meals, drinks, and water sports. AE, DC, MC, V.

This is the largest hotel in Jamaica, the much-publicized combination of two high-rise beachfront properties constructed in 1975 and 1976. The place is long on theatrics and special effects—meant to overwhelm guests, like a Hollywood production—but is short on pure Jamaican style. In 1993, a breezeway and an elaborate cluster of waterfalls and swimming pools were inserted into what had been parking lots between the towers, and the entire complex unified into a coherent whole. Today, the end result contains more beachfront than any other hotel in Ocho Rios. The comfortable array of public rooms is usually crammed with tour groups and conference attendees from around the world. The standard bedrooms are tile-floored and furnished with Caribbean furniture. Each opens onto a private balcony.

Dining/Entertainment: The four restaurants include the Dragon (Chinese) and the L'Allegro (Italian), and the less formal Café Jamique and Mallard's Court (international). There's also a beachfront grill and a total of eight bars scattered throughout the premises. The hotel operates a casino (slot machines only). Every Thursday the Jamaica Grande is transformed into a village for Jump Up Carnival, with Jamaican food, a live band, and shopping. There's also the "Me Crazy" Disco.

Services: Daily activities programs.

Facilities: Tennis courts lighted for nighttime play, full range of free water sports.

Sandals Dunn's River

Along the A3 (5 minutes west of town; P.O. Box 51), Ocho Rios, Jamaica, W.I. ☎ **809/ 972-1610** or 800/SANDALS. Fax 809/972-1611. 246 rms, 10 suites. TV TEL. 3-night stay in winter $1,660–$2,040 double; $2,180–$2,495 suite for two. 3-night stay in off-season $1,575– $1,935 double; $2,070–$2,370 suite for two. Rates include all meals, snacks, unlimited wine and drinks, airport transfers, tax, and services. Three-night minimum stay required. AE, MC, V.

Having known various incarnations as the Jamaica Hilton and Eden II, this luxury all-inclusive resort found its latest identity in 1991 as a member of Butch Stewart's rapidly expanding Sandals empire. Some guests who have sampled them all consider this to be the finest of the Sandals resorts. Only male/female couples are allowed.

Set on the seafront between Ocho Rios and St. Anne's Bay, this very sports-oriented resort occupies 25 well-landscaped acres and offers attractively furnished and often quite spacious accommodations. All the rooms were reconstructed architecturally after the Sandals takeover. Italianate/Mediterranean styling was added, and in some respects the hotel seems more European than any of the other Ocho Rios properties. Rooms are scattered among the six-story main building, two lanai buildings, and a five-story west wing.

Dining/Entertainment: Before retreating to the disco, guests choose between several dining options. The International Room, named because of its cuisine, is elegant, with emerald and rose fabric-covered walls and rosewood furniture. West Indian Windies serves Caribbean specialties, such as curried mutton or grilled red snapper. D'Amore offers Italian cuisine, and Restaurant Teppanyaki serves Chinese, Polynesian, and Japanese dishes.

Services: Tours to Dunn's River Falls, round-trip transfers to the airport, hourly shuttles to Sandals Ocho Rios, complimentary massage.

Facilities: Three Jacuzzis, two whirlpool baths, fitness center, jogging course, beach bar, pitch-and-putt golf course, one of the most spectacular swim-up bars (in the lagoon-shaped pool), transport to the Sandals Golf & Country Club.

Sandals Ocho Rios

Main Street (1 mile west of town center along A3; P.O. Box 771), Ocho Rios, Jamaica, W.I. ☎ **809/974-5691** or 800/SANDALS. Fax 809/974-5700. 237 rms. TV TEL. 3-night stay in winter $1,470–$1,810 double. 3-night stay in off-season $1,410–$1,740 double. Rates include all meals, snacks, unlimited wine and drinks, airport transfers, and services and facilities listed below. 3-night minimum stay required (6-night minimum at Christmas). AE, MC, V.

This is another Jamaican addition to the ever-expanding couples-only empire of Gordon "Butch" Stewart, who pioneered similar all-inclusive properties in Montego Bay and Negril. With an array of sports options, Sandals Ocho Rios attracts a mix of coupled singles and married folk, including honeymooners. On 13 well-landscaped acres, it offers comfortably furnished rooms with either ocean or garden views, and there are some cottage units, too. All rooms are reasonably large with king-size beds, along with hair dryers and radios.

Dining/Entertainment: You can sip your free drinks at an oceanside swim-up bar, and nightly theme parties and live entertainment take place in a modern amphitheater. A unique feature of the resort is an open-air disco. For dining, St. Anne's is the resort's main dining room. There's also Michelle's for Italian food and the Reef Terrace Grill for gourmet Jamaican cuisine and fresh seafood.

Services: Round-trip airport transfers, tours to Dunn's River Ralls, massage, laundry.

Facilities: Three freshwater pools; private artificial beach; sporting equipment and instruction, including waterskiing, windsurfing, sailing, snorkeling, and scuba; paddleboats, kayaks, glass-bottom boat; Jacuzzi, saunas, fully equipped fitness center, two tennis courts. Guests can play at Sandals Golf & Country Club.

✪ Sans Souci Lido

On the A3 (P.O. Box 103), Jamaica, W.I. ☎ **809/974-2353**, or 800/859-7873 in the U.S. Fax 809/974-2544. 12 rms, 90 suites, 9 penthouses. A/C MINIBAR TV TEL. 3-night stay in winter $2,070 double; from $2,280 suite for two; from $3,280 penthouse for two. 3-night stay in off-season $1,760 double; from $1,870 suite for two; from $2,730 penthouse for two. Rates are all-inclusive. AE, DC, MC, V.

Sans Souci, French for "without a care," is one of the most luxurious and tasteful hotels in Ocho Rios and is a renowned spa. It's east of town on a forested plot of land whose rocky border abuts the sea. A cliffside elevator brings guests to an outdoor bar. There's a freshwater pool, plus a mineral bath big enough for an elephant, and a labyrinth of catwalks and bridges stretching over rocky chasms filled with surging water.

Each accommodation features a veranda or patio, copies of Chippendale furniture, plush upholstery, and subdued colonial elegance. Some contain Jacuzzis.

Dining/Entertainment: The resort offers guests The Casanova (see "Where to Dine," below). In addition, there's the Ristorante Palazzira by the beach, and the Balloon Bar tries to bring back some of the 1920s art of cocktailing. There are also several terraces for drinking.

Services: Room service, laundry/valet, massage, baby-sitting.

Facilities: Established in 1987, Charlie's Spa grew out of the hotel's mineral springs, frequented for medicinal benefits since the 1700s. Considered effective for treating certain skin disorders, arthritis, and rheumatism, the spa is considered the finest place in Jamaica for a health-and-fitness vacation, and one of the finest in the entire Caribbean.

Sports lovers appreciate the hotel's three Laykold tennis courts (two lighted), and the nearby croquet lawn. Scuba, snorkeling, windsurfing, deep-sea fishing, and Sunfish and catamaran sailing are available at the beach. Guests can golf on an 18-hole course and watch polo matches while they take afternoon tea at the St. Anne Polo Club, Drax Hall.

OTHER ACCOMMODATIONS

Very Expensive

✪ Jamaica Inn

Main Street (1¹/₂ miles east of the town center along A3; P.O. Box 1), Ocho Rios, Jamaica, W.I. ☎ **809/974-2514** or 800/837-4608. Fax 809/974-2449. 41 rms, 4 suites. A/C TEL. Winter (including all meals) $385–$475 double, from $490 suite for two. Off-season (including breakfast and dinner) $220–$275 double, from $290 suite for two. No children under 14 accepted. AE, MC, V.

Built in 1950, the Jamaica Inn is a series of long, low, U-shaped buildings set near the sea and surrounded by grass and palm trees with oleander and bougainvillea. The clear water immediately offshore makes for easy snorkeling.

The rooms benefited from a large-scale renovation and upgrade in 1993. Lovely patios open onto the lawns, and the bedrooms are reached along garden paths. The handsomely furnished rooms open onto balconies. The White Suite here was a favorite of Winston Churchill. The full meal plan is required in the winter, half-board in the summer.

Dining/Entertainment: The inn is proud of its cuisine. The European-trained chef lends his expertise to the production of dishes both international and Jamaican. The management requires men to wear a jacket and tie at night.

Services: Laundry, room service.

Facilities: There is a small pool almost at the water's edge, where a wide, white sand beach invites you to swim or lounge. For nonaquatic types there is tennis, with golf close by at the Sandals Golf Club.

Expensive

✪ Plantation Inn

Main Street (1¹/₂ miles east of town along A3; P.O. Box 2), Ocho Rios, Jamaica, W.I. ☎ **809/974-5601** or 800/752-6824. Fax 809/974-5912. 61 rms, 15 suites. A/C TEL. Winter $195–$270 double; $235–$310 triple; from $345 suite for two. Off-season $130–$150 double, $170–$190 triple; from $180 suite for two. MAP $55 extra per person per day. No children under 12 in winter; no children under 7 in summer. AE, DC, MC, V.

Opened in 1957 and set in gardens above the beach on the eastern edge of town, the Plantation Inn evokes a Southern antebellum mansion in the United States (or at least a Southern antebellum mansion with lots of water sports) and is reached by a sweeping driveway and entered through a colonnaded portico.

All bedrooms open off balconies and offer their own patios overlooking the sea. The double rooms are attractively decorated with chintz and comfortable furnishings, and there are also junior suites. Apart from the regular hotel, there are two units that provide lodgings: Plantana Villa above the east beach sleeps two to six people; Blue Shadow Villa on the west side accommodates up to eight guests.

Dining/Entertainment: There is an inside dining room, but most of the action takes place outside under the tropical sky. You can have breakfast on your own balcony, lunch is outdoors, and English tea is served on the terrace every afternoon. On Thursdays guests can enjoy a cultural folk show while dining.

Services: Facials, massage, waxing, room service.

Facilities: Two private beaches (36 steps down from the garden; seats on the way provide resting spots). Snorkeling, Sunfish sailing, and windsurfing are available, and there is a glass-bottom boat on one of the two private beaches. The hotel has a jungle gym offering exercise equipment, a sauna, and two tennis courts. Golf is available for hotel guests at the Upton Golf Course, a 15-minute drive away.

Inexpensive

ⓢ Hibiscus Lodge Hotel

87 Main St. (in the town center along Mallards Bay shore; P.O. Box 52), Ocho Rios, Jamaica, W.I. ☎ **809/974-2676.** Fax 809/974-1874. 27 rms. Winter $76 double, $113 triple; off-season $66 double, $95 triple. Rates include breakfast. AE, DC, MC, V.

The Hibiscus Lodge Hotel offers more value than any resort at Ocho Rios. It's an intimate little inn with character and charm, perched precariously on a cliffside three blocks from the Ocho Rios Mall. All bedrooms, either doubles or triples, contain private baths, ceiling fans, and verandas opening to the sea. Singles can be rented for the double rate.

After a day spent swimming in a pool suspended over the cliffs, with a large sun deck, guests can enjoy a drink in the unique swinging bar. On the three-acre site are a Jacuzzi and tennis court, along with conference facilities. The owners, Richard Powell and Alfred Doswald, also provide a good restaurant, Almond Tree (see "Where to Dine," below). The Grotto is a piano bar open daily from 5pm to 2am.

A NEARBY PLACE TO STAY

Blue Harbour

On the north coast road (A4) 80 miles west of Montego Bay and 60 miles north of Kingston (P.O. Box 50), Port Maria, St. Mary's, Jamaica, W.I. ☎ **809/994-2262,** or 505/586-1244 in Questa, New Mexico. 3 villas. $150 double, or $4,000 weekly in winter, $2,800 weekly in summer for entire complex (all-inclusive). No credit cards.

This retreat was once owned by Sir Noël Coward (see the box in this chapter), who entertained the rich and famous of his day here. Coward dubbed Blue Harbour, his first Jamaica retreat, "Coward's Folly." Eventually the place became so popular that Coward built Firefly, a "retreat from his retreat," and stopped staying at Blue Harbour (See "Noël's 'Folly,'" later in this chapter).

Today the compound is rented in whole or part to paying guests. The compound can accommodate 10 to a dozen guests comfortably, although the actual bed count is 18. The main house is the Villa Grande, with two bedrooms and two baths, along with a kitchen, dining room, and terrace. Villa Rose, a guesthouse, contains two large bedrooms, and the smaller Villa Chica is a one-bedroom, one-bath cottage once favored by Marlene Dietrich. Meals, both Jamaican and international, are cooked by a friendly, helpful staff who run the place and see to the needs of guests, some of whom book in here like a house party, renting the entire compound. At other times, individual units are rented separately.

WHERE TO DINE

Since nearly all the major hotels in Ocho Rios have gone all-inclusive, smaller independent restaurants are being smothered. There are some, however, struggling to survive.

VERY EXPENSIVE

The Casanova

At the Sans Souci Lido, A3, 2 miles east of Ocho Rios. ☎ **809/974-2353.** Nonguest evening pass of $75 includes dinner, entertainment, and drinks (Tues and Fri beach buffet). AE, DC, MC, V. Daily 7–9:30pm. INTERNATIONAL.

In the all-inclusive Sans Souci Lido, one of the most elegant enclaves along the north coast, The Casanova's meals are included for the resort's houseguests, but nonresidents who purchase an evening pass can also dine and be entertained here. The pass includes all drinks. In the late 1960s, Harry Cipriani (of Harry's Bar fame in Venice) taught the staff some of his culinary techniques, and a little more care, even today, seems to go into the cuisine here, as opposed to the mass-market chow-downs at some of the other all-inclusives.

The pasta is still made fresh daily, along with many of the other staples. Performers sometimes set up in the lattice-roofed gazebo to provide jazz to accompany your meal. Typical dishes, served by polite, formally dressed waiters, include smoked chicken breast in a continental berry sauce as an appetizer, or else a small vegetable mousse with a Fontina cheese sauce. For your main course, you might prefer *osso buco* (braised veal shanks) or roasted Cornish hen with citrus and mild spice. Desserts are sumptuous, and might be followed by one of the house's four special coffees.

EXPENSIVE

✪ Plantation Inn Restaurant

In the Plantation Inn, Main Street. ☎ **809/974-5601.** Reservations required. Main courses $17–$25; 3-course table d'hôte $35; lunch from $15. AE, DC, MC, V. Daily 7:30–10am, 12:30–1:30pm, 4:30–5:30pm (afternoon tea), and 7:30–10:30pm. JAMAICAN/CONTINENTAL.

You'll think you've arrived at Tara in *Gone with the Wind.* An evening here offers one of the most romantic experiences for dining in Ocho Rios. You dine and dance by candlelight. The continental cuisine is spiced up a bit by Jamaican specialties. You're seated at beautifully laid tables with crisp linen, and after the dinner plates are cleared, a band plays for dancing. It's definitely the pampered life. The restaurant is divided into the indoor Dining Room and the outdoor Bougainvillea Terrace. Afternoon tea is served daily in The Peacock Pavilion annex.

Appetizers are always spicy and zingy, our favorite being "Fire and Spice," a chicken-and-beef kebab with a ginger pimiento sauce. Baked West Indian crab backs are often featured. For the main course, we always ask the chef to prepare a whole roast fish—based upon the catch of the day. The always perfectly cooked fish is served boneless and seasoned with island herbs and spices. It's slowly roasted in the oven and presented with fresh country vegetables. Since traditionally the place attracts a lot of meat eaters, the chefs always prepare the classics, lamb chops Provencale and the like—all the food that Sir Winston and others loved in the '50s. The table d'hôte menu featured every evening is also good value. One of the most delectable dishes we encountered on this menu was a combination of shrimp, conch, lobster, and fresh fish with lemon butter. Opt for the banana cream pie for dessert, if featured. It's creamy and good.

Ruins Restaurant, Gift Shop and Boutique

Turtle River, DaCosta Drive. ☎ **809/974-2442.** Reservations required. Main courses $12–$35. AE, DC, MC, V. Mon–Sat noon–2:30pm and daily 6–9:30pm. In the town center off Main Street. CHINESE/INTERNATIONAL.

At Ruins, you dine at the foot of a series of waterfalls that can be considered a tourist attraction in its own right. In 1831 a British entrepreneur constructed a sugar mill on the site, using the powerful stream to drive his waterwheels. Today, all that remains is a jumble of ruins—hence the restaurant's name. After you cross a covered bridge, perhaps stopping off for a drink at the bar in the outbuilding first, you find yourself in a fairyland where the only sounds come from the tree frogs, the falling water from about a dozen cascades, and the discreet clink of silver and china. Tables are set on a wooden deck leading all the way up to the pool at the foot of the falls, where moss and other vegetation line the stones at the base. As part of the evening's enjoyment you may want to climb a flight of stairs to the top of the falls, where bobbing lanterns and the illuminated waters below afford one of the most delightful experiences on the island.

Come here for this dramatic setting, not for the cuisine, which is really Chinese-American rather than authentic Chinese. Here you get several kinds of chow mein or chop suey as well as such familiar fare as sweet-and-sour pork. Lobster in a stir-fry is the house specialty and is the best item on the menu. Dishes such as chicken Kiev justify the international in the restaurant's cuisine, but stick to the Chinese selections or all-vegetarian dishes; some of the latter aren't bad.

MODERATE

✪ Almond Tree Restaurant

In the Hibiscus Lodge Hotel, 87 Main St. (in the town center along the shore). ☎ **809/974-2813.** Reservations recommended. Main courses $12.50–$36. AE, DC, MC, V. Daily noon–2:30pm and 6–9:30pm. INTERNATIONAL.

Overlooking the Caribbean, the Almond Tree Restaurant is a two-tiered patio restaurant (with a tree growing through its roof) in the Hibiscus Lodge Hotel (see "Where to Stay," above), 3 blocks from the Ocho Rios Mall. Lobster thermidor is the most delectable item on the menu, and lobster Almond Tree is a specialty, but we prefer their bouillabaisse (with not only pieces of conch, but lobster). Also excellent are the roast suckling pig, médaillons of beef Anne (Annie) Palmer, and a fondue bourguignonne. Jamaican plantation rice is a local specialty. The wine list offers a variety of vintages, including Spanish and Jamaican. Have an aperitif in the unique "swinging bar" (swinging chairs, that is).

Dock "On the Bay"

Fisherman's Point (in the town center). ☎ **809/974-7168.** Reservations recommended. Main courses $13–$27. MC, V. Daily 11am–2:30pm and 3–11pm. JAMAICAN/INTERNATIONAL.

Part of a complex of Fisherman's Point rental units "on the bay" in the heart of Ocho Rios near Turtle Beach, this rather elegant dining spot was launched in 1987.

For dinner, you can always count on today's catch, perhaps Caribbean lobster, and certainly seafood chowder and shrimp in garlic butter. One section of the menu is devoted to Jamaican specialties, including curried goat. You can also order such international dishes as paella, beef Stroganoff, and chicken cordon bleu. But we'd skip these and go instead for either the Jamaican specialties or the fresh fish. Dock "On the Bay" occupies a point near the end of the peninsula jutting seaward; it's the closest restaurant to the cruise-ship pier, so steer clear when ships are in port. Its most attractive feature is a sun-flooded garden-style patio.

✪ Evita's Italian Restaurant

Eden Bower Road (directly south of Main Street, a few steps from The Enchanted Garden resort). ☎ **809/974-2333.** Reservations recommended. Main courses $7.50–$21. AE, MC, V. Daily 11am–11pm. ITALIAN.

A 5-minute drive south of the commercial heart of Ocho Rios, in a hillside residential neighborhood enjoying a panoramic view over the city's harbor and beachfronts, stands the premier Italian restaurant in Ocho Rios. This is the most fun restaurant along the north coast of Jamaica. Its soul and artistic flair come from Eva Myers, convivial former owner of some of the most legendary bars of Montego Bay, who established her culinary headquarters within this store-fronted Jamaican house in 1990. An outdoor terrace adds additional seating and enhanced views.

More than half the menu is devoted to pastas—any of which might make a meal in itself—and the selection includes almost every variety known in northern and southern Italy. If you're not in the mood for pasta, the fish dishes are excellent, especially snapper stuffed with crabmeat, and lobster and scampi in a buttery white cream sauce. Italian and other wines by the bottle might accompany your menu choice. You can sample jerk spaghetti, snapper stuffed with crabmeat, lobster and scampi in a white cream sauce, and a combination of spicy chicken and shrimp.

INEXPENSIVE

Little Pub Restaurant

59 Main St. (in the town center). ☎ **809/974-2324.** Reservations recommended. Main courses $13–$28. AE, MC, V. Daily 7am–4:30pm and 6pm–midnight. JAMAICAN/INTERNATIONAL.

Located in a red-brick courtyard with a fountain and a waterfall surrounded by gingerbread-fretwork souvenir shops, this indoor/outdoor pub's centerpiece is a restaurant in the dinner-theater style. Top local and international artists are featured, as well as Jamaican musical plays. No one will mind if you just enjoy a drink while seated on one of Little Pub's barrel chairs. But if you want dinner, you can proceed to one of the linen-covered tables capped with cut flowers and candlelight. Many items include very familiar fare (too familiar say some critics), and that means grilled kingfish, stewed snapper, barbecue chicken, and the inevitable and overpriced lobster. The cookery is competent, but many go here for the convivial atmosphere instead of the food.

⑤ Parkway Restaurant

60 DaCosta Dr. (in the town center near the post office). ☎ **809/974-2667.** Main courses $8–$20. AE, MC, V. Daily 8am–11:30pm. JAMAICAN.

This popular spot couldn't have a much plainer facade. Inside, Parkway continues to look unpretentious, but many local families and businesspeople know that they can come here for some of the best-tasting and least expensive local dishes in Ocho Rios. On clean napery, amid a serviceable decor, hungry diners are fed Jamaican-style chicken, curried goat, and filet of red snapper, and to top it off, banana cream pie. Lobster and fresh fish are usually featured. The food is straightforward, honest, and sometimes rises above the mundane.

BEACHES, GOLF, FISHING & TENNIS

BEACHES Most visitors to Ocho Rios head for a beach. The most visited is the often overcrowded **Mallards Beach,** shared by hotel guests and cruise-ship passengers. Locals may also steer you to **Turtle Beach** in the south.

GOLF **Sandals Golf & Country Club (☎ 809/974-0119)** is free to residents of Sandals properties at Dunn's River and Ocho Rios (see "Where to Stay," above). If you're not staying at one of them, you can still play for $25 for nine holes, $35 for 18 holes year-round. The golf course lies about 700 feet above sea level, a 5-minute drive from Ocho Rios.

DEEP-SEA FISHING The **Sans Souci Hotel and Club (☎ 809/974-2353)** offers deep-sea fishing for $350 for a half day for four to five participants. See "Where to Stay," above.

TENNIS **Ciboney Ocho Rios,** Main Street, Ocho Rios (☎ **809/974-1036**), focuses more on tennis than any other resort in the area (see "Where to Stay," above). It offers three clay surface and three hard-surface courts, all lit for nighttime play. Residents play free either day or night, but nonresidents must call and make arrangements with the manager. A pro on site offers lessons for $15 an hour. Pan-Caribbean competitions are held here, as well as pan-parish playoffs. Ciboney also sponsors twice-a-day clinics for both beginners and advanced players.

Frequent guest tournaments are also staged, including handicapped doubles and mixed doubles. One of their most bizarre tournaments is the pot-bellied one. If you don't have a pot belly, the staff will pad you with towels to simulate one.

SEEING THE SIGHTS

A pleasant drive south of Ocho Rios along the A3 will take you inland through **Fern Gully.** This was originally a riverbed, but now the main road winds up some 700 feet among a profusion of wild ferns, a tall rain forest, hardwood trees, and lianas. For the botanist, there are hundreds of varieties of ferns to examine. Roadside stands offer fruit and vegetables, carved wood souvenirs, and basketwork. The road runs for about 4 miles, sometimes with a large pool of sunlight, sometimes fingers of light just penetrating the overhanging vegetation. Then at the top of the hill, you come to a right-hand turn, onto a narrow road leading to Golden Grove.

Head west when you see the signs pointing to Lydford. You'll pass the remains of **Edinburgh Castle,** built in 1763, the lair of a Scot named Lewis Hutchinson, who used to shoot passersby and toss their bodies into a deep pit built for the purpose. The authorities got wind of his activities, and although he tried to escape by canoe, he was captured by the navy under the command of Admiral Rodney and was hanged. Rather proud of his achievements (evidence of at least 43 murders was found), he left £100 and instructions for a memorial to be built. It never was, but the castle ruins remain.

Continue north on the A1 to **St. Anne's Bay,** the site of the first Spanish settlement on Jamaica, where you can see the statue of Christopher Columbus—cast in his hometown of Genoa—erected near St. Anne's Hospital on the west side of town, close to the coast road. There are a number of Georgian buildings in the town: The Court House near the parish church, built in 1866, is most interesting.

Following are additional sights in the Ocho Rios region, first east of town, then west.

EAST OF OCHO RIOS

Brimmer Hall Estate

2 miles from Port Maria, St. Mary's (21 miles east of Ocho Rios). ☎ **809/994-2309.** Tours $15. Tours are offered Thurs at 2pm.

This 1817 estate is an ideal place to spend a day. You can relax beside a pool and sample a wide variety of brews and concoctions, including a rum punch or lemonade. The Plantation Tour Eating House offers typical Jamaican dishes for lunch, and there is a souvenir shop with a good selection of ceramics, art, straw goods, wood carvings, rums, liqueurs, and cigars. All this is on a working plantation where you are driven around in a tractor-drawn jitney to see the tropical fruit trees and coffee plants, and learn from the knowledgeable guides about the various processes necessary to produce the fine fruit of the island. You are also taken on a tour of the great house.

Coyaba River Garden and Museum

Shaw Park Road. ☎ **809/974-6235.** Admission $4.50 for those over 13; $2.25 children 6–12, free for children 5 and under. Daily 8:30am–5pm. Take the Fern Gully/Kingston Road and turn right at St. John's Anglican Church. Follow signs to Coyaba just a further half mile away.

A mile from the center of Ocho Rios, at an elevation of 420 feet, this park and museum were built on the grounds of the former Shaw Park plantation. The name, *Coyaba,* comes from the Arawak name for paradise. Coyaba is a Spanish-style museum with a river and gardens filled with native flora, a cut-stone courtyard, fountains, an art gallery, and a crafts shop and bar. The museum boasts a collection of artifacts from the Arawak, Spanish, and English settlements in the area.

Firefly

Grant's Pen in St. Mary, 20 miles east of Ocho Rios above Oracabessa (signposted). ☎ **809/ 997-7201.** Admission $10. Daily 9am–5pm.

Firefly was the home of Sir Noël Coward and his longtime companion, Graham Payne, who, as executor of Coward's estate, donated it to the Jamaica National Heritage Trust (see "Noël's 'Folly'" later in this chapter). The recently restored house has not been a residence since Sir Noël died in 1973. The library contains his large collection of books, and the living room is warm and comfortable with big armchairs and two grand pianos where he composed several famous songs. Paintings by the noted playwright, actor, author, and composer adorn the walls. An open patio looks out over the pool and the sea. On the premises are a gift shop, bar, and restaurant where high tea, sandwiches, and drinks are served. The property is leased by Chris Blackwell, the president of Island Records and the impresario behind such musical luminaries as Bob Marley, Robert Palmer, and U2.

Goldeneye

Oracabessa, 13 miles east of Ocho Rios. ☎ **809/974-5833.** Not open to the public.

Sir Noël Coward was a frequent guest of Ian Fleming at Goldeneye, which was a fashionable estate in the 1950s. It was here that the secret agent 007 was born in 1952. Fleming built the house in 1946, and wrote each of the 13 original Bond books during his holidays here. Through the large gates, with bronze pineapples on the top, came a host of international celebrities such as Evelyn Waugh, Truman Capote, and Graham Greene.

The house was closed and grew dilapidated for some time after the writer's death. Its present owner, music publisher Christopher Blackwell, has restored the property. It is furnished with "just the basics," the way Fleming wanted it, and the beachfront house is occasionally rented by the owner.

Noël's "Folly"

Arriving in Jamaica in 1944, the gay English playwright, songwriter, raconteur, and actor Noël Coward discovered his dream island.

He returned in 1948 and rented Goldeneye from his friend Ian Fleming, the real-life spy who later created the James Bond character at this estate. During this stopover, Coward found a "magical spot" 10 miles down the coast at St. Mary's. The land was once owned by Sir Henry Morgan, the notorious buccaneer who had built a small fortress on the property so he could spy on any stray galleon entering local waters. It was here that Coward began construction on what he called his "folly"—Blue Harbour, which can be rented today (see "Where to Stay," earlier in this chapter).

Once settled in, Coward sent out invitations to his "bloody loved ones." They included Laurence Olivier, Vivien Leigh, Alfred Lunt, Lynn Fontane, Errol Flynn, Katharine Hepburn, Mary Martin, Claudette Colbert, and John Gielgud, among others. Some stayed an entire month.

Blue Harbour became so popular on the North Coast cocktail circuit that in 1956 Coward fled it and built Firefly on a panoramic nearby hilltop. It still stands today much as he left it (see "What to See & Do"). Coward lived at Firefly with his long-time companion, Graham Payne.

In 1965, the Queen Mother came to visit Coward, who prepared a lobster mousse for her only to have it melt in the hot sun. He quickly rushed to the kitchen and opened a can of split-pea soup. She found it "divine"—perhaps because Coward had hastily laced it with sherry.

Sir Winston Churchill, who also loved Jamaica, visited Coward several times at Firefly. He told the playwright: "An Englishman has an inalienable right to live wherever he chooses."

Coward died at Firefly and is buried on the grounds. You can still see his plain, flat white marble gravestone, which is inscribed simply: "Sir Noël Coward, born December 16, 1899, died March 26, 1973."

Unless you're a guest of the tenant, you aren't allowed to visit, as it is private property. But all 007 fans in this part of the world like to go by, hoping for a look. Look for the Esso (not Exxon) sign and take the narrow lane nearby going to the sea.

Harmony Hall

Tower Isle (on A3, 4 miles east of Ocho Rios). ☎ **809/460-4120.** Free admission. Gallery daily 10am–6pm.

Harmony Hall was built near the end of the 19th century as another one of the great houses of Jamaica, this one connected with a pimiento estate. Today, after a restoration, it's a center for a gallery selling paintings and other works by Jamaican artists. High-quality arts and crafts are also sold, not the usual junky assortment you often find at the beach. In addition, a bamboo factory makes furniture from a special trademark technique known as "plugging." You can also purchase Sharon McConnell's Starfish Oils, 100% pure essential-oil blends. On the ground floor is a clothing line, Reggae to Wear, designed and made in Jamaica from Balinese fabrics. Watson's shopping shuttle, calling at various hotels, makes a lunchtime trip Monday through Saturday.

On site is Alexander's Café, serving simple fare such as burgers, seafood, chicken, and sandwiches along with daily specials. They cater to vegetarians as well. Hours are daily from 10am to 6pm.

Prospect Plantation

On A3. ☎ **809/974-2058.** Tours $12 adults, free for children under 12; 1-hour horseback ride $20. Tours Mon–Sat 10:30am, 2 and 3:30pm; Sun 11am, 1:30 and 3pm.

Three miles east of Ocho Rios along the A3, adjoining the 18-hole Prospect Mini Golf Course, is a working plantation. A visit can be both educational and relaxing. On your leisurely ride by covered jitney through the scenic beauty of Prospect, you'll readily see why this section of Jamaica is called "the garden parish of the island." You can view the many trees planted by such visitors as Sir Winston Churchill, Henry Kissinger, Charles Chaplin, Pierre Trudeau, and Sir Noël Coward. You will learn about and see growing pimiento (allspice), bananas, cassava, sugarcane, coffee, cacao, coconut, pineapple, and the famous leucaena "Tree of Life." You'll see Jamaica's first hydroelectric plant, and sample some of the exotic fruit and drinks.

Horseback riding is available on three scenic trails at Prospect. The rides vary from 1 to $2^1/_4$ hours. Advance booking of 1 hour is necessary to reserve horses.

WEST OF OCHO RIOS

Dunn's River Falls

On A3. ☎ **809/974-2857.** Admission $5 adults, $2 ages 2–12; free for children under 2. Cruise-ship arrival days 8am–5pm; otherwise daily 9am–5pm.

A few miles west of Ocho Rios is the impressive Dunn's River Falls. There is plenty of parking space, and for a small charge you can relax on the beach or climb with a guide to the top of the 600-foot falls. You can splash in the waters at the bottom of the falls or drop into the cool pools higher up between the cascades of water. The beach restaurant provides snacks and refreshing drinks, and dressing rooms are available. If you're planning to climb the falls, wear old tennis shoes—anything to protect your feet from the sharp rocks and to prevent slipping.

SHOPPING

See "Shopping" in Montego Bay in Chapter 4. The same warnings given there apply when you're shopping in Ocho Rios. Prepare yourself for some aggressive selling when you venture into the shopping centers mentioned below. We don't recommend these centers; we mention them because they are there. Is shopping fun in Ocho Rios? A resounding no. Do cruise ship passengers indulge in it anyway? A decided yes.

Warning: Some so-called "duty-free" prices are actually lower than Stateside prices, but then the government hits you with a 10% General Consumption Tax on all items purchased.

THE CENTERS & MALLS

There are seven main shopping plazas. The originals are Ocean Village, Pineapple Place, and Coconut Grove. Newer ones include the New Ocho Rios Plaza, in the center of town, with some 60 shops. Island Plaza is another major shopping complex, as is the Mutual Security Plaza with some 30 shops. Opposite the New Ocho Rios Plaza is the Taj Mahal, with 26 duty-free stores.

OCEAN VILLAGE SHOPPING CENTRE   Here are numerous boutiques, food stores, a bank, sundries purveyors, travel agencies, service facilities—what have you. The **Ocho Rios Pharmacy** (☎ 809/974-2398) sells most proprietary brands, perfumes, plasters for sore heels, and suntan lotions, among its many wares. You can call the shopping center at 809/974-2683. Open Monday through Saturday 8:30am to 7:30pm and Sunday 9am to 5pm.

PINEAPPLE PLACE SHOPPING CENTRE   Just east of Ocho Rios, this is a collection of shops in cedar-shingle-roofed cottages set amid tropical flowers.

OCHO RIOS CRAFT PARK   This is a complex of some 150 stalls through which to browse. An eager seller will weave you a hat or a basket while you wait, or you can buy from the mixtures of ready-made hats, hampers, handbags, placemats, and lampshades. Other stands stock hand-embroidered goods and will make up small items while you wait. Wood carvers work on bowls, ashtrays, wooden-head carvings, and statues chipped from lignum vitae, and make cups from local bamboo.

COCONUT GROVE SHOPPING PLAZA   This collection of low-lying shops is linked by walkways and shrubs. The merchandise consists mainly of local craft items. Many of your fellow shoppers may be cruise-ship passengers.

ISLAND PLAZA   This shopping complex is right in the heart of Ocho Rios. Some of the best Jamaican art is to be found here, all paintings by local artists. You can also purchase local handmade crafts (be prepared to do some haggling over price and quality), carvings, ceramics, even kitchenware, and most definitely the inevitable T-shirts.

SPECIALTY SHOPS

In general, the shopping is better at Montego Bay if you're going there. If not, wander the Ocho Rios crafts markets, although much of the merchandise is monotonous.

Among the few places that deserve special mention are **Casa de Oro,** Pineapple Place (☎ **809/974-2577**), specializing in selling duty-free watches, fine jewelry, and the classic perfumes. It's open Monday through Saturday from 9am to 5pm. **Caribbean Camera Centre,** Pineapple Place (☎ **809/974-2421**), is the best place for cameras and photographic supplies. Open Monday through Saturday from 9am to 5pm.

Swiss Stores, in the Ocean Village Shopping Centre (☎ **809/974-2519**), sells all the big names in Swiss watches, including Juvenia, Tissot, Omega, Rolex, Patek Philippe, and Piaget—and here the Rolex watches are real, not those fakes touted by hustlers on the streets of Ocho Rios. The Swiss outlet also sells duty-free handcrafted jewelry, some of dubious taste but some really exquisite jewelry as well. Open Monday through Saturday from 9am to 5pm.

If you'd like to avoid the hassle of the markets, but still find some local handcrafts or art, head for **Beautiful Memories,** 9 Island Plaza (☎ **809/974-2374**), which has a limited but representative sampling of Jamaican art, as well as an exhibit of Jamaican crafts, pottery, woodwork, and hand-embroidered items. Open Monday through Friday from 9am to 5pm and Saturday from 10am to 5pm.

OCHO RIOS AFTER DARK

Hotels in Ocho Rios often provide live entertainment to which nonresidents are invited. Ask at your hotel desk where the action is on any given night.

Otherwise, you may want to look in on **Silks Nightclub,** in the Shaw Park Beach Hotel, Cutlass Bay (☎ **809/974-2552**), which attracts visitors with well-upholstered banquettes, a smallish dance floor, and a green-and-red decor whose contrasting tones seem to add energy to the sometimes-animated crowd of drinkers and dancers. Nonresidents of this well-known hotel can enter for $3 each; beer costs another $1.50. The club is open Wednesday through Monday from 10pm until 3am.

3 Port Antonio

Port Antonio is a verdant and sleepy seaport 63 miles northeast of Kingston (you may have seen it already, since it was the locale for Tom Cruise's film *Cocktail*). Here you can still catch a glimpse of the Jamaica of 100 years ago. The titled and the wealthy have come here before you—European duchesses and barons, along with film stars like Linda Evans, Raquel Welch, and Peter O'Toole. You may even spot Whoopi Goldberg, who came here to film *Clara's Heart*.

The small, bustling town itself is like many on Jamaica—clean but ramshackle, with sidewalks around a market filled with vendors; tin-roofed shacks competing with old Georgian and modern brick and concrete buildings; lots of people busily shopping, talking, and laughing, others sitting and playing dominoes—loudly banging the pieces on the table, which is very much part of the game. The colorful market is a place to browse for local craftwork, spices, and fruits.

In the old days, visitors arrived by banana boat and stayed at the Titchfield Hotel (since burned down) in a lush, tropical part of the island unspoiled by modern tourist gimmicks. Captain Bligh landed here in 1793 with his cargo of breadfruit plants from Tahiti, and Port Antonio claims that the breadfruit grown here are the best on the island (see "Strange Fruit" in Chapter 2). Visitors still arrive by water, but now it's on cruise ships, which moor close to Navy Island and send their passengers ashore just for the day.

Navy Island and the long-gone Titchfield Hotel were owned for a short time by film star Errol Flynn. The story is that after suffering damage to his yacht, he put into Kingston for repairs, visited Port Antonio by motorbike, fell in love with the area, and in due course acquired Navy Island (in a gambling game, some say). Later, he either lost or sold it and bought a nearby plantation, Comfort Castle, which is still owned by his widow, Patrice Wymore Flynn, who spends most of her time there. He was much loved and admired by the Jamaicans and was totally integrated into the community. They still talk of him in Port Antonio, especially the men, who refer to his legendary womanizing and drinking in reverent tones.

To reach Port Antonio from Kingston, you can take A4 through Port Morant and up the east coast. You can also drive north on A3 through Castleton, and then approach Port Antonio along the north coast.

WHERE TO STAY

Despite its reputation as an enclave of the rich and famous, you'll find a good range of accommodations in Port Antonio.

VERY EXPENSIVE

✪ Trident Villas & Hotel

Route A4 (P.O. Box 119), Port Antonio, Jamaica, W.I. ☎ **809/993-2602,** or 800/237-3237 in the U.S. Fax 809/993-2590. 8 rms, 18 suites. TEL. Winter $350 double, $620 suite; off-season $220 double, $340 suite. MAP $65 per person per day extra. AE, MC, V. Take Allan Avenue east of town 2¹/₂ miles.

On the coast toward Frenchman's Cove stands this elegant rendezvous for the very affluent. The deluxe Trident complex is the most tasteful and refined on the north shore. Sitting regally above jagged coral cliffs with a seaside panorama, the hotel is the personal and creative statement of Earl Levy, scion of a prominent Kingston family. Nearby he has erected a multimillion-dollar reproduction of a European château, known as Trident Castle, which can be rented as one unit. Here, guests are grandly housed in eight large bedrooms beautifully furnished in plantation style.

The hotel's main building is furnished with many antique and well-chosen pieces, and flowers decorate the lobby, which is cooled by sea breezes. Your accommodations will be a studio cottage or tower, reached by a pathway through the gardens. In a cottage, a large bedroom with ample sitting area opens onto a private patio with nothing between you and the sea except grass and a low stone wall. All cottages and tower rooms offer baths with tubs, showers, and toilets, plus ceiling fans and plenty of storage space. Jugs of ice and water are constantly replenished, and fresh flowers grace the dressing table. Singles are accommodated in either junior or deluxe villa suites, whereas two or three guests are lodged in junior, deluxe villa, prime minister's, or imperial suites.

There's a small private sand beach, and the gardens embrace a pool and a ginger-bread gazebo.

Dining/Entertainment: For breakfast or lunch, you can go to the main building where there are two patios, one covered. You can have your breakfast there or have it served on your private patio by your own butler. Men are required to wear jackets and ties to dinner, served in a wing of the main block. Silver service, crystal, and Port Royal pewter sparkle on the tables. Dinner is a many-course, fixed-price meal, so if you are concerned with dietary restrictions, you should make your requirements known early so that alternative food can be prepared.

Services: Laundry, baby-sitting, room service.

Facilities: Tennis, horseback riding, and such water sports as sailing and snorkeling included in rates; swimming pool.

EXPENSIVE

Fern Hill Club

Mile Gully Road, San San (P.O. Box 100), Port Antonio, Jamaica, W.I. ☎ **809/993-3222**, or 416/620-4666 in Toronto for all reservations. Fax 809/993-2257. 31 units. A/C TV. Winter $300 double, $380 suite for two; off-season $190 double, $230 suite for two. Rates include meals, sports, and Jamaican liquor products. AE, MC, V. Head east along Allan Avenue and watch for signs.

Attractive, airy, and panoramic, Fern Hill occupies 20 forested acres high above the coastline, attracting primarily a British or Canadian clientele. Accommodations come in a wide range of configurations, including standard rooms, junior suites, spa suites, and villas with cooking facilities. Technically classified as a private club, the establishment comprises a colonial-style clubhouse and five outlying villas, plus a comfortable annex at the bottom of the hill. The accommodations are private, drawing a large patronage among honeymooners. Many of the rooms are furnished in a rather standard, bland style, and there is no air-conditioning. We think this is a less elegant choice than its main competitor, Goblin Hill (see below).

Dining/Entertainment: There is the Blue Mahoe Bar (named after the wood that sheaths it) and a patio for dining. The hotel restaurant offers an international menu (see "Where to Dine," below).

Services: Shuttle bus down steep hillside to beach.

Facilities: Four swimming pools, tennis court.

Goblin Hill Villas at San San

San San (5 miles east of Port Antonio; P.O. Box 26), Port Antonio, Jamaica, W.I. ☎ **809/993-3286**, or 809/925-8108 in Kingston for reservations. Fax 809/925-6248. 28 villas. A/C MINIBAR. Winter $1,850 one-bedroom villa per week, $2,130 two-bedroom villa for four per week; off-season $1,710 one-bedroom villa per week, $1,885 two-bedroom villa for four per week. Rates include transfers and rental car. AE, MC, V.

This green and sun-washed hillside, once reputed to shelter goblins, is now dotted with vacation Georgian-style homes on the 12-acre San San Estate. Everything about the place is relaxing. The swimming pool is surrounded by a vine-laced arbor, which lies just a stone's throw from an almost impenetrable forest. A long flight of steps leads down to the crescent-shaped sands of San San Beach. Backgammon and Scrabble tournaments are held quite often; the reading and games room comes equipped with a video and TV; and there's a shady garden terrace.

Port Antonio

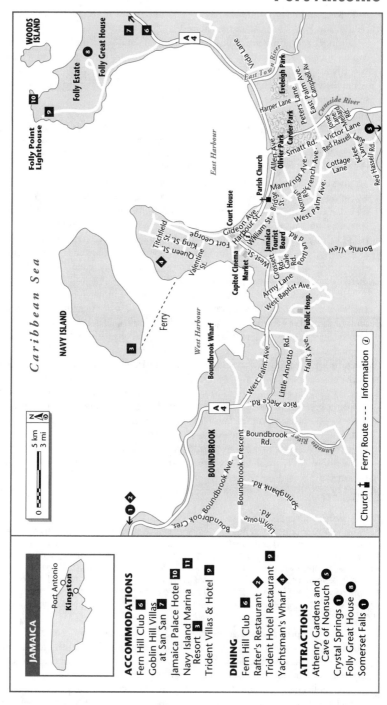

The accommodations are townhouse style, housed in stucco villas, and feature ceiling fans, king-size beds, and kitchens.

Dining/Entertainment: Housekeepers prepare and serve meals and attend to chores, but guests pay for their own food. Guests gather for the manager's rum punch and calypso party in the leafy Tree Bar.

Facilities: Swimming pool and a pair of lighted Laykold tennis courts, plus snorkeling, windsurfing, and scuba diving on San San Beach.

Jamaica Palace Hotel

Williamsfield (P.O. Box 277), Port Antonio, Jamaica, W.I. ☎ **809/993-2021** or 800/423-4095; 312/883-1020 in Chicago. Fax 809/993-3459. 21 rms, 59 suites. A/C TV TEL. Winter $140 double, $230 suite; off-season $160 double, $210 suite. MAP $45 extra per person per day. AE, MC, V. Head 1 mile east on Allan Avenue and watch for signs.

Set on 5 acres of tropical landscaping, the Jamaica Palace opened in 1989. Rising like a stately mansion, the deluxe hotel commands a coastal view of Port Antonio (though note that the property doesn't have its own beach). Its owner, German-born Siglinde von Stephani-Fahmi, set out to combine the elegance of a European hotel with the relaxed atmosphere of a Jamaican resort. The public rooms contain furnishings and art from Europe, including a 6-foot Baccarat crystal candelabra and a pair of Italian ebony-and-ivory chairs from the 15th century. Outside, there are Tara-style white marble columns and sunny patios and balconies.

The accommodations consist of 21 deluxe rooms, 52 junior suites, six full suites, and an imperial suite. Most rooms are large, with $12^1/2$-foot ceilings and oversize pink-hued marble bathrooms. Some, however, are rather small but still elegantly furnished. Suites are individually furnished with crystal chandeliers, Persian rugs, and original works of art. TVs are available upon request.

Dining/Entertainment: Both continental and Jamaican food is served, especially in the chic main dining room with its lighted "waterwall" sculpted from Jamaican cave stones. Men are requested to wear jacket and tie. There's also a poolside cafe with a barbecue area. Live dance music and calypso bands are featured at Jamaica Palace.

Services: Massage facilities; fashion boutique operated by Patrice Wymore Flynn, widow of Errol Flynn; complimentary shuttle service and admission to three nearby white sandy beaches. Room service, laundry, baby-sitting.

Facilities: An unusual 114-foot-long swimming pool shaped just like the island of Jamaica.

MODERATE

Navy Island Marina Resort

Navy Island (P.O. Box 188), Port Antonio, Jamaica, W.I. ☎ **809/993-2667.** Fax 809/993-2667. 1 rm, 10 villas. Year-round $60 double, $80 one-bedroom villa for one, $100 one-bedroom villa for two, $140 one-bedroom villa for three, $180 two-bedroom villa for three, $200 two-bedroom villa for four, $240 two-bedroom villa for five, $260 two-bedroom villa for six. Additional person (maximum of six in a unit) $20 extra. All rates include breakfast. AE, MC, V. To reach the resort, you'll have to take a short ferry ride across the harbor from the dockyards of Port Antonio on West Street. Hotel guests travel free, but temporary visitors pay $2 for the round-trip. The ferry runs daily 24 hours.

Jamaica's only private island getaway, Navy Island Marina Resort is on that "bit of paradise" once owned by actor Errol Flynn, who came here for his off-screen adventures. Today this cottage colony and yacht club is one of the best-kept travel secrets in the Caribbean. In what had been the swashbuckling movie star's Garden of Eden, a memorabilia room has stills from some of Flynn's pictures.

Each accommodation is designed as a studio villa or rondavel branching out from the main club. Ceiling fans and trade winds keep the cottages cool, and mosquito netting over the beds adds a plantation touch. There is only one hotel room, which can be rented as a single or double.

One of the resort's beaches is a secluded clothing-optional stretch of sand known as Trembly Knee Cove. You can wander at leisure, exploring the island, whose grounds are dotted with hybrid hibiscus, bougainvillea, and royal and coconut palms (many planted by Flynn himself).

Dining/Entertainment: At night, after enjoying drinks in the HMS *Bounty* Bar, guests can dine in the Navy Island Restaurant. One can order a five-course dinner, served nightly.

Services: Free ferry service.

Facilities: Swimming pool; two beaches; water sports, including scuba diving and windsurfing.

INEXPENSIVE

De Montevin Lodge Hotel

21 Fort George St. (in the town center on Titchfield Hill), Port Antonio, Jamaica, W.I. ☎ **809/ 993-2604.** 13 rms (3 with bath). $39 double without bath; $52 double with bath. Rates include breakfast. No credit cards.

De Montevin, the most ornate and best-maintained gingerbread house in town, stands on a narrow back street whose edges are lined with architectural reminders (some not well-preserved) of colonial days. Built as a sea captain's house in 1881, the hotel is really worth a photograph. Cast-iron accents and elongated red-and-white balconies set a tone for the charm you find inside: cedar doors, art deco cupboards, a ceiling embellished with lacy plaster designs, and the most elaborate cove moldings in town. Don't expect modern amenities here; your old-fashioned room might be a study of another, not-yet-renovated era.

WHERE TO DINE

An array of atmospheric choices awaits you in Port Antonio. All hotels welcome outside guests for dinner, but reservations are required.

EXPENSIVE

Fern Hill Club

Mile Gully Road. ☎ **809/993-3222.** Reservations required. Lunch $10; dinner $30. AE, MC, V. Daily 1–2pm and 7:30–9:30pm. Head east on Allan Avenue. INTERNATIONAL/JAMAICAN.

Fern Hill features such a sweeping view of the rugged coastline that the best sunset-watching in Port Antonio is found here. Depending on who's in the kitchen at night, the food here can be quite satisfactory, as well. Some nights, however, especially in the off-season, it doesn't live up to the view. Specialties include jerk chicken, jerk pork, grilled lobster, and Créole fish. Ask about beach barbecues.

✪ Trident Hotel Restaurant

Route A4. ☎ **809/993-2602.** Reservations and jacket and tie for men required. Lunch $15– $25; six-course dinner $50. AE, MC, V. Daily 8am–4pm and 8–10pm. Head east on Allan Avenue. INTERNATIONAL.

The Trident Hotel Restaurant has for a long time been frequented by those seeking high-level cuisine. In the main hotel building, the restaurant has an air of elegance. The high-pitched wooden roof set on white stone walls holds several ceiling fans that gently stir the air. The antique tables for two, four, or more are set with old china, English silver, and Port Royal pewter. Dinner is served from 8pm.

A waiter, resplendent in uniform—including white starched shirt and pristine white cotton gloves—will help you choose your wine. The waiter whispers the name of each course as he serves it: Jamaican salad; coconut soup; dolphin with mayonnaise and mustard sauce; steak with broccoli and sautéed potatoes; peach Melba and Blue Mountain coffee with Tía Maria, a Jamaican coffee liqueur. The six-course menu is changed every day. The cuisine is always fresh and prepared with first-class ingredients, but the setting and the white-gloved service are generally more memorable than the food. Tip at your discretion.

MODERATE

Rafter's Restaurant

St. Margaret's Bay (signposted 5 miles west of Port Antonio). ☎ **809/993-2778.** Reservations not required. Main courses $7. AE, MC, V. Daily 11am–6pm. JAMAICAN.

Rafter's lies at the edge of the river, where still waters provided a convenient resting point for the commercial raft operators who formerly floated goods downstream. Jean McGill and Beverley Dixon are the managers of this establishment. The neoclassical pavilion housing the establishment was built in 1954 by a local architect for the earl of Mansfield. The house drink is a Rio Grande special, which combines four kinds of rum with fresh juices. Lunch is the usual selection of sandwiches, burgers, and an array of salads, chicken, and, if available, grilled lobster. A fish dinner in the evening might be more substantial. Freshly caught fish can be requested served grilled, steamed, or pan-fried. Vegetables that go along with main courses are generally fresh and not cooked to death.

INEXPENSIVE

De Montevin Lodge Restaurant

21 Fort George St. (in the town center on Titchfield Hill). ☎ **809/993-2604.** Reservations recommended. Fixed-price menus $10.50–$19.50. No credit cards. Daily 12:30–2pm and 7–9pm. JAMAICAN.

At De Montevin you'll be able to order an authentic Jamaican dinner. Start with pepperpot or pumpkin soup; follow with curried lobster and chicken Jamaican style with local vegetables; and top the meal off with coconut or banana cream pie, washed down with coffee. We suggest an ice-cold Red Stripe beer with the meal, too. The menu changes according to the availability of fresh supplies, but the standard of cooking and the full Jamaican character of the meal are constant. Call the day before to make a reservation, or else just show up unannounced and take potluck.

Yachtsman's Wharf

16 West St. (near departure point for the ferries to Navy Island). ☎ **809/993-3053.** Main courses $6–$13. No credit cards. Daily 7:30am–10pm, or later. INTERNATIONAL.

Beneath a thatch-covered roof at the end of an industrial pier, this rustic bar and restaurant is a favorite of expat crewmembers of ultra-expensive yachts, many of whom have dined here and have pinned their ensigns on the roughly textured planks and posts. Yachtsman's opens for breakfast and stays open all day. Menu items include the usual array of tropical drinks, burgers, seafood ceviche, curried chicken, and ackee with saltfish; main dishes include vegetables. Come here for the setting, the camaraderie, and the good times. The food is only secondary.

BEACHES, FISHING & RIVER RAFTING

BEACHES   Port Antonio boasts several public white sand beaches; some are free and some charge a fee for use of their facilities.

The best of them all is the famous **San San Beach,** with its white sands. **Boston Beach** is free, and often has light surfing; there are picnic tables as well as a restaurant and snack bar. Before heading to the beach, stop nearby and get the makings for a picnic lunch at the most famous center for peppery jerk pork and chicken in Jamaica. These rustic shacks also sell the much rarer jerk sausage. The dish was said to originate with the Maroons who lived in the hills beyond and occasionally ventured out to harass plantation owners. The location is east of Port Antonio and the Blue Lagoon.

Also free is **Fairy Hill Beach** (Winnifred), with no changing rooms or showers. **Frenchman's Cove Beach** attracts a chic crowd to its white sand beach combined with a freshwater stream. Nonhotel guests are charged a fee.

Navy Island, once Errol Flynn's personal hideaway, is a fine choice for swimming (one beach is clothing-optional) and snorkeling (at **Crusoe's Beach**). Take the boat from the Navy Island dock on West Street across from the Exxon station. It's a 7-minute ride to the island, and a round-trip costs $2. The ferry runs 24 hours a day on the half hour.

DEEP-SEA FISHING　A 30-foot long sportfishing boat with a tournament rig, the **Bonita II** is available for rental at Port Antonio. Taking out up to four passengers at a time, it charges $150 per half day or $280 per day, with crew, bait, tackle, and soft drinks included. It docks at Port Antonio's main marina, off West Palm Avenue, in the center of town. Call **809/993-3086** for bookings.

✪ **RIVER RAFTING**　Rafting started on the Rio Grande as a means of transporting bananas from plantations to waiting freighters. In 1871 a Yankee skipper, Lorenzo Dow Baker, decided that a seat on one of the rafts was better than walking, but it was not until Errol Flynn arrived that the rafts became popular tourist attractions. Flynn hired the craft for his friends, and he encouraged the drivers to race down the Rio Grande, spurred on by bets on who would win. Now that bananas are transported by road, the raft skipper makes one or maybe two trips a day down the waterway.

The rafts are some 33 feet long and only 4 feet wide, and are propelled by stout bamboo poles. There is a raised double seat about two-thirds of the way back for the two passengers. The skipper stands in the front, trousers rolled up to his knees, the water washing his feet, and guides the lively craft down the river, about 8 miles between steep hills covered with coconut palms, banana plantations, and flowers, through limestone cliffs pitted with caves, through the Tunnel of Love—a narrow cleft in the rocks—then on to wider, gentler water.

Rio Grande Attractions Limited (☎ **809/993-2778**) can arrange a raft trip for you. The day starts at Rafter's Restaurant, west of Port Antonio at Burlington on St. Margaret's Bay. Trips last 2¹/₂ hours and they're offered from 8:30am to 4:30pm daily at a cost of $40 per raft, which is suitable for two people. From the restaurant, a fully insured driver will take you in your rented car to the starting point at Grants Level or Berrydale, where you board your raft. The trip ends at Rafter's Restaurant, where you collect your car (brought here by the driver). If you feel like it, take a picnic lunch, but bring enough for the skipper, too. He'll find a peaceful spot, regaling you with lively stories of life on the river.

SEEING THE SIGHTS

Athenry Gardens and Cave of Nonsuch
Portland. ☎ **809/993-3740**. Admission $5 adults, $2.50 children under 12 (includes guide for gardens and cave). Daily 9am–5pm (last tour 4:30pm).

It's an easy drive and an easy walk to see the stalagmites, stalactites, fossilized marine life, and evidence of Arawak civilization as well as signs of 1¹/₂ million years of volcanic activity. Athenry Gardens afford panoramic views of the island and sea; the gardens are filled with coconut palms, flowers, and trees. Complete guided tours are given.

These sights are a 20-minute drive south–southeast of Port Antonio: From Harbour Street in Port Antonio, turn south in front of the Anglican church onto Red Hassel Road and proceed approximately 1 mile to Breastworks community (fork in road). Take the left fork, cross a narrow bridge, go immediately left after the bridge, and proceed approximately 3 1/2 miles to the village of Nonsuch.

Crystal Springs

Buff Bay, Portland. ☎ **809/929-6280.** Admission $2.60 adults, $1.30 children. Daily 9am–5pm.

Crystal Springs is a tract of forested land whose borders were originally recorded in 1655. Then it was attached to a nearby plantation whose great house is now under separate (and private) ownership. Visitors, however, can trek through the organization's 156 acres of forest much beloved by birds and wildlife. A simple restaurant, usually open daily from 8am to 5pm, is on the premises, as well as a series of cottages erected in the early 1990s. These are usually rented to visiting ornithologists who can do without the amenities or distractions of a traditional resort.

Folly Great House

On the outskirts of Port Antonio on the way to Trident Village, going east on A4. No phone. Free admission. Open 24 hours a day.

This house reputedly was built in 1905 by Arthur Mitchell, an American millionaire, for his wife, Annie (daughter of Charles Tiffany, founder of the famous New York jewelry store). Sea water was used in making the concrete for its foundations and mortar, and the house began to crumble only 11 years after the family moved in. Because of the beautiful location, it is easy to see what a fine great house it must have been, but the years and vandals have not added to its attractiveness. Decay and graffiti mar the remains of the two-story mansion.

Somerset Falls

8 miles west of Port Antonio on A4, just past Hope Bay. ☎ **809/926-2952** (Albert Shaw). Tour $2. Daily 9am–5pm.

The waters of the Daniels River pour down a deep gorge through the rain forest, with waterfalls and foaming cascades. You can take a short ride in an electric gondola to the hidden falls. This is one of Jamaica's most historic sites, used by the Spanish before the English capture of the island, and it is a stop on the daily Grand Jamaica Tour from Ocho Rios. Phone Albert Shaw at the above number or check with your Ocho Rios hotel or travel agent. At the falls, you can swim in the deep rock pools and buy sandwiches, light meals, beer, soft drinks, and even liquor at the snack bar. The guided tour includes the gondola ride and a cave, as well as a visit to the freshwater fish farm.

7

Kingston & the Blue Mountains

With 660,000 inhabitants, Jamaica's capital of Kingston is the largest English-speaking community in the Caribbean. This busy city occupies some 40 square miles on the south coast plains between the Blue Mountains and the sea. With the world's seventh largest harbor, it is the country's hub of transportation, industry, finance, and public administration. It's also Jamaica's main cultural center, with a campus of the University of the West Indies at its edge. The buildings here are a mixture of very modern, graceful old, and plain ramshackle.

Unfortunately, squalid living conditions in parts of the city have helped foster crime and political violence, and visitors should be cautious. All leading hotels employ guards to help ensure your safety.

Nearby Port Royal and Spanish Town are well worth a visit; Kingston's history is linked to both of these historic towns. It was founded by survivors of the great 1692 earthquake which destroyed Port Royal. In 1872 it replaced Spanish Town as Jamaica's capital.

1   Where to Stay

When you inquire about a reservation, ask whether the room tax is included in the rate quoted. The following rates are year-round, unless noted otherwise. Prices are quoted in U.S. dollars.

EXPENSIVE

Jamaica Pegasus

81 Knutsford Blvd. (in the center of New Kingston, off Oxford Rd.; a 12-mile taxi ride from the airport), Kingston 5, Jamaica, W.I. ☎ **809/926-3690,** or 800/225-5843 in the U.S. and Canada. Fax 809/929-5855. 325 rms, 18 suites. A/C TV TEL $190–$200 double; $291–$597 suite for two. AE, DC, MC, V. Free parking.

A favorite with business travelers, Jamaica Pegasus outclasses its nearest rival, the Wyndham New Kingston, in a close race. It's located in the banking area—and a fine residential section—of Kingston. After a major renovation, the hotel is now better than ever, and is the site of many conventions and social events.

The hotel combines English style with Jamaican warmth. The staff makes an effort to provide vacation-related activities, such as arranging water sports and sightseeing.

What's Special About Kingston

Beaches
- Gunboat Beach, the most popular choice for Kingstonians who like to frolic in the water, especially on weekends.
- Fort Clarence, in the Hellshire Hills, southwest of the center, a black sandy beach with clothes-changing facilities. Noted for its spontaneous reggae concerts.
- Lysson's Beach, Morant Bay, a good sandy beach that many Kingstonians consider worth the 32-mile drive to the east to enjoy sunning and swimming.
- Lime Cay, a tiny island beyond Kingston Harbour—ideal for picnicking and swimming. Reached by boat from Morgan's Harbour Marina at Port Royal.

Great Towns/Villages
- Port Royal, a 20-minute ferryboat ride from Kingston, the former stamping ground of such swashbuckling pirates as Henry Morgan. Destroyed in a 1692 earthquake.
- Spanish Town, west of Kingston. Founded by Spaniards, it was from 1662 to 1872 the capital of Jamaica.

Memorable Sights
- The Bob Marley Museum, the most popular tourist spot in Kingston, the famous reggae singer's home and recording studio until his death.
- Fort Charles, the only remaining of Port Royal's six forts. Built in 1656, it has withstood attack, earthquake, fire, and hurricane.
- Devon House, a striking building of classical style and the former home of one of the first black millionaires in the Caribbean.
- Hope Botanical Gardens, sprawling across 60 acres on the grounds of a former sugarcane estate, with more than 600 different types of tropical trees.

Shopping
- Things Jamaican, at Devon House, premier showplace of Jamaican handcrafts—every item in the store, from pewter to rum, made in Jamaica.

Each of the well-furnished bedrooms contains coffee-making equipment, satellite color TV, and a radio. Several floors of luxuriously appointed suites form the Knutsford Club, which offers special executive services.

Dining/Entertainment: The 4pm tea service is considered a bit of a social event among some residents. The premier restaurant is The Port Royal (see "Where to Dine," below). The Brasserie is the hotel's informal restaurant that opens to the swimming pool where a splashing fountain cools the air. It adjoins a circular bar near the pool at which occasional barbecues are prepared, featuring such dishes as grilled fish and jerk pork.

Services: Laundry and dry-cleaning, 24-hour room service, baby-sitting, therapeutic massage.

Facilities: Jogging track, health club, tennis courts, outdoor pool.

Wyndham Kingston Hotel

77 Knutsford Blvd. (in the center of New Kingston, near Oxford Rd.; P.O. Box 112), Kingston 5, Jamaica, W.I. ☎ **809/926-5430,** or 800/822-4200 in the U.S. Fax 809/929-7439. 303 rms, 13 suites. A/C TV TEL $180–$210 double; from $315–$575 suite. Children under 12 stay free in parents' room. AE, DC, MC, V. Free parking.

After massive renovations in 1994, the Wyndham Kingston rises as an imposing mass of pink-colored stucco pierced with oversized sheets of tinted glass. The main core of the hotel is a 17-floor tower, containing 220 guest rooms and suites. In addition, poolside units add to the diversity of the hotel's accommodations. Completely refurbished, bedrooms feature up-to-date amenities, including coffee makers and remote-control satellite TV.

Dining/Entertainment: Fine cuisine is offered at the Terrace Café, providing à la carte Jamaican and international food. The health-conscious appreciate the fare served from the cafe's popular salad and pasta bars. The Rendezvous Bar and Palm Court Restaurant offers more elegant dining and fine wines. For details on the hotel's nightclub, refer to the Jonkanoo under "Evening Entertainment," below.

Services: Laundry, valet, baby-sitting, massage.

Facilities: Olympic-size swimming pool, floodlit tennis courts, health club, tour desk.

MODERATE

Terra Nova Hotel

17 Waterloo Rd. (near West Kings House Road), Kingston 10, Jamaica, W.I. ☎ **809/926-2211**, or 800/74-CHARMS in the U.S. or Canada. Fax 809/929-4933. 35 rms. A/C TV TEL $96–$106 double. AE, DC, MC, V. Free parking.

Built in 1924 as a wedding present for a young bride, this house on the western edge of New Kingston has had a varied career. It was once the family seat of the Myers rum dynasty, and the birthplace and home of Christopher Blackwell, promoter of many Jamaican singers and musical groups, such as Bob Marley and the Wailers and Millie Small. In 1959 the house was converted into a hotel. Set on $2^1/_2$ acres of well-kept gardens with a backdrop of greenery and mountains, it is now considered one of the best small Kingston hotels. The rooms are rather basic, however; this is definitely not a resort.

Most of Terra Nova's bedrooms are in a new wing, and all feature balconies or patios looking onto the gardens. The Spanish-style El Dorado Room, with a marble floor, wide windows, and spotless linen, offers local and international food. Your à la carte breakfast is served on the coffee terrace, and there is a swimming pool at the front of the hotel.

INEXPENSIVE

Hotel Four Seasons

18 Ruthven Rd. (near Half Way Tree Road), Kingston 10, Jamaica, W.I. ☎ **809/929-7655**, or 800/742-4276. Fax 809/929-5964. 39 rms. A/C TV TEL. $78 double. AE, DC, MC, V. Free parking.

Small and respectable, this hotel (not affiliated with the famous Four Seasons chain) is an old house on the western outskirts of New Kingston with a colonial-style veranda along the front, with a view of mango trees and a garden through which you drive. Old mahogany woodwork enhances the appearance of the reception area, the bar, and the formal dining room. Guestrooms are decorated in wicker or plantation-style furniture, although they are more likely to remind you of a motel. By the time you check in, more modern and up-to-date rooms should have been added. Meals are served to both guests and nonresidents, either on the terrace or in the formal dining room; a buffet lunch Monday through Friday attracts the city's business leaders. The hotel also has two bars (one inside, the other outside). Guests can arrange to swim in a pool at a nearby hotel.

Indies Hotel

5 Holborn Rd. (near the intersection of Trafalgar Road), Kingston 10, Jamaica, W.I. ☎ **809/926-2952**. Fax 809/926-2879. 15 rms. A/C TV TEL. $58–$62 double; $77 triple. AE, MC, V. Free parking.

Kingston Area

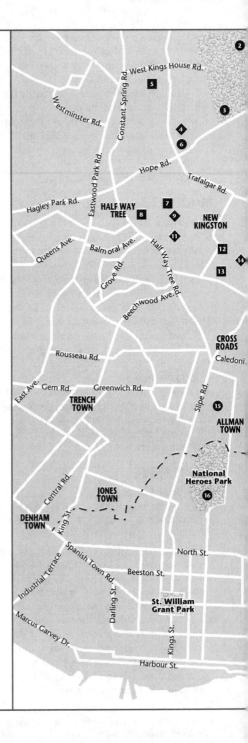

JAMAICA

Negril

Kingston

ACCOMMODATIONS
Hotel Four Seasons **8**
Indies Hotel **7**
Jamaica Pegasus **13**
Terra Nova Hotel **5**
Wyndham Kingston Hotel **12**

DINING
Blue Mountain Inn **25**
Chelsea Jerk Centre **11**
Devonshire Restaurant/
 The Grogg Shoppe **4**
El Dorado Room **5**
Hot Pot, The **14**
Indies Pub and Grill **9**
Jade Garden **4**
Port Royal Restaurant, The **13**

ATTRACTIONS
Coke Church **20**
Devon House **6**
Hope Botanical Gardens **24**
Institute of Jamaica **19**
Jamaica House **3**
King's House **2**
Kingston Crafts Market **17**
Kingston Mall **18**
Mico College **15**
National Arena **22**
National Heroes Park **16**
National Library
 of Jamaica **19**
National Stadium **21**
University of
 West Indies **23**

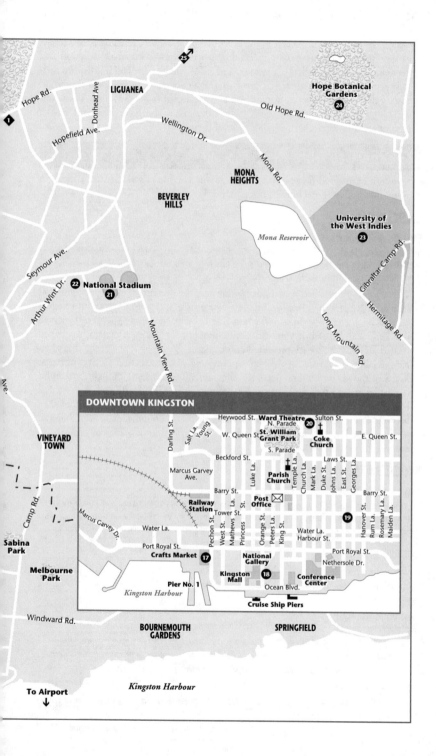

DOWNTOWN KINGSTON

Kingston Harbour

Kingston Harbour

On one of the small side streets in the heart of New Kingston, opening onto a flower garden, this half-timber building with double gables features a small reception area decorated with potted plants, a lounge, and a TV lounge. The barely adequate bedrooms, restaurant, and bar are grouped around a cool patio. Indies has a reputation among the locals for friendly atmosphere and good-quality budget meals. Their fish-and-chips are good, and they specialize in pizza. They also serve steak with all the trimmings, and when they get fancy, lobster thermidor.

2 Where to Dine

Kingston has a good range of places to eat, whether you're seeking stately meals in plantation houses, hotel buffets, or fast-food shops.

EXPENSIVE

The Port Royal Restaurant

In the Jamaica Pegasus Hotel, 81 Knutsford Blvd. (in New Kingston, off Oxford Road). ☎ **809/ 926-3690.** Main course $16–$30; fixed price lunch $15.80. AE, DC, MC, V. Mon–Fri 12:30– 3pm; Mon–Sat 7–11pm. SEAFOOD/CONTINENTAL.

This elegantly furnished restaurant is your best bet if you're looking for upmarket seafood. It's a favorite place for local business people hoping to impress out-of-town clients. We prefer to begin with the Jamaican baby lobster as an appetizer. It's served in a shell with a salad. If you want something hot for a starter, make it the baked stuffed Jamaican crab back presented on vermicelli. *Doubloon* is one of the chef's better specialties—a medley of chicken suprême and veal presented on a layer of pasta. Many of the main meat and poultry dishes are quite ordinary, although the seafood specialties are more radiant, especially the snapper filet filled with crab mousse and baked in parmesan and fresh herbs. The Créole shrimp is also good—simmered in beer and flavored with Cajun spices. Service is first class. You might also visit "In Vino Veritas," the hotel's wine cellar offering a wide selection of exclusive wines from around the world.

MODERATE

Devonshire Restaurant/The Grogg Shoppe

26 Hope Rd., in Devon House (near Trafalgar Park). ☎ **809/929-7046** and 809/929-7027. Reservations recommended in the Devonshire, not necessary in the Grogg Shoppe. Devonshire main courses $6–$24 at lunch, $8–$28 at dinner. Grogg Shoppe main courses $4–$10 at lunch, $6–$28 at dinner. A 10% service charge is added to all bills. AE, MC, V. Mon–Sat 10am– midnight. JAMAICAN.

These two restaurants are in the brick-sided former servant's quarters of Kingston's most-visited mansion, Devon House. The more formal of the two is the Devonshire,

Impressions

It would be idle to pretend that Kingston is an attractive city. It is bigger and uglier than any other town in the British West Indies. It was a relief to discover, after a few days, that it is quite unrepresentative of the rest of this beautiful island.
—Patrick Leigh Fermor, *The Traveller's Tree,* 1951

The slums of Kingston are beyond description. Even the camera glamorises them, except in shots taken from the air.
—V. S. Naipaul, *The Middle Passage,* 1962

where you can eat on patios under trees, in view of the royal palms and the fountain in front of the historic great house. For true Jamaican flavor, head here, as the kitchen turns out the most authentic dishes in Kingston. Appetizers include a "tidbit" of jerk pork or a bowl of soup (perhaps Jamaican red pea—really bean—or pumpkin). Main dishes include Jamaican ackee and saltfish, barbecued chicken, and curried seafood. Also tasty are unusual homemade ice creams flavored with local fruits, such as soursop. Blue Mountain tea or coffee is also served. The bars for both restaurants serve 11 different rum punches and 10 fruit punches, such as a tamarind fizz or a papaya (pawpaw) punch. Many aficionados opt for these drinks on one of the Grogg Shoppe's two different terraces, labeled "mango" or "mahogany" after nearby trees. Especially popular is the "Devon Duppy," combining into one pastel-colored glass virtually every variety of rum in the bartender's inventory.

Jade Garden

106 Hope Rd., in Sovereign Centre (north of the town center, west of National Stadium). ☎ **809/978-3476.** Reservations recommended. Main courses $8.20–$32. AE, MC, V. Daily noon–1pm. CHINESE.

The best Chinese restaurant in Kingston, Jade Garden serves well-prepared food in an elegant, formal setting. The menu is so large we wonder how they manage. The typical chow mein and chop suey dishes are here, but we'd ignore them to concentrate on the more challenging offers from the chefs. On a recent visit, the beef with oyster sauce was delectable, as was the pork with ham choy. For unusual flavors, go shopping in the "China Gems" section of the menu where you'll find some really savory offerings, including Pi Paw bean curd with chopped Chinese sausage, shrimp, black mushrooms, and water chestnuts. Also excellent is Subgum War Bar, a combination of meats sautéed with Chinese vegetables and served on a sizzling hot platter. Count on several good seafood specialties always being featured, especially deep-fried prawns stuffed with prawn mousse and served in a garlic butter sauce.

INEXPENSIVE

ⓢ Chelsea Jerk Centre

7 Chelsea Ave. (between the New Kingston Shopping Centre and the Wyndham New Kingston Hotel). ☎ **809/926-6322.** Reservations not accepted. Jerk half-chicken $3.50; pound of jerk pork $6. AE, MC, V. Mon–Thurs 11:30am–11pm, Sat–Sun 11:30am–12:30am. JAMAICAN.

Chelsea Jerk Centre is the city's most popular seller of the Jamaican delicacies jerk pork and jerk chicken. Set in a low-slung angular concrete building, it offers food to take out or to eat in the comfortably battered dining room. Although no formal appetizers are served, you might order a side portion of what the scrawled blackboard refers to as "Festival," which is fried cornmeal dumplings. The best bargain is Chelsea's Special, which is like an old-fashioned "blue plate" special at a U.S. roadside diner. It consists of rice, peas, and vegetables, along with jerked pork or chicken.

El Dorado Room

In the Terra Nova Hotel, 17 Waterloo Rd. (on the western edge of New Kingston, near West Kings House Road). ☎ **809/926-9334.** Reservations recommended. Main courses $9–$26 at lunch, $12–$26 at dinner. AE, DC, MC, V. Daily noon–2:30pm and 7–10pm. INTERNATIONAL/JAMAICAN.

Situated in one of the small, respectable hotels of Kingston (see "Where to Stay," above), this restaurant hosts a crowd of local businesspeople and dignitaries. The grandeur of the portico, the elaborate moldings of the hotel reception area, and the formal dining room are vestiges of the wealthy former owners.

The restaurant emphasizes finfish and shellfish dishes, and the chef is noted for flambé and fondues. We've found smoked marlin and Jamaican pepperpot soup to be the most tasty starters, followed by one of the specialties such as a blackened snapper, which is evocative of New Orleans kitchens. The best items may emerge from the grill, including grilled lobster or a jerk pork loin. The latter is a real "taste of Jamaica," having been marinated with herbs, then "jerked," and served with yams and honey-baked plantain. Among the seafood selections, we gravitate to the steamed ginger snapper with onions and garlic, plus a garnish of okra.

Indies Pub and Grill

8 Holborn Rd. (in New Kingston, off Hope Road). ☎ **809/926-5050**. Main courses $4.15–$17.70; pizzas $6.50–$9.90. AE, V. Mon–Wed 11am–midnight, Thurs–Sat 11am–1:30am, Sun 4pm–midnight. JAMAICAN.

Indies, an informal neighborhood restaurant across the street from the Indies Hotel (see "Where to Stay," above), was designed around a garden terrace, which on hot nights provides the best (and coolest) place to sit. You can also dine in the inner rooms, which are haphazardly but pleasantly decorated with caribou horn, tortoiseshell, half-timber walls, an aquarium sometimes stocked with baby sharks, and even a Canadian moosehead.

There's a full sandwich menu at lunchtime. In the evening you can enjoy grilled lobster, fish-and-chips, barbecued quail, chicken Kiev, or roast beef. It's a little better than standard pub grub. Pizza is a specialty. A bottle of Red Stripe, the Jamaican national beer, is the preferred beverage here.

The Hot Pot

2 Altamont Terrace. ☎ **809/929-3906**. Main courses $1.70–$3.25. V. Daily 8am–10pm. JAMAICAN.

Set within a short walk of both the Pegasus and Wyndham hotels, this is a simple local restaurant with an animated crowd of regulars and straightforward, unfussy cuisine. Within a green-and-white interior, near a view of a modest garden, you can drink Red Stripe beer or rum drinks. Menu items include red pea soup, beef stew, roast chicken, steaks, mutton, and fish. The place stays open throughout the day, serving breakfast, lunch, and dinner without interruption. The food is what you'd be served in a typical Jamaican home—nothing fancy, but satisfying and filling—and the prices are astonishingly low.

Queen of Sheba

56 Hope Rd. ☎ **809/978-0510**. Main courses $5.80–$7.80. No credit cards. Daily 10am–10pm. JAMAICAN/ETHIOPIAN.

On the grounds of the Bob Marley Museum (see "What to See & Do," below) is this Ethiopian restaurant honoring the late emperor Haile Selassie whom the Rastas view as their Messiah, a descendant of King Solomon and the Queen of Sheba (hence, the restaurant's name). On the grounds where the famous reggae star once walked—today you are likely to see his also famous son, Ziggy—you can enjoy an exotic cuisine served with equally exotic natural juices. The Jamaican dishes include beef, chicken, or fish, although most of the Ethiopian cuisine is vegetarian. Steamed fish with Ethiopian sauces is a regular feature, but it might be more appetizing to order any number of the vegetarian plates, ranging from lentils with garlic and herbs to steamed callaloo with herbs and sesame. Excellent cakes are served for dessert.

Service is slow and the staff is blasé, but as a cultural experience it's unmatched anywhere else in Kingston. Amid posters of Selassie, African art, and homages to Bob Marley, you sit on a carpeted floor, cross-legged, beneath low Ethiopian-style wooden tables.

3 What to See & Do

Even if you're staying in one of Jamaica's resort towns, such as Montego Bay or Ocho Rios, you may want to sightsee in Kingston and visit nearby Spanish Town and Port Royal. Following are notable places of interest in Kingston; Spanish Town and Port Royal are described in "Side Trips to Spanish Town & Port Royal," later in this chapter.

✪ **Devon House,** 26 Hope Rd. (☎ 809/929-6602), was built in 1881 by George Stiebel, a Jamaican who, after mining in South America, became one of the first black millionaires in the Caribbean. A striking classical building in the Georgian style, the house has been restored to its original beauty by the Jamaican National Trust. The grounds contain craft shops (see "Shopping," below), boutiques, restaurants (see "Where to Dine," above), shops that sell the best ice cream in Jamaica in exotic fruit flavors, and a bakery and pastry shop with Jamaican puddings and desserts. The main house also displays furniture of various periods and styles. Admission to Devon House is $2. The house is open Tuesday through Sunday from 10am to 5pm.

Almost next door to Devon House are the sentried gates of **Jamaica House,** residence of the country's prime minister. It is a fine, white-columned building set well back from the road.

Continuing along Hope Road, at the crossroads of Lady Musgrave Road and King's House Road, turn left and you'll see a gate on the left with its own personal traffic light. This leads to **King's House,** the official residence of the governor-general of Jamaica, the British monarch's representative on the island. The outside and front lawn of the gracious residence, set on 200 acres of well-tended parkland, is sometimes open to view Monday through Friday from 10am to 5pm. The secretarial offices are housed next door in an old wooden building set on brick arches. In front of the house is a gigantic banyan tree in whose roots, legend says, duppies (as ghosts are called in Jamaica) take refuge when they're not living in the cotton trees.

Between Old Hope Road and Mona Road, a short distance from the Botanical Gardens, is the **University of the West Indies** (☎ 809/927-1660) built in 1948 on the Mona Sugar Estate, the third of the large estates in this area. Ruins of old mills, storehouses, and aqueducts are juxtaposed with modern buildings on what may be the most beautifully situated college campus in the world. The chapel, an old sugar-factory building, was transported stone by stone from Trelawny and rebuilt on the campus close to another old sugar factory, the remains of which are well-preserved and give a good idea of how sugar was once made.

The entrance to **National Stadium,** Briggs Park, of which Jamaica is justly proud, features an aluminum statue of Arthur Wint, a national athlete. The stadium is used for soccer, field sports, and cycling. Beside the stadium is the **National Arena,** used for indoor sports, exhibitions, and concerts, and there is an Olympic-size pool. Admission prices vary according to activities.

A mile above Kingston, if you go north on Duke Street, lies **National Heroes Park,** formerly known as George VI Memorial Park. This was the old Kingston racecourse. An assortment of large office blocks, including the Ministries of Finance and Education, overlooks the park. There are statues of Simón Bolívar, of Nanny of the Maroons, and of George Gordon and Paul Bogle, martyrs of the Morant Bay revolt. Norman Manley and Alexander Bustamante, national heroes of Jamaica, are buried here, as is Sir Donald Sangster, a former prime minister.

Just north of Heroes Park, on Marescaux Road, is **Mico College** (☎ 809/929-5260), a coeducational post-secondary teacher-training institution. Lacy Mico, a rich London widow, left her fortune to a favorite nephew on the condition that he marry one of her six nieces. He did not, and the inheritance was invested, the interest being used to ransom victims of the Barbary pirates. With the end of piracy in the early 19th century, it was decided to devote the capital to founding schools for newly emancipated enslaved persons, and Mico College was established.

The central administrative offices of the **Institute of Jamaica,** founded in 1879, are between 12 and 16 East St. (☎ **809/922-0620**), close to the harbor. Open from 8:30am to 5pm Monday through Thursday, until 4pm on Friday, the institute fosters and encourages the development of culture, science, and history in the national interest. The institute has responsibility for several divisions and organizations, of which Junior Centre, the Natural History Division (repository of the national collection of flora and fauna), and the National Library are at the East Street headquarters. Those located elsewhere are the Cultural Training Centre, 1 Arthur Wint Dr., with schools of music, dance, art, and drama; the African-Caribbean Institute, 12 Ocean Blvd., which conducts research on cultural heritage; the Museums Division, with sites in Port Royal and Spanish Town, which has responsibility for the display of artifacts relevant to the history of Jamaica; the National Gallery, 12 Ocean Blvd.; and the Institute of Jamaica Publications Ltd., 2A Suthermere Rd., which publishes a quarterly, the *Jamaica Journal,* as well as other works of educational and cultural merit.

The **National Library of Jamaica** (formerly West India Reference Library), Institute of Jamaica, 12 East St. (☎ **809/922-0620**), a storehouse of the history, culture, and traditions of Jamaica and the Caribbean, is the world's finest working library for West Indian studies. It holds the most comprehensive, up-to-date, and balanced collection of materials—including books, newspapers, photographs, maps, and prints—to be found anywhere in the Caribbean. Of special interest to visitors are regular exhibitions that attractively and professionally highlight different aspects of Jamaican and West Indian life. From September through June, it is open Monday through Thursday from 9:30am to 5pm and Friday until 4pm.

Cays & Mangroves

Although close to the urban sprawl of Kingston, you can return to nature by taking a boat tour leaving from Morgan's Harbour Hotel Marina in Port Royal (call 809/967-8061 to reserve). The nearby mangroves are a natural habitat for Jamaica's bird life, especially pelicans and frigates which use the area as a breeding ground. Entirely surrounded by water, it is also an important haven for other water-loving birds and wildlife.

Close to Morgan's Harbour and the Kingston airport, the mangroves have survived hurricanes and earthquakes. Jamaican officials created a waterway, allowing small boats to enter. During this trip you can see oyster beds, fish-breeding grounds, and a wide assortment of mangroves, along with wrecks never removed from Hurricane Gilbert's visit in 1988. If you're lucky, you may even spot a pod of dolphins.

After the mangroves you're taken on a tour of some of Jamaica's most famous cays, including Lime Cay and Maiden Cay. Close to them is Gun Cay, so aptly named for the remains of cannons and large guns. Many a "bloody war" among notorious pirates were fought here.

The cost of this tour is $10, lasting 1 hour. Departures can usually be arranged at your convenience.

The **Bob Marley Museum** (formerly Tuff Gong Studio), 56 Hope Rd. (☎ 809/927-9152), is the most-visited sight in Kingston. The clapboard house, painted in Rastafarian green, yellow, and red, with its garden and high surrounding wall, was the famous reggae singer's home and recording studio until his death. The museum is open Monday, Tuesday, Thursday, and Friday from 9:30am to 4:30pm and Wednesday and Saturday from 12:30 to 5:30pm. Admission is $3.10 for adults and 40¢ for children 4 to 12, free for children 3 and under. It is reached by bus no. 70 or 75 from Halfway Tree.

4 Shopping

Downtown Kingston, the old part of the town, is centered around Sir William Grant Park, formerly Victoria Park, a showpiece of lawns, lights, and fountains. North of the park is Ward Theatre, the oldest theater in the New World, where traditional Jamaican pantomime is staged from December 26 to early April. To the east is Coke Methodist Church and to the south, the equally historic Kingston Parish Church.

Cool arcades lead off King Street, but everywhere are many people going about their business. There are some beggars and the inevitable peddlers who sidle up and offer "hot stuff, mon"—which frequently means highly polished brass lightly dipped in gold and fraudulently offered at high prices as real gold. The hucksters accept a polite but firm "no," but if you let them keep you talking, you may end up buying. They're very persuasive!

On King Street are the imposing General Post Office and the Supreme Court buildings.

ART

For many years the richly evocative paintings of Haiti were viewed as the most valuable contribution to the arts in the Caribbean basin. But there's a rapidly growing perception that Jamaica is one of the artistic leaders of the developing nations. An articulate group of Caribbean critics is focusing attention of the art world on the unusual, eclectic, and sometimes politically motivated painting produced in Jamaica.

Frame Centre Gallery
10 Tangerine Place. ☎ **809/926-4644.**

Frame Centre is one of the most important galleries in Jamaica. The founder and guiding force, Guy McIntosh, is widely respected today as a patron of Jamaican arts. Committed to presenting quality Jamaican works, the gallery has three viewing areas and carries a varied collection of more than 300 pieces. It represents both pioneer and contemporary artists, some of whom are internationally known. Younger, newer talents are always on display. Open Monday to Friday from 8:30am to 5pm, Saturday from 10am to 2pm.

Mutual Life Gallery
Mutual Life Centre, 2 Oxford Rd. ☎ **809/926-9025.**

One of Jamaica's most prominent art galleries is in the corporate headquarters of this major insurance company. After you pass a security check, you can climb to Mutual Life's mezzanine level for an insight into the changing face of Jamaican art. The gallery's exhibitions are organized by Pat Ramsay, who encourages unknowns and showcases established artists with flair. Exhibitions change once a month, but there are usually long-term exhibits as well. The Mutual Life Insurance Company donates the space as part of its effort to improve the status of Caribbean arts. The gallery is a not-for-profit institution. Open Monday to Friday from 10am to 6pm.

HANDCRAFTS

Kingston Crafts Market
At the west end of Harbour Street, downtown.

A large, covered area of individually owned small stalls, Kingston Crafts Market is reached through thoroughfares like Straw Avenue, Drummer's Lane, and Cheapside. All kinds of Jamaican crafts are on sale—wooden plates and bowls, trays, ashtrays, and pepperpots made of mahoe, the national wood. Straw hats, mats, and baskets are on display, as are batik shirts and cotton shirts with gaudy designs. Banners for wall decoration are inscribed with the Jamaican coat-of-arms, and wood masks often have elaborately carved faces. Apart from being a good place to buy worthwhile souvenirs, the market is where you can learn the art of bargaining and ask for a *brawta,* a free bonus. Open Monday to Saturday from 9am to 6pm. Sunday hours vary by stall.

The Shops at Devon House
26 Hope Rd. (at Devon House). ☎ **809/929-7029.**

Associated with one of the most beautiful and historic mansions in Jamaica, a building operated by the Jamaican National Trust, these shops ring the borders of a 200-year-old courtyard once used by slaves and servants. Although about 10 shops operate from these premises, 4 of the largest are operated by Things Jamaican, a nationwide emporium dedicated to the enhancement of the country's handcrafts. Shops include the Cookery, selling island-made sauces and spices; the Pottery, selling crockery and stoneware; and Country Crafts and The Jacaranda, both of which sell handcrafts, gifts, and furniture items. Look for pewter knives and forks, based on designs of pewter items discovered in archeological digs in the Port Royal area in 1965, and—when in inventory—reproductions of antique furniture based on items culled from historic great houses throughout the country. Open Tuesday to Saturday from 9:30am to 5pm.

LIQUOR

Sangster's Old Jamaica Spirits
17 Holborn Rd. ☎ **809/926-8888.**

Sangster's has a full array of unusual rum-based liqueurs available in this well-scrubbed factory outlet on a side street off the modern uptown New Kingston business area. The entrance isn't well-marked, but once you're in the showroom, the hundreds of bottles tell you that you're in a rum lovers' mecca. The prices vary, based on the quality and size of the container. You can purchase such tempting flavors as coconut, coffee-orange, coffee cream, and coconut cream rums, plus Blue Mountain coffee liqueurs. There's a large trolley filled with samples of rums and liqueurs, and you can sample from small cups before buying. Open Monday to Friday from 8:30am to 4:30pm.

A SHOPPING CENTER

New Kingston Shopping Centre
30 Dominica Dr., New Kingston.

One of the most modern shopping centers in Jamaica, New Kingston is known for its overall merchandise rather than for a particular merchant. It is sleek and contemporary, and stores are centered around a Maya-style pyramid, down the sides of which cascades of water irrigate trailing bougainvillea. Fast-food outlets, fashion boutiques, and shops selling many other items are here. Free concerts are often presented in the open-air theater. Open Monday to Saturday from 10am to 6pm.

5 Kingston After Dark

Kingston offers a variety of nighttime entertainment. Most entertainment is listed in the daily press, along with a host of other attractions, including colorful carnivals and festivals held islandwide throughout the year.

Caution: The city is unsafe at night. Be careful!

THE PERFORMING ARTS

Kingston is a leading cultural center of the West Indies. Notable theaters include **Ward Theatre,** on North Parade Road (☎ **809/922-0453**), and the **Little Theatre,** on Tom Redcam Drive near the National Stadium (☎ **809/926-6129**). Both stage local or imported plays and musicals, light opera, revues, and internationally acclaimed Jamaican dance and choral groups and pop concerts. Ticket prices vary. From downtown Kingston (Parade) and Cross roads, buses nos. 90A and 90B run here to the Creative Arts Centre.

THE CLUB & BAR SCENE

Red Hills Strip, a suburban area of Kingston, has a number of nightclubs, but we avoid them all like the plague.

On the other hand, the Wyndham Kingston Hotel's **Jonkanoo,** 75 Knutsford Blvd. (☎ **809/926-543**) offers a contemporary and elegant venue whose entertainment changes according to the night of the week, ranging from sports events shown on a big-screen TV to live reggae bands. There's a $6 cover charge, and beers cost $1.30. Open Tuesday to Sunday from 5pm to 2am.

6 Side Trips to Spanish Town & Port Royal

Historic Spanish Town and Port Royal can both be reached easily from Kingston, and are well worth a visit.

SPANISH TOWN

Spanish Town, some 10 miles west of Kingston, was the capital of Jamaica from 1662 to 1872, and was founded by the Spanish as Villa de la Vega. But all traces of Roman Catholicism were obliterated by Cromwell's men in 1655.

The English cathedral, surprisingly retaining a Spanish name, **St. Jago de la Vega,** was founded in 1666 and rebuilt shortly after being destroyed by a hurricane in 1712. As you drive into the town from Kingston, the ancient cathedral catches your eye, with its brick tower and two-tiered wooden steeple, added in 1831. Because the cathedral was built on the foundation and remains of the old Spanish church, it is half-English, half-Spanish, showing two definite styles—one Romanesque, the other Gothic.

Of cruciform design and built mostly of brick, St. Jago (Spanish for St. James) de la Vega is one of the most interesting historic buildings in Jamaica. The black-and-white marble stones of the aisles are interspersed with ancient tombstones, and the walls are heavy with marble memorials that almost form a chronicle of Jamaica's history, dating back as far as 1662. Episcopalian services, held regularly on Sundays at 7 and 10:30am and at 6:30pm, are sometimes conducted by the bishop of Jamaica, whose see this is.

Beyond the cathedral, turn right and go two blocks to Constitution Street and the **Town Square.** Graceful royal palms surround this little square. On the west side is Old **King's House,** residence of Jamaica's British governors until 1872, when the capital was transferred to Kingston. It hosted many celebrated guests—among them

Lord Nelson, Admiral Rodney, Captain Bligh of HMS *Bounty* fame, and King William IV stayed here. Gutted by fire in 1925, its facade has been restored.

Behind the house is the **Jamaica People's Museum of Craft & Technology,** Old King's House, Constitution Square (☎ **809/922-0620**), whose garden contains examples of old farm machinery, an old water-mill wheel, a hand-turned sugar mill, a coffee pulper, an old hearse, and a fire engine. An outbuilding houses a museum of crafts and technology, together with a number of smaller agricultural implements. In the small archeological museum are old prints, models (including one of King's House based on a written description), and maps of the town's grid layout from the 1700s. Open Monday through Thursday from 9am to 5pm, and on Friday from 9am to 4pm. Admission is $1.

On the north side of the square is the **Rodney Memorial,** the most dramatic building on the square, commissioned by a grateful assembly to commemorate the victory in 1782 of British admiral Baron George Rodney over a French fleet, which saved the island from invasion.

The remaining side of the square, the east, contains the most attractive building, the **House of Assembly,** with a shady brick colonnade running the length of the ground floor, above which is a wooden-pillared balcony. This was the stormy center of the bitter debates for Jamaica's governing body. Now the ground floor is the parish library. Council officers occupy the upper floor, along with the Mayor's Parlour, all closed to the public.

The streets around the old Town Square contain many fine Georgian town houses intermixed with tin-roofed shacks. Nearby is the market, so busy in the morning you will find it difficult, almost dangerous, to drive through. It provides a bustling scene of Jamaican life.

Driving to Spanish Town from Kingston on the A1 (Washington Boulevard), at Central Village you come to the **Arawak Museum,** on the right. It lies in the hamlet of White Marl, just outside Spanish Town. There is no phone on the premises, but it is run by the Institute of Jamaica (☎ **809/922-0620**). The entrance appears to lead to a quarry, but don't be put off. Drive down to the museum, a hexagonal building on the site of one of the largest Arawak settlements on the island. The small, well-planned museum contains drawings, pictures, and diagrams of Arawak life, plus old flints and other artifacts that help you to understand the early history of Jamaica. Tobacco smoking seems to have been a habit even in 1518, when Arawak were recorded as lighting hollow tubes at one end and sucking the other. The visitor can also see signs of an original Arawak settlement at White Marl, around the museum's main building. It is open Monday through Thursday from 10am to 5pm and Friday until 4pm. Admission is free but contributions are appreciated.

PORT ROYAL

From West Beach Dock, Kingston, a ferry ride of 20 to 30 minutes takes you across the harbor to Port Royal, which conjures up images of swashbuckling pirates, led by Henry Morgan, swilling grog in harbor taverns. Blackbeard stopped here regularly on his Caribbean trips.

The town was once one of the largest trading centers of the New World, but the whole thing came to an end at 11:43am on June 7, 1692, when a devastating earthquake shoved one-third of the town underwater. With its rich heritage, Port Royal has been designated by the government for redevelopment as a tourist attraction.

As you drive along the Palisades, you arrive first at **St. Peter's Church.** It's usually closed, but you may persuade the caretaker, who lives opposite, to open it if you want to see the silver plate, said to be a spoil captured by Henry Morgan from the

---

The Wickedest City on Earth

As the notorious pirate Henry Morgan made his way through the streets in the late 17th century, the prostitutes hustled customers, the rum flowed, and buccaneers were growing rich and sassy. The town was Port Royal, at the entrance to the world's seventh largest natural harbor. It was filled with drinking parlors, gambling dens, billiard rooms, brothels, and joints offering entertainment such as cock fights, target shoots, and bear baiting. Buccaneers not only got drunk—they fought duels and pursued "foul vices" after long months at sea. All this earned for Port Royal the title of "The Wickedest City on Earth."

All this came to a thundering end on the hot morning of June 7, 1692. Without warning, a severe earthquake sunk most of the town, killing some 2,000 people. The skies turned copper over this once-vibrant pirate city. To this day it is known as the famous "Sunken City" of Port Royal.

Today Port Royal is a small fishing village at the end of the Palisades strip. Some 2,000 residents—and a lot of ghosts—live here. Its seafaring traditions continue, and the town is famous for both its fresh seafood and quaint architecture of old days. Once there were six forts here with a total of 145 guns; some of the guns remain today, but only Fort Charles still stands.

Actually, the 1692 earthquake was only one of nine that descended upon Port Royal. And that's not all: 16 of the worst hurricanes to hit the Caribbean and three devastating fires ravaged the town. It's a wonder anything is still standing today.

Norman Manley International Airport shares the same thin peninsula with Port Royal, but otherwise, all is quiet in the town today. It's easy to conjure up images not only of Morgan but of another buccaneer, Roche Brasiliano, who liked to roast Spaniards alive. To celebrate he'd break out a keg of wine on the streets of Port Royal; whether they wanted to or not, he forced passersby to have a drink with him at gunpoint.

What happened to Henry Morgan after piracy was outlawed here in 1681? He was knighted in England and sent back to arrest his old hell-raising mateys.

---

cathedral in Panama. In the ill-kept graveyard is the tomb of one Lewis Galdy, a Frenchman swallowed up and subsequently regurgitated by the 1692 earthquake.

Fort Charles, the only one of Port Royal's six forts still standing, has withstood attack, earthquake, fire, and hurricane. Built in 1656 and later strengthened by Morgan for his own purposes, the fort was expanded and further armed in the 1700s, until its firepower boasted more than 100 cannons, covering both land and sea approaches. After subsequent earthquakes and tremors, the fort ceased to be at the water's edge and is now well inland. In 1779 Britain's naval hero, Lord Horatio Nelson, commanded the fort and trod the wooden walkway inside the western parapet as he kept watch for the French invasion fleet. It is administered by the Institute of Jamaica (☎ **809/922-0620**).

Giddy House, once the Royal Artillery storehouse and part of the Fort Charles complex, is another example of what earthquakes can do. Walking across its tilted floor is an eerie and strangely disorienting experience.

Fort Charles Maritime Museum (☎ **809/924-8782**) is in the former British naval headquarters where Nelson served. Scale models of the fort and ships of past eras are in this small museum. Open daily from 9:30am to 5:30pm. Admission is $2 for adults, $1 for children.

At Morgan's Harbour in Port Royal, **Buccaneer Scuba Club** (☎ **809/924-8148**) is one of Jamaica's leading dive and water sports operators. It offers a wide range of dive sites to accommodate various divers' tastes—from the incredible *Texas Wreck* to the unspoiled beauty of the Turtle Reef. PADI courses are also available. There's also a wide array of water sports offered including waterskiing, body-boarding, ring-skiing, and even a banana boat ride. One-tank dives cost from $35, and the other sports mentioned are $15 per person for 15 minutes.

WHERE TO STAY

Morgan's Harbour Hotel and Beach Club

Port Royal, Kingston 1, Jamaica, W.I. ☎ **809/967-8030**, or 800/44-UTELL in the U.S. Fax 809/967-8073. 50 rms, 6 suites. A/C MINIBAR TV TEL. $159 double; $184–$306 suite. AE, MC, V. Free parking. A public ferryboat (5¢ per person) departs every 2 hours from Victoria Pier on Ocean Blvd. Many visitors arrive by car or taxi, or pay $12 for the hotel's private boat to fetch them from any of the piers in downtown Kingston.

This is the most visible building within the historic ruin of Port Royal, once known as "the wickedest city on earth." Rebuilt after Hurricane Gilbert in 1988, Morgan's lies near the end of a long sandspit whose rocky and scrub-covered length shelters the harbor of Kingston. Set on 22 acres of this flat seashore, the resort has the largest marina facility around Kingston and a swimming area carefully defined by docks and buoys. On the premises is a 200-year-old red-brick building originally constructed to melt pitch for sailing ships of His Majesty's navy. The hotel has a rambling series of wings whose eaves are accented with hints of neo-Victorian gingerbread. The resort contains a breezy and popular restaurant, Henry Morgan's, where ghost stories about old Port Royal seem especially lurid as the liquor flows on Friday nights.

The hotel rents well-furnished bedrooms, each with furniture whose design is derived in part from an 18th-century Chippendale-Jamaican motif. The Buccaneer Scuba Club is on site, organizing dives to some of the 170-odd wrecks lying close to shore. Deep-sea fishing charters and trips to outlying cays can also be arranged.

WHERE TO DINE

Sir Henry Morgan's Restaurant

In Morgan's Harbour Hotel and Beach Club, Port Royal. ☎ **809/967-8075.** Main courses $5.80–$26 at lunch, $8.45–$26 at dinner. AE, MC, V. Daily noon–3pm and 7–10:30pm. INTERNATIONAL/JAMAICAN.

The bar and restaurant offer guests both a Jamaican and international cuisine, with panoramic views over Kingston Bay and the Blue Mountains. Except for the elegant lobster or seafood salad, lunch is a relatively simple affair. You can order various sandwiches and desserts, along with a daily luncheon special, a traditional Jamaican dish. The catch of the day is steamed or fried. You get more of a choice at dinner; your best bet is either the fresh Jamaican lobster which can be prepared in a number of ways—everything from thermidor to grilled with garlic butter. The traditional Jamaican pepper steak, with hot and sweet peppers, is excellent, as is the selection of homemade ice creams to finish your meal.

7 Exploring the Blue Mountains

Jamaica has some of the most varied and unusual topography of any island in the Caribbean. Part of its appeal to 18th-century mariners derived from its ample amounts of fresh water, which pours in the form of rivers, streams, and waterfalls, from the heights of a mountain ridge appropriately named the Blue Mountains.

These lie within the 192-acre Blue Mountain–John Crow Mountain National Park, which is maintained by the Jamaican government.

They provide a rich environment for coffee production, producing a blended version that is among Jamaica's leading and most expensive exports. But for the nature enthusiast, the mountains reveal an astonishingly complex series of eco-systems which change radically as a trekker climbs from sea level to the mountain's fog-shrouded peaks.

The most popular climb begins at Whitfield Hall, a high-altitude hostel and coffee estate about 6 miles from the hamlet of Mavis Bank near Kingston (see "Where to Stay" in this chapater). The summit of Blue Mountain Peak (3,000 feet above sea level) requires from between 5 and 6 hours, each way, to reach it. En route, hikers pass through acres of coffee plantations and forest, where temperatures are cooler (sometimes much cooler) than one might have expected, and where high humidity encourages a rampant growth of vegetation. Bird life en route includes hummingbirds, many species of warblers, rufous-throated solitaires, yellow-bellied sapsuckers, and Greater Antillean pewees.

The best preparation for the wide ranges of temperature you'll encounter is to dress in layers. Carry a soft-sided rucksack for storage, and bring some bottled water. Take a flashlight if you opt for a 2am departure in anticipation of watching the sunrise from atop the peak. Sneakers are usually adequate, although many climbers bring their hiking boots to Jamaica solely in anticipation of their trek up Blue Mountain. Be aware that even during the "dry" season (from December to March) rainfall is common. During the "rainy" season (the rest of the year), these peaks can receive up to 150 inches of rainfall a year, and fogs and mists are frequent.

Considering the social unrest in Jamaica, and the tendency for hiking paths to become obscured by vegetation and tropical storms, it's a very wise idea to hire a guide for your ascent of the mountain. Worthy contenders include **Sunventure Tours** (☎ 809/929-5694), and **SENSE Adventures Ltd.** (☎ 809/927-1097), operating out of Kingston. Depending on the time of departure (that is, day or night), and the accoutrements which are included, the price of a guide for a trek up Blue Mountain ranges from $50 to $150 per person.

WHERE TO STAY

✪ Strawberry Hill

Irish Town, Blue Mountains, Jamaica, W.I. ☎ **809/944-8400** or 800/OUTPOST. Fax 809/944-8408. 18 rms in one-, two-, and three-bedroom units. A/C. Winter (including continental breakfast) $250–$775 double; off-season $175–$575 double. AE, DC, MC, V. Guests are personally escorted to the hotel in a customized van or via a 7-minute helicopter ride.

The area's best place to stay, Strawberry Hill sits 3,100 feet up in the Blue Mountains overlooking the turbulent city. Kingston seems far removed from this lush, botanical-garden setting, which is a 50-minute drive from the Kingston airport or 30 minutes (15 miles) via mountain roads from the center of the city.

A self-contained facility with its own power and water purification system, this cottage complex was built on the site of a 1600s great house which Hurricane Gilbert destroyed in 1988. The property was conceived by multimillionaire Chris Blackwell, the impresario whose Island Records launched reggae's Bob Marley into worldwide fame. One former guest found this all-inclusive establishment to be a "home-away-from-home for five-star Robinson Crusoes." Local craftspeople fashioned the cottages and furnished them in a classic plantation style, with canopied four-poster beds and louvered windows. In one case, a doorway was carved with figures inspired by Madonna's book *Sex.*

Activities include coffee-plantation tours, hiking and mountain biking through the Blue Mountains, and even such spa services as massages and aroma therapy.

Dining/Entertainment: Better than anything you'll find in Kingston, the "new Jamaican cuisine" here includes such local dishes as curried cho-cho soup with grilled shrimp and fresh cilantro, fresh grilled fish with jerk mango and sweet pepper salsa, or sweet potatoes and dasheen gnocchi with roasted leeks and callaloo in a herby lime cream sauce.

Whitfield Hall

c/o John Allgrove, 8 Armon Jones Crescent, Kingston 6, Jamaica, W.I. ☎ **809/927-0986.** 7 rms (none with bath), 2-bedroom cottage. $12 per person; $50 cottage for up to 4. No credit cards. See below for directions.

One of the most isolated places in Jamaica, this hostel is located more than halfway up Blue Mountain at some 4,000 feet above sea level. The main allure here is the opportunity to see the Blue Mountains from a hillclimber's point of view. Whitfield Hall is a coffee plantation dating from 1776, and it is the last inhabited house from that period. It provides basic accommodation for 30 guests in rooms containing two or more beds. Blankets and linen are provided, but personal items, such as towels, soap, and food, are not. There is no restaurant, but there's a deep freeze, a refrigerator, and good cooking facilities including crockery and cutlery. All water comes from a spring, and lighting is by kerosene pressure lamps called Tilleys. A wood fire warms the hostel and its guests, for it gets cold in the mountains at night. You bring your own food and share the kitchen.

To get there, you can drive to Mavis Bank, about 20 miles from Kingston. Head northeast along Old Hope Road to the suburb of Papine, then proceed to Gordon Town. At Gordon Town, turn right over the bridge near the police station, and drive into the hills for some 10 miles until you reach Mavis Bank. You can also reach Mavis Bank by bus from the Kingston suburb of Papine. The bus departs from the northeast edge of town, at the end of Old Hope Road. Mavis Bank is the terminus of this bus line. Transportation from Mavis Bank to Whitefield costs $20 each way. Most guests simplify matters by requesting pickup in Kingston by the hostel's Land Rover, which costs $40 each way for up to six passengers.

WHERE TO DINE

✪ Blue Mountain Inn

Gordon Town Road. ☎ **809/927-1700.** Reservations and jackets for men required. Main courses $17.60–$41.60. AE, DC, MC, V. Daily 7–11pm. Head north on Old Hope Road, into the mountains. CARIBBEAN/SEAFOOD/STEAK.

About a 20-minute drive from downtown Kingston, this 18th-century coffee-plantation house sits high on the slopes of Blue Mountain, surrounded by trees and flowers on the bank of the Mammee River. Blue Mountain Inn is one of Jamaica's most famous restaurants, not only for food but also for atmosphere and service. Log fires blaze on cold nights, and the dining room gleams with silver and sparkling glass under the discreet table lights.

Menus change monthly and feature Caribbean dishes, fresh seafood, and U.S. steaks, all served with a selection of fresh vegetables. Examples might include New Orleans bourbon and garlic shrimp, chicken Kiev, or an array of lobster dishes. Top off your meal with tropical fruit salad and ice cream, Tía Maria parfait, baked Alaska, or a more ambitious banana or pineapple flambé. The menu is decidedly old fashioned but still alluring after many years. The wine list includes European varieties together with local beverages.

Getting to Know Barbados

8

In 1751 a young American major named George Washington visited Barbados with his half-brother, Lawrence, who had developed tuberculosis. Regrettably, the future American president contracted smallpox here, and it left him marked for life. Barbados is said to have been the only place outside the United States that George Washington ever visited.

In the 19th century Barbados became famous as the sanatorium of the West Indies. Mainly British guests suffering from "the vapors" came here for the perfect climate and the relaxed, unhurried life.

The smallpox danger long gone, Barbados remains salubrious to the spirit, with its lush vegetation, its coral reefs, and its seemingly endless miles of pink-and-white sandy beaches. The most easterly of the long chain of Caribbean islands, it retains old-world charm, an imprint of grace and courtesy left from 300 years of British tradition.

Barbados is renowned for its hospitable people. In a way, Barbados is like an England in the tropics, with bandbox cottages set in neat little gardens, centuries-old parish churches, and a scenic, hilly area in the northeast known as the Scotland District, where a mist rises in the morning. Narrow roads ramble through the sugarcane fields trimmed with hedgerows. In Barbados, sugar is king, and rum is queen.

1 The Regions in Brief

An uplifted coral island, Barbados is flat, especially when compared to the wild, volcanic terrain of the Antilles. It is about 21 miles long and 14 miles wide, with an area of 166 square miles. Barbados lies 200 miles from Trinidad, 1,610 miles southeast of Miami, 575 miles southeast of Puerto Rico, and 600 miles northeast of Caracas, Venezuela. Most hotels are on the western side, a sandy shoreline. The eastern side, fronting the Atlantic, is a breezy coastline lapped by white-capped rollers. Experienced surfers like it, but it's not safe for amateur swimmers.

The beaches of Barbados are among the most beautiful in the Caribbean, and all open to the public. White sandy beaches start in the north at Hey at the Almond Beach Club—about a mile of sand—and continue almost unbroken to Brighton Beach, a local favorite, in the south. Needham's Point, with a lighthouse, is the one

What's Special About Barbados

Beaches
- Paynes Bay, almost everyone's favorite West Coast beach, with plenty of white sand and one of the island's prettiest bays. Good for snorkeling and water sports.
- The Beaches at Fresh Water Bay, directly south of Paynes Bay, include Brighton Beach, Paradise Beach, and Brandon's Beach. These three are the pick of the litter, but they're so good and so well-known that they are likely to be overcrowded.
- Church Point, north of St. James Church, also on the West Coast. One of the most scenic bays in Barbados, with some of the best swimming.
- Casuarina Beach, a wide stretch of sand with lots of trade winds churning up the biggest waves along the South Coast, making it a haven for windsurfers.
- Sandy Beach, another South Coast favorite, especially of families with young children. They're drawn to the shallow and tranquil waters and the Blue Lagoon atmosphere.
- Crane Beach, on the southwest coast. Set against cliffs and dunes, the pink-tinged sands make this a favorite of many locals and sometimes-visitor Prince Andrew, who has a house overlooking the beach. The seas, however, can be rough at times.

Great Towns/Villages
- Bridgetown, the capital, with colonial buildings, modern offices, and a statue of Horatio (Lord Nelson), its most-photographed landmark.
- Holetown, a small old St. James coast village that's near the site of the first settlement. The ship *Olive Blossom* landed here on May 14, 1625, and the island was claimed in the name of James I of England. Then, on February 17, 1627, the vessel *William and John* arrived with settlers.

Memorable Sights
- The Gold Coast, a nickname for the gilded shoreline of St. Peter and St. James, site of posh hotels and homes of the wintering wealthy.
- Harrison's Cave, magnificent caverns graced with underground pools, waterfalls, and streams, and an array of crystal chambers.
- Barbados Wildlife Reserve, home of the rare green monkey, believed to have been imported from West Africa 300 years ago. Deer, exotic birds, and tortoises live in this mahogany forest.

Parks and Gardens
- Farley Hill, a national park dedicated by Queen Elizabeth II—rich with exotic planting.
- Andromeda Tropical Gardens, a showplace of the Caribbean, noted for terraces of lush tropical plants gathered from all over the world.

An Ancient Monument
- St. Nicholas Abbey (ca. 1650), near Cherry Tree Hill, the oldest great house in Barbados. Known for its Jacobean architecture and antiques.

of the most typical beaches on the heavily built-up South Coast. Local beach lovers flock here on weekends, although we have other favorites.

The island is divided, for administrative purposes, into several parishes. The most interesting for visitors include the following:

Bridgetown & St. Michael   On the southwestern corner of the island, the capital **Bridgetown** is small but pulsating with life—in fact, it's one of the liveliest capitals in the Caribbean, although there's nowhere near the activity (or danger) of bustling Kingston, Jamaica. Colonial buildings and contemporary office blocks go hand and hand—for some, mere backdrops to the vendors hawking their wares. The city is reached by two bridges, both in the east, including one spanning the Constitution River (it's not actually a river) and Chamberlin Bridge, which will take you to the waterfront, called the Careenage.

The surrounding **parish of St. Michael** traditionally has been the hub of Bajan business activity and culture. Although Barbados has far more interesting parishes from a traveler's point of view, St. Michael is visited for shopping in Bridgetown and for its **Barbados Museum,** directly south of Bridgetown. Standing across the street from the museum is **Garrison Savannah,** one of the finest parade grounds in the Caribbean.

St. James (Gold Coast)   This is the heart of the West Coast tourist district, sometimes referred to as the Gold Goast or the Platinum Coast. Most of its posh tourist establishments stretch along Highway 1, which runs up the west coast from Bridgetown. Nearly all the deluxe resorts are found here, including the Colony Club; the rich and famous have hung out at Sandy Lane. Over the years everyone from Princess Margaret to Mick Jagger, from Jacqueline Onasis to permanent resident Claudette Colbert have passed along this coast's too-narrow highway. The parish embraces some of the best beaches along the coast and the town of **Holetown,** where an obelisk marks the spot where the British ship *Olive Blossom* landed the first settlers in 1627.

St. Peter   Wedged between the Gold Coast to the south and seldom-visited St. Lucy parish at the top of the island, St. Peter spans Barbados and opens onto the Caribbean Sea in the west and the Atlantic Ocean in the east. Many of the finest homes on the island are found here, along with such tourist attractions as **St. Nicholas Abbey, Farley Hill National Park,** and **Barbados Wildlife Reserve,** home of the rare green monkey. It is also home to the town of **Speightstown,** once a major sugar port and now a fishing center with a bustling waterfront, old houses, and restored **Church of St. Peter's.** People in the north of the island do their shopping in Speightstown.

Christ Church   South and east of Bridgetown, the southernmost parish of Christ Church embraces **Oistins,** the fishing capital of the island, and **Hastings** and **Worthing,** where you will find many of the least expensive accommodations and restaurants on Barbados. Accordingly, Christ Church attracts vacationers of more modest means than does posh St. James/Gold Coast. It has a string of white sandy beaches and a surf that lures windsurfers from around the world. The parish is also a center of commercial activity, although nothing to equal that of St. Michael.

St. Philip   In the southeastern corner of Barbados, bordered by Christ Church in the west and St. John to the north, St. Philip geographically is the biggest parish in Barbados. It is a long way from Bridgetown, however, so it has been allowed to sleep. Since it borders the rough Atlantic Ocean—not the tranquil Caribbean Sea— it hasn't been overtaken by developers' bulldozers. It is visited mainly by travelers who want to see **Sam Lord's Castle,** one of the major attractions of Barbados. However, developers are coming in fast, so you'd better go now before its rural charms disappear.

St. John   Site of the east coast sugar plantations, St. John is home to **Hackleton's Cliff,** which at 1,000 feet offers some of the most panoramic Atlantic Ocean vistas. In many ways, this is the most ideal parish for wandering about, or even getting lost.

Barbados

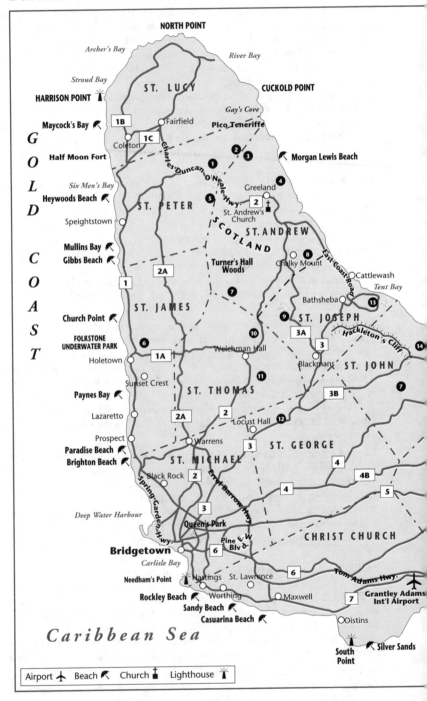

Caribbean Islands

Barbados

Andromeda
  Botanical Gardens ⑬
Barbados Wildlife Reserve ❶
Chalky Mount Potteries ❽
Cherry Tree Hill ❸
Codrington College ⑮
Farley Hill National Park ❺
Flower Forest
  of Barbados ❾
Gun Hill Signal Station ⑫
Harrison's Cave ⑪
Morgan Lewis Sugar
  Windmill & Museum ❹
Sam Lord's Castle ⑯
St. James Church ❻
St. John's Church ⑭
St. Nicholas Abbey ❷
Sunbury Plantation House ⑰
Villa Nova ❼
Welchman Hall Gully ⑩

Atlantic Ocean

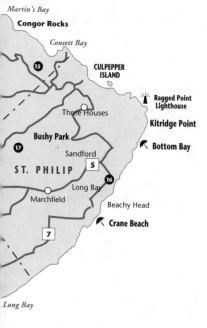

Martin's Bay
Congor Rocks

Consett Bay

⑮

**CULPEPPER
ISLAND**

*Ragged Point
Lighthouse*

Three Houses

Kitridge Point

Bushy Park

⑰   Sandford

ST. PHILIP   ❺

          ⑯

Bottom Bay

Long Bay

Marchfield

Beachy Head

❼   **Crane Beach**

Long Bay

0 ▬▬▬ 3 km
        1.9 mi

N

There's always something to discover down every road. Highways 4 and 3B split through the parish. Follow 3B to **St. John's Paris Church,** set upon a cliff fronting the Atlantic. One of the major attractions here is **Villa Nova,** which was visited by Queen Elizabeth II and Prince Philip.

St. Joseph   Windswept St. Joseph, in the middle of the east coast, is the site of **"Little Scotland,"** with rolling hills, tiny hamlets, grazing sheep, and valleys. Its main target is the fishing village of **Bathsheba** and nearby **Tent Bay,** major destinations for both visitors and Bajans, who head here for Sunday picnics at the beach. Visitors often pass through here heading for lunch at the world-famous (although extremely modest) **Atlantic Hotel.** The parish is also the site of **St. Joseph Anglican Church,** above Horse Hill, and **Andromeda Gardens,** one of the island's choice beauty spots.

St. Thomas   To the west of St. James, this landlocked parish lies in the heart of the island. It is traversed by Routes 2 and 2A from St. Michael, and Route 1A coming from St. James. The major attractions here are natural wonders such as **Welchman Hall Gully** and **Harrison's Caves** (more about these attractions later). **Bagatelle Great House** is your best choice for a restaurant stopover.

St. Andrew   With a small population—unique on overpopulated Barbados—this parish still maintains a lot of its rustic charm characterized by hills and dales. It lies directly northwest of St. Joseph. It has many attractions to lure visitors, including **Cherry Tree Hill** and **Chalky Mount Village,** where residents live mainly in wooden houses and earn their living making pottery.

2 Barbados Today

The Human Development Report of the United Nations in 1993 placed Barbados first among all developing nations in the world—the third time in a row that the island nation had received that distinction. This was a long overdue acknowledgment that Barbados is one of the most cosmopolitan and sophisticated destinations in the West Indies.

Its hotel and restaurant boom has been phenomenal—almost too phenomenal for some, especially restaurateurs facing empty dining rooms because of the severe competition, or hoteliers with empty rooms at certain slow periods of the year.

By Caribbean standards, unemployment remains reasonably low (but don't tell that to someone out of work); the government is stable; and business is always paramount. Visitors are genuinely welcomed by most of the population, and you won't be confronted with the awful poverty of some destinations, although most Bajans are far from rich (most live in small wooden houses).

A very British but not stuffy atmosphere prevails. Only Sandy Hotel, a deluxe hotel, maintains a more straightlaced British ambience.

Barbados has been independent since 1966, but it's never completely eradicated the former influence of empire—it just doesn't want to. Although most people on the island opted for independence, British customs remain: cricket games, afternoon tea, Nelson's statue on Trafalgar Square in Bridgetown, and even the island's system of education, justice, and government, all led by a prime minister.

Barbados doesn't have the turmoil and strife of Jamaica, and certainly not the violence. For that reason, it remains in the vanguard of islands attracting visitors to its shores. Crime is on the rise, but it's mainly in the form of petty robberies and muggings. Violent attacks on tourists continue to be rare. Even through the island is hardly perfect or free of problems, it remains one of the more tranquil destinations in the Caribbean, especially for a nation with such a large population.

3   History 101

The first known inhabitants of Barbados were the Arawak, who immigrated from South America some 400 years before the birth of Christ. They had disappeared by A.D. 1200, perhaps wiped out by the Carib, who dominated Barbados for 300 years.

All Indians had disappeared by the time the first British expedition arrived in 1625, claiming the island for England. The British found only wild hogs left by early Portuguese explorers. A Portuguese navigator, Pedro a Camoes, had come ashore in 1536 and named the island Los Barbados, "the bearded ones," after the shaggy fig trees along the shoreline. He did not establish a settlement.

On February 17, 1627, a ship called *William and John,* captained by Henry Powell, brought 80 Englishmen and 10 Africans (captured from a Spanish galleon) to the west coast of Barbados. This landing is celebrated annually at the Holetown Festival. The early settlers imported about 40 Arawak to teach them how to cultivate Caribbean crops.

To the British, Barbados was reminiscent of the rolling downs of Cornwall and Devon. They soon turned the island into a Little England, tropical style. It became the most British colony in the New World, never having existed under any other flag. In 1639 a parliament along English lines was established, and the island was divided into the 11 parishes that exist today.

A thriving colony of Europeans and African slaves, predominantly male, turned Barbados into a prosperous land, based on trading in tobacco and cotton. By the 1640s, sugarcane production, an industry established by Sir James Drax, dominated the economy. More and more slaves were imported to work these sugar plantations.

Many English families settled here in the 18th and 19th centuries, in spite of outbreaks of yellow fever and intermittent wars. Because of the early importation of so many black laborers, Barbados is the most densely populated of the West Indian islands. No English-speaking visitor ever achieved the fame of George Washington, who arrived in 1751 on his only overseas trip. He promptly caught smallpox.

In 1766, a raging fire—a curse of the Caribbean—struck Bridgetown, destroying most of the capital. A monstrous hurricane devastated the island in 1780.

Dateline

- **1625** First English landing in Barbados at Holetown.
- **1627** First English settlement established near Holetown.
- **1639** First legislature established.
- **1640** Sugar industry begun by Sir James Drax.
- **1751** George Washington visits Barbados on his only overseas trip, catches smallpox.
- **1766** Bridgetown destroyed by fire.
- **1834** Slavery abolished.
- **1838** Complete freedom granted to former slaves.
- **1876** Black Bajans riot.
- **1884** Franchise Act passed.
- **1905** British garrison withdraws.
- **1937** Island-wide riots erupt.
- **1938** Grantley H. Adams heads Barbados Labour Party.
- **1962** West Indies Federation dissolves after four years.
- **1966** Barbados becomes independent nation in the Commonwealth of Nations. Country joins United Nations.
- **1967** Barbados joins Organization of American States.
- **1973** First Barbados national currency issued.
- **1982** U.S. President and Mrs. Ronald Reagan visit Barbados.
- **1985** Prime Minister J. M. G. M. Tom Adams dies in office.
- **1986** Errol Barrow becomes prime minister for second time.
- **1987** Barrow dies in office, L. Erskine Sandiford becomes prime minister.
- **1989** 350th anniversary of Barbados Parliament observed.
- **1991** 25th anniversary of independence observed.

Once Barbados was the most heavily defended fortress island in the Caribbean, with 26 forts ringing its 21 miles of coast. Perhaps for that reason, the island was never invaded by another nation.

Slavery was abolished in 1834, and by 1838 complete freedom had been granted to former slaves. Their descendants would eventually take over the island politically. Of the original English settlers, about 20 of their families dominated the island's history and economic development during the early colonial period. Descendants of many of these families still rank among the island's elite and heavily influence its cultural life. Some of their beautiful and well-preserved plantation houses bear witness to the pattern of English country life they re-created in Barbados.

Although black and white Bajans live in relative peace today, that was not always the case. For example, in the spring of 1876 riots erupted as black Bajans protested against the rule of the white "plantocracy." That riot ended with eight dead and 400 in jail. One of the injustices the Bajans protested was that only 1,300 of the island's 160,000 inhabitants were eligible to vote.

The constitution was amended in 1884 with a Franchise Act that allowed people who owned less land to vote in elections. Many of the island's nonwhites still did not qualify, however, since whites owned 90% of the land.

Barbadians emigrated to avoid the harsh conditions on the island, thousands going to Central America to help build the Panama Canal. The sugar industry had deteriorated into a depressed state by this time.

In 1905 the last of the British garrison left Barbados, although the island was still decades away from independence.

Riots in the streets continued in the years between the world wars, notably in 1937 when unrest lasted for 3 days. Fields were raided and shops broken into. These disturbances led to social change and the first lasting labor parties.

Much of the social and political change was directed by Grantley H. Adams, who from 1938 to 1945 was a spokesman for most people on the island. Adams headed the Barbados Labour Party. His first victory came in 1940, when the Labour Party won five seats in the House of Assembly.

Adams represented Barbados at the 1958 inauguration of the Federation of the West Indies, and served as its prime minister. The federation never really gained political clout, and it came to an end in 1962.

In 1961 Barbados was run by Errol Barrow, who succeeded Adams as prime minister of Barbados. His liberal Democratic Labour Party (DLP) carried out a number of public works programs.

Barrow led the island to independence on November 30, 1966. Barbados was now a sovereign state in the Commonwealth of Nations, and the little island entered the United Nations. Barrow was the first prime minister. The following year, Barbados joined the Organization of American States, and by 1973 the island issued its own currency. Barrow served for more than a decade as prime minister.

J. M. G. M. Tom Adams, son of Grantley Adams, led Barbados into the 1980s. In 1985, however, Adams died in office. Barrow became prime minister for the second time in 1986, but he died in office the following year. L. Erskine Sandiford then became prime minister. Sandiford's DLP won a strong parliamentary majority in elections in 1991, and he continued as prime minister.

In 1989, Barbados observed the 350th anniversary of the establishment of its parliament, and in 1991 festivities marked the 25th anniversary of island independence.

In the early 1990s Barbados had a population of about 255,000, almost all of whom were at least partly of black African descent. The yearly birth rate was 16 per 1,000 people, while the yearly death rate was 9 per 1,000 people. Life expectancy at birth was 76 years for females and 70 years for males. There was an annual migration out of Barbados of 6 persons per 1,000 inhabitants.

In the same period, the Barbados economy was growing, but the unemployment rate was high. Leading industries were tourism, farming (principally sugarcane), fishing, light manufacturing (notably clothing, furniture, electronic equipment, and medical supplies), and financial services (including "offshore" financial institutions).

4 Bajan Religion & Folklore

About 40% of the island's population is Anglican. In addition, there are many other Christian denominations and sects, including Pentecostal, Methodist, Moravian, and Roman Catholic. There are small groups of Muslims, Jews, and Hindus.

That wasn't the case when the first Bajans, as the island's residents are known, were brought in slavery from West Africa, carrying with them their folk traditions, tales, and beliefs, which in the absence of writing were orally passed from generation to generation.

Sometimes African gods, such as Shango, were kept alive, enjoying cult status. West African folktales, the Anancy stories (similar to the tradition of Jamaica) were the tall tales told on dark nights. *Obeah* (witchcraft) and *voodoo* spread fear among the local slaves who whispered tales of power and magic. Many early folktales concerned the ability of some people to transform themselves into animals, such as donkeys.

Grandmothers pass on to their offspring stories of *duppies*, or spirits of deceased persons. A *Conrad* is said to take possession of someone's body, forcing the person to do mean things against their neighbors. The Conrad is like a ghost returning to earth to seek revenge for some past wrong that happened to it in life.

The dreaded *heartmen* are reputed to appear at sugarcane harvest time. They are accused of killing young Bajan children and presenting their hearts to the devil as a kind of trophy.

The *baccoo* is one of the more mysterious creatures, a little man who, it is claimed, can live in a bottle. The baccoo can be either good or evil, depending on how he is treated.

Because of the strong and unifying role of western religions on the island, folklore and various superstitions are not as strong as they once were, but they still exist. Today, young Bajan writers record early folk tradition, and West Indian folklore stories are broadcast regularly over the radio.

5 Local Arts & Crafts

Just as the slaves brought many of their traditions and lore to Barbados from Africa, so too is that continent still evident in much the island's present-day arts and crafts. Rastafarian craftspeople turn out items made from clay, wood, leather, and straw. Sometimes the line between what is art and what is craft becomes blurred, however, since many items produced on the island, including images of local birds or fish, are little more than tourist souvenirs. On the other hand, purses, shoes, leather bags, and other items have more use.

The majority of craftspeople display their wares at Pelican Village (see "Shopping" in Chapter 11). Some of the finest works of Bajan artists is displayed there in the art gallery of the Barbados Art Council, which might be your best introduction to the art of Barbados. Bajan art is not as well-known as the art of Haiti and Jamaica, but it is a movement attracting new artists every year.

Miss Rachel & the Prince

Rachel Pringle was born in 1753, the daughter of a schoolmaster from Scotland, William Lauder, and his slave mistress. According to reports of the day, Lauder was vicious to Rachel and mistreated her. Fleeing from his tyrannical household, Rachel was aided by Captain Thomas Pringle, who took a fancy to her and paid an awesome sum to Lauder for her freedom. When the captain installed his new "sex toy" in a house in Bridgetown, Rachel took his name.

The captain wanted a child by his new mistress but she apparently couldn't have one; their liaison remained fruitless. When Pringle sailed away on a voyage, however, Rachel decided to pretend she was pregnant. During his absence, she borrowed a child from another Bajan woman. When Pringle returned home, she presented him with "his" newborn. Pringle accepted the child as his own—until its mother showed up to reclaim her baby. Infuriated with Rachel's deception, Pringle walked out on her.

Ever resourceful, Rachel didn't waste time finding herself another "guardian," a man known only as Polgreen. Taverns on the island were often run by mulatto women who were actually the paramours of the island's wealthy, so sometime in the 1780s Rachel launched the island's first hotel. Now long gone but originally on St. George Street, her ill-reputed establishment quickly became popular with the British Royal Navy.

Her most prominent guest—or should we say client—was Prince William Henry. The prince in the 1780s wasn't the staid figure he later became as King William IV. Fueled by Barbados rum, he joined in a night of hell-raising debauchery, smashing furniture and breaking the plates. At one point the future king turned over Rachel's chair, sending her sprawling onto the floor.

Before the prince sailed away, she presented his future Highness with a bill for 700 British pounds. That was an awful lot of money back then, but surprisingly, William Henry agreed to pay.

Rachel used the money to restore her establishment and renamed it the Royal Naval Hotel. Its reputation and clientele remained unchanged, but during her lifetime this hot bed hotel made the enormously fat Miss Rachel a good living entertaining the pride of the British fleet.

Chief among the Bajan artists who have distinguished themselves in the West Indies is Karl Broodhagen, whose Bridgetown sculpture *The Freed Slave* is his best-known work, celebrating the 150th anniversary of emancipation.

The overseer of Bajan handcrafts is the Industrial Development Corporation, which has a Handicraft Sales Shop at Pelican Village and at Grantley Adams International Airport, among other outlets. The best of island handcrafts is displayed at its shops. IDC also has training workshops for young Bajans wanting to enter the field.

Barbados has long had a distinguished reputation for its clay pottery. Originally items such as pots or lamps were intended for island consumption, but today visitors also can purchase pottery to take home. Pottery displays of various craftspeople can be seen at Pelican Village.

Bajans have also entered the West Indies fashion market, with batik and silk-screen dressings, some of which have been discovered by U.S. fashion magazines. Fabrics are sometimes turned into artistic statements in the form of wall hangings. Jill Walker prints are particularly sought after (see Walker's Caribbean World under "Shopping" in Chapter 11). Walker's prints represent island life, sometimes satirically.

The National Cultural Foundation often organizes art exhibits at the Queen's Park Gallery (see "Shopping" in Chapter 11).

6 Bajan Architecture

Many of the historic buildings and homes of Barbados—products of European colonization—have long since disappeared. Some were simply torn down to make way for less distinguished structures, and others were destroyed by nature, such as the great hurricane of 1780. Most remaining distinguished buildings are either Georgian or Victorian, but at least eight 17th-century great houses remain.

The main architectural legacy today is Georgian. Since coral limestone covers much of the island, it was the natural building material, although the first houses were wooden. Quarrying of coral limestone from oceanfront cliffs was relatively easy, especially with the cheap labor available at the time.

Much of the Georgian architecture had to be adapted to the climate, which led to the creation of the spacious verandas, the Guyana-inspired Demerara window, tall and well-ventilated gables, and the "tray" ceiling. Squat, horizontal structures were erected, the better to withstand rather frequent hurricanes. Parapet roofs came into existence. Built of stone, they had a concave curve on each side and followed the sloping line of the shed-roof on the front porch or veranda. Gabled or hipped roofs were thus protected from high winds.

The most common architectural legacy of long ago—still seen all over Barbados— is the chattel house, small makeshift homes built by rural people. This is a pioneering version of the mobile home, as it was constructed on a foundation of loose stones

---

❷ Did You Know?

- There is nothing but ocean between Barbados and Africa.
- Fine red sand from the Sahara can tint Bajan sunsets.
- The Arawak established villages on Barbados 400 years before the birth of Christ.
- Ninety-four percent of the original immigrants from England were male—mostly in their teens and twenties.
- In the 1640s, 23,000 British colonials and 20,000 slaves from Africa lived on Barbados.
- Barbados is governed by the third-oldest parliament in the Commonwealth of Nations. Only those of Great Britain and Bermuda are older.
- Rachel Pringle, a Bajan, once operated the most successful house of prostitution in the Caribbean, catering at times to royalty.
- Barbados is the only place outside the United States visited by George Washington. He contracted smallpox here.
- Church and state at one point tried to ban calypso music in Barbados because of its political content.
- Barbados is the most densely populated island in the West Indies.
- About 38% of tourists to Barbados come from the United States, about 22% from Great Britain, and about 14% from Canada.

and could be dismantled and moved elsewhere. These movable houses once had an economic necessity. They could be hastily assembled on plantations as work dictated, then moved to other plantations where new workers were needed. Each window of these houses supports a trio of wood shutters, and these could be adjusted to keep out the rain, hot sun, or heavy wind. The shutters were an early form of jalousies. Chattel houses are much beloved by today's photographers because they are painted in many different hues of vivid, floral colors.

Of the 17th-century great houses, the most outstanding is the St. Nicholas Abbey (not a church), which is now one of the major attractions of the island. Perhaps built from 1650 to 1660, this house in St. Peter resembles an English Jacobean manor house.

As Bridgetown expanded, spilling over into such communities as Hastings and Spooner's Hill, a new Palladian-inspired architecture arose. A symmetrical facade was devised, with a pedimented main portico. Often these newly developing houses had a large double staircase that led from the main-floor reception area to the upstairs bedrooms. Late in the 19th century, homes betrayed a heavy Victorian influence, but with Barbadian adaptations that evolved into sash windows, alternating jalousies, and a big, wide veranda ideal for sipping local drinks such as mauby.

Much of the architectural legacy of Barbados has already been destroyed, giving way in part to modern concrete-block constructions, but lately there has been a renewed interest in preserving what is left of the island's old architecture.

7 The Music of Barbados

Although many Bajans today listen to reggae music—most often from Jamaica—calypso is still dominant on the island. Calypso was brought to Barbados from West Africa in the early 17th century. The early songs spoke of hardships and sorrows suffered as the slaves labored in the sugarcane fields. The British overlords looked upon this music as "pagan" or "barbarous." In 1688 the assembly passed a law banning drums or local musical instruments, as they feared it was an incitement to violence and rioting. Only through secret rituals could the slaves keep alive their music and African traditions. Even after emancipation, calypso music was still viewed with distaste by the ruling elite in Barbados, and it remained largely underground until a white Bajan group, the Merrymen, revived it in the 1960s.

Today, calypso music is heard all over the world. Much of the calypso music of Barbados was early influenced by Trinidad, which has far deeper calypso roots, but Barbados's Mighty Gabby has emerged as the premier calypso performer. Gabby (his real name is Tony Carter) often sings songs of protest, and many of his calypso songs have won awards. In the late '70s, he was voted "Folksinger of the Year" for 3 consecutive years. His major rival today is another calypsonian, Red Plastic Bag, who first achieved recognition in 1982 with his "Mr. Harding Can't Burn." Most visitors hear calypso as strictly entertainment, but to Bajans it is often a singing newspaper, full of social comment and political satire.

To many, calypso music is best represented by the charismatic Eddy Grant, who was born in Guyana. This singer/producer preserves and promotes calypso music from his studio on Bayler's Plantation in the parish of St. Philip, where he has lived since 1981. Grant has been called the most charismatic singer in the entire Caribbean Basin, and his records are widely played on Barbados. He promotes local calypsonians on his Ice Records label; Grant has been an enormous backer and promoter of Gabby.

The tuk band became an island tradition. The name derives from a large log drum that gives out a sound like "boom-a-tuk." The rhythm is viewed as somewhat martial, like a marching military band.

With the advent of Radio Barbados in 1963, local calypso music received a greater audience, and many singers emerged from oblivion. Along came not only Mighty Gabby, as mentioned, but Mighty Dragon, Mighty Viper, and Lord Summers.

Sometimes theater in Barbados is a street scene, with drummers providing African rhythms as they march along. But there is organized theater as well, although rather fledgling. The island has local dance performances, plays, and concerts, often presented at annual festivals.

Although attempts were made to suppress West African–inspired dances, the forced laborers continued "working up," as they called their pelvic gyrations and traditional dances.

More formal modern dancing was introduced to Barbados in 1968 by Mary Stevens, who founded the Barbados Dance Theatre Company. Since then, several workshops have been formed, encouraging youth in various types of dance— even ballet, which was once considered the private domain of the white upper class.

Theater dates from the 17th century in Barbados. George Washington in his diary mentions attending *The Tragedy of George Barnwell* on December 15, 1751. Originally, Shakespeare and other English plays were presented. Only plantation whites attended. Black Bajans didn't stage theatrical performances until after World War II, with the emergence of the Green Room Players, who offered local productions using themes of black Bajan life. Since 1979, Stage One Theater Productions has carried on island theatrical tradition. Community Theatre Productions sponsors training workshops for aspirant Bajan actors, and many theatrical performances are staged at annual festivals.

8 Bajan Food & Drink

Today's traveler will find an extensive selection of fine restaurants in Barbados serving French, Italian, and other continental cuisines, as do the dining rooms of the island's many hotels. If possible, however, escape the dining rooms of your hotel and sample the island's own cuisine, which is interesting but not exotically spicy. Bajan cuisine is a culinary hybrid, primarily drawn from Africa and England, but also heavily influenced by Spanish, French, East Indian, Chinese, and American cooking techniques brought to the island by visitors and immigrants.

The famous flying fish appears on every menu, and when prepared right it's a delicacy, moist and succulent, nutlike in flavor, approaching the subtlety of brook trout. Bajans boil it, steam it, bake it, stew it, fry it, stuff it, or whatever.

Try also the sea urchin, or *oursin,* which Bajans also often call "sea eggs." Crab-in-the-back is another specialty, as is langouste, the Barbadian all-tail lobster. Dolphin (the fish known elsewhere at mahi mahi, not the mammal) and saltfish cakes are other popular items on the menu. Also typical are yams, sweet potatoes, and eddoes, dark-brown, thick-skinned underground parts of the taro plant. And Barbadian fruits, including papaya, passion fruit, and mangoes, are luscious.

If you hear that any hotel or restaurant is having a *cohobblopot,* or more commonly, a Bajan buffet, make a reservation. This is a Barbadian term that means to "cook up," and it inevitably will produce an array of local delicacies.

Pepperpot, stews, and curries are made with local chicken, pork, beef, and fish.

The secret of the flavorful dishes, as any Bajan cook will tell you, is in the "season-ing up." It is said that seasoning techniques have changed little since the 16th century.

At Christmas, when many U.S. visitors come to Barbados, roast ham or turkey is served with *jug-jug,* a rich casserole of Scottish derivation that includes salt beef, ground corn flour, green pigeon peas, and spices. *Cou-cou,* a side dish made from okra and cornmeal, accompanies fish, especially the flying fish of Barbados.

Note: Barbados is one of the few places in the Caribbean where barracuda is con-sidered a safe and acceptable food item. In other parts of the region, it is sometimes poisonous because of its diet of other fish that feed on certain kinds of plankton.

When it came time to invite a friend for a drink, old-time Bajans used to say, "Let's fire a grog."

Beer, perhaps more so than rum, has now become virtually the national drink. For many, Banks and beer are virtually the same word. Banks refers to the bottled lager that has been produced on the island since 1961. Throughout the island you'll hear Bajans ordering, "Banks thanks."

Barbados rum, including Mount Gay, the most popular brand name, has been the traditional drink of the island since the days of the planter aristocracy. Colors of rum range from clear to mahogany brown.

A drink unique to Barbados is falernum, made from rum, lime juice, sugar syrup, and various essences. Falernum, which is thick and syrupy, is often added to rum cocktails, although others prefer to drink it as a liqueur.

Mauby—colloquially "mabee"—is another traditional drink of Barbados, its fla-vor coming from the imported bark of a tree. In olden days, mauby vendors hawked the drink on the streets of Bridgetown, but today it comes in bottles.

9 Recommended Books & Recordings

BOOKS
HISTORY

The Civilized Island Barbados: A Social History (1750-1816), by Karl Stewart Watson (Caribbean Graphics, 1979), covers a wide range of history of the white landed aristocracy and the enslaved population. Everything from race attitudes to death rites of the forced laborers is intelligently reviewed.

The Barbados-Carolina Connection, by Warren Alleyne and Henry Fraser (Mac-millan Caribbean, 1988), tells of the exploration of the Carolina coast by Bajan adventurers and the part played in the settlement of Charles Town in 1670. This is a little known aspect of the American connection between Barbados and the United States.

Historic Bridgetown, by Warren Alleyne (Barbados National Trust, 1978), tells the exciting saga of the capital of Barbados, much of it swept away today by modern de-velopments. From the Careenage to Nelson's Statue, this book by a former RAF member in World War II is filled with background, including the true story of how Rachel Pringle, the island's most famous madam, came to acquire her infamous hotel.

Barbados: A History from the Amerindians to Independence, by F. A. Hoyos (Macmillan Caribbean, 1978), is one of the best statements on the island's background—from the sugar revolution and the eventual fall of the planter class, to the final stirring of the masses and independence.

Times Remembered in Africa and the Caribbean, by John Stow (Metlock Printers, 1991), is a memoir of the last British governor of Barbados. After independence he was appointed the first governor-general of the island, retiring in 1967. Some of his reflections on Barbados include the arrival of such famous visitors as Sir Winston Churchill and Queen Elizabeth II.

An Outline of Barbados History, by P. F. Campbell (Caribbean Graphics, 1974), is for those who like their history short and condensed. It traces the island's history in just 27 pages.

GENERAL

A-Z of Barbadian Heritage, by Henry Fraser, Sean Carrington, Addinton Forde, and John Gilmore (Heinemann, 1990), answers in alphabetical order everything you want to know about Barbados, and even provides some data about questions that might never have occurred to you. From history to culture, from aphrodisiacs to the saga of rum—it's all here.

The Barbadian Male, Sexual Attitudes & Practice, by Graham Dann (Macmillan Caribbean, 1987), is a unique work. Much data has been compiled on the role of the Caribbean woman as homemaker and child supporter, but this pioneering work focuses on the male—from gender attitudes to current attitudes about premarital sex.

FICTION

It So Happen, by Timothy Callender (Heinemann, 1991), is a collection of compelling tales by this deceased writer, considered the leading storyteller of the island. Filled with zany characters—and their dialect—the stories, ranging from "Obeah for the Obeah Man" to "A Deal with the Devil," overflow with humor.

Caribbean, by James A. Michener (Fawcett, reprint 1989), begins with the conquest in A.D. 1310 of the peaceful Arawak by the fierce Carib and ends seven centuries later with Fidel Castro of Cuba. It has some good background on Barbados.

LANGUAGE

Barbadian Dialect, by Frank A. Collymore (Barbados National Trust, 1970), is not dull like a dictionary, but contains lots of local lore, as you learn the meanings of such words as "lick mouth"—a popular dispenser of local gossip or one who kisses and tells.

ARCHITECTURE

Historic Houses of Barbados, by Henry Fraser and Ronnie Hughes (Barbados National Trust and Art Heritage Publications, 1986), with excellent drawings by Fraser, is the best architectural survey of Barbadian buildings from chattel houses to Georgian great houses.

Historic Churches of Barbados, by Barbara Hill (Art Heritage Publications, 1984), is a work of love by a woman (now deceased) who came to Barbados in 1955 and left a rough draft of a manuscript, which was later edited and considerably amplified. The book traces the design and development of the island's church buildings.

TRAVEL

Barbados The Visitor's Guide, by F. A. Hoyos (Macmillan, 1988), is a standard travel guide that covers history, geography, and cultural heritage. The same author also penned for Macmillan in 1960 *Barbados Our Island Home,* in which the history of the island is interwoven with its geography and plant and animal life.

RECORDINGS

Calypso is the dominant music form on Barbados, although some younger people today listen to reggae from Jamaica.

The internationally famous Merrymen, all citizens of Barbados, performed in the music capitals of the world before recently disbanding. Ironically, this all-white Bajan group is credited with keeping alive the tradition of calypso in Barbados in the 1960s when the music had started to wane. A good introduction to the group is *The Best of the Merrymen* (BTR 5 2451).

The king of calypso on the island is The Mighty Gabby. His songs are often a form of political protest. One of his more popular songs, "Miss Barbados" (1985), satirized the selection of a Canadian beauty to represent Barbados in an international beauty pageant. Singing since he was six, Gabby (real name: Tony Carter) lived for a while in New York but returned to Barbados where today he is considered to Bajan calypso what Bob Marley was to Jamaican reggae. Two of his best albums—available in local music stores—are *Gabby Across the Board* (no identifying number) and *Gabby: One in the Eye* (BG1-1001).

A current top-selling recording is Gabby, Grynner, and Square One's *Large and in Charge.* It includes such songs as "Zook Me" and "We Cheating."

Grynner, Gabby's sometimes-colleague, is a noted singer in his own right. He is best explored on his own tape: *Grynner: The Road March King* (no identifying number).

A new group coming into prominence in calypso is Spice and Company. It can be heard on the recording, *The First Fifteen* (WK-340).

Planning a Trip to Barbados

9

This chapter is devoted to the where, the when, and the how of your trip to Barbados—all those advance-planning tips that can ensure a smooth vacation. Many items mentioned in Chapter 3, "Planning a Trip to Jamaica," are equally applicable to Barbados. This is especially true of health and insurance, tips for travelers with special needs, and advice about homestays and home exchanges. We will not repeat these topics here, so refer to Chapter 3 for more complete information.

1 Visitor Information & Entry Requirements

VISITOR INFORMATION

In the **United States,** you can obtain information before you go at the following offices: 800 Second Ave., New York, NY 10017 (☎ 212/986-6516); and 3440 Wilshire Blvd., Suite 1215, Los Angeles, CA 90010 (☎ 213/380-2198 or 800/221-9831). In **Canada,** offices are at 5160 Yonge St., Suite 1800, North York, ON M2N 6L9 (☎ 416/512-6569); and 615 René Lévesque Blvd. West, Suite 460, Montreal, PQ H3B 1P5 (☎ 514/861-0085). The toll-free number for Canada is (☎ 800/268-9122). In the **United Kingdom,** the Barbados Tourism Authority is at 263 Tottenham Court Rd., London W1P 9AA (☎ 0171/636-9448).

Once you arrive, check with the **Barbados Tourism Authority** on Harbour Road, in Bridgetown (☎ 809/427-2623).

ENTRY REQUIREMENTS

A U.S. and Canadian citizen coming directly from North America to Barbados for a period not exceeding three months must have proof of identity and national status, such as a passport, which is always preferred. However, a birth certificate (either an original or a certified copy) is also acceptable, providing it is backed up by a photo ID. For stays longer than three months, a passport is required. An ongoing or return ticket is also necessary.

British subjects need a valid passport.

Vaccinations are not required to enter Barbados if you're coming from the United States or Canada.

What Things Cost in Barbados	U.S. $
Taxi from airport to a West Coast hotel	20.00
Average bus ride	.75
Local telephone call	.15
Double room at Glitter Bay (very expensive)	395.00
Double room at Divi Southwinds Beach Resort (moderate)	185.00
Double room at Fairholme (inexpensive)	30.00
Lunch for one at Koko's (moderate)	16.00
Lunch for one at The Ship Inn (inexpensive)	10.50
Dinner for one at Bagatelle Restaurant (expensive)	45.00
Dinner for one at Château Créole Restaurant (moderate)	8.00
Dinner for one at T.G.I. Boomers (inexpensive)	18.00
Bottle of beer in a bar	2.50
Coca-Cola in a cafe	1.25
Glass of wine in a restaurant	3.00
Roll of ASA 100 color film, 36 exposures	7.00
Admission to Tyrol Cot Heritage Village	5.00
Movie ticket	3.00
Admission to *1627 and All That*	45.00

2 Money

The Barbados dollar, the official currency, circulates in $100, $20, $10, and $5 notes, and $1, 25¢, and 10¢ silver coins, and 5¢ and 1¢ copper coins. The Bajan dollar is worth about 50¢ in U.S. currency.

U.S. dollars are widely accepted, as are traveler's checks.

If you need to get cash from your own bank account, or a cash advance from your credit card, there are ATMs at the major shopping malls and at all banks. For specific locations of Cirrus locations on Barbados, call **800/424-7787.** To learn of Plus locations in Barbados, call **800/843-7587.**

If you do need to change money, most banks and hotel desks can accommodate you.

Note: Currency quotations in this guide are in U.S. dollars ($) unless specified as Barbados dollars (BD$).

3 When to Go

THE CLIMATE Trade winds keep humidity low on Barbados. More than 3,000 hours of sunshine mix with enough rain to produce bumper crops of fruit and vegetables.

The climate here is pleasantly tropical and varies little throughout the year. Average high temperatures in the popular winter months, November through March, range from 83° to 86°F; average lows, 70° to 73°F. Average highs April through October are 85° to 87°F; average lows, 72° to 74°F. The rainy season is June to November, when the island gets about 75% of its annual precipitation. This period is also the hurricane season.

HOLIDAYS   Bajans celebrate the following public holidays: New Year's Day (January 1), Errol Barrow Day (January 21), Good Friday, Easter Monday, Labor Day (early May), Whitmonday, Kadooment Day (first Monday in August), United Nations Day (October 7), Independence Day (November 30), Christmas Day (December 25), and Boxing Day (December 26).

BARBADOS CALENDAR OF EVENTS

Because the dates of many of the following events can vary from year to year, check with a Barbados Tourist Authority office for exact dates (see "Visitor Information," above). You might also contact the Barbados Board of Tourism, 800 Second Ave., New York, NY 10017 (☎ 212/986-6516, or 800/221-9831 in the U.S.; 213/360-2198 in Los Angeles).

January

- **Barbados International Windsurfing.** This annual event draws some of the world's most skilled windsurfers, who consider surfing off Barbados the best this side of Hawaii. Events revolve around the Barbados Windsurfing Club. January 13–21.
- **Barbados National Trust Open House Program.** This program allows noteworthy houses on the island to be viewed by the public. Houses are selected by the National Trust on the basis of historical and architectural interest and decorative beauty. Call the National Trust at **809/426-2421** for more details. Mid-January to April 3.
- **Barbados Horticultural Society's Annual Flower Show,** Balls Plantation, Christ Church. A wide variety of exotic flowers and plants are displayed by regional horticultural societies. January 27–29.

February

- **Holetown Festival,** St. James. This week-long event commemorates the landing of the first European settlers, at Holetown in 1627. Highlights include street fairs, a Royal Barbados Police Band concert, a music festival in the historic parish church, a road race, and the crowning of a queen. February 18–25.

March–April

- **Cockspur Gold Cup Race,** Garrison Savannah. Horses from Barbados, Jamaica, Martinique, and Trinidad and Tobago participate in an invitational race at this historic site. March 2.
- **Oistins Fish Festival.** This festival commemorates the signing of the charter of Barbados and celebrates the life and contribution made by this fishing town to the development of the island. The program features fishing, boat racing, fish-boning competitions, a Coast Guard exhibition, food stalls, arts and crafts, dancing, singing, and road races. April 5–8.

July–August

- ✪ **Crop Over Festival.** The island's major national festival celebrates the completion of the sugarcane harvest. Revived in 1974, it recognizes the hardworking men and women of the sugar industry. Communities all over the island participate in fairs, concerts, calypso competitions, cart parades, and other cultural activities. Crop Over including in a grand costume parade, Kadooment Day, a national holiday on the first Monday in August. June 30–August 25.

August

- **Banks Barbados International Hockey Festival.** Men's, women's, and mixed teams from many countries join Bajan clubs for a week of field hockey competition. For a listing of events and locations, contact the Barbados Hockey Federation, P.O. Box 66B, Britton Hill, St. Michael (☎ 809/426-3721). August 18–24.

November

- **National Independence Festival of Culture and Arts.** In 1966, Barbados became an independent country in the Commonwealth of Nations, and that achievement is marked by celebrations, with competitions and performances in dance, drama, singing, and acting. The festival begins in early November and culminates November 30, Independence Day, a national holiday. For information on the various events, contact Barbados National Cultural Foundation, West Terrace, St. James (☎ 809/424-0907).

December

- **Run Barbados Series.** This series is comprised of a 10-kilometer race and a 26-mile, 385-yard marathon, attracting runners from around the world. The 10k race is held in and around Bridgetown, and the marathon begins at the Grantley Adams International Airport and finishes at Heywoods, north on the West Coast. December 7–8.

4 Flying to Barbados

More than 20 daily flights arrive in Barbados from not only mainland North America and Puerto Rico, but from neighboring islands, some South American capitals, and several European hubs (notably London).

From North America, the major gateways to Barbados are New York, Miami, and Toronto. There also are flights from San Juan, Puerto Rico, the major Caribbean hub. Flying time to Barbados from New York is $4^1/2$ hours; from Miami, $3^1/2$ hours; from Toronto, 5 hours; and from San Juan, $1^1/2$ hours. Grantley Adams International Airport is south of Bridgetown.

American Airlines (☎ 800/433-7300) has dozens of connections via San Juan. In addition, one flight usually departs New York's JFK in the morning and flies nonstop to Barbados, arriving in midafternoon. There's also a daily direct flight from Miami. A nonstop Airbus 300 (a very large aircraft that carries approximately 350 people) departs Barbados each afternoon for a return flight heading for San Juan. Passengers can usually speed through U.S. Customs clearance in San Juan rather than in their home cities, saving time and inconvenience.

Travelers via New York and Miami also can opt for nonstop flights offered daily by **BWIA** (☎ 800/538-2942), the national airline of Trinidad and Tobago. BWIA also offers many flights between Barbados and Trinidad.

Air Canada (☎ 800/363-5440 in the U.S. or 800/268-7240 in Canada) offers nonstop service from Canada, featuring convenient evening departures. Service from Toronto is on Tuesday, Friday, and Saturday, with a flight from Montreal on Sunday. In the winter there is an additional flight from Toronto on Thursday, with an additional Sunday flight from Toronto in the summer only.

Barbados is a major hub of the Caribbean-based airline known as **LIAT** (Leeward Islands Air Transport; ☎ 809/434-5428 for reservations, or 809/428-0986 at the Barbados airport). Frankly, LIAT provides generally poor service from Barbados to a handful of neighboring islands, including Dominica, Antigua, and St. Vincent and the Grenadines.

British Airways (☎ 800/247-9297) offers nonstop service to Barbados from both of London's major airports (Heathrow and Gatwick). In fact, more Europeans fly to Barbados on BA than on any other airline.

The Babe Ruth of Barbados

As in Jamaica and most other former outposts of the British Empire, cricket is the national pastime in Barbados. First made popular about 1870, the game is played by virtually every schoolboy. Some Bajans simply live for cricket.

The late cricket star Sir Frank Worrell, whom might be described as the Babe Ruth of Barbados, became the country's first nonpolitical national hero. He scored 3,860 runs in 51 tests at an average of 49.48 runs—a truly outstanding accomplishment. Sir Frank died in 1967 of leukemia. Sir Garfield Sobers is another great Bajan cricket player whose name you may hear.

Cricket matches can last from a day for one inning to 5 days for two innings (obviously we're not talking about baseball innings here). If you'd like to see all or part of a local match, watch for announcements in the newspapers or ask at the tourist board.

---

5 Package Tours

Many companies offer package tours to Barbados. These usually include air transport as well as hotel accommodations and, in some cases, meals.

Among the most attractive are packages offered by the airlines themselves, most notably **American** (☎ 800/433-7300), whose frequent flights and high-volume buying power can bring substantial savings for someone booking all aspects of a Caribbean getaway at the same time. The best deals are available to those wishing to remain in the same hotel, on the same island, for between three days and three weeks. On Barbados, there's a wide array of hotels from which to choose, often at very attractive rates.

From St. Louis, one of North America's most visible tour operators, **Go-Go Tours** (☎ 800/821-3731) flies package-tour customers on American Airlines to any of 30 different Bajan hotels for package-deal stays of between three days and a month.

Other deals are widely available. Read the travel section in your newspaper, and/or talk to a reputable travel agent.

6 Getting Around

From Grantley Adams International Airport, it costs about $20 by taxi to most hotels along the West Coast, and about $11 to a South Coast destination.

Once you've settled in and are ready to start exploring, you have a number of options: You can take a very inexpensive bus, hire an expensive taxi, rent an expensive car or an inexpensive bike or scooter, or stroll around sunny Barbados for free. See "The Regions in Brief" in Chapter 9 for a description of the island's layout.

BY TAXI

Taxis aren't metered, but rates are fixed by the government. Taxis on the island are identified by the license plate letter "Z." One to five passengers can be transported at the same time, and the fare can be shared. Overcharging is infrequent; most drivers have a reputation for courtesy and honesty. Taxis are plentiful, and drivers will produce a list of standard rates. The rate per hour is a standard $16. Most drivers are familiar with the island and will be happy to drive you around to see the sights for an entire day.

BY RENTAL CAR

If you don't mind *driving on the left side of the road*, you may find that having your own car is ideal for a Bajan holiday. None of the major U.S.-based car-rental companies maintains affiliates in Barbados, but a host of well-managed local companies work hard to fill the needs of the island's car-renting public. Except in the peak mid-winter season, cars are usually readily available without prior reservation.

Consequently, most visitors wait until arrival to book a rental car. Lots of people pay for a taxi from the airport to their hotel, then, after settling in, arrange for their car to be delivered to them. This is a good idea, since there's often a delay if you wait for a rental car to become available at the Barbados airport.

Many other visitors throw up their hands at the idea of driving on the left-hand side of the narrow and not-very-well-lighted island roads, and opt simply for a taxi whenever they need to be transported anywhere.

The island's most frequently recommended car-rental firm is **National,** Bush Hall Main Road, St. Michael (☎ **809/426-0603**), which offers a wide selection of Mokes and well-maintained cars. This company will deliver and pick up a car at your hotel. Located near the island's national stadium (the only one on the island), it is 3 miles northeast of Bridgetown. Maintaining an all-Japanese fleet of Toyotas, Mitsubishis, Suzukis, and Hondas, they charge from $55 to $70 per day for rentals of everything from open-sided fun cars to relatively luxurious cars with automatic transmission and air-conditioning. No taxes apply to car rentals in Barbados. Extra insurance coverage, however, is recommended, at a cost of BD$10 ($5) per day, which reduces the responsibility of any renter to only BD$500 ($250) in the event of an accident. Cars will be delivered to any location on the island on request, and the driver who delivers it will carry the necessary forms for issuance of the Bajan driver's license (see "Driving Rules," below). This company is not affiliated in any way with the U.S. car-rental giant with the same name.

Other frequently recommended companies operating in Barbados, which charge approximately the same prices and offer the same services, include **Sunny Isle Motors,** Dayton, Worthing Main Road, Christ Church (☎ **809/435-7979**); and **P&S Car Rentals,** Pleasant View, Cave Hill, St. Michael (☎ **809/424-2052**). One company convenient to hotels on the remote southeastern end of Barbados is **Stoutes Car Rentals**, Kirtons, St. Philip (☎ **809/435-4456**). Closer to the airport than its competitors, it can theoretically deliver a car to the airport within 10 minutes if you call when you arrive. Stoutes rents from an all-Japanese inventory, and also offers a handful of Portuguese-manufactured Mini-Mokes.

A temporary permit is needed if you don't have an International Driver's License. The rental agencies listed below will issue you a visitor's permit or you can go to the police desk upon arriving at the airport. You're charged a registration fee of BD$10 ($5), and you must have your own valid license. The speed limit is 20 m.p.h. within city limits, 30 m.p.h. elsewhere on the island.

BY BUS

Barbados has a reliable bus system fanning out from Bridgetown to almost every part of the island. Buses run on most major routes every 15 minutes or so. Fares are BD$1.75 (90¢) wherever you go, and exact change is required.

The government-owned buses are blue with yellow stripes. They are not numbered, but destinations are marked in front. Departures are from Bridgetown, leaving from Fairchild Street for the south and east; from Lower Green and the Princess

Alice Highway for the north going along the West Coast. Call **809/436-6820** for bus schedules and information.

Privately operated minibuses cover shorter distances and travel more frequently. They are bright yellow, with destinations displayed on the bottom left corner of the windshield. Minibuses in Bridgetown are boarded at River Road, Temple Yard, and Probyn Street. They, too, cost BD$1.75 (90¢).

BY SCOOTER OR BICYCLE

The best place in Barbados renting small machines is **Fun Seekers, Inc. Motorscooter and Bicycle Rental,** Rockley Main Road, Christ Church (☎ **809/ 435-6852**). Located on the coastal road, about 2 miles southeast of Bridgetown, it rents Honda motorscooters and big-wheeled, single-speed bicycles, and offers detailed maps and recommended scenic itineraries free. A deposit of $100 or $50 is required for rentals of scooters and bicycles, respectively. Two-seater motorcycles rent from $30.50 per day, and bicycles go for $10 per day. Discounts are offered for weekly rentals.

To rent a motorscooter, you must present a valid driver's license issued from your state or country of residence; Fun Seekers will issue you a Barbadian driver's license, priced at BD$10 ($5).

In addition to bike and scooter rentals, the company also arranges day cruises on a pair of well-maintained boats.

FAST FACTS: Barbados

American Express   The American Express affiliate in Barbados is located in the heart of Bridgetown. Contact the **Barbados International Travel Services,** Horizon House, P.O. Box 605C, McGregor Street, Bridgetown (☎ **809/431-2423**). Hours are Monday through Friday 9am to 5pm, and Saturday 9am to 1pm.

Bookstores   The island's best bookstore is **Cloister Bookstore Ltd.,** Hincks Street (☎ **809/426-2662**). It carries a full line of travel, history, textbooks, and resources on island lore. Another choice is **A. S. Bryden & Sons Ltd.** (or simply Bryden's). Hours of both bookstores are Monday through Friday from 8am to 1pm and Saturday from 8am to 1pm.

Business Hours   Most banks in Barbados are open from 9am to 3pm Monday to Thursday and from 9am to 1pm and 3 to 5pm Friday. Stores are open 8am to 4pm Monday to Friday and 8am to noon Saturday. Most government offices are open from 8:30am to 4:30pm Monday to Friday.

Car Rentals   See "Getting Around" earlier in this chapter.

Climate   See "When to Go," earlier in this chapter.

Consulates   Contact **the U.S. Consulate,** in the ALICO Building, Lower Broad Street, Cheapside in Bridgetown (☎ **809/431-0225**); **Canadian High Commission,** Bishop Court, Hill Pine Road (☎ **809/429-3550**); or **British High Commission,** Lower Collymore Rock, St. Michael (☎ **809/436-6694**).

Currency   See "Money," earlier in this chapter.

Dentist   Barbados might be served by more dentists than any other Caribbean island. One who is particularly well-recommended is Dr. Derek Golding, who maintains a busy practice with two colleagues at the Beckwith Shopping Mall, in

Bridgetown (☎ 809/426-3001). He accepts most emergency dental problems from the many cruise ships that dock in the waters off Barbados; the ships' pursers call in advance on ship-to-shore radios. The practice will accept any emergency, often remaining open late for last-minute problems. All members of the dental team received their training in the U.S., Britain, Canada, or New Zealand.

Doctor   Take your pick; there are dozens on Barbados. Your hotel might have a list of physicians on call, although some of the best recommended are Dr. J. D. Gibling (☎ 809/432-1772) and Dr. Adrian Lorde or his colleague, Dr. Ahmed Mohamad (☎ 809/424-8236), any of whom will make house calls to patients in their hotel rooms.

Documents Required   See "Visitor Information and Entry Requirements," earlier in this chapter.

Drugs   Penalties are severe for either possessing or selling drugs—heavy fines, a jail term, and most definitely deportation. Some drug pushers along the beachfronts may in fact be informants for the police.

Drugstores   Many hotels sell basic toiletries, including the much-requested suntan lotion. Medications can be obtained at the many pharmacies scattered throughout Bridgetown. One of the biggest is **Gill's Pharmacy,** Chapel Street near Tudor Street in Bridgetown (☎ 809/427-2654), which is open Monday through Friday from 8:30am to 12:30pm and Saturday from 8:30am to 2pm. It is also open Sunday from 8:30 to 11am. Another recommended drugstore is **Connolly's Pharmacy,** Prince Alfred Street at George Street in Bridgetown (☎ 809/426-4045). It is open Monday through Thursday from 8am to 5pm, Friday from 8am to 6pm, Saturday from 8am to 1pm, and Sunday from 9am to 12:30pm.

Electricity   The electricity is 110 volts AC, 50 cycles, so at most hotels you can use U.S.-made appliances.

Emergencies   The number to call in an emergency is 119. Other important numbers include police, 112; fire department, 113; and ambulance, 61113.

Eyeglasses   The island's largest opticians can produce eyeglasses or contact lenses in a reasonably short time. All are in the vicinity of Bridgetown. Try **Harcourt Carter Optical,** corner of George Street and 5th Avenue in the Belleville district (☎ 809/429-5565); or Imperial Optical, St. Michael's Row (☎ 809/426-4074). Hours for both are Monday to Friday from 8am to 4pm.

Hospitals   The 600-bed **Queen Elizabeth Hospital** (☎ 809/436-6450) is on Martinsdale Road in Bridgetown. This is the major hospital to head to on Barbados in case of an emergency. There are several private clinics as well, one of the best recommended and expensive being **Bayview Hospital,** St. Paul's Avenue, Bayville, St. Michael (☎ 809/436-5446).

Information   See "Visitor Information & Entry Requirements," earlier in this chapter.

Laundry and Dry Cleaning   Try **Steve's Dry Cleaning,** Coles Garage Building, Bay Street, Bridgetown (☎ 809/427-9119). It is open Monday through Friday from 7:30am to 6pm and Saturday from 7:30am to 2pm. A good self-service laundry near many of the inexpensive South Coast hotels is **Hastings Village Laundermat,** Balmoral Gap, Hastings (☎ 809/429-7079). You can go there any time from 8am to 7pm Monday through Saturday and from 8am to 2:30pm Sunday.

Liquor Laws   These are amazingly relaxed in Barbados. You can obtain a drink at virtually any time, provided a place is open for business. There seems to be no age limit, although a proprietor of an establishment would not necessarily serve drinks to a child. But some 15-year-olds—"who look older," in the words of one bartender—seem to have no problem.

Mail   Most hotel desks can attend to your mail, which takes 3 to 6 days to reach the United States. You can also use various mailboxes—painted red—throughout the island. Post offices are open Monday to Friday from 7:30am to 5pm. If you don't know where you'll be staying (not a good idea, incidentally), you can have your mail sent c/o General Delivery, **Barbados Post Office Department,** Cheapside Street, Bridgetown, W.I. (☎ 809/436-4800). At this post office, you can purchase stamps, send faxes, and mail packages. An airmail letter to the U.S. or Canada costs BD90¢ (45¢), an airmail postcard, BD65¢ (35¢). An airmail letter to Britain costs BD$1.10 (55¢), an airmail postcard BD70¢ (35¢).

Maps   At bookstores (see above), you can purchase various maps of Barbados, but one of the best, *Barbados Holiday Map,* is distributed free at many hotels. It's free because it's subsidized by advertisers. All the major roads of Barbados are shown clearly on this map, one part of which includes descriptions of major places of interest.

Money   See "Money," earlier in this chapter.

Newspapers and Magazines   The leading daily newspapers are *The Nation* and *Barbados Advocate,* both of which lean moderately to the right of the political spectrum. The *International Herald Tribune* and *USA Today* are flown in daily.

Photographic Needs   Most hotels sell film in their gift shops, and many can arrange for it to be sent out to be developed if enough time is alloted. Otherwise, you can patronize one of the three outlets of **C.L. Gibbs,** each offering photo finish 1-hour labs. They're found on the West Coast at Sunset Mall, Sunset Crest (☎ 809/432-6167); at Worthing along the South Coast (☎ 809/435-7357), and in Bridgetown on Broad Street (☎ 809/437-3497). All outlets are open Monday to Friday from 9am to 5pm and on Saturday from 9pm to 1pm.

Police   Call 112.

Post Office   See "Mail," above.

Radio   Barbados is served by three major radio broadcasters. Barbados Broadcasting Service operates an FM station; Barbados Rediffusion Service runs YESS Ten-Four (104 on the FM dial), a news and music service; and CBC Radio operates Radio Liberty FM and Radio 900, both of which broadcast news, music, and public-interest programs.

Safety   The people of Barbados seem to know that much of the island's livelihood depends on the goodwill of its tourists (the mainstay of its economy), so crimes against visitors are highly discouraged and severely punished. Nevertheless, crime has come to Barbados in recent years, because of rising unemployment among the island's youth. Purse-snatching and pickpocketing exist in Bridgetown, so take precautions. Although it's not a "crime," you still might be annoyed by the unwanted attention you get from various hawkers and peddlers on the beach. A firm and resounding "No!" should get rid of them. In any case, safeguard your possessions and never leave them unattended on the beach. And never go walking along the beach at night.

Shoe Repairs   Harry's Heel Bar and Shoe Repair Centre, Cowell Street, St. Michael, Bridgetown (☎ **809/427-5578**), will repair most shoes, luggage, and handbags while you wait. The same company also maintains a collection point in the Gertz Shopping Plaza, Collymore Rock, St. Michael (☎ **809/436-6764**), which accepts items for repair and redelivery several days later. Both branches are open Monday to Friday from 9am to 5pm and Saturday from 8:30am to 1pm.

Taxes   When you leave, you'll have to pay a BD$25 ($12.50) departure tax. By the time you arrive, the government of Barbados should have introduced a Value-Added Tax (VAT) on nearly all goods and services, including sightseeing attractions, food, and hotel rooms.

Taxis   See "Getting Around," earlier in this chapter.

Telephone, Telex, and Fax   You should have no trouble with telecommunications out of Barbados. Telegrams can be sent at your hotel front desk or at the **Barbados External Telecommunications Ltd. Office,** Wildley Main Rd., St. Michael (☎ **809/427-5200**), which is open from 8am to 6pm Monday to Friday and from 8am to 1pm Saturday. International telephone, fax, telex, and data-access services are also available at this office.

Television   CBC TV (Caribbean Broadcasting Corp.), Channel 8 on the dial, is broadcast from Barbados. News and entertainment are also imported every day on the popular TNT (Turner Broadcasting), which appears on Channel 26.

Time   Barbados is on Atlantic time, 1 hour ahead of New York (eastern standard time). Unlike Jamaica, Barbados switches to daylight savings time.

Tipping   Most restaurants and hotels add a 10% service charge, and you need not tip more unless service has been good. Many visitors or locals routinely add another 10% in those cases. Maids get about $1 per day, and bellboys are tipped from $1 per bag, porters about $1 per piece of luggage.

Transit Info   Taxis line up in front of most major hotels. If you need to call one, try **Johnson's Stables** at 809/426-5186 or **Dear's Garage** 809/427-7853.

Water   Barbados has a pure water supply. It's pumped from underground sources in the coral rock, which underlies six-sevenths of the island, and it's safe to drink.

Weddings   It's relatively easy to tie the knot in Barbados, although it calls for some advance planning. Couples can marry the same day they arrive on Barbados, but must first obtain a marriage license from the **Ministry of Home Affairs** (☎ **809/ 431-7600;** fax 809/431-7768). Bring either a passport, or birth certificate and photo I.D., $50 in fees, and $12 for the revenue stamp (which can be obtained at the local post office), a letter from the authorized officiant who will perform the service, plus proof, if applicable, of pertinent deaths or divorces of former spouse(s). A Roman Catholic wedding on Barbados carries additional requirements. For more information, contact the **Barbados Tourism Authority,** 800 Second Ave., New York, NY 10017 (☎ **212/986-6516** or 800/221-9831).

Where to Stay & Dine on Barbados

Barbados has some of the best hotels in the West Indies. You can be pampered in elegant comfort, and enjoy an atmosphere like that of an English house party. Most hotels are small and personally run, with a quiet, restrained dignity.

The biggest recent change has been a tendency for hotels to charge all-inclusive rates. Even some that have not gone this route insist that you take two meals with them every day.

The bad news is that because of the island's popularity, especially with groups, its big hotels are often extremely expensive in high season. There has been little hotel development here in recent years, with few new openings, so there has been no competition to keep prices down. The price you pay for a moderately priced room here could get you a lavish suite in many parts of the world, including many U.S. cities.

Most of our recommendations are at St. James Beach, the island's fashionable and expensive Gold Coast, but there should be a hotel or resort tailored for you somewhere in Barbados. Even though the upper end is *very* expensive, there are hostelries in all sizes and to suit most wallets—from simple inns to palatial suites or luxurious cottages. To escape $500-a-night prices at some hotels, many visitors opt for apartment rentals or time-share units. Others head south from Bridgetown to places like Hastings and Worthing where they find the best bargains, often in self-contained efficiencies or studio apartments, in which you can save by cooking some or all of your meals.

1 Where to Stay

Although rates are high in the winter, they generally drop from 20% to 60% from mid-April to mid-December. With certain variations, so-called summer rates apply from mid-April to mid-December, and winter rates are in effect from December 15 to April 15.

Generally, **very expensive** in this chapter means more than $350 a night for a double room in the winter season; **expensive,** $250 to $350; **moderate,** $150 to $250; **inexpensive,** under $150. These categories are high, that's true, but they reflect reality on Barbados.

The rates are in U.S. dollars unless otherwise indicated. A 5% government tax and a 10% service charge are added to all rates.

Barbados Accommodations

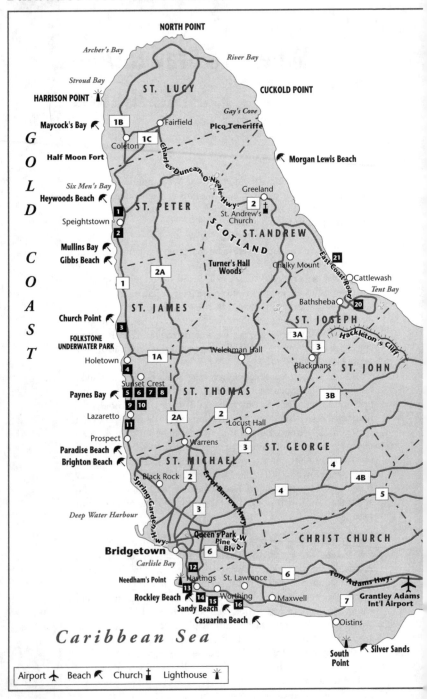

NORTH POINT

Archer's Bay

River Bay

ST. LUCY

CUCKOLD POINT

Stroud Bay

HARRISON POINT

Gay's Cove

1B Fairfield

Maycock's Bay

Pico Teneriffe

1C Coleton

Half Moon Fort

Morgan Lewis Beach

Six Men's Bay

Greeland

Heywoods Beach

2 St. Andrew's Church

ST. PETER

Speightstown

1

2

SCOTLAND

ST. ANDREW

Mullins Bay

Gibbs Beach

Turner's Hall Woods

Chalky Mount

21 Cattlewash

2A

Tent Bay

1

Bathsheba

20

Church Point

ST. JAMES

ST. JOSEPH

FOLKSTONE UNDERWATER PARK

Welchman Hall

3A

3

Holetown

1A

Blackmans

ST. JOHN

4 Sunset Crest

5 6 7 8

Paynes Bay

ST. THOMAS

3B

9 10

Lazaretto

11

2A

2

Locust Hall

Prospect

Warrens

3

ST. GEORGE

Paradise Beach

Brighton Beach

ST. MICHAEL

4

Black Rock

2

4B

3

4

5

Deep Water Harbour

Queen's Park

CHRIST CHURCH

Bridgetown

6

Pine Blvd.

Carlisle Bay

12

Hastings

6

Needham's Point

13 St. Lawrence

Rockley Beach

14

15 Worthing

Tom Adams Hwy.

7 Grantley Adams Int'l Airport

Sandy Beach

16 Maxwell

Casuarina Beach

Oistins

Caribbean Sea

South Point

Silver Sands

GOLD COAST

Charles Duncan O'Neale Hwy.

East Coast Road

Hackleton's Cliff

Errol Barrow Hwy.

Spring Garden Hwy.

| Airport ✈ | Beach 🏖 | Church ✝ | Lighthouse 🕯 |

202

Atlantic Ocean

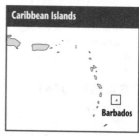

Caribbean Islands

Barbados

Almond Beach Club **5**
Almond Beach Village **1**
Bagshot House Hotel **16**
Barbados Hilton **13**
Casuarina Beach Club **16**
Cobblers Cove Hotel **2**
Coconut Creek Club **6**
Colony Club **3**
Coral Reef Club **3**
Crane Beach Hotel **18**
The Crystal Cove **11**
Divi Southwinds Beach Resort **16**
The Edgewater Inn **20**
Fairholme **17**
Glitter Bay **3**
Grand Barbados Beach Resort **12**
Kingsley Club **21**
Marriott's Sam Lord's Castle **19**
Ocean View **14**
Royal Pavilion **3**
Sandpiper Inn **4**
Sandy Beach Hotel **16**
Sandy Lane **7**
Settlers Beach **3**
Southern Palms **16**
Tamarind Cove **10**
Traveller's Palm **9**
Treasure Beach **8**
Woodville **15**

Martin's Bay

Congor Rocks

Consett Bay

CULPEPPER ISLAND

Ragged Point Lighthouse

Three Houses

Kitridge Point

Bushy Park

Bottom Bay

Sandford

ST. PHILIP **5**

19

Long Bay

Marchfield

18 Beachy Head

7 **Crane Beach**

Long Bay

0 ━━━━ 3 km
      1.9 mi

N

203

One of the most common hotel and resort rates is **MAP,** meaning Modified American Plan. MAP usually includes room, breakfast, and dinner. If we give the room rate separately, it means the additional charge is for breakfast and dinner. **CP** means Continental Plan, room and a light breakfast. **EP** is European Plan: room only. The **AP,** or American Plan, is the most expensive rate, because it includes room plus three meals a day.

ON THE WEST COAST
VERY EXPENSIVE
Cobblers Cove Hotel

Road View (¹/₂ mile south of Speightstown on Highway 1), St. Peter, Barbados, W.I. ☎ **809/ 442-2291,** or 800/223-6510 in the U.S., 800/424-5500 in Canada, 0181/367-5175 in London. Fax 809/422-1460. 40 suites. A/C MINIBAR TEL. Winter $500–$850 double; $1,400 Camelot or Colleton Suite for two. Off-season $330–$470 double, $710 Camelot or Colleton Suite for two. Rates include MAP. AE, MC, V. Closed late Sept to mid-Oct.

One of the small, exclusive hotels of Barbados, Cobblers Cove grew out of a beachfront mansion that was built like a fort, with mock-medieval touches that appealed to its original plantation owners. The home, now a Relais & Châteaux, was erected over the site of a former British fort that protected vessels entering the harbor at nearby Speightstown. Today, after an extensive overhaul, the hotel is a favorite honeymoon retreat, offering first-class suites in a series of 10 Iberian-style villas placed in the gardens in horseshoe patterns.

Each unit is outfitted inside with tropical woods and contains a spacious living room, private balcony or patio overlooking a white sand beach, and a kitchenette. Two of the most exclusive accommodations you can rent in all Barbados are the Camelot and Colleton Suites on the rooftop of the original mansion. They are beautifully decorated and offer panoramic views of both the beach and the garden.

Dining/Entertainment: The open-air, shingle-roofed, award-winning Terrace Restaurant overlooks the sea (see "Where to Dine," below). Nearby is the resort's social center, its bar.

Services: Laundry, baby-sitting, arrangements for island tours.

Facilities: A tennis court and a swimming pool plus water sports including waterskiing, Sunfish sailing, snorkeling, glass-bottomed-boat rides, and windsurfing.

Glitter Bay

Porters (1 mile north of Holetown on Highway 1), St. James, Barbados, W.I. ☎ **809/422-5555,** or 800/283-8666 in the U.S., 800/567-5327 in Canada, 0181/367-5175 in London. Fax 809/ 422-3940. 83 suites. A/C MINIBAR TEL. Winter $395–$415 double, $485–$555 one-bedroom suite for two, from $960–$995 two-bedroom suite for four. Off-season $195–$285 double, $220–$405 one-bedroom suite, $415–$675 two-bedroom suite. MAP $60 per person per day. AE, DC, MC, V.

This carefully maintained resort has discreet charm and Mediterranean style, although it isn't quite as sophisticated and spectacular as its next-door sibling, Royal Pavilion (see below). Built in 1981 by a The Pemberton Group, a small Barbados-based hotel chain, Glitter Bay occupies a 10-acre plot of manicured lowlands near a sandy beachfront. Units are in a white-walled minivillage of Iberian inspiration, whose patios, thick beams, and red terra-cotta tiles surround a garden containing a swimming pool, an artificial waterfall, and a simulated lagoon. Most units feature unusual artwork, built-in furniture, and louvered doors reminiscent of a thick-walled refuge in a Moroccan casbah. The suites contain small kitchenettes. Glitter Bay is more geared to families than is Royal Pavilion.

Dining/Entertainment: Glitter Bay's social center is the Piperade Restaurant, whose curved sides ride beneath a terra-cotta roof amid a garden. Offering both American and international cuisine, along with West Indian specialties, it contains its own bar. The Sunset Beach Bar is a popular rendezvous spot for a sundowner. Sheltered by shrubbery and tropical trees, guests can dance under the stars on an out-door patio, and enjoy local entertainment, such as a steel band or calypso.

Services: Laundry, baby-sitting, and a concierge.

Facilities: A full range of complimentary water sports includes waterskiing, windsurfing, snorkeling, aerobics classes, and catamaran sailing. Many other activities, such as golf and horseback riding, can be arranged, and two tennis courts are lighted at night.

Royal Pavilion

Porters (1 mile north of Holetown on Highway 1), St. James, Barbados, W.I. ☎ **809/422-4444,** or 800/283-8666 in the U.S., 800/567-5327 in Canada, 0181/367-5175 in London. Fax 809/422-3940. 72 junior suites, 3 villas. A/C MINIBAR TEL. Winter $545 double, $1,060 villa for four, $1,595 villa for six. Off-season $230 double, $465 villa for four, $695 villa for six. MAP $60 per person extra. No children under 12 in winter. AE, DC, MC, V.

A spectacular place to stay, this Pemberton hotel shares gardens with neighboring Glitter Bay, which is part of the same chain. British grace and Bajan hospitality blend happily in this aristocratic property, which became one of the finest resorts in Barbados the moment it opened. We think it's far superior to the more famous Sandy Lane (see below), for example. The architects of Royal Pavilion created a California-hacienda style for their waterfront junior suites and villas. There are eight acres of beautifully landscaped gardens. TV is available on request in any room.

Dining/Entertainment: There are two oceanfront restaurants, including Tabora's, which serves breakfast and lunch. The more formal Palm Terrace, set below the seaside columns of an open-air loggia, is open only for dinner (see "Where to Dine," below).

Services: Laundry, baby-sitting, and a concierge.

Facilities: Freshwater swimming pool, fitness center at Glitter Bay, two tennis courts (complimentary for guests day and night), and a water sports program including complimentary snorkeling, waterskiing, sailing, and windsurfing. The best golf on the island is at Pemberton's Westmoreland Golf and Country Club.

Sandy Lane

St. James (less than 1 mile south of Holetown on Highway 1), Barbados, W.I. ☎ **809/432-1311,** or 800/225-5843 in the U.S. and Canada. Fax 809/432-2954. 90 rms, 30 suites. A/C MINIBAR TEL. Winter $850–$1,395 double, from $1,400 suite. Off-season $545–$645 double, from $695 suite. Rates include MAP. AE, DC, DISC, MC, V.

If you have to ask the astronomical cost of a room here, you probably can't afford it. The last remaining outpost of British colonialism in Barbados, the place is stiffly formal and "veddy" British. Sandy Lane was established in 1961, on the 380-acre site of a bankrupted sugar plantation. During its aristocratic heyday the hotel attracted many of the grandest names in Britain. In 1991, after a period of much-publicized decline, the hotel received a multimillion dollar infusion from the Forte chain, its present owners. Despite the massive overhaul, we don't feel it has kept pace with the other properties here. Nevertheless, it offers well-furnished suites and rooms (all doubles and all with refrigerators), a private beach, and one of the most prestigious golf courses in Barbados, among many other sports facilities. The swimming pool is surrounded by Italianate gardens, Roman fountains, and colonnaded verandas.

Dining/Entertainment: You can order a cool salad at Sandy Lane's pool at lunch, and later enjoy a continental-inspired candlelight dinner. Buffet tables are frequent, as is regular Barbados entertainment, such as calypso. You can also dine on Italian cuisine in the Seashell Restaurant, or munch on club sandwiches and hamburgers at either the Oasis Beach Bar or an informal bar/snack bar beside the golf course. Scattered in various corners of the place, you'll find five different bars. Live entertainment (usually a dance band) is presented nightly, and a Bajan floor show and cabaret is offered once a week.

Services: 24-hour room service, baby-sitting, laundry and dry cleaning, concierge, valet.

Facilities: 18-hole golf course, free-form outdoor swimming pool, five all-weather tennis courts (two lighted for night play), an array of water sports including scuba, windsurfing, sailboat rentals, snorkeling; rental bicycles, activities center for children 2–11.

Settlers Beach

St. James (directly north of Holetown on Highway 1; 8 miles from Bridgetown), Barbados, W.I. ☎ 809/422-6510 or 800/223-1108. Fax 809/422-1937. 22 villas. A/C TEL. Winter $550–$650 double, $600–$650 triple, $650–$700 quad. Off-season $240 double, $260 triple, $280 quad. Children under 18 stay free in parents' room. MAP $50 per person extra. AE, DC, MC, V.

Settlers Beach is a seaside collection of comfortable two-story villas situated on 4¹/₂ acres of beachfront property. Each apartment is self-contained, with two bedrooms, two bathrooms, a spacious tile-floored lounge and dining room, and a fully equipped kitchen. The apartments are decorated in sunny colors and were built in 1967. All units were last refurbished in 1995. This resort, squeezed between larger properties, appeals to those who are more independent instead of clients who like to be coddled. Frankly, it's dated, but it still wins lots of repeat business, attracting American families in the summer and English visitors in the winter.

Dining/Entertainment: The square-roofed dining room has won awards and is considered one of the finer hotel restaurants on the island. A bar is nearby.

Services: Laundry, baby-sitting, room service (8am to 9pm).

Facilities: Swimming pool, two tennis courts, and a sandy beach.

Treasure Beach

St. James (about ¹/₂ mile south of Holetown on Highway 1), Barbados, W.I. ☎ 809/432-1346, or 800/223-6510 in the U.S., 800/424-5500 in Canada. Fax 809/432-1094. 24 suites. A/C TEL. Winter (including breakfast) $420–$550 one-bedroom suite, $700–$840 two-bedroom penthouse suite. Off-season $155–$215 one-bedroom suite, $280–$310 two-bedroom penthouse suite. MAP $45 per person extra. AE, DC, DISC, MC, V.

Set on an acre of sandy beachfront land, in a mini-village of two-story buildings arranged into a horseshoe pattern around a pool and garden, Treasure Beach has one of the most loyal clienteles of any hotel on the island. It's small but choice, known for its well-prepared food and the comfort and style of its amenities. The atmosphere is intimate and relaxed, and the well-trained staff prides itself on offering personal service. The hotel is set in tropical gardens at the edge of a white sandy beach in the glittery St. James hotel belt. The accommodations are beautifully furnished in a tropical motif and open onto private balconies or patios. All units have refrigerators and sinks; one has a kitchen. Guests are about evenly divided between North Americans and Britishers. Children under 12 are accepted only by special request.

Dining/Entertainment: Even if you aren't staying here, try to sample some of the culinary specialties at the Treasure Beach Restaurant, including freshly caught seafood and favorites from the Bajan culinary repertoire. The evening entertainment is discreet and low-key, in respect for calm and privacy.

Services: Valet and laundry service, room service, safety-deposit boxes, and a concierge who arranges car rentals and island tours.

Facilities: Rental of sailboats, access to nearby golf and tennis courts.

EXPENSIVE

Almond Beach Club

Vauxhall (less than 1 mile south of Holetown on Highway 1), St. James, Barbados, W.I. ☎ **809/432-7840,** or 407/4-ALMOND in the U.S. Fax 809/432-2115. 95 rms, 65 suites. A/C TV TEL. Winter $430–$475 double, $490–$560 suite for two. Off-season $315–$410 double, $380–$450 suite for two. Rates are all-inclusive. No children under 6. AE, DC, MC, V.

Set on flat and sandy acreage about a 2-minute walk from its more famous neighbor, Sandy Lane, this hotel lies on the island's West Coast, south of Holetown, opening onto Paynes Bay. The narrow beach here is less than ideal. An overhauled restoration of an older property, this place was turned into the first of Barbados's all-inclusive resorts in 1991 as part of the $2 million refurbishment. Accommodations are spread among seven low-rise three-story buildings (no elevators). Poolview units open onto three freshwater swimming pools and the gardens, planted with frangipani trees and palms. Beachfront units open onto the Caribbean. Island motifs form the room decor, with tropical fabrics and tile floors.

Dining/Entertainment: The all-inclusive program offers a dine-around option: guests can take one lunch and one dinner per week-long stay at one of three neighboring hotels. On the premises is a continental restaurant (the Almond Beach), a West Indian/Bajan restaurant (Enid's), and a beachfront snack bar. The Rum Shop Bar evokes 19th-century colonial days and offers a sampling of virtually every kind of distilled rum on Barbados. There is live nightly entertainment—jazz bands, steel-drum bands, Bajan folk dancing, and up-to-date music, as well as piano bar entertainment until 2am.

Services: Island tours, laundry, baby-sitting.

Facilities: Three freshwater swimming pools, tennis and squash courts, fitness center with sauna, fishing, windsurfing, waterskiing, reef fishing, kayaking, and "banana boating."

Almond Beach Village

Speightstown (15 miles north of Bridgetown along Highway 2A), St. Peter, Barbados, W.I. ☎ **809/422-4900** or 800/822-4200. Fax 809/422-1581. 288 rms, 23 suites. A/C TV TEL. Winter $430–$475 double, $490–$560 suite. Off-season $315–$365 double, $380–$550 suite. Rates are all-inclusive. AE, DC, MC, V.

Set near the northern tip of a string of more expensive Gold Coast resorts, this hotel occupies the site of a 19th-century sugarcane plantation. In 1994, it was acquired by the largest industrial conglomerate on the island (Barbados Shipping and Trading, Ltd.) and benefited from $13 million worth of renovations. Today, it's the most desirable all-inclusive resort on the island; all meals, drinks, and most sporting activities are included in one net price.

The relatively isolated position makes leaving the premises awkward, although that doesn't seem to bother most guests, who remain occupied on the 30 acres of tropically landscaped gardens and prime beachfront. Accommodations are clustered into seven different compounds for something akin to a miniature, self-contained village.

Dining/Entertainment: Four different restaurants add diversity to the dining options. There's the specialty Italian restaurant La Smarita, most formal of the lot. The main dining room is The Horizons, largest on the premises. Least formal and casual is Enid's for Bajan food. Other choices are The Reef (a burger-and-hot-dog joint) and a more formal seafood venue by candlelight at nighttime.

Services: Laundry facilities, baby-sitting, room service.

Facilities: Five floodlit tennis courts, a nine-hole par-3 golf course that's too easy for professionals, but well-tuned for beginners, two air-conditioned squash courts. Exchange privileges are available with the hotel's all-inclusive twin, the Almond Beach Club (see above).

Coconut Creek Club

Derricks (about 1 mile south of Holetown on Highway 1), St. James, Barbados, W.I. ☎ 809/432-0803. Fax 809/438-4697. 53 rms. A/C TEL. Winter $310–$350 double. Off-season $220–$265 double. Rates include MAP. AE, DC, MC, V.

Small, intimate, and famous as a discreet retreat for European celebrities escaping the paparazzi, Coconut Creek is an elegant but informal Gold Coast retreat. Its developers re-created a three-acre corner of England here; completely renovated in 1995, it resembles a country retreat in Devon. About half the rather small accommodations lie atop a low bluff overlooking the two most secluded beaches on the island's West Coast. Because of the configuration of the nearby coastline, access to these beaches is possible only by boat from the hotel and a handful of nearby privately owned villas. Many of the bedrooms are built on the low cliff edge, overlooking the ocean, whereas others open onto the pool or the flat, tropical garden. Each bedroom offers a veranda or balcony where breakfast can be served. Baths are cramped.

Dining/Entertainment: The owners have created an outpost of Britannia in the only restaurant, The Cricketers, which was modeled after an upscale English pub. Bajan buffets and barbecues are served in the restaurant's vine-covered open pergola, overlooking the gardens and the sea. The inn's food has been praised by *Gourmet* magazine. There's dancing to West Indian calypso and steel bands almost every night. Clients on MAP are encouraged to dine at the restaurants connected to this chain's three other properties—Crystal Cove Hotel, Tamarind Cove Hotel, and the Colony Club—all at no additional charge.

Services: Room service (7:30am to 10pm), baby-sitting.

Facilities: Freshwater swimming pool; complimentary water sports include waterskiing, windsurfing, snorkeling, and free use of Hobie Cats. Scuba can be arranged for an extra charge, and tennis is available nearby.

Colony Club

Porters (1 mile north of Holetown on Highway 1), St. James Beach, Barbados, W.I. ☎ 809/422-2335. Fax 809/422-0667. 64 rms, 34 junior suites. A/C TEL. Winter $365–$495 double, $430–$495 suite. Off-season $270–$310 double, $320–$340 suite. Rates include MAP. AE, DC, MC, V.

Established by an English expatriate in the 1950s, and today a charter member of a British-owned hotel chain based in Barbados, Colony Club is one of the well-respected and discreetly elegant hotels on the western coast, catering mainly to Brits. Set behind an entrance lined with Australian pines, it seems more like a residential club than a traditional hotel. It occupies an enviable site beside one of the island's best-known beaches. An elegant feeling prevails, even though the Colony has grown from a small "English country house party"–type establishment to a complex of carefully maintained rooms that overlook shaded verandas and handsomely landscaped grounds. About a third of the rooms lie beside the sea; the others are scattered along the flat and densely tropical gardens. All units have private patios. Your opinion of this resort is likely to be shaped by your room assignment, since some look a bit dowdy while others are up-to-date and spiffy. Accommodations are clustered in two- and three-story Mediterranean-style bungalows with red-tile roofs. Sliding glass doors open onto sun terraces.

Dining/Entertainment: The open-sided Laguna Restaurant is set between the beachside freshwater pool and the main building. Orchids, the hotel's formal restaurant, offers an international cuisine (see "Where to Dine," below). The dance floor is reached by a footbridge to an "island" in the middle of the pool. There is nightly entertainment.

Services: Room service (7:30am to 9:30pm), laundry, baby-sitting, arrangements for outings and excursions.

Facilities: Three freshwater swimming pools, hairdressing/beauty salon, complimentary water sports, chauffeured speedboat and catamaran rides, air-conditioned fitness center, two floodlit tennis courts.

Coral Reef Club

St. James Beach (a 5-minute drive north of Holetown on Highway 1), Barbados, W.I. ☎ **809/ 422-2372** or 800/223-1108. Fax 809/422-1776. 69 units. A/C TEL. Winter $485–$685 double; off-season $300–$350 double. Rates include MAP. AE, MC, V.

Family owned and managed, this inn set standards that are hard for competitors to match, as Coral Reef Club is one of the best and most respected hotels on the island. Set on elegantly landscaped and flat land beside the sea, it offers veranda-fronted private cottages that surround a main building and clubhouse. This building contains the reception area, a reading room, a dining area and bar, and four deluxe bedrooms on the second floor. The accommodations are scattered about a dozen handsomely landscaped acres with machineels and casuarinas, fronting a long strip of white sandy beach that's ideal for swimming. All units open onto private patios, but they vary greatly. Some rooms provide separate dressing rooms. Not all are in cottages. Some, not in the main building, are in small coral stone wings in the gardens.

Dining/Entertainment: You can enjoy a lunch buffet in an open-air area. Dinner is served in a room open to ocean views on three sides, and a first-class continental chef runs the kitchen. There's a weekly folklore show and barbecue every Thursday. The Bajan buffet on Monday evening features an array of food, along with whole baked fish and lots of local entertainment.

Services: 24-hour room service, laundry, massage, and a reception staff able to help arrange almost anything.

Facilities: Freshwater swimming pool, hair salon, lighted tennis court, water sports including windsurfing, snorkeling, scuba, sailing.

The Crystal Cove

Fitt's Village (4 miles north of Bridgetown), St. James, Barbados, W.I. ☎ **809/432-2683** or 800/ 223-6510. Fax 809/424-0996. 56 rms, 32 suites. A/C TV TEL. Winter $305–$365 double, $355– $475 suite; off-season $200–$260 double, $235–$335 suite. AE, DC, MC.

Once this was the much complained-about Barbados Beach Village, but now it's become The Crystal Cove, and it's much better than before. Set on a four-acre beachfront site, it is a member of the Barbados-based St. James Beach Hotels, which owns some of the best properties on the island, including Colony Club, Coconut Creek, and Tamarind Cove. Guests have access to the other hotels' combined facilities, and a water taxi is provided for transportation among the different properties. This, in fact, is one of the major reasons for staying here. If you get bored or tired of the treacherous pilings and offshore rocks at the beach here, you can hop over to the next venue of the St. James group.

Rooms are either standard, somewhat like a motel, or more upscale with separate living areas from the bedrooms. Most of them have high ceilings, and more than two dozen units have kitchenettes.

Dining/Entertainment: The food at the two restaurants is above average, though you probably wouldn't drive across the island to sample it. Entertainment is provided most nights.

Facilities: Three swimming pools, two tennis courts.

Sandpiper Inn

Holetown (just north of town on Highway 1), St. James, Barbados, W.I. ☎ **809/422-2251** or 800/223-1108. Fax 809/422-1776. 21 rms, 24 suites. A/C MINIBAR TEL. Winter $360–$460 double, $600–$820 suite; off-season $180–$280 double, $330–$430 suite. MAP $45 per person extra. Children not accepted in February. AE, MC, V.

The Sandpiper has more of a South Seas look than most of the hotels of Barbados. Affiliated with the Coral Reef Club (see above), it is a self-contained, intimate resort on the waterside, and has a refreshing lack of pretense. Avoiding any decoration that might seem sterile or modern, the resort maintains a truly Bajan flavor. It is situated in a small grove of coconut palms and flowering trees right on the beach. The cluster of rustic-chic units surrounds the swimming pool, and some have a fine sea view. The rooms open onto little terraces that stretch along the second story, where you can order drinks or have breakfast.

Dining/Entertainment: Dining is under a wooden ceiling, and the cuisine is both continental and West Indian. Once a week in the winter, big buffets are spread out for you, with white-capped chefs in attendance. There are two bars, one of which sits a few paces from the surf.

Services: Laundry, room service, baby-sitting.

Facilities: Swimming pool, two tennis courts.

Tamarind Cove

Paynes Bay (1¹/₂ miles south of Holetown on Highway 1), St. James Beach (mailing address: P.O. Box 429, Bridgetown), Barbados, W.I. ☎ **809/432-1332**. Fax 809/432-6317. 59 rms, 107 suites. A/C TEL. Winter $375–$395 double, $430–$550 suite; off-season $270–$290 double, $300–$370 suite. Rates include MAP. AE, DC, MC, V.

Tamarind Cove was established in 1969, when Janet Kidd, daughter of British newspaper magnate Lord Beaverbrook, built a small and glamorous hotel on her own land to accommodate friends who flew in for matches on her world-class polo grounds. Shortly after construction, it was acquired by a small British-based hotel chain (St. James Beach Properties, Ltd.), which soon transformed it into their flagship property. It is a major challenger to the Coral Reef/Sandpiper properties, and attracts the same upmarket clientele. In 1990, an $8 million restoration enlarged and expanded it into one of the most noteworthy hotels in Barbados. In 1995 a new south wing, with some 49 luxurious rooms and suites—some with private plunge pools and Jacuzzis—was added, along with a freshwater swimming pool with a beachfront terrace.

Designed in an Iberian style, with pale pink walls and red terra-cotta roofs, Tamarind Cove occupies a desirable site beside St. James Beach. The stylish and comfortable accommodations are in a series of hacienda-style buildings interspersed with vegetation. Each unit features a patio or balcony overlooking the gardens or ocean.

Dining/Entertainment: In addition to an informal beachfront restaurant, Tamarind contains two elegant restaurants; the more memorable is Neptune's, which specializes in sophisticated seafood dishes. The Flamingo is the main restaurant. A handful of bars are scattered throughout the property, and there's musical entertainment every night.

Services: Room service, baby-sitters, laundry, massage, concierge.

Facilities: Immediately adjacent white-sand beach, and four palm-shaded freshwater swimming pools; complimentary water sports including waterskiing, windsurfing, catamaran sailing, and snorkeling. Golf, tennis, horseback riding, and polo are available nearby.

INEXPENSIVE

Traveller's Palm

265 Palm Ave. (a 5-minute drive south of Holetown on Highway 1), Sunset Crest, St. James, Barbados, W.I. ☎ **809/432-7722.** 16 apts. A/C. Winter $75 apt for up to four; off-season $50 apt for up to four. Service and tax extra. AE, MC, V.

Designed for the independent traveler, Traveller's Palm is a choice collection of simply furnished apartments with fully equipped kitchens. Apartments also offer living and dining room areas, as well as patios where you can eat breakfast or enjoy a candlelit dinner. The apartments are filled with bright, resort colors and handcrafted furniture, and they open onto a lawn with a swimming pool. Serviced by maids, they contain one bedroom but can sleep up to four people. A handful of beaches lie within a 5-minute walk. Hamburgers and cheese toasties are served from a snack bar beside the pool.

SOUTH OF BRIDGETOWN

Barbados Hilton

Needham's Point (directly south of Bridgetown off Highway 7; P.O. Box 510), St. Michael, Barbados, W.I. ☎ **809/426-0200,** or 800/HILTONS in the U.S. Fax 809/436-8946. 182 rms, 2 suites. A/C MINIBAR TV TEL. Winter $245–$275 double, $576 suite; off-season $148–$170 double, $266–$358 suite. AE, DC, MC, V.

On more than 14 acres of landscaped gardens, the Barbados Hilton International is a self-contained resort, although it lies on the heavily populated southern edge of Bridgetown near an oil refinery whose odors sometimes drift over the beach. The competition has long ago edged the Hilton from the topnotch ranks, and it looks a bit worn and tired. But it remains a favorite of business travelers and conventioneers, and is often packed every night. Built in 1966 and overhauled and redecorated several times since, it occupies the rugged peninsula where the English built Fort Charles in the 18th century. The Hilton's architecture incorporates porous blocks of bleached coral interspersed with jutting balconies and wide expanses of glass.

The bedrooms are arranged around a central courtyard that's filled with tropical gardens and covered by a skylight. Each of the comfortable units offers a balcony with a view of Carlisle Bay on the north side or the Atlantic on the south, and vines cascade down from the balconies.

Several kinds of water sports are offered on the milk-white sands of the nearby beach, whose outermost edge is protected from storm damage by a massive breakwater of giant rocks.

Dining/Entertainment: The Verandah restaurant, whose backdrop is a row of diminutive clapboard-sided Bajan houses, serves your basic island and international specialties to the accompaniment of live music. The hotel has a gaming room with slot machines, and both a beachfront daytime bar and snack restaurant (The Gazebo) and a nighttime bar (The Flambeau).

Services: Masseur, room service, laundry, concierge who arranges sports and other diversionary activities.

Facilities: Four lighted tennis courts, 1,000-foot-wide manmade beach, sauna, health club; access to horseback riding and golf.

Grand Barbados Beach Resort

Aquatic Gap, Bay St. (about 1 mile southeast of Bridgetown off Highway 7; P.O. Box 639), Bridgetown, St. Michael, Barbados, W.I. ☎ **809/426-0890.** Fax 809/436-9823. 128 rms,

5 suites. A/C MINIBAR TV TEL. Winter $245–$275 double, $500–$650 suite; off-season $145–$190 double, $300–$350 suite. MAP $47 extra per person per day. AE, DC, MC, V.

This stylish and imaginative hotel is an airy and well-designed eight-story resort incorporating lots of space and light, opening onto Carlisle Bay. It is the result of a radical overhaul of a property built in 1969. In 1986, a Trinidad-based insurance company spent several million dollars to renovate the four-acre resort, adding a cosmopolitan kind of zest. Like the Hilton, it's near an oil refinery. Today, the well-furnished but often small bedrooms all provide balconies, in-room movies, hair dryers, and safes. The higher prices listed above are for units on the two Aquatic Club executive floors, the two top stories of the hotel, where the rooms come with extra amenities such as complimentary cocktails, continental breakfast, and pastries with coffee in the executive lounge at night.

Dining/Entertainment: Perhaps its most unusual feature is the massive pier jutting out into the sea, at the end of which is a seafood restaurant, the Schooner, known for its buffets. The Boardwalk Café is on the pier, where nightly entertainment is provided. There is also the Coral Garden cocktail lounge.

Services: Room service from 7am to 1pm, laundry, concierge for the arrangement of car rentals and island tours.

Facilities: Water sports, outdoor swimming pool, Jacuzzi, sauna, Sunfish sailing, free use of the hotel's fitness center; complimentary day/night tennis nearby; complimentary glass-bottom boat rides; sports, such as golf, water-skiing, and horseback riding, can be arranged.

ON THE SOUTH COAST
MODERATE

Divi Southwinds Beach Resort

St. Lawrence Gap (midway between Bridgetown and Oistins, off Highway 7), Christ Church, Barbados, W.I. ☎ **809/428-7181** or 800/367-3484. Fax 809/428-4674. 33 studios, 127 suites. A/C TV TEL. Winter $185–$200 double occupancy of a studio, $205–$230 double occupancy of a one-bedroom suite. Off-season $110–$125 studio, $140–$155 one-bedroom suite. MAP $40 extra per person per day. AE, DC, MC, V.

The Divi Southwinds was created when two distinctly different resorts (an older unit on the beachfront and a newer one built a short walk inland near a pair of swimming pools) were combined into a single coherent although architecturally undistinguished whole. Scattered over sandy flatlands of about 20 acres, the resorts were built in 1975 and 1986, respectively. Each has its own virtues and each enjoys a loyal clientele. The showplace of the resort are the newer (inland) buildings consisting of suites with full kitchens—ideal for families. This section looks like an interconnected series of town houses, with spacious wooden balconies and views of a large L-shaped swimming pool. From these buildings, visitors need only cross through two groves of palm trees and a narrow lane to reach the resort's beach. The more older, more modest but fully renovated units lie directly on the palm-ringed beachfront near an oval-shaped swimming pool of their own.

Dining/Entertainment: The Aquarius Restaurant, which rises like a cedar-sided Tahitian teepee above the largest of the resort's swimming pools, is the main dining and drinking emporium. The food is pretty standard. A satellite snack bar/drink bar lies beside the beach, near the resort's older units.

Services: Morning room service, laundry, arranging island tours.

Facilities: Three swimming pools (one a wading pool reserved for children), sailboat rentals, putting green, hair salon, snorkeling equipment.

ⓗ Family-Friendly Hotels

Glitter Bay *(see p. 205)*   If you can afford it, the best place is Glitter Bay with its cottagelike suites and kitchenettes. Children can play on the beach or in the swimming pool. They're charged from $35 to $55 per day when sharing a suite with their parents.

Divi Southwinds Beach Resort *(see p. 215)*   On 20 acres, this modern resort offers two-bedroom suites with full kitchens—ideal for families. A swimming pool is reserved for children.

Sandy Beach Hotel *(see p. 216)*   Children get reduced rates at this South Coast beach resort, with its one- and two-bedroom suites, suitable for families, with fully equipped kitchenettes.

Casuarina Beach Club *(see p. 217)*   This family-run choice caters to families with reasonably priced suites offering kitchenettes and a pair of swimming pools.

Sandy Beach Hotel

Worthing, Christ Church, Barbados, W.I. ☎ **809/435-8000.** Fax 809/435-8053. 89 suites. A/C TV TEL. Winter $95 double; $205–$280 one-bedroom suite; $335–$475 two-bedroom suite. Off-season $85 double; $115–$150 one-bedroom suite; $225–$290 two-bedroom suite. Additional person $30 extra in winter, $25 extra off-season. Children under 12 stay free in parents' room. MAP $40 per adult extra. Service and taxes extra. AE, MC, V.

Definitely not be confused with Sandy Lane (see above), this Bajan-owned hotel was established in 1980 on two acres of beachfront land. It rises around an architectural centerpiece, a soaring conical-shaped *palapa*. A good choice for families with children, Sandy Beach contains only one- and two-bedroom suites, plus 16 honeymoon suites with queen-size beds and completely private patios. All the tastefully decorated and spacious accommodations provide fully equipped kitchenettes and private balconies or patios. All the furniture at this informal place was made in Barbados. Facilities for the disabled are provided in four of the ground-floor suites. It may not be a glamorous choice, but it's reliable.

Dining/Entertainment: The Beachfront Restaurant, specializing in seafood and steak, lies under the previously mentioned palapa and opens onto a view of the beach and swimming pool. The open-air design and use of wood and hanging plants give the restaurant a natural look by day that becomes romantic by candlelight at night. Outsiders are welcomed every Monday at a rum punch party with a Trinidad-style steel band and a Bajan buffet.

Services: Room service, laundry, dry cleaning, concierge who arranges island tours.

Facilities: Guests pay extra for water sports including 3-hour snorkeling trips, windsurfing, paddleboats, Sailfish, scuba lessons, and use of air mattresses, snorkels, fins, and masks. There's also a swimming pool for adults, and a children's play area with wading pool.

Southern Palms

St. Lawrence (midway between Bridgetown and Oistins on Highway 7), Barbados, W.I. ☎ **809/428-7171,** or 800/424-5500 in the U.S. Fax 809/428-7175. 73 rms, 20 suites. A/C TEL. Winter $180–$220 double, $270 suite; off-season $95–$115 double, $150 suite. MAP $40 extra per person per day. AE, DC, MC, V.

A seafront club with a distinct personality, Southern Palms lies on Pink Beach, midway between the airport and Bridgetown. The core of the resort is a mid-20th-century pink-and-white manor house, built in a Dutch style with a garden-level colonnade of arches. Spread along the sands are multiarched two- and three-story buildings, on grounds planted with oleander, bougainvillea, and hibiscus. Italian fountains and statues add to the Mediterranean feeling.

In its more modern block, an eclectic mixture of rooms includes some with kitchenettes, some facing the ocean, others opening onto the garden, and some with penthouse luxury. The decor is the standard motel-like tropical motif. A cluster of buildings that contain the restaurant and bars links the accommodations together.

Dining/Entertainment: The Khus-Khus Bar and Restaurant serves both West Indian and continental cuisine. A local orchestra often entertains by providing merengue and steel-band music.

Services: Laundry, room service, arranging island tours.

Facilities: Terrace for sunning, two beachside freshwater swimming pools, sailboat rentals, snorkeling, and scuba.

INEXPENSIVE

Bagshot House Hotel

St. Lawrence (a 15-minute drive southeast of Bridgetown on Highway 7), Christ Church, Barbados, W.I. ☎ **809/435-6956.** 16 rms. TEL. Winter $130 double; off-season $90 double. Rates include breakfast. No credit cards.

Custom-built in 1956 and renovated in 1995, this small, family-managed hotel sports flowering vines tumbling over balcony railings and an old-fashioned and unhurried kind of charm. The hotel was named after the early 19th-century manor house that once stood on this site. That house was demolished, and this concrete-sided hotel was built in its place; it was named after Bagshot, the town in England where the original builder was born. In front, the beach stretches out before you. Some of the well-kept, simply furnished units boast views of the water. Only two units are air-conditioned. For an extra charge, a TV can be placed in your room. A sunbathing deck, which doubles as a kind of living room for the resort, is perched at the edge of a lagoon. A deckside lounge is decorated with paintings by local artists, and there's a restaurant on the premises.

Casuarina Beach Club

St. Lawrence Gap, Christ Church, Barbados, W.I. ☎ **809/428-3600,** or 800/223-9815 in the U.S. Fax 809/428-1970. 123 studios, 20 one-bedroom, 14 two-bedroom suites. A/C TEL. Winter $160–$170 studio for two; $190 one-bedroom suite; $320 two-bedroom suite. Off-season $90–$100 studio for two; $120–$135 one-bedroom suite; $180–$195 two-bedroom suite. Children under 12 stay free in parents' room. MAP $35 per person extra. AE, MC, V.

The South Coast resorts are rather lackluster as a group, but this one is the best. It's a good choice for those who prefer to cook for themselves. You approach Casuarina through a forest of palm trees, which sway above a well-maintained lawn. Established in 1981, with substantial additions and improvements in 1991, the resort is pleasant, family-run, and unpretentious. Designed in the Iberian styel, with red-tile roofs and white walls, the main building has a series of arched windows leading onto verandas. To get to your accommodation, you pass through the outlying reception building and beside the pair of swimming pools. These are separated from the wide sandy beach by a lawn dotted with casuarina and bougainvillea. On the premises is an octagonal-roofed open-air bar and restaurant, two floodlit tennis courts, and a fitness room. The front desk can arrange most seaside activities through outside agencies. Each accommodation is equipped with a ceiling fan and rattan furniture, and each suite contains a kitchenette for preparing snacks and meals. The hotel is decorated with local artwork, including paintings, terra-cotta pots, sculptures, and unusual baskets, many produced in Barbados or elsewhere in the West Indies.

Fairholme

Maxwell (6 miles southeast of Bridgetown on Highway 7), Christ Church, Barbados, W.I. ☎ **809/428-9425.** 11 rms, 20 studio apts. A/C. Winter $30 double, $55 studio apt; off-season $28 double, $35 studio apt. No credit cards.

Fairholme is a converted plantation house whose sleeping quarters have been enlarged during the past quarter century by a handful of interconnected annexes. The main house and its original gardens are just off a major road, a 5-minute walk to the beach, and across from its neighboring hotel, the Sherringham Beach, which has a waterfront cafe and bar that Fairholme guests can patronize. The older part has 11 double rooms, each with a living-room area and a patio overlooking an orchard and swimming pool. Beside the pool is a grassy lawn for sunbathing and a bar for island beverages. More recently added are 20 Spanish-style studio apartments, all with kitchen and balcony or patio. Each features high cathedral ceilings, dark beams, and traditional furnishings. The restaurant has a reputation for wholesome home-cooking—nothing fancy, but the ingredients are fresh. On the premises are the remnants of a very old wall, part of the ruined foundation of the original plantation complex. A note about the air-conditioning: Someone from the reception desk will sell you a brass token for $3. When you insert it into a slot in your air conditioner, it will give you around 8 hours of cooling.

Ocean View

Hastings (4 miles southeast of Bridgetown on Highway 7), Christ Church, Barbados, W.I. ☎ **809/427-7821.** Fax 809/427-7826. 28 rms, 4 suites. TEL. Winter $95–$145 double, $175–$225 suite; off-season $65–$75 double, $150 suite. MAP $40 extra per day. AE, MC, V.

An old-timer that seems just as good as ever, Ocean View was founded in 1901, making it the oldest hotel in Barbados. Built between the busy road and the beach, the pink-and-white resort has some of the graciousness of a colonial English house, including an open staircase with an old balustrade and a seaside porch that's good for lounging. Every bedroom is different—some are large, others small and cozy. Island antiques add special touches. Most rooms have air-conditioning, and all have ceiling fans.

This vintage hostelry also serves good food. You can dine at a table overlooking the sea, helping yourself at the well-known Sunday planters' buffet lunch in the winter for $27.50. As in the olden days, there is a big spread of Bajan specialties. Ernest Hemingway attended some buffets here, enjoying especially the callaloo soup, flying fish, and pepperpot, according to local legend.

Woodville Beach Hotel

Hastings (2¹/₂ miles southeast of Bridgetown on Highway 7), Christ Church, Barbados, W.I. ☎ **809/435-6694.** Fax 809/435-9211. 31 apts. TEL. Winter $85–$100 studio, $110 one-bedroom apt, $150 two-bedroom apt; off-season $56–$66 studio, $75 one-bedroom apt, $110 two-bedroom apt. No credit cards.

These apartments, last renovated in 1995, are one of the best bargains in Barbados, ideal for families on a budget. Situated directly at a rocky shoreline in the heart of Hastings village, on slightly less than an acre of land, this U-shaped apartment complex is built around a pool terrace overlooking the sea. Functional and minimalist in decor, it is clean and comfortable. The tiny kitchenettes in each accommodation are fully equipped, and a variety of rental units are offered, ranging from a studio to a two-bedroom apartment. All feature balconies or decks, and 12 contain air-conditioning. Supermarkets, stores, and banks are within easy walking distance. Although a handful of athletic guests swim off the nearby rocks, most opt for a 5-minute walk to the white sands of Rockley (Accra) Beach. The first of this complex's apartments was built in 1967, with many improvements and additions since. A small restaurant is on site.

ON THE EAST COAST
MODERATE

Crane Beach Hotel

Crane Bay (near the easternmost end of the island about 14 miles from Bridgetown, a 15-minute drive northeast of the airport via Highway 7), St. Philip, Barbados, W.I. ☎ **809/423-6220**, or 800/223-6510 in the U.S. and Canada. Fax 809/423-5343. 14 rms, 4 suites. TEL. Winter $180 double, $250–$295 suite, $450 two-bedroom suite. Off-season $100 double; $140–$175 suite; $260 two-bedroom suite. MAP $40 per person extra. Honeymoon packages available. AE, DC, MC, V.

On a remote hilltop property on a cliff, Crane Beach was called by one writer "the most beautiful spot on earth." At least Prince Andrew thought so when he built his clearly visible house on a nearby cliff. The location may be beautiful, but the hotel has some drawbacks. Time-share units are hawked in the lobby, and housekeeping appears lax. Rubberneckers can pay an entrance fee to enter the property, and patronize the area around the swimming pool and the bar, often disturbing the tranquility (everyone has to pay $2.50 to enter the property, but that money is redeemable if you make purchases at either the bar or restaurant). In other words, it's not for everybody, but yet is one of the most famous hostelries in the Southern Caribbean. Near Marriott's Sam Lord's Castle, the hotel opens onto one of the best beaches in Barbados (reached by walking down some 200 steps); the water at times can be too rough for swimming. Canopied beds and antique furnishings are found in many of the bedrooms, and often the views are panoramic. Some units are air-conditioned, and a few have kitchenettes.

Dining/Entertainment: Many visitors for the day head here just to have a drink on the panoramic terrace or order a meal. An international cuisine is served with West Indian flair. At night the tables are candlelit. Its Sunday brunch is a well-attended event.

Services: Room service, baby-sitting, laundry.

Facilities: The Roman-style swimming pool with columns, separating the main house from the dining room, has perhaps been used as a backdrop for more fashion layouts than any other place in the Caribbean. The resort also has tennis courts.

Marriott's Sam Lord's Castle

Long Bay (near the easternmost end of the island, about 14 miles from Bridgetown, a 15-minute drive northeast of the airport via Highway 7), St. Philip, Barbados, W.I. ☎ **809/423-7350** or 800/223-6388. Fax 809/423-5918. 234 rms. A/C MINIBAR TEL. Winter $225–$275 double; off-season $115–$145 double. MAP $44 per person per day. AE, DC, MC, V.

This resort's architecturally acclaimed centerpiece was built in 1820 by one of Barbados's most notorious scoundrels. According to legend, Samuel Hall Lord (the "Regency Rascal") built the estate with money acquired by luring ships to their doom on the jagged but hard-to-detect rocks of Cobbler's Reef. Only seven rooms are in the Main House, and these have garnered all the style, with canopied beds and tasteful furnishings. The rest of the accommodations are in cottages and wings, either two or four floors high, villas built at the edge of the cliff, and some rather tacky motel rooms with a *faux*-castle theme. Some of these units evoke southwest Miami in the

1950s, no great compliment. For privacy's sake and to get more light, try to avoid ground-floor units if possible. The best and most expensive accommodations are in structures 7, 8, and 9.

The great house was built in the pirate's more mellow golden years. To create its dignified interior, craftsmen were imported from England to reproduce selected sections of the monarchy's castle at Windsor. The ceilings look down on the dubiously acquired but nonetheless beautiful art of Reynolds, Raeburn, and Chippendale.

Today, amid 72 acres landscaped with rare flowering trees, the estate has a wide, lengthy private sandy beach edged by tall coconut trees. The staff seems more concerned with the demands of the group traffic—the hotel is a favorite for conventions—than for the solo traveler.

Dining/Entertainment: Three meals a day are served in the Wanderer Restaurant, and you can order a hamburger at Sam's Place, right on the beach. There are many bars as well. A Fiesta night in the hotel's Bajan Village is offered once a week, as is a shipwreck barbecue and beach party with a steel-drum band, a limbo show, and fire-eaters on South Beach.

Services: Beauty shop/barbershop, laundry, baby-sitters, concierge who arranges island tours.

Facilities: In addition to three free-form pools, other facilities include a game room, an exercise room, shuffleboard, table tennis, and a library. In addition, golf, sailing, horseback riding, snorkeling, waterskiing, fishing, luncheon and nighttime cruises, and other activities available on the island can be arranged by the activities director.

INEXPENSIVE

The Edgewater Inn

Bathsheba (13 miles northeast of Bridgetown on Highway 3), St. Joseph, Barbados, W.I. ☎ **809/433-9900,** or 213/389-5291 in the U.S. Fax 809/433-9902. 20 rms. Winter $75–$110 double; off-season $55–$90 double. AE, DISC, MC, V.

Built as a dramatically isolated private home on the site of a much older colonial building, and converted into a hotel in 1947, this inn is set directly on the Atlantic seacoast, a short drive southeast of the island's "Scotland District." Lying in a tropical rain forest on top of a low cliff, the property opens onto ocean views, and a nearby wildlife sanctuary invites exploration. Cozy and intimate, the small inn is decorated with beveled leaded glass windows from Asia, and furnishings reflect an island motif, with mahogany pieces handcrafted by local artisans.

The freshwater swimming pool, shaped like the island of Barbados, is the focal point of the resort. Surfers are attracted to the hotel and nonresidents are also invited to drop by, either for a meal or a drink. The restaurant, serving West Indian cuisine, is open daily from 11am to 4pm for lunch and from 6 to 9pm for dinner. A Bajan buffet is staged every Sunday from noon to 3:30pm, costing $18.

Kingsley Club

Cattlewash-on-Sea (just north of Bathsheba on Highway 3), St. Joseph, Barbados, W.I. ☎ **809/433-9422.** Fax 809/433-9226. 8 rms. Winter $101 double; off-season $84 double. Rates include breakfast. AE, MC, V.

Kingsley may be that hidden-away little West Indian inn you've been hoping to find far from the bustle of the tourist-ridden West Coast. It is often a favorite stopover for the Bajans themselves. The rooms are simply furnished and very modest but clean and comfortable. In the foothills of Bathsheba, opening onto the often-turbulent Atlantic, the resort lies on the northeast coast. Cattlewash Beach is one of the longest, widest, and least crowded in Barbados. But please note: Swimming here can be extremely dangerous.

At night, you can sit back and enjoy a rum punch made from an old planter's recipe. Kingsley enjoys a reputation for good cooking, and its Bajan food is recommended for those traveling to the East Coast just for the day (see "Where to Dine," below).

2　Where to Dine

Gourmet cuisine, prepared by chefs from Europe and North America, is commonplace at the posher places on Barbados. There has been an explosive growth in the number of new restaurants in the mid-90s.

If you want authentic Bajan cuisine, head for the local taverns, where callaloo soup, cou-cou, and pepperpot stew will be on the menus, all indicating the West African heritage of many Barbadians. We'll share our own favorite finds below.

Flying fish, kingfish, snapper, and dolphin (mahi mahi, not the mammal) are better than most meat dishes, many of which are made from frozen meat shipped in from the north.

Most top restaurants require a reservation in the winter. It's always a good idea to call a place before trekking across the island, because of unexpected closings.

In this chapter, meals considered **expensive** cost from $40 per person; **moderate,** $25 to $40; and **inexpensive,** under $25, plus wine and drinks. A 10% service charge is added to most restaurant tabs, but it's customary to tip more than this, especially if service has been good. Prices are given below in U.S. dollars.

ON THE WEST COAST
EXPENSIVE

✪ Bagatelle Restaurant

Highway 2A, St. Thomas Parish. ☎ **809/421-6767.** Reservations recommended. Lunch $12; fixed-price dinner $45. AE, MC, V. Mon–Sat 11am–2:30pm; daily 7–9:30pm. Closed Sun in May–Nov. Cut inland on Highway 2A near Paynes Bay, north of Bridgetown, 3 miles from both Sunset Crest and Sandy Lane hotels. FRENCH/CARIBBEAN.

Bagatelle is housed in one of the most historic and impressive buildings on Barbados. Located a 15-minute drive north of Bridgetown, and originally built in 1645 as the residence of Lord Willoughby, the island's first governor, the restaurant is situated on five acres of forest, illuminated by some of the best lighting in the Caribbean. This sylvan retreat is in the cool uplands, just south of the island's center, and retains the charm of its original construction. Walls, fashioned from blocks of chiseled coral, are at least 3 feet thick. The setting seems to complement the presentation of the island's finest and most elegant French cuisine, which has a dash of Caribbean flavor. Candles and lanterns illuminate the menu as well as the white coral walls, the old archways, and the ancient trees. Service is gracious, among the best we've found on Barbados. You might get personal suggestions from the the British-born owners, Richard and Val Richings.

While seated on massively carved baronial chairs, you could try homemade duck liver pâté, deviled Caribbean crab backs, or smoked flying fish mousse with horseradish mayonnaise. The beef Wellington Bagatelle-style with a chausseur sauce is a favorite, as is the crisp roast duckling with an orange and brandy sauce. The local catch of the day—perhaps the most popular item on the menu—can be prepared grilled, barbecued, or in the style of Baxters Road (that is, spicily seasoned and sautéed in deep oil). A different list of homemade desserts is featured nightly, and coffee can be served on the terrace. Cruise-ship passengers can take advantage of a light lunch here before their ships sail at sunset.

✪ Carambola

Derricks (1 mile south of Holetown on Highway 1; 3 miles north of Bridgetown), St. James. ☎ **809/432-0832.** Reservations recommended. Main courses $19–$45. AE, MC, V. Mon–Sat 6:30–9:30pm. Closed Aug. FRENCH/CARIBBEAN/ASIAN.

Built atop the upper edge of a 20-foot seaside cliff, Carambola offers one of the most panoramic terraces for dining in the Caribbean. You must have a very early dinner to see the view, since Carambola doesn't serve lunch. Contained in the shadow of a much-enlarged Bajan house, originally built during the 1950s as a private home, the restaurant has quickly moved to the forefront of the island's dining scene. Owner Robin Walcott's creative, prize-winning cuisine is a blend of French, Caribbean, and a medley of inspirations from Asia. You might begin with a chicken breast salad with warm glass noodles, and follow with a filet of local barracuda. Or you can enjoy a more French selection, perhaps traditional loin of lamb with an herb crust resting on a ragoût of mushrooms and golden polenta. The impressive wine list features mostly French vintages.

✪ The Cliff

Highway 1, Derrick, St. James. ☎ **809/432-1922.** Reservations recommended. Main courses $21–$48. AE, DISC, DC, MC, V. Mon–Sat 6:30–10pm. INTERNATIONAL/CARIBBEAN.

Before it opened in 1995, its owners lavished time and money on blasting a niche from a coralstone cliff to create a perch for their open-air restaurant. What you'll see today is a four-level area, crafted from terra-cotta tiles and coral stone, set above a 10-foot cliff adjacent to the Coconut Creek Hotel. Despite the fact that the English/Bajan partners who own it don't consider it exclusive, posh, or even particularly formal, it has attracted Prince Andrew, Steven Segal, and the assorted titled and bejeweled clients of the nearby upscale hotels. Despite all this, no one will mind if you wear well-tailored shorts—the place really is surprisingly informal.

The food here was accurately praised by *Gourmet* reader Dr. Stephen C. Bandy of Princeton, N.J., who wrote, "The Cliff offers a menu of the highest quality: best cuts of meat, the freshest and most interesting vegetables and greens I have ever eaten on the island, and dessert confections that would not be looked down on in New York restaurants like Bouley and Lespinasse." How right he is! Menu items include grilled snapper drizzled in three types of coriander sauce (cream-based, oil-based, and vinaigrette style) and accompanied with garlic-infused mashed potatoes; and Thai-style curried shrimp. Sushi is presented (when available) as a starter complete with wasabi and portions of fresh local tuna, scallops, and snapper. As you dine, watch for manta rays, which glide through the illuminated waters below. The seas are usually calm enough to see them, and catching a glimpse is considered a sign of very good luck.

La Cage aux Folles

Summerland Great House (between Batts Rock and Tamarind Cove), Prospect, St. James. ☎ **809/424-2424.** Reservations recommended, especially in winter. Main courses $20–$45. MC, V. Wed–Mon 7–10:30pm. Closed June. ASIAN/INTERNATIONAL.

La Cage aux Folles is the latest statement of two entrepreneurs who have established several other restaurants in both London and Barbados since their careers began in the early 1970s. Located in an old-fashioned island house, the decor is evocative of a plantation house, with tall ceilings, impressive crystal chandeliers, and a balcony for sundowners. The most impressive room, reserved for groups and wedding receptions, centers around a reflecting pool and is lined with Bajan antiques or antique reproductions. In spite of the name, which might make you think this restaurant was about

Barbados Dining

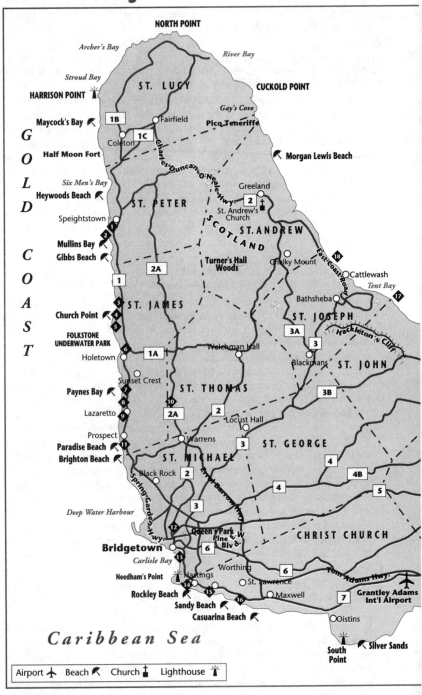

NORTH POINT

Archer's Bay

River Bay

ST. LUCY

CUCKOLD POINT

Stroud Bay

HARRISON POINT

Gay's Cove

1B ○Fairfield

MAYCOCK'S BAY

Pico Teneriffe

1C ○Coleton

Half Moon Fort

Morgan Lewis Beach

Six Men's Bay

G O L D   C O A S T

Heywoods Beach

ST. PETER

Greeland

Speightstown

St. Andrew's Church

1

2

SCOTLAND

Mullins Bay

ST. ANDREW

Gibbs Beach

2A

Turner's Hall Woods

Chalky Mount

18

Cattlewash

1

Tent Bay

3 ST. JAMES

Bathsheba

17

Church Point **4**

5

ST. JOSEPH

FOLKSTONE UNDERWATER PARK

3A

Hackleton's Cliff

6

3

Holetown **1A** Welchman Hall

Blackmans **ST. JOHN**

Sunset Crest

Paynes Bay **7**

ST. THOMAS

8

10

3B

Lazaretto **9**

2A **2** Locust Hall

Prospect

Warrens **3** **ST. GEORGE**

Paradise Beach **11**

Brighton Beach

2 **ST. MICHAEL** **4**

Black Rock

4B

3 **4** **5**

Deep Water Harbour

12

CHRIST CHURCH

Bridgetown Queen's Park

13 Pine Blvd **6**

Carlisle Bay Worthing

6

Needham's Point Hastings

Tom Adams Hwy.

14 St. Lawrence

7 Grantley Adams Int'l Airport

Rockley Beach **15** Maxwell

Sandy Beach **16**

Casuarina Beach

○Oistins

Caribbean Sea

South Point Silver Sands

Airport ✈ Beach 🏄 Church ⚓ Lighthouse

Atlantic Ocean

Martin's Bay
Congor Rocks

Consett Bay

CULPEPPER ISLAND

Three Houses

Ragged Point Lighthouse

Kitridge Point

Bushy Park

Sandford

Bottom Bay

ST. PHILIP 5

Long Bay

Marchfield

Beachy Head

7

Crane Beach

Long Bay

Caribbean Islands

Barbados

0   3 km / 1.9 mi

N

show "girls" in drag, this is among the stellar dining choices on the island, venturing around the world for its culinary inspirations.

Try the sesame prawn pâté, sweet-and-sour shrimp, or Créole fish soup. Other courses include crispy aromatic duck and a dish inspired by the cuisine of India: tikka makhani, a creamy and spicy chicken cooked slowly in a tandoori and served with stir-fried vegetables. For dessert, profiteroles with chocolate sauce and an old-fashioned English syllabub are the best choices.

La Maison

Holetown (north of Bridgetown on Highway 1, near Paynes Bay), St. James. ☎ **809/432-1156.** Reservations recommended. Main courses $22–$40; lunch from $10. MC, V. Tues–Sat noon–2:30pm; Tues–Sun 6:30–9:30pm. FRENCH/CARIBBEAN.

Located on the beach, a 3-minute walk south of Holetown, La Maison was established in 1990 in a coral-sided structure built in the 1970s as a copy of an older Barbadian home constructed long ago for members of the Cunard family. Open on two sides to the sea and to a flowering courtyard, whose centerpiece is a mermaid-capped fountain, the restaurant derives most of its decor from the exposed coral of its walls and the glow of its intricate ceiling, crafted solely of a Guyanan hardwood called greenheart. The award-winning cuisine is served with quiet dignity.

For appetizers, the chef offers an array of dishes, including blackened flying fish filets set on a sweet-potato salad. Main courses include such exotica as barracuda steamed with passion fruit or a trio of flying fish prepared in three different ways. If you don't want anything too exotic, try the broiled chicken breast stuffed with sun-dried tomatoes or the grilled sirloin with cracked peppercorns. The restaurant knows how to do the simpler dishes well, too.

✪ Neptune's

At the Tamarind Cove Beach Resort, Paynes Bay, St. James Beach. ☎ **809/432-1332.** Reservations recommended. Main courses $21–$40. AE, DC, MC, V. Daily 6:30–10pm. Closed Tues in off-season. SEAFOOD.

By anyone's standards, Neptune's is the best seafood restaurant in Barbados. Contained in the pink hacienda-style walls of one of the island's most respected resorts, it abandons completely the "ocean breezes blowing through the hibiscus blossoms" mode that characterizes most of Barbados's other restaurants. Instead, you'll find a stylish octagonal room sheathed in *faux* malachite, whose emerald-green tones reflect the colors of an illuminated aquarium in the room's center. Service is impeccable.

Appetizers range from Bajan fish terrine to fresh local fish set in a champagne jelly scented with peppercorns. Another delectable choice is the kebab of scallops on a bed of confit leeks. Neptune's catch is a selection of island fish, often served in a light orange sauce flavored with herbs. You can also order that island favorite, filet of red snapper, or splurge on lobster medallions in a red pepper sauce. Chicken is served here Caribbean-style—in this case, wrapped in filo pastry and baked with a mango sauce. The dessert menu is one of the most elaborate in Barbados, ranging from a classical tiramisu to a coconut and mango parfait or a trio of rich chocolate mousse.

✪ Olives Bar & Bistro

2nd Street (at the corner of Highway 1), Holetown. ☎ **809/432-2112.** Reservations recommended. Main courses $14–$28. AE, DC, MC, V. Daily 5:30–10:30pm. MEDITERRANEAN/CARIBBEAN.

Established in 1994 by a couple from New Zealand, this restaurant occupies the site of the first two-story house ever built in Holetown. Its name is a reference to the fact that only olive oil is used to prepare the cuisine. Additionally, olives are the only snack served in the bar, which is welcoming and rowdy. The street-level dining room (no-smoking and air-conditioned) spills out from its original coral-stone walls and scrubbed-pine floorboards into a pleasant garden.

The cuisine celebrates the warm-weather climates of southern Europe and the Antilles and does so exceeding well. Even some local chefs like to dine here on their nights off. Best menu items include yellowfin tuna, marinated and seared rare, and served on a bed of roasted-garlic mashed potatoes with grilled ratatouille. More Caribbean in its flavors is a jerk tenderloin of pork with roasted-garlic mashed potatoes. Don't overlook the possibility of a cocktail in the cozy upstairs bar area.

✪ The Orchid Room

In the Colony Club Hotel, Porters, St. James. ☎ **809/422-2335.** Reservations recommended. Main courses $19–$35. AE, DC, MC, V. Daily 6:30–10pm. CARIBBEAN/FRENCH.

The Orchid Room blends a plantation house ambience with velvet glove service and finesse in the kitchen. It's even won the approval of the earl of Bradford, head of the Master Chefs of Great Britain, who found his last meal here "beautifully presented and perfectly prepared." Beneath sparkling chandeliers and surrounded by period furnishings, main courses are served with a dash of showmanship as silver domes are removed to reveal their treasures.

The award-winning chef brings Gallic flare to his creations, which are composed mostly of local ingredients. Appetizers are likely to include a salad of lobster with mango, delicate but full-flavored. Goat cheese is set on a sweet-potato pancake and scattered with walnuts, or else a soup may be an inventive cold lettuce with peppercorns or else hot pumpkin with smoked salmon. Main courses are varied, ranging from grilled dorado laid on a purée of eggplant and potato and dressed with lime and olive oil, or Washington state lamb filet gift-wrapped in a cornmeal crêpe with a deeply reduced cabernet sauvignon sauce.

The Palm Terrace

In the Royal Pavilion Hotel, Porters, St. James. ☎ **809/422-4444.** Reservations required. Main courses $25–$45. AE, DC, MC, V. Daily 7–9:30pm. CARIBBEAN/INTERNATIONAL.

North of Bridgetown between Sunset Crest and Gibbs Beach, in an elegant setting on a pink marble terrace evocative of the Mediterranean, this dramatic restaurant opens onto the oceanfront. The Palm Terrace has a French chef who oversees a Bajan staff. Together they turn out some of the more delectable cuisine offered at any West Coast hotel. To the sounds of music, with the trade winds sweeping in, you can sample chicken liver parfait served with a pear chutney and walnut brioche as an appetizer, or perhaps smoked fish tacos and black beans with a chili pepper sauce. Pastas are generally excellent, or else you may prefer grilled red snapper with roasted garlic. We were recently won over by the Thai green chicken curry. Each evening the chef prepares a prime roast carved at your table.

MODERATE

Château Créole

2 miles north of Holetown on Highway 1, St. James. ☎ **809/422-4116.** Reservations recommended. Main courses $15–31. AE, MC, V. Mon–Sat 6:30–9pm. BAJAN/CRÉOLE.

Built about 1975, this stucco-and-tile house is situated in a tropical garden dotted with classical urns and gazebos. After passing under an arbor, you'll be invited to order a drink, served on one of the flowered banquettes that fill various parts of Château Créole.

Go here for zesty dishes packed with island flavors. Menu specialties include Créole dishes such as stuffed crab backs, which—at least in this kitchen—prove the gastronomic potential of this often mishandled dish. Begin, perhaps, with red bean soup or else a succulent version of fish chowder. The chef manages to come up with such simple dishes as baked whitefish stuffed with crabmeat, given its artistry by the use and selection of fresh herbs. For a real taste of Barbados, make it chicken with fresh mangoes seasoned with ginger. Meals are taken al fresco on the rear terrace, by candlelight.

The Fathoms

Paynes Bay (10-minute drive south of Holetown on Highway 1), St. James. ☎ **809/432-2568.** Reservations recommended for dinner. Main courses $8–$10 at lunch, $15–$32 at dinner. AE, MC, V. Daily 11:30am–3pm and 6:30–10pm (last order). INTERNATIONAL.

The Fathoms is housed in a stucco-sided, red-roofed structure close to the surf of the island's western coastline, near one of the island's fish markets. The pleasant restaurant serves meals on an outdoor terrace shaded by a vast and primeval mahogany tree or an interior decorated with exposed accents of terra cotta, wood, and decorative pottery.

The restaurant offers a fairly ambitious menu, and does itself proud with such dishes as shrimp and crab etouffé, herbed conch cakes, or blackened shrimp with mango—all appearing as appetizers. For a main dish, it's caramelized barracuda (just like mother made) or else local rabbit stewed with onions, rum, rosemary, and raisins. Dorado fish Hunan has zesty and winning flavors, but the New Zealand lamb rack left us as cold as it was. Upstairs is a Sante Fe–style tapas bar, primarily for drinks, wines, and finger foods. A pool table and board games help you pass the evening away at this attractive watering hole, open daily from 5pm until the crowd finally departs for the night.

Koko's

Prospect (north of Bridgetown on Highway 1, between Batts Rock and Tamarind Cove), St. James. ☎ **809/424-4557.** Reservations recommended. Main courses $8–$22. MC, V. Daily 6:30–10pm. BAJAN.

Koko's is an award-winning restaurant, known for its excellent Caribbean cookery, a kind of Bajan *cuisine moderne.*

The location alone is appealing: It's in a charming once-private house, built on coral blocks on a terrace overlooking the sea. If you're tired of the typical bland surf-and-turf dinners and you want authentic island flavors, this is the place for you. You might begin with a homemade local soup, perhaps pepperpot, made with "roots of the Caribbean," or stir-fried squid with lime-and-mayonnaise sauce as an appetizer. Shrimp and crab fritters are served with a fiery dip. Main dishes include the chef's "ketch of de day," as well as West Coast–style island rabbit served with a tamarind-and-ginger sauce. Each dessert is homemade and luscious.

⑤ Nico's Champagne & Wine Bar

Derrick's, St. James. ☎ **809/432-6386.** Reservations recommended. Lunch main courses $10–$25; dinner main courses $10–$30. AE, MC, V. Mon–Sat 11:30am–10:30pm. INTERNATIONAL.

Set on the landward side of a road that bisects some of the most expensive residential real estate on Barbados, this is an informal bistro inspired by the wine bars of London. Set within a 19th-century building originally constructed in the 1800s as the headquarters for a plantation, it does a thriving business from within its air-conditioned bar area, where about a dozen kinds of wine are sold by the glass. Meals are served without napery and without fuss at tables protected with a shed-style roof in the garden in back. Food is flavorful, and designed to accompany the wine: Examples include deep-fried blue brie with passionfruit sauce; lemon pepper chicken kebabs; local red snapper with herb and white wine sauce, and some of the best lobster (grilled simply and served with garlic butter) in Barbados. Chris Millward and Cheryl

---

ⓜ Family-Friendly Restaurants

Shakey's Restaurant *(see page 232)*   Here you get the best pizzas on the island, including almost any kind you could want, including a gargantuan one for $35 for the family with the killer appetite. It's noisy and fun, and also serves fried chicken and subs.

The Ship Inn *(see page 232)*   This is one of the best family restaurants, lying at St. Lawrence Gap along the South Coast, site of many budget hotels. Its all-you-can-eat carvery lunches and similar help-yourself dinners make it a favorite of the family with a lean purse and a big appetite.

T.G.I. Boomers *(see page 233)*   Another family favorite at St. Lawrence Gap, this restaurant might be the bargain of Barbados. It offers both Bajan and American cuisine, along with the hamburgers and seafood that kids crave. It also serves the best American breakfast on Barbados.

Wiltshire, your hosts, seemed to have devoted a lot of care and attention to what you eat and drink.

✪ Raffles

First Street, Holetown. ☎ **809/432-6557.** Reservations recommended. Main courses $20–$32.50. AE, DC, MC, V. Daily 6–10pm (last order). CARIBBEAN.

Set amid the weather-beaten buildings along the main street of Holetown, in a pink-and-white, much-renovated older building, this cozy enclave has a relatively unusual list of specialties. A decor of *faux* leopardskin and safari-derived artifacts adds to the exotic atmosphere. The food here is rich, zesty, and spicy; appetite-rousing appetizers include the herb-flavored shrimp set on a bed of local greens. Proof of the talent of the chef is to take that old wives' favorite, Bajan saltfish cakes, and get the tourists to ask for a second helping. Jamaican ackee with saltfish is a favorite in Kingston, but our dining companion found it "an acquired taste." To go all the way to Africa, ask for *babouttie*, ground and heavily curried beef baked in custard and served with sliced bananas. If all that is *too* much, barbecued pork and tenderloin steaks also appear on the menu. The place is also known for its changing array of local fish—dolphin, barracuda, kingfish, the inevitable flying fish, and sea trout—prepared blackened, grilled, or sautéed.

The Terrace Restaurant

In the Cobblers Cove Hotel, Road View (¹/₂ mile south of Speightstown on Highway 1), St. Peter. ☎ **809/422-2291.** Reservations recommended. Main lunch courses $10–$20; main dinner courses $18–$25; fixed-price dinner $50. AE, MC, V. Daily 12:30–2pm and 7–9pm. CONTINENTAL.

This award-winning restaurant in the deluxe Cobblers Cove Hotel (see "Where to Stay," above) is open to nonguests, too, and you might come here to enjoy dining overlooking the ocean and a West Coast beach. Before dinner, guests often stop at the poolside bar to order the specialty drink, Cobblers Cooler, an extra-tall drink blending Caribbean fruits with the rum of Barbados.

The menu changes daily to take advantage of fresh local produce. A team of French-trained chefs work in the kitchen. You might begin with gazpacho of shrimp or duck pâté with orange sauce. The catch of the day is usually featured, and it can be either poached or grilled and flavored with Bajan seasoning. A *plat végétarien* is also featured, and meat courses include Bajan ham braised with pineapple and honey in a Madeira sauce. Many guests prefer to finish their meal with an Irish coffee. Although not always exciting, the food is reliable, solid, and always perfectly prepared with first-class ingredients.

INEXPENSIVE

Pizza House

Highway 1, Holetown, St. James. ☎ **809/432-0227.** Reservations not accepted or needed. Pizzas, pastas, subs, and salads $7–$28. AE, DISC, MC, V. Sun–Thurs 10:30am–11pm, Fri–Sat 10:30am–midnight. PIZZA.

If you're staying at one of the expensive West Coast hotels and get a sudden craving for pizza, head here. The place is squat and simple, and also functions as a bar with all kinds of liquor available. The place has a social life too, with lots of Bajans hanging out. The $28 pizza is the "ridiculous pie," with everything on it.

SPEIGHTSTOWN

Mango's

2 West End, Queen Street, Speightstown. ☎ **809/422-0704.** Reservations recommended. Main courses $11–$37.50. AE, MC, V. Tues–Sat 6–9:30pm. INTERNATIONAL.

Speightstown was never noted for its dining choices until this cafe, restaurant, and bar overlooking the water opened right on its main street. Run by a couple from Montreal, the restaurant offers entertainment on some nights, and features daily specials. It is best known for its seafood, and the owners buy directly from the fishers' boats. The catch of the day might be red snapper, dolphin, swordfish, grouper, or barracuda, depending on the season. It can be served grilled, blackened, or Bajan (breaded). Grilled lobster with lemon butter is also featured. If you don't want fish, opt for the 8-ounce U.S. of A. tenderloin steak cooked to perfection or the fall-off-the-bone barbecued baby back ribs. Chicken breast appears with a mango sauce and a very tasty vegetarian spaghetti. Appetizers might be anything from an intriguing green peppercorn pâté to pumpkin soup. Top the meal with a key lime pie or an even more interesting French orange rum cake. The food is exceedingly pleasing, and the seasonings do not overpower the flavor of the main ingredient, as they do at many Bajan restaurants. Seasonal market-fresh ingredients are used to good advantage.

BRIDGETOWN

Fisherman's Wharf

The Careenage, Bridgetown. ☎ **809/436-7778.** Reservations recommended. Main courses $12–$20; lunch from $10. Mon–Fri 11:30am–10pm, Sun 6–11pm. MC, V. CARIBBEAN.

The Careenage is the most colorful part of Bridgetown, and this restaurant and bar opens onto the waterfront action. Set on the upper floor of a restored warehouse dating from the turn of the century, this popular watering hole and dining choice is run by Diana Hamilton-Glover. Live jazz is featured on Sunday nights from 7 to 10:30pm, when the Fisherman's Wharf becomes one of the liveliest places to be in all of Barbados. It's a bit raffish and politicized, but very useful for an insight into local culture.

For an appetizer, try the stuffed crab backs. One of the best-known West Indian soups, callaloo 'n' dumplings, is also offered, made with callaloo greens, okra, and pig's tail, seasoned with fresh coconut and hot peppers, and studded with "tiny" dumplings. Fish is the most popular item, including a Coconut Bay dolphin or beer-batter shrimp; seafood pizzas are also popular. In the bar you can order from a sandwich menu, including all-beef burgers, Monday through Friday from noon to 6pm.

SOUTH OF BRIDGETOWN

Brown Sugar

Aquatic Gap (directly south of Bridgetown on Highway 7), St. Michael. ☎ 809/426-7684. Reservations recommended. Fixed-price buffet lunch $14; main dinner courses $11–$30. AE, DC, MC, V. Sun–Fri noon–2:30pm; daily 6–9:30pm (last order). BAJAN.

Hidden behind lush foliage, Brown Sugar is a beautiful al fresco restaurant in an old-fashioned clapboard-sided island house. The ceiling is latticed, with slow-turning fans, and there's an open veranda for dining by candlelight in a setting of hanging plants. The chefs prepare some of the tastiest Bajan specialties on the island. For an unusual and imaginative opening, try Salomon Gundy, a spicy-hot Jamaica favorite—a pâté of smoked herring, allspice, wine vinegar, onion, chives, and hot bonnie peppers, served with Jamaican water crackers. Among the soups, we suggest hot gungo-pea soup (pigeon peas cooked in chicken broth and zested with fresh coconut milk, herbs, and a touch of white wine). Among the most recommendable main dishes, Créole orange chicken is popular, or perhaps you'd like stuffed crab backs. A selection of locally grown fresh vegetables is also offered. For desserts—called confections here—we recommend the walnut rum pie with rum sauce. The restaurant is known for its good-value lunches, which are served buffet style to most of the businessmen and women of the surrounding district. Dinners are romantic and leisurely, drawing numerous visitors from the surrounding hotels.

ON THE SOUTH COAST

EXPENSIVE

David's Place

St. Lawrence Main Road (directly south of Bridgetown on Highway 7, between Rockley Beach and Worthing), Worthing, Christ Church. ☎ 809/435-9755. Reservations recommended. Main courses $14–$30. AE, MC, V. Daily 6–10pm (last order). BAJAN/INTERNATIONAL.

Owner/operators David and Darla Trotman deliver on their promise that you'll sample "Barbadian dining at its best." Their restaurant is in an old-fashioned Bajan house, with strongly contrasting black-and-white tones both inside and outside. Tables are positioned so diners enjoy a view over the Caribbean. Everybody's favorite, pumpkin or cucumber soup, might get you going or else you can select the more prosaic fish cakes or even pickled chicken wings, a tangy alternative to this much overserved dish.

If you're afraid to venture to Baxter's Road at night, you can order Baxter's Road chicken here. It's seasoned the Bajan way—that is, marinated in lime, salt and herbs, then deep fried. Pepperpot is a hot and spicy dish made with God only knows what, but definitely beef, salt pork, chicken, and lamb. Steak fish, perhaps the best item to order, might be dolphin, kingfish, barracuda, shark, or red snapper. It's served in a white wine sauce or deep fried the Bajan way. And at last a restaurant that offers that old drugstore favorite of the 1940s and '50s, a banana split, for dessert.

✪ Ile De France

In the Windsor Arms Hotel (a 12-minute drive southeast of Bridgetown center on Highway 7), Hastings, Christ Church. ☎ 809/435-6869. Reservations recommended. Main courses $18–$37.50. AE, MC, V. Tues–Sun 6:30–9:30pm (last order). CLASSIC FRENCH.

By anyone's standards, Ile de France offers the finest and most authentic French cuisine in Barbados. Place yourself in the capable hands of Michel and Martine Gramaglia, two French-born expatriates who handle their kitchen and dining room with an enviable *savoir faire*. Meals are served on a candlelit outdoor terrace overlooking a manicured garden, beside one of the oldest and most venerable hotels on the island.

Menu specialties involve ingredients obtained fresh on Barbados or flown in from France or French-owned Martinique. These might include *escargots de Bourgogne*, a flavorful version of *soupe de poissons avec langoustines* (also known as *une petite soupière de la mer*), a *marinade aux trois poissons* whose exact composition depends on the catch of the day, imported *foie gras* of goose or duckling, and a dish for which the establishment is deservedly becoming famous, a *tresse d'agneau* (rack of lamb enveloped in an herb-laden croûte accompanied by its own juices). The atmosphere is charming, traditional, and evocative of the French mainland, especially when music by Edith Piaf or Yves Montand pervades the dining room.

Josef's

St. Lawrence Gap. ☎ **809/435-6541.** Reservations recommended. Main lunch courses $9–$13; main dinner courses $20–$28. AE, DC, MC, V. Mon–Fri noon–2:30pm; daily 6:30–10pm. CARIBBEAN/CONTINENTAL.

Set within the garden of a carefully refurbished pink-and-white Bajan house, between the road and the sea, this is one of the longtime favorites among the upscale restaurants in Barbados. Established in the 1980s by an expatriate Austrian, and leased out in the early 1990s to a Swede, it focuses on carefully contrived upscale food at nighttime, and less expensive, simpler fare during lunch. Actually, some dishes are roughly equivalent at lunch and dinner, so you can save a bit of money by opting for a midday meal here. Swedish specialties include meatballs in traditional gravy with traditional garnish, and Swedish-style filet steak. More tropical dishes include garlic shrimp, jerk shrimp, blackened kingfish, seafood crêpes, and curried chicken. Filet Marco Polo is made from strips of filet steak floating in a pool of red wine sauce. Although some of the Swedish fare may be too heavy for the tropics, the chef is pleasing when he shows a lighter touch. The cookery is characterized by rural good sense rather than citified refinements that get in the way of eating pleasures.

Luigi's Restaurant

Dover Woods, St. Lawrence Gap, Christ Church. ☎ **809/428-9218.** Reservations recommended. Main courses $12.50–$16.50. MC, V. Daily 6–10:30pm (last order). ITALIAN.

Since 1963, this open-air Italian trattoria has operated in a green-and-white building built as a private house. The feeling is contemporary, airy, and comfortable. Miles and Lisa Needham are the owners and managers. Pizzas are offered as appetizers, along with more classic choices such as half a dozen escargots, or when available, a Caesar salad. Half orders of many pastas are also available as starters. The baked pastas, such as creamy lasagne, are delectable, and you can also order the fresh fish or veal special of the day, among other dishes. For dessert, try the zabaglione or one of the wide selection of coffees, ranging from Italian to Russian or Turkish.

Pisces

St. Lawrence Gap, Christ Church. ☎ **809/435-6564.** Reservations recommended. Main courses $14–$33. AE, DC, MC, V. Daily 6–9:30pm (last order). From Bridgetown, take Highway 7 south for about 4 miles, then turn right toward St. Lawrence Gap. BAJAN.

Pisces offers al fresco dining at water's edge. A beautiful restaurant with a tropical decor, it serves primarily a Caribbean seafood menu, as its astrology-sign name suggests. All dishes are created from scratch, using herbs and fruit from the restaurant's own garden. Popular dishes are snapper Caribe, broiled fresh lobster, and a Pisces platter, which combines three kinds of fish (red snapper, Bajan flying fish, grilled kingfish) with butterfly prawns on a single platter. New restaurants come and go in Barbados, but this old favorite still hangs in.

Secrets

In Bagshot House, St. Lawrence Coast Road., Christ Church. ☎ **809/428-9525.** Reservations recommended. Main courses $16–$30. AE, MC, V. Mon–Sat 6–10pm (last order). Closed Sept. INTERNATIONAL.

Set behind the pink facade of one of the island's most historic hotels, this is one of the best restaurants on the southwestern coast. The hotel is old but the restaurant was founded only in 1992. Its owners are the Bajan-British husband-and-wife team of Mark and Amanda Evelyn, who maintain an elegant dining room outfitted with lattices and a beachfront terrace, both with lots of potted plants. Service and decor are relatively formal, but the only dress code is that visitors shouldn't wear shorts.

Many dishes are based on fresh seafood, and include at least four different preparations (blackened, Créole, provencal, or grilled) of grouper, flying fish, snapper, and dolphin. Also available are at least three different versions of lobster, and an array of chicken dishes. A beef specialty is beef Armand, which is prepared in a style similar to beef Wellington. The kitchen wisely does not overextend itself, and we've never been served a bad meal here.

Witch Doctor

St. Lawrence Gap (4 miles south of Bridgetown on Highway 7), Christ Church. ☎ **809/435-6581.** Reservations recommended. Main courses $11–$30. MC, V. Daily 6:15–9:45pm. BAJAN/AFRICAN.

The Witch Doctor hides behind a screen of thick foliage. The decor, in honor of its name, features African and island wood carvings of witch doctors. The place purveys a fascinating cuisine with some unusual concoctions that are tasty and well-prepared, a big change from bland hotel fare. For an appetizer, try the split pea-and-pumpkin soup. You'll also be offered ceviche (cold raw fish soused in lime). Chef's specialties include various flambé dishes such as steak, shrimp Créole, fried flying fish, and chicken piri-piri (inspired by Mozambique).

INEXPENSIVE

Shakey's Restaurant

Hastings Main Road, Hastings. ☎ **809/435-7777.** Reservations not accepted. Pizzas and platters $1.50–$35. AE, MC, V. Daily 11am–11pm. FAST FOOD/PIZZAS.

Place your order at the countertop of this pink-and-white mimic of a Stateside pizza parlor, and when the food is ready, a staff member will carry it to your table. There's virtually every kind of pizza you could conceive of, including a gargantuan model (priced at $35) that almost no one ever orders simply because it's too unwieldy. Be prepared for a minimum of fuss from the staff, and a lot of noise from families with children who sometimes arrive here in groups. Also offered is fried chicken with piquant sauce, and submarine sandwiches.

⊗ The Ship Inn

St. Lawrence Gap (south of Bridgetown on Highway 7, between Rockley Beach and Worthing), Christ Church. ☎ **809/435-6961.** Reservations recommended for the carvery. Main courses $8–$13; all-you-can-eat carvery lunches $10.50; all-you-can-eat carvery dinners $20, plus $7.50 for appetizer and dessert. AE, MC, V. Sun–Fri noon–3pm; daily 6–10:30pm (last order). ENGLISH PUB/BAJAN.

The Ship Inn is a traditional English-style pub that contains an attractive, rustic decor with dark ceiling beams, ships' engravings, and other nautical memorabilia displayed under the muted lighting of ships' lanterns. As an alternative, you can sip a rum drink in the tropical atmosphere of the garden bar. Many guests come for darts and to meet friends, certainly to listen to the live music presented nightly by some of the island's top bands.

The Ship Inn serves substantial bar food, such as homemade steak-and-kidney pie, shepherd's pie, and chicken, shrimp, and fish dishes. For more formal dining, visit the Captain's Carvery, where you can have your fill of succulent cuts from prime roasts on a nighttime buffet table, and an array of traditional Bajan food such as filets of flying fish. You can drink in the pub until 2am daily, sampling beers from Jamaica, Trinidad, and Europe. Diners come here to drink and chow down on the big, filling, and hearty portions—not for any nouvelle stuff.

ⓈT.G.I. Boomers

St. Lawrence Gap, Christ Church. ☎ **809/428-8439.** Reservations not required. Main courses $9–$22.50; lunch specials $4.50–$6; American breakfast 6.50; daiquiris $3–$5. AE, DISC, MC, V. Daily 8am–10pm. AMERICAN/BAJAN.

T.G.I. Boomers offers some of the best bargain meals on the island. A Bajan-run operation, it has an active bar, and a row of tables where food is served, usually along with frothy pastel-colored drinks. The cook prepares a special catch of the day, and the fish is served with soup or salad, rice or baked potato, and a vegetable. You can always count on seafood, steaks, and hamburgers. For breakfast, you might want two eggs with bacon, toast, and coffee. For lunch, try a daily Bajan special or a jumbo sandwich. This is simple fare; most people come for a belt-busting good time with tried-and-true dishes that never go out of favor. Be sure to try one of the 16-ounce daiquiris, which come in six flavors—but don't attempt to drive back to your hotel!

ON THE EAST COAST

ⓈAtlantis Hotel

Bathsheba (13 miles northeast of Bridgetown on Highway 3), St. Joseph. ☎ **809/433-9445.** Reservations required for Sun buffet, recommended at all other times. Two-course fixed-price lunch or dinner $16.50; Sun buffet $17.25. AE. Daily 1–3pm and 7pm (and don't be late). BAJAN.

This place will give you some insight into the old-fashioned Barbados before all the tourism development. The slightly run-down Atlantis Hotel is often filled with both Bajans and visitors. In the sunny, breeze-filled interior, with a sweeping view of the turbulent ocean, the elderly Enid I. Maxwell has been welcoming visitors from all over the world ever since she opened the place in 1945. Her copious buffets are considered one of the best food values on the island. From loaded tables, you can partake of such traditional and uncomplicated Bajan foods as pumpkin fritters, peas and rice, macaroni and cheese, chow mein, souse, or a Bajan pepperpot. No one ever leaves here hungry, and no one has thought of adding anything new to the repertoire since World War II ended.

Kingsley Club

Cattlewash-on-Sea (¼ mile northeast of Bathsheba on Highway 3), St. Joseph. ☎ **809/433-9422.** Reservations required for dinner, recommended for lunch. Main courses $8–$16; fixed-price four-course menu $25–$35. AE, MC, V. Daily noon–3pm and 6–7:30pm (last order). BAJAN.

A historic inn (see "Where to Stay," earlier in this chapter), the Kingsley Club serves terrific Bajan food in a turn-of-the-century house cooled by Atlantic breezes. You're greeted and shown to your table. They invite you to "come tuck in" and enjoy your fill of split pea-and-pumpkin soup, dolphin meunière, or planters fried chicken, followed by one of their homemade desserts, perhaps coconut pie. The cuisine always struck us as what a Bajan might prepare for a dinner at home with the family. The inn lies amid the rolling hills of the northeast coast of Barbados, the Scotland District, about 15 miles from Bridgetown.

What to See & Do on Barbados

In addition to a host of water sports and other outdoor activities to keep you busy on the beach, Barbados is one of the more interesting islands in the West Indies to explore, either in your own rented car or with a taxi driver as a guide. There are formal gardens, stately great houses, white sandy beaches, noted museums, excellent shopping, topnotch restaurants, and much more.

The principal activities on Barbados are swimming, sunning, windsurfing, boating, and other activities that go along with a tropical beach vacation. All these are best on the western coast in the clear, buoyant waters. You may also want to visit the surf-pounded Atlantic waters in the east, which are better for scenery than for swimming.

With visibilities in excess of 100 feet most of the year, and with more than 50 varies of fish swimming above and around its coral reefs, Barbados beckons scuba divers and snorkelers. The sea also teems with dolphin, marlin, wahoo, barracuda, and sailfish, to name only the most popular catches, making for first-rate deep-sea fishing.

A SUGGESTED ITINERARY

Following is a suggested way to spend a week on Barbados. If you're lucky enough to have more time than that, spend the rest of your visit relaxing, enjoying the good life, and sampling as many of the beaches as time allows.

Day 1 Barbados is practically in South America, so if you're flying from North America, especially Canada or New York, you'll need the better part of a day just to get there, often with a stopover in San Juan. Unwind the first night, enjoy a Bajan buffet, listen to a local calypso band, and go to bed early.

Day 2 In the morning or afternoon, explore Farley Hill National Park in the northern St. Peter Parish and visit Barbados Wildlife Reserve. Then relax on the beach. In the evening (if it's a Thursday) attend a performance of *1627 And All That . . .* or a similar Bajan show.

Day 3 Cruise on the *Bajan Queen,* modeled after a Mississippi riverboat. Enjoy swimming and snorkeling. You can also take the cruise at night, enjoying a Bajan buffet and listening to local bands.

Day 4 Head for Bridgetown and go on a shopping spree, browsing for local crafts, especially those at Pelican Village.

Day 5 If your budget allows, enjoy submerged sightseeing aboard the *Atlantis II* submarine with its 16 2-foot-wide viewing ports. The entire trip takes 2 hours (45 minutes actually in the submarine). Then, after an afternoon on the beach, attend the Plantation Restaurant and Garden show, a dinner theater with a Bajan cabaret.

Day 6 Go on a driving tour of the island, seeing the major sights, including Sam Lord's Castle, Villa Nova, St. Nicholas Abbey, and the Welchman Hall Gully.

Day 7 Visit Harrison's Cave and explore the East Coast of Barbados, with a typically Bajan lunch at the Atlantis Hotel. Take the rest of the day off to relax and prepare for the flight home.

1 Beaches

Barbadians say they have a beach for every day of the year. If you're only visiting for a short time, you'll probably be happy with the ones that are easy to find. They're all open to the public, even those in front of the big resort hotels and private homes. The government requires public access to all beaches, via roads along the property line or through the hotel entrance.

THE WEST COAST

Waters are calmest on the western shore, which faces the Caribbean Sea.

The major beaches border **Paynes Bay,** with access across from the Coach House or the Bamboo Beach Bar. This is a good beach for water sports, especially snorkeling. There is also a parking area. The sands can get rather crowded, but the beautiful bay somehow makes it seem worth the effort to get there. Three of the best beaches here include **Paradise Beach, Brighton Beach,** and **Brandon's Beach.**

Church Point lies north of St. James Church, opening onto Heron Bay, site of the Colony Club Hotel. This is one of the most scenic bays in Barbados, and the swimming is ideal, although the beach can get overcrowded. There are some shade trees when you've had enough sun. You can also order drinks at the beach terrace operated by the Colony Club.

Mullins Beach, a final West Coast selection, is the third most recommendable beach. Its blue waters are glassy, and snorkelers in particular seek it out. There's parking on the main road. Again, the beach has some shady areas. At the Mullins Beach Bar, you can order food and drink.

THE SOUTH COAST

Good spots here include **Casuarina Beach,** with access from Maxwell Coast Road, going across the property of Casuarina Beach Hotel. This is one of the wider beaches of Barbados, and we've noticed that it's swept by trade winds even on the hottest days of August. Windsurfers are especially fond of this one. Food and drink can be ordered at the hotel.

Silver Sands Beach, to the east of Oistins, is near the very south point of Barbados, directly east of South Point Lighthouse and near the Silver Rock Hotel. This white sandy beach is a favorite with many Bajans, who probably want to keep it a secret from as many tourists as possible. Windsurfing is excellent here if you're advanced. Drinks are sold at Silver Rock Bar.

Sandy Beach, reached from the car park on the Worthing main road, has tranquil waters opening onto a lagoon, a cliché of Caribbean charm. This is a family favorite, with lots of screaming and yelling on the weekends especially. Food and drink are sold here.

THE SOUTHEAST COAST

The southeast coast is the site of the big waves, especially at **Crane Beach,** the white sandy beach set against a backdrop of palms that usually appears in Sunday travel magazines. The beach is spectacular, as Prince Andrew, who has a house overlooking it, might agree. It offers excellent body surfing, but at times the waters might be too rough for all but the strongest swimmers. The beach is set against cliffs, and the Crane Beach Hotel towers above it. This is ocean swimming, not the calm Caribbean, so take precautions.

Bottom Bay is one of our all-time Bajan favorites. It is north of Marriott's Sam Lord's Castle. You park on the top of a cliff then walk down steps to this much-photographed tropical beach, with its grove of coconut palms. There's even a cave. The sand is brilliantly white, a picture-postcard version of a beach with an aquamarine sea.

THE EAST COAST (ATLANTIC)

There are miles and miles of uncrowded beaches along the east coast, but this is the Atlantic side, and swimming here is potentially dangerous. Many visitors like to walk along the sands here, especially those in the Bathsheba/Cattlewash areas, enjoying the splendid rugged scenery. Waves are extremely high on these beaches, and the bottom tends to be rocky. Currents are also unpredictable. The beaches are great if you don't go into the water.

2 Outdoor Activities

DEEP-SEA FISHING

The fishing is first-rate in the waters off Barbados, where fishers pursue dolphin, marlin, wahoo, barracuda, and sailfish, to name only the most popular catches. There's also an occasional cobia. **The Dive Shop,** Pebbles Beach, Aquatic Gap, St. Michael (☎ 809/426-9947), can arrange half-day charters for one to six people (all equipment and drinks included), costing $350 per boat. Under the same arrangement, the whole-day jaunt goes for $700. In other words, no discount.

GOLF

The Royal Westmoreland Golf & Country Club, Westmoreland, St. James (☎ 809/422-4653), is the island's premier golf course, usurping a position formerly held by Sandy Lane. Designed in 1994 by Robert Trent Jones Jr., this $30 million, 27-hole course is spread across 500 acres overlooking the Gold Coast. It is part of a private residential community and can only be played by guests of the Royal Pavilion, Glitter Bay, Colony Club, Tamaraind Cove, Coral Reef, Crystal Cove, Cobblers Cove, Sandpiper Inn, and Sandy Lane. It costs $85 for nine holes, or $145 for 18 holes, including a cart.

Open to all is the 18-hole championship golf course of the **Sandy Lane Hotel,** St. James (☎ 809/432-1311), on the West Coast. Greens fees are $85 in the winter and $60 in the summer for 18 holes, or $55 in the winter and $40 in the summer for nine holes.

HIKING

The **Barbados National Trust** offers Sunday morning hikes throughout the year. The program, which gives participants an opportunity to learn about the natural beauty of Barbados, are cosponsored by the Duke of Edinburgh's Award Scheme and the Barbados Heart Foundation, and attracts more than 300 participants weekly.

Into the Green Hills

Unless visitors make special efforts to explore the lush interior, most of their time on Barbados might be confined to the island's densely populated coastal plain. But much of Barbados's true beauty can only be appreciated through treks, tours, or hillclimbs through such rarely visited parishes as St. Thomas and St. George (both of which are landlocked) and the Atlantic-coast parishes of St. Andrews and St. John (where the rough surf of the Atlantic usually discourages sailing and swimming.)

Until recently, most visitors were requested to restrict their sightseeing in these relatively undeveloped parishes to the sides of the highways and roads. But a locally owned tour operator, **Highland Outdoor Tours,** conducts a series of tours across privately owned land. With its verdant, rolling hills and many dramatic rock outcroppings, much of the terrain might remind you of a windswept but balmy version of Scotland.

You'll have the option of conducting your tour on horseback, on foot, or as a passenger in a tractor-drawn jitney. Horseback rides and walking tours last anywhere from 2 to 5 hours. As you traverse what used to be some of the most productive sugar plantations in the British Empire, your guide will describe the geology, architecture, and historical references you'll see en route. A wide range of add-ons can be arranged as part of your experience, including barbecued dinners or picnic lunches prepared over the open hearth of a historic Bajan home.

All tours depart from the Highland Outdoor Tour Center in the parish of St. Thomas (in north central Barbados). Transportation to and from your hotel is included in the price of horseback tours (from $50), hiking tours (from $50), and tractor-drawn jitney tours (from $25). For more information, contact Highland Outdoor Tours, Canefield, St. Thomas Parish, Barbados, W.I. (☎ **809/438-8069**).

Led by young Barbadians and members of the National Trust, the hikes cover a different area of the island each week. Tour escorts also give brief educational talks on various aspects of the hikes such as geography, history, geology, and agriculture.

The hikes are free and open to participants of all ages. They are divided into three categories: fast, for those who wish to hike for the exercise; medium, for those wishing exercise but at a slower pace than the fast walk; and slow, fondly known as "stop and stare," for those wishing to walk at a leisurely pace.

All the hikes start promptly at either 6:30am or 3:30pm and begin and end in the same place, where parking is available. Each hike is about 5 miles long and takes about 3 hours. Visitors needing transportation should contact the Barbados National Trust at **809/426-2421.** The staff there will tell you where to meet for the hike.

HORSEBACK RIDING

A different view of Barbados is offered by the **Caribbean International Riding Centre,** c/o the Roachford family, Auburn, St. Joseph (☎ **809/433-1453**). Maintained by Swedish-born Elizabeth Roachford and her four daughters, it boards nearly 40 horses, more than most other riding stables on the island. Mrs. Roachford or one of her daughters (each trained according to the Swedish equestrian traditions) offer a variety of trail rides for equestrians of any level of experience. Their shortest ride provides a 75-minute escorted trek through tropical forests, followed by relaxation over a cool drink in the clubroom. The $30 price includes transportation to and from your hotel and a complimentary beverage. The most scenic tour takes you through the

Gully Ride and continues out to the cliff where riders can enjoy a panoramic view of almost the entire east coast. Advance reservations are strongly advised.

SCUBA DIVING & SNORKELING

The clear waters off Barbados have visibility of more than 100 feet most of the year, and more than 50 varieties of fish are found on the shallow inside reefs. On night dives, sleeping fish, night anemones, lobsters, moray eels, and octopuses can be seen.

On a mile-long coral reef 2 minutes by boat from **Sandy Beach,** sea fans, corals, gorgonias, and reef fish are plentiful. *J.R.,* a dredge barge sunk as an artificial reef in 1983, is popular with beginners for its coral, fish life, and 20-foot depth. The *Berwyn,* a coral-encrusted tugboat that sank in Carlisle Bay in 1916, attracts photographers because of its variety of reef fish, shallow depth, good light, and visibility.

The **Asta Reef,** with a drop of 80 feet, has coral, sea fans, and reef fish in abundance. It's the site of a Barbados wreck sunk in 1986 as an artificial reef. Dottins, the most beautiful reef on the West Coast, stretches 5 miles from Holetown to Bridgetown and has numerous dive sites at an average depth of 40 feet and dropoffs of 100 feet. The SS *Stavronika,* a Greek freighter, is a popular dive site for advanced divers. Crippled by fire in 1976, the 360-foot freighter was sunk a quarter mile off the West Coast to become an artificial reef in **Folkstone Underwater Park.** The mast is at 40 feet, the deck at 80 feet, and the keel at 140 feet. It's encrusted with coral.

The Dive Shop, Pebbles Beach, Aquatic Gap, St. Michael (☎ **809/426-9947**), offers some of the best scuba diving in Barbados (costing about $43 per one-tank dive). Every day, two dive trips go out to the nearby reefs and wrecks. In addition, snorkeling trips and equipment rentals are possible. Visitors with reasonable swimming skills who have never dived before can sign up for a resort course. Priced at $50, it includes pool training, safety instructions, and a one-tank open-water dive. The operation is NAUI- and PADI-certified. It is open daily from 9am to 5pm.

Good **snorkeling spots** on the West Coast include the beaches along Paynes Bay and Mullins Beach. See also the cruises and boat trips listed below; some of them include stops for snorkeling.

TENNIS

Sandy Lane, St. James (☎ **809/432-1311**), places more emphasis on tennis than any other resort in Barbados, with two pros on hand, along with five courts and an open-door policy to nonresidents. Two of the five courts—all of which are well-maintained—are lit for night games. One of the courts is carpeted with a substance that emulates the feel of grass, whereas the other four are hard-surfaced. Court no. 1 is the most frequently used, because of its position adjacent to the clubhouse, bar, and restaurant. It's advised to play early or late, although the courts are still wide open during the "hot times" between 10am and 3pm. Court rentals are $20 per hour, or $10 per half hour. Lessons with a pro cost $25 per half hour or $50 per hour.

The **Barbados Hilton,** Needham's Point (☎ **809/426-0200**), maintains four hard-surface courts, each of which is lit for night play. Hilton's courts are not nearly as clubby or gracious as those of Sandy Lane, but they're closer to Bridgetown, and more convenient for many visitors. Guests play for free, while nonresidents pay $20 per half hour. At night, all players are charged $5 per half hour for illumination of the courts.

WINDSURFING

Experts say that the windsurfing off Barbados is as good as any this side of Hawaii, and it certainly turns into a very big business between November and April.

Thousands of windsurfers from all over the world now come here from as far as Finland, Argentina, and Japan. The shifting of the trade winds between November and May and the shallow offshore reef off **Silver Sands** create unique conditions of wind and wave swells. This allows windsurfers to reach speeds of up to 50 knots and do complete loops off the waves. Silver Sands is rated the best spot in the Caribbean for advanced windsurfing (skill rating 5-6). In other words, one needs skills similar to a professional downhill skier's to master these conditions. Nearby **Casuarina Beach** is another excellent choice.

An operation set up especially to handle the demand is the **Barbados Windsurfing Club,** Silver Sands Hotel, Christ Church (☎ 809/428-6001). It rents boards and gives lessons. Club Mistral, a company run by Mistral A.G. of Germany, manufacturer of fine windsurfing boards, provides the rental fleet for the Barbados facility. This fleet consists of up to 100 boards, all current models with a selection of 200 sails. Board rentals cost $20 per hour, or $40 for a half day.

3 Exploring Bridgetown

Often hot and clogged with traffic, Bridgetown, the capital, is an architectural hodgepodge that merits little more than a morning's shopping jaunt (see Section 7 of this chapter for our specific recommendations).

Once you arrive, check with the **Barbados Tourism Authority** on Harbour Road, in Bridgetown (☎ 809/427-2623).

You might begin your Bridgetown tour at The Careenage, the waterfront area whose name derives from "careening" vessels over on their sides in order to clean their bottoms. The harbor was a haven for the clipper ship, and even though today it doesn't have its former color, it's still worth exploring.

The long period of British colonization is evident at **Trafalgar Square.** The monument honoring Lord Nelson was executed by Sir Richard Westmacott and erected in 1813. The **Public Buildings** on the square are of the great, gray Victorian-Gothic variety that you might expect to find in South Kensington, London. The east wing contains the meeting halls of the Senate and the House of Assembly, with

✪ Frommer's Favorite Barbados Experiences

Touring the Great Houses. From mid-January through the first week of April, you can tour a different great house every Wednesday afternoon. You can get a feel for the elegant colonial lifestyle and see plantation antiques. Watch for announcements in the local papers or call the National Trust at 809/426-2421.

An Evening at *1627 and All That.* See "Barbados After Dark," later in this chapter. While dining on Bajan specialties, you can enjoy a musical celebration of the island experience.

Nighttime Stroll Along Baxters Road. Nothing is more authentically Bajan than a promenade along this famous Bridgetown road, sampling the specialties of its food stalls (the fried chicken's terrific) and washing everything down with Banks beer. Things don't really heat up before 10pm.

Sunday Lunch with Enid Maxwell. Since 1945, Enid's Atlantis Hotel on the East Coast has set the best Sunday noonday spread on the island. Try the Bajan delicacies—pumpkin fritters, flying fish, dolphin, spinach cakes, and pickled breadfruit. Everything is homemade.

Bridgetown

stained-glass windows depicting sovereigns of England from James I to Queen Victoria. Look for the Great Protector himself, Oliver Cromwell.

Behind the Financial Building, **St. Michael's Cathedral,** south of Trafalgar Square, is a symbol of the Church of England. This Anglican church was first built in 1655 but was completely destroyed in the 1780 hurricane. Reconstructed in 1789, it was again damaged—though not completely demolished—by a hurricane in 1831. George Washington is said to have worshipped here on his Barbados visit.

For years, guides pointed out a house on Upper Bay Street where Washington allegedly slept during his only trip outside the United States, although historians seriously doubted the claim. Nevertheless, beginning in 1910, the building was called "The Washington House." Now, after careful investigation, the house where Washington slept has been identified by historians as **Bush Hill House** in the Garrison, which lies about a half mile south of the Upper Bay Street location. This real Washington building is used for business offices and is not open to the public.

Bridgetown Synagogue, on Synagogue Lane (☎ 809/432-0840), one of the oldest synagogues in the Western Hemisphere, is surrounded by a burial ground of early Jewish settlers. The present building dates from 1833. It was constructed on the site of a synagogue erected by Jews from Brazil in 1654. Sometime in the early 20th century the synagogue was deconsecrated, and the structure served various roles. In 1983 the government of Barbados seized the deteriorating building, intending to raze it and build a courthouse on the site. An outcry went up from the small Jewish community on the island, and money was raised for its restoration. The building was saved and is now part of the Barbados National Trust; it is a synagogue once more. It is open Monday through Friday from 9am to 4pm.

At this point, you can hail a taxi if you don't have a car and visit **Garrison Savannah,** just south of the capital. Cricket matches and other games are played in this open space of some 50 acres. Horse races are often held here, as well.

Barbados Museum, St. Ann's Garrison, St. Michael (☎ 809/427-0201), is housed in the former military prison at the impressive St. Ann's Garrison. In the exhibition "In Search of Bim," extensive collections show the island's development from prehistoric to modern times. "Born of the Sea" affords fascinating glimpses into the natural environment. There are also fine collections of West Indian maps, decorative art, and fine art. The museum sells a variety of quality publications, reproductions (maps, cards, prints), and handcrafts; it also has a children's gallery with changing exhibits. Its Courtyard Café is a good place for a snack or light lunch. The museum is open from 10am to 6pm Monday through Saturday. It charges $5 for adults, $2.50 for children.

Nearby, the russet-red **St. Ann's Fort,** on the fringe of the Savannah, garrisoned British soldiers in 1694. The fort wasn't completed until 1703. The Clock House survived the hurricane of 1831.

A DRIVING TOUR
Around the Island

Start: Bridgetown.
Finish: Bridgetown.
Time: 6 hours, excluding stopovers.
Best Time: Any sunny day.
Worst Time: When cruise ships are in harbor, as roads and attractions are at their most congested then.

If you can afford it, the ideal way to take this tour is with a local taxi driver who will generally negotiate a fair rate, somewhere around $50.

Of course, you can tour on your own, but you'll have to rent an expensive car, and you won't know the often unmarked roads like the locals do. If you do explore on your own, you can count on getting lost, at least several times. Although Barbados contains many signposted directions, highway authorities will often leave you stranded at strategic junctions, and it's very easy to take a wrong turn if you don't know the way—even people who live in Barbados often get confused. No clear, concise map of Barbados has yet been devised. Maps only help you with general directions; when you're looking for the route to a specific destination, they can often be most unhelpful.

Having said that, know that part of the fun of exploring Barbados is the discovery of the island. So if you do get lost a few times, and miss an attraction or two, no great harm should befall you. And the local people in the countryside are generally quite friendly and helpful.

After leaving Bridgetown (see above), head south along Highway 7, passing through the resorts of Hastings, Rockley, Worthing, and St. Lawrence, all of which contain any number of inexpensive to medium-priced hotels, as opposed to the most expensive and deluxe hotels north of Bridgetown.

After passing through Worthing (and providing you can find this badly marked road), turn right along:

1. **St. Lawrence Gap,** which is the restaurant row of Barbados, including such well-established places as Witch Doctor and The Ship Inn (see "Where to Dine" in Chapter 10). There are also several budget and medium-priced hotels located along this strip, which is generally lively both day and night.

At the end of St. Lawrence Gap, resume your journey along Highway 7 by taking a right turn. You'll bypass the town of:

2. **Oistins,** a former shipping port that today is a fishing village. Here the Charter of Barbados was signed at the Mermaid in 1652, as the island surrendered to Commonwealth forces. The Mermaid Inn, incidentally, was owned by a cousin of John Turner, who built the House of the Seven Gables in Salem, Massachusetts.

At the signpost, take a left for Providence and the Grantley Adams airport, a continuation of Highway 7. You'll pass the airport on your right. After bypassing the airport, follow the signs to Sam Lord's Castle. At the hamlet of Spencers, leave Highway 7 and turn onto Rock Hall Road, going through the villages of St. Martins and Heddings until you come to the signposted Crane Beach Hotel.

☕ **TAKE A BREAK**   **The Crane Beach Hotel,** Crane Bay, St. Philip (☎ **809/423-6220**). Virtually everyone touring the South Coast stops at this remote hilltop property. The view of the Atlantic and the Roman-style swimming pool charm all the visiting cruise-ship passengers; some climb down the steep steps to Crane Beach. The house on the hill overlooking the beach is owned by Britain's Prince Andrew. You pay $2.50 to enter the property, but that money is redeemable if you make purchases at either the bar or restaurant.

After leaving the hotel, follow Crane Road east. Turn right at the signpost and continue to the end of the road to:

3. **Sam Lord's Castle,** a Marriott hotel (see "Where to Stay" in Chapter 10) but also one of the major sightseeing attractions in Barbados. You may want to have a drink or a snack if you didn't already stop at Crane Beach Hotel. Built by slaves in 1820,

and furnished in part with Regency pieces, the "castle" is like a Georgian plantation mansion. Take note of the ornate ceilings, said to be the finest example of
stucco work in the Western Hemisphere. At the entrance to the hotel are shops
selling handcrafts and souvenirs. If you're not a guest, you'll have to pay $2.50 to
enter.

After leaving Sam Lord's Castle, take a right onto Long Bay Road and continue
east. Go right via the village of Wellhouse and continue along the main road that
skirts the coastline but does not adjoin the coast. Turn right down a narrow road
to:

4. **Ragged Point Lighthouse,** on a rugged cliff on the easternmost point of Barbados. Built in 1885, the lighthouse sends its beacon as a warning to ships approaching the dangerous reef, called "The Cobblers." The view from here is panoramic.

After leaving the lighthouse, continue straight along Marley Vale Road (don't
expect proper signs). At the signpost to Bayfield, go right and pass Three Houses
Park. Take a right at the signpost to Bridgetown onto Thickets Road. Take a right
again at the signpost to Bathsheba. When you come to another signpost, turn left
toward Bathsheba and follow a sign to:

5. **Codrington College,** opened in 1745. A cabbage-palm-lined avenue leads to old
coral-block buildings. Today the college is a training school for men and women
from the entire Caribbean to enter the ordained ministry of the Anglican church.
The college is under the auspices of the Dioceses of the West Indies. Entrance is
$2.50.

After leaving the college, go right, then take the next left up the steep Coach
Hill Road where you'll see excellent views of the East Coast and the lighthouse you
just visited. At the top of the hill, continue right and follow the signposts to:

6. **St. John's Church,** perched on the edge of a cliff opening on the East Coast some
825 feet above sea level. The church dates from 1836 and in its graveyard in the
rear rests Fernando Paleologus, a descendant of Emperor Constantine the Great,
whose family was driven from the throne in Constantinople (Istanbul) by the
Turks. The royal relative died in Barbados in 1678.

After leaving the church, go left and then take the next right onto Gall Hill
Road. Stay on this road until you reach Four Roads Junction, at which point you
follow the signposts for Villa Nova, following along Wakefield Road. At the
signpost for Villa Nova, turn left and then take the next right into the grounds.

7. **Villa Nova,** was built in 1834 as a fine sugar plantation great house (☎ 809/
433-1524). It is furnished with period antiques in Barbadian mahogany and surrounded by 6¹/₂ acres of landscaped gardens and trees. Its most famous association
was with the late Sir Anthony Eden (later the earl of Avon), former prime minister of Great Britain, who purchased it from the government in 1965. Along with
the countess of Avon (Clarissa Churchill), Sir Anthony lived in this winter home
for six years. In 1966, he and the countess entertained Queen Elizabeth II and
Prince Philip at the great house. It has since been sold. Visiting hours are Monday through Friday from 9am to 4pm, and the admission is $4 per person.

After leaving Villa Nova, turn left and pass through the hamlet of Venture. At
the next intersection, continue left until you see the signpost pointing right toward
Easy Hall, another East Coast hamlet. At the next signpost, pointing in the direction of Flower Forest, go left along Buckden House Road. Take the next right and
head down Highway 3, a steep, curvy road toward the ocean. Turn right toward
Bathsheba and follow the signs to:

8. **Andromeda Botanical Gardens,** on a cliff overlooking Bathsheba on the rugged
East Coast (☎ 809/433-9261). Limestone boulders make for a natural eight-acre

Driving Tour — Around Barbados

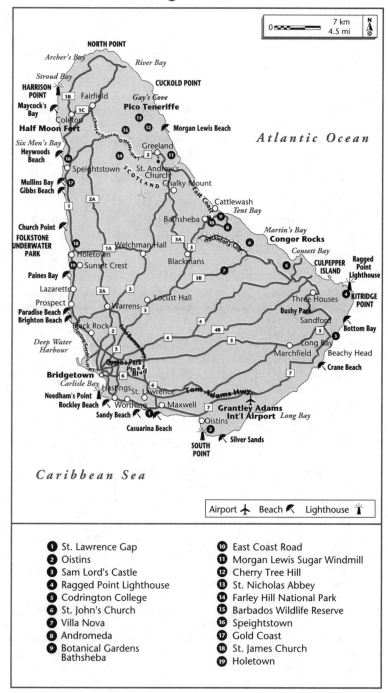

0 ━━━━━ 7 km
4.5 mi

N

NORTH POINT

Archer's Bay

River Bay

Stroud Bay

CUCKOLD POINT

HARRISON POINT   1B   Fairfield

Gay's Cove

Maycock's Bay   1C

Coleton   **Pico Teneriffe**   13

Half Moon Fort

Six Men's Bay   15   12   ← *Morgan Lewis Beach*

Heywoods Beach   16

Greeland   2   11

Speightstown   14

SCOTLAND   St. Andrew's Church

Mullins Bay   17

Gibbs Beach

Chalky Mount

Atlantic Ocean

Cattlewash

Tent Bay

Bathsheba   10   9

8

Church Point

FOLKSTONE UNDERWATER PARK   18   1A   Welchman Hall

Martin's Bay

Congor Rocks

Consett Bay

CULPEPPER ISLAND

Ragged Point Lighthouse

Holetown   3

Blackmans   3A

Paines Bay   19   Sunset Crest

3B   7

6   5

Lazaretto   2A   2

Prospect   Locust Hall

KITRIDGE POINT

Paradise Beach

Brighton Beach   Warrens   3

Three Houses

Bushy Park

Sandford

Black Rock

4

4B   5

Bottom Bay

Deep Water Harbour

3

4

5   Long Bay

Marchfield   *Beachy Head*

Queen's Park   Pine Blvd

Bridgetown   6

Carlisle Bay   6

Crane Beach

Needham's Point   Hastings   St. Lawrence

7

Tom Adams Hwy

Rockley Beach   Worthing   Maxwell

Sandy Beach   1

7   **Grantley Adams Int'l Airport**   *Long Bay*

Casuarina Beach   Oistins   2   ← *Silver Sands*

SOUTH POINT

Caribbean Sea

Airport ✈   Beach 🏖   Lighthouse 🗼

1 St. Lawrence Gap
2 Oistins
3 Sam Lord's Castle
4 Ragged Point Lighthouse
5 Codrington College
6 St. John's Church
7 Villa Nova
8 Andromeda
9 Botanical Gardens Bathsheba

10 East Coast Road
11 Morgan Lewis Sugar Windmill
12 Cherry Tree Hill
13 St. Nicholas Abbey
14 Farley Hill National Park
15 Barbados Wildlife Reserve
16 Speightstown
17 Gold Coast
18 St. James Church
19 Holetown

241

rock-garden setting, where thousands of orchids bloom in the open air every day of the year, along with hundreds of hibiscus and heliconia. Other plants are more seasonal, including the flamboyant frangipani, jade vine and bougainvillea, lipstick tree, candlestick tree, mammee apple, and many more. Many varieties of ferns, bromeliads, and other species that are houseplants in temperate climates grow here in splendid profusion. A section is a palm garden, with more than 100 species. A simple guide helps visitors to identify many of the plants. The garden was started in 1954 by the late Iris Bannochie, on land that had belonged to her family for more than 200 years. On the grounds you'll occasionally see frogs, herons, guppies, and sometimes a mongoose or a monkey. Charging $5 for admission, the gardens are open 9am to 5pm daily. On the grounds is The Best of Barbados gift shop and the Hibiscus Café.

After leaving the gardens, turn right and follow the signs to a great place to stop for lunch.

🍵 **TAKE A BREAK**   The **Atlantis Hotel,** Bathsheba, St. Joseph (☎ 809/ 433-9445), is one of the oldest hotels in Barbados, where Enid Maxwell has been serving her favorite Bajan dishes, including flying fish and pickled breadfruit, for longer than she cares to remember. Tattered but respectable, this hotel was once a villa built by a wealthy planter in 1882. It is set directly on the seacoast, just south of the "Scotland District." It offers a set menu at lunch and features a well-attended Sunday buffet, an event among the Bajans themselves. See "Where to Dine" in Chapter 10 for details.

Now continue north along the coast road to the town of:
9. **Bathsheba,** where ocean rollers break, forming cascades of white foam. This place has been called Cornwall (England) in miniature. Today the old fishing village is a favorite low-cost resort for Bajans, although the waters of the Atlantic Ocean are considered dangerous for swimmers.
   The trail north from Bathsheba takes you along the:
10. **East Coast Road,** which runs for many miles, opening onto dramatic views of the Atlantic. Chalky Mount rises from the beach to a height of 500 feet, forming a trio of peaks, and a little to the south Barclays Park is a 15-acre natural wonder presented as a gift to the people of Barbados by the British banking family. There's a snack bar and a place to picnic here.
   Further north, in St. Andrew, just south of Cherry Tree Hill, is the:
11. **Morgan Lewis Sugar Windmill and Museum** (☎ 809/426-2421), typical of the wind-driven mills that extracted juice from sugarcane from the 17th to the 19th centuries, helping produce sugar that made Barbados one of Britain's most valuable possessions in the Americas. (And it was from Barbados sugarcane that rum was first made.) Admission is $2 for adults, $1.25 for children under 14. Open Monday to Friday from 9am to 5pm.
   Now climb Morgan Lewis Hill on Highway 1 to reach:
12. **Cherry Tree Hill,** offering one of the finest views in Barbados. You can look right down the eastern shore past Bathsheba to the lighthouse at Ragged Point. The crest is about 850 feet above sea level, and from its precincts you'll see out over the Scotland District. The cherry trees from which the hill got its name no longer stand here, having given way to mahogany.
   On Cherry Tree Hill, signs point the way to:
13. **St. Nicholas Abbey,** a Jacobean plantation great house and sugarcane fields that have been around since about 1650 (☎ 809/422-8725). It was never an abbey—

an ambitious owner in about 1820 simply christened it as such. More than 200 acres are still cultivated each year. In the parish of St. Peter, the structure—at least the ground floor—is open to the public Monday through Friday from 10am to 3:30pm, charging an admission of $5 per person, free for children under 13. The house is believed to be one of three Jacobean houses in the Western Hemisphere, and it's characterized by curved gables. Lt. Col. Stephen Cave, the owner, is descended from the family that purchased the sugar plantation and great house in 1810. Light refreshments are offered for sale.

After leaving the abbey, follow the road to Diamond Corner, where you go left. Take another left onto the Charles Duncan O'Neal Highway to:

14. **Farley Hill National Park,** in northern St. Peter Parish. Farley Hill House, used in filming of the 1950s motion picture *Island in the Sun*, starring Harry Belafonte, was gutted by fire. This movie is now largely forgotten by the world, but it still brings back many memories for Barbadians familiar with it. The park, dedicated by Queen Elizabeth in 1966, is open daily from 8:30am to 6pm. You pay a vehicular entrance fee of $1.50 for cars. After disembarking in the parking area, you can walk the grounds and enjoy the tropical flowers and lush vegetation.

Across the entrance from the park lies the:

15. **Barbados Wildlife Reserve,** a project operated by the Barbados Primate Research Center in St. Peter (☎ **809/422-8826**), standing in a mahogany forest across the road from Farley Hill National Park. From 10am to 5pm daily, for an admission charge of $5 (half price for children), you stroll through what is primarily a monkey sanctuary. Besides uncaged monkeys, you can see wild hares, deer, tortoises, otters, caymans, wallabies, and a variety of tropical birds.

From Farley Hill Park and the wildlife reserve, backtrack to the junction of Highways 1 and 2. From here, head west along Highway 1, signposted to:

16. **Speightstown,** founded around 1635. For a time it was a whaling port and is now the second city of Barbados. The community contains colonial buildings constructed after the devastating hurricane of 1831. The parish church, rebuilt in a half-Grecian style after the hurricane, is one of the places of interest. Its chancel rail is of carved mahogany.

After exploring Speightstown if you have time, turn left in the direction of the:

17. **Gold Coast,** the protected western shoreline that opens onto the gentle Caribbean. Along the shoreline of the parishes of St. James and St. Peter are the island's plushest hotels (see "Where to Stay" in Chapter 10).

On Highway 1, directly north of Holetown, lies:

18. **St. James Church,** St. James, an Anglican church rebuilt in 1872 on the site of the early settlers' church of 1660. On the southern porch is an old bell, bearing the inscription of "God Bless King William, 1696." Locals still recall the 1982 visit of Ronald and Nancy Reagan. Continue south on Highway 1 to:

19. **Holetown,** the main center of the West Coast; it takes its name from the town of Hole on the Thames River in England. The first English settlers landed here

---

Impressions

I was irresistibly made to think of the frog that would blow itself out and look as large as an ox.
—Anthony Trollope, *The West Indies and the Spanish Main,* 1859

That prosperous and civilized little cane-garden.
—Charles Kingsley, *At Last, A Christmas in the West Indies*

in the winter of 1627. An obelisk marks the spot where the *Olive Blossom* two years earlier had landed the first Europeans, who did not stay. For some reason, the monument gives the date erroneously as 1605.

Chances are you may be staying in a hotel north of Bridgetown. If so, you may want to end this driving tour at your hotel. If you're staying in less expensive digs south of Bridgetown, you can continue south along the coast, passing through Bridgetown until you reach your hotel.

5 Exploring Inland

HISTORIC SIGHTS IN ST. MICHAEL & ST. GEORGE PARISHES

Tyrol Cot Heritage Village

Codrington Hill, St. Michael. ☎ **809/424-2074.** Admission $5. Mon–Sat 9am–5pm.

If you arrive at the airport, you'll recognize the name of Sir Grantley Adams, the leader of the Bajan movement for independence from Britain. This was once his home, and his wife, Lady Adams, lived in the house until her death in 1990. Once viewed as a highly prized invitation, it is now open to all who pay the admission. The date of construction was sometime in the mid-1850s, and the style was Palladian, made of coral stone. The grounds of the former political leader have been turned into a museum of Bajan life, including small chattel houses where potters and artists work.

Francia Plantation

On ABC Highway, St. George, Barbados. ☎ **809/429-0474.** Admission $4. Mon–Fri 10am–4pm. Turn east onto Highway 4 at the Norman Niles Roundabout (follow signs to "Gun Hill" and Highway X). After going 1/2 mile, turn left onto Highway X (follow signs to Gun Hill and Francia Plantation). After another mile turn right at the Mobil gas station and follow Highway X past St. George's Parish Church and up the hill for a mile, turning left at the sign to Francia.

A fine home, this house stands on a wooded hillside overlooking the St. George Valley, and is still owned and occupied by descendants of its original occupants. Inside, you can explore several rooms, including the dining room with family silver and an 18th-century James McCabe bracket clock. On the walls are antique maps and prints, including a map of the West Indies printed in 1522.

Gun Hill Signal Station

Highway 4. ☎ **809/429-1358.** Admission $4 adults, $2 children under 14. Mon–Sat 9am–5pm. Take Highway 3 from Bridgetown and then go inland from Highway 4 toward St. George Church.

One of two such stations owned and operated by the Barbados National Trust, Gun Hill Signal Station is strategically placed on the highland of St. George and commands a panoramic view from the east to the west. Built in 1818, it was the finest of a chain of signal stations and was also used as an outpost for the British army stationed there at the time.

TROPICAL GARDENS & SPECTACULAR CAVES

✪ Harrison's Cave

Welchman Hall, St. Thomas. ☎ **809/438-6640.** Admission $7.50 adults, $3.75 children 3–16, free 2 and under. Daily 9am–4pm. From Bridgetown, take Highway 2 and follow the signposted directions.

This cave is the number-one tourist attraction of Barbados, and visitors have the chance to view this beautiful, natural, underground world from aboard an electric tram and trailer. Before the tour, a video of the cave is shown in the presentation hall. During the tour, visitors see bubbling streams, tumbling cascades, and deep pools, which are subtly lighted, while all around stalactites hang overhead like icicles. Stalagmites rise from the floor. Visitors may disembark and get a closer look at this natural phenomenon at the Rotunda Room and the Cascade Pool.

Flower Forest of Barbados

St. Joseph. ☎ **809/433-8152.** Admission $5 adults, $2.50 children 5–16. Daily 9am–5pm. Take Highway 2 from Bridgetown and follow it to Welchman Hall Gully, which is signposted. The Flower Forest is nearby.

At Richmond Plantation, an old sugar estate, Flower Forest of Barbados stands 850 feet above sea level near the western edge of the Scotland District, a mile from Harrison's Cave. Set in one of the most scenic parts of Barbados, it is more than just a botanical garden, for people and nature came together here to create something beautiful. After viewing the grounds, visitors can purchase handcrafts at Best of Barbados.

Welchman Hall Gully

St. Thomas. ☎ **809/438-6671.** Admission $5 adults, $2.50 children 6–12, free under 6. Daily 9am–5pm. Take Highway 2 from Bridgetown and follow the signs.

This is a lush tropical rain forest operated by the Barbados National Trust. Here are found specimens of plants growing when the English settlers landed in 1627. Many plants are labeled—clove, nutmeg, tree fern, and cacao among others—and occasionally you'll spot a wild monkey. A series of caves were here until their roofs fell in. Breadfruit trees are claimed to be descended from seedlings brought from the South Pacific by Captain William Bligh of H.M.S. *Bounty* fame.

6 Cruises & Tours

CRUISES

The *Bajan Queen,* the largest of the coastal cruising vessels, is modeled after a Mississippi riverboat. It is the only cruise ship offering table seating and dining on local fare, produced fresh in the on-board galley. There is also cover available from sun or rain. Day cruises include two anchor stops for swimming (with snorkeling equipment provided), a buffet luncheon, water sports, open bar, and dancing to calypso music and international records. The *Bajan Queen* becomes a showboat at night, with local bands providing all kinds of music for dancing under the stars. You are treated to a dinner of roast chicken, barbecued steak, and seasoned flying fish with a help-yourself buffet of fresh side dishes and salads. Cruises are usually sold out, so book early to avoid disappointment. Each cruise costs $55 and includes transportation to and from your hotel. For reservations, contact **Bajan Queen Ltd.,** Dunford House, Fontabelle, St. Michael (☎ **809/436-6424**).

The same company also owns two motorized replicas of pirate frigates, the *Jolly Roger I* and the *Jolly Roger II.* You can enjoy drinks from an open bar, a full steak barbecue lunch, and nonstop music for dancing on the spacious sun deck. Later, the boat stops at a sheltered cove where passengers can strip to their bathing suits and go for a swim. Lunch cruises are from 10am to 2pm Monday through Saturday. The cost is $55 per person; children under 12 pay half price. For information, call **809/436-6424,** or visit the berth at Bridgetown Harbour.

Patrick Gonsalves skippers the *Limbo Lady* (☎ 809/420-5418), his classic 44-foot yacht, while his wife, Yvonne, a singer and guitarist, serenades you on a sunset cruise. Daily lunch cruises are also possible, with a stop for swimming and snorkeling (equipment provided). Both lunch and sunset cruises offer a complimentary open bar and transportation to and from your hotel. Lunch cruises lasting 4¹/₂ hours cost $50, and 3-hour sunset cruises go for $42, including a glass of champagne. Moonlight dinner cruises can also be arranged (call the number above for more information).

RUM TOURS

Tours, with or without lunch included, are offered at **The Mount Gay Distilleries, Ltd.,** Spring Garden Highway, Brandon's St. Michael's (☎ 809/425-9066). Founded in 1703, and today noted as the oldest rum distillery in the world, it offers 45-minute tours of the rum-making process Monday to Friday from 9am to 3:45pm, departing at 30-minute intervals. Tours cost $5 per person, and include a complimentary rum punch, access to a souvenir stand, and a highly informative tour of the distillery. A more elaborate version of the tour, which includes lunch, is available Monday to Friday for $20 per person, including free transport to and from your hotel, a tour of the distillery, a welcome rum punch, and a lunch which is prepared either à la carte or buffet style, depending on the number of participants. It usually requires advance reservations.

SUBMERGED SIGHTSEEING

You don't have to be an experienced diver to see what lives 150 feet below the surface of the sea around Barbados. You can view these wonders aboard *Atlantis II,* a sightseeing submarine. The air-conditioned submersible seats 28 passengers, and, with two crew members, makes 11 dives daily from 9am to 7pm. Passengers are transported from the Careenage in downtown Bridgetown aboard *Yukon II,* a 48-foot boat, to the submarine site, about a mile off the West Coast hotel district. The ride offers a view of the Gold Coast.

The submarine has 16 2-foot-wide viewing ports, 8 on either side, plus a 52-inch port at the front. Besides the rainbow of colors, tropical fish, and plants, you'll see an intact shipwreck that lies upright. The total time of the trip is about 2 hours, including 45 minutes in the submarine, and it costs BD$139 ($69.50). Children 4 to 12 are charged half fare. For reservations, call **Atlantis Submarines (Barbados) Inc.,** Horizon House, McGregor Street, Bridgetown (☎ 809/436-8929).

SIGHTSEEING TOURS

Nearly all Bajan taxi drivers are familiar with the entire island, and like to show it off to visitors. If you can afford it, touring by taxi is far more relaxing than—and preferable to—taking one of the standardized bus tours. The average day tour by taxi costs $50 but, of course, that figure has to be negotiated in advance.

Instead of a private taxi, you can also book a tour with **Bajan Tours,** Glenayre, Locust Hall, St. George (☎ 809/437-9389), a locally owned and operated tour company. Their best bet for the first-timer is the exclusive island tour, costing $50 per person, with departure between 8:30am to 9am, and return from 3:30 to 4pm daily. It covers all the highlights of the island, including the Barbados Wildlife Reserve, the Chalky Mount Potteries, and the rugged East Coast. On Friday for the same price they conduct a heritage tour—mainly of the major plantations and museums on the island—and on Tuesday and Wednesday they offer an Eco Tour, which takes in the natural beauty of the island. It too costs $50 and leaves at the same time as the other two tours. A full buffet lunch is included in all tours.

7 Shopping

Barbados merchants can sometimes offer duty-free merchandise at prices 20% to 40% lower than in the United States and Canada. But, of course, you've got to be a smart shopper to spot bargains and also be familiar with prices back in your hometown. Duty-free shops have two prices listed on merchandise, the local retail price and the local retail price less government tax. You can avoid paying the tax if you have your purchase sent directly to the airport or cruise-ship dock; otherwise, if you're using the goods while in Barbados, you must pay the tax.

Some of the best duty-free buys include cameras (such as Leica and Fuji), watches (names like Omega, Piaget, Seiko), crystal (such as Waterford and Lalique), gold (especially jewelry), bone china (such names as Wedgwood and Royal Doulton), cosmetics and perfumes, and liquor (including Barbados-produced rums and liqueurs), along with tobacco products and cashmere sweaters, tweeds, and sportswear from Britain.

The outstanding Barbados handcraft item is black coral, fashioned into attractive earrings, pendants, and rings. Clay pottery is another Bajan craft. In Barbados you'll find a selection of locally made vases, pots, pottery mugs, glazed plates, and ornaments.

Wall hangings are made from local grasses and dried flowers. Island craftspeople also turn out straw mats, baskets, and bags with raffia embroidery. Still in its infant stage, leatherwork is also found in Barbados, particularly such items as handbags, belts, and sandals. Cruise passengers generally head for the **Bridgetown Cruise Terminal** at Bridgetown Harbour, where there are some 20 duty-free shops and at least 13 merchandise stores specializing in local and regional products.

Articrafts

Broad Street, Bridgetown. ☎ **809/427-5767.**

Here John and Roslyn Watson have assembled one of the most impressive displays of Bajan arts and crafts on the island. Roslyn's woven wall hangings are decorated with objects from the island including sea fans and coral; they make a distinctive handcrafted design, especially if you have a home in Florida or California. Straw work, handbags, and bamboo items are also sold. Hours are Monday to Friday from 8:30am to 5pm, Saturday from 8:30am to 1pm.

Best of Barbados

At the Southern Palms Hotel, St. Lawrence Gap. ☎ **809/428-7171.**

Part of an islandwide chain of 12 stores, Best of Barbados sells only products designed and/or made in Barbados. The best shop on the island for local products, it was established in 1975 by an English-born painter, Jill Walker, whose prints are best-sellers, and her husband, Jimmy. They sell articles celebrating aspects of island life, including coasters, mats, and trays with scenes of local life, T-shirts, pottery, dolls and games, and cookbooks, among other items. This tasteful shop is in a pink-and-white building around the corner from the entrance to Southern Palms.

A more convenient location might be the outlet in Bridgetown at Mall 34, Broad Street (☎ **809/436-1416**). Hours for both shops are Monday to Saturday from 9am to 5pm and Sunday from 9am to 1pm.

Cave Shepherd

10-14 Broad St., Bridgetown. ☎ **809/431-2121.**

The best place to shop for tax-free merchandise is Cave Shepherd, which has branches at Sunset Crest in Holetown, Da Costas Mall, Grantley Adams International Airport, and the Bridgetown Cruise Terminal. If your time is limited and you want a preview of what's for sale in Barbados, try this outlet. Cave Shepherd is the largest department store in Barbados and one of the most modern in the Caribbean, and it has the widest selections of goods islandwide. It was established in 1906, when the Cave family was the sole owner, but after a disastrous fire in 1969, it went public and was rebuilt with the financial assistance of more than 2,000 Barbadians. The store offers perfumes, cosmetics from the world's leading houses, fine full-lead crystal and English bone china, sweaters, cameras, gold and silver jewelry, swimwear, leather goods, designer clothing for men, handcrafts, and souvenirs. More than 70 brands of liqueurs are sold, as well as other spirits. After you finish shopping, relax on the top floor in the cool comfort of the Ideal Restaurant. Hours are Monday to Friday from 9am to 5pm, Saturday from 8:30am to 1:30pm.

Colours of De Caribbean
The Waterfront Marina, Bridgetown. ☎ **809/436-8522.**

Next to the Waterfront Café on the Careenage, this unique store has a very individualized collection of tropical clothing—all made in the West Indies—and other collections including jewelry and decorative objects. Original hand-painted and batik clothing may hold the most interest for you. The collection was assembled by owner/designer Dianne Butcher, who sees to it that her collection "reflects the music, dance, and culture" of Barbados. She answers the question how to look elegant even though casually dressed. Hours are Monday to Friday from 9am to 6pm, Saturday from 9am to 2pm.

Cotton Days
Bay Street, St. Michael. ☎ **809/427-7191.**

Boutiques abound in Barbados, and Cotton Days is one of the best known and most stylish. It inventories a wide array of casually elegant one-of-a-kind garments suitable for cool nights in hot climes. The collection has been called "wearable art." For inspiration, the in-house designers turn to the flora and fauna of the island and the underwater world. The sales staff is skilled at selecting whimsical accessories to accompany the dresses, blouses, and shirts sold here. Magazines like *Vogue* and *Glamour* have praised this collection. Open Monday to Friday from 9am to 5pm and Saturday from 9am to 1pm.

Earthworks Pottery/Otherworks
Edgehill Heights 2, St. Thomas Paris. ☎ **809/425-0223.**

Some serious shoppers consider this one of the artistic highlights of Barbados. Deep in the island's central highlands, its modern building was erected in the 1970s by Canadian-born Goldie Spieler. Trained as an art teacher and ceramic artist, Ms. Spieler and her son, David, create whimsical plates, cups, saucers, and serving vessels whose blue and green colors emulate the color of the Bajan sea and sky. Some of their fans claim that a breakfast of corn flakes in a cerulean-blue porringer on a snowy Stateside morning re-creates the warmth of a Caribbean holiday. Many objects are decorated with Antillean-inspired swirls and zigzags, and can be shipped virtually anywhere. On the premises is the studio where the objects are crafted, and a showroom that sells the output of at least half a dozen other island potters. Prices range from $3 to $400. Open Monday to Friday from 9am to 5pm, Saturday from 9am to 1pm.

The Great House Gallery
In the Bagatelle Restaurant, Highway 2A, St. Thomas. ☎ **809/421-6767.**

Set within the airy upper floor of one of the most historic great houses in Barbados, this art gallery combines a sophisticated inventory of artworks with West Indian graciousness. Displayed on high white walls amid the reflected glow of an antique mahogany floor, the gallery maintains the same hours as the restaurant downstairs (see "Where to Dine" in Chapter 10), adding a cultivated gloss to the rituals of dining and drinking. Established by Richard and Valerie Richings, the gallery sells oils and watercolors by Caribbean, South American, and British artists priced from $20 to $2,000. Among them are included the award-winning works of the owners themselves. Open Monday to Friday from 10am to 5pm.

Harrison's
1 Broad St., Bridgetown. ☎ **809/431-5500.**

In addition to this main shop, Harrison's has 14 branch stores, all selling a wide variety of duty-free merchandise, including china, crystal, jewelry, leather goods, sweaters, and perfumes, all at fair prices. We've been able to find good buys here in the range of Baccarat, Lalique, Royal Doulton, and Waterford crystal. They also sell some state-of-the-art leather products handcrafted in Columbia. They've been in business since the 19th century. Harrison's is the major competitor to Cave Shepherd on the island, but we'd give the edge to Cave Shepherd. Open Monday to Friday from 9am to 5pm, Saturday from 9am to 1pm.

Louis Bayley Shoppe
Da Costas Mall, Broad Street, Bridgetown. ☎ **809/431-0029.**

At this outlet, you'll find a selection of fine china from manufacturers throughout Europe (such as Aynsley and Belleek giftware, Waterford crystal, Lladró and Florence figurines), all at tax-free prices. Prices are usually less expensive than similar items you might pick up on a tour of Europe. This shop also carries a wide range of European jewelry, gemstones, and 18-karat gold, famous watch names (such as Rolex, Omega, Raymond Weil, Citizen, Tag Heuer, Ebel, and Swatch), and the distinctive Mont Blanc pens. Open Monday to Friday 9am to 5pm, Saturday from 9am to 1:30pm.

Mall 34
Broad Street. ☎ **809/429-9235.**

Bridgetown's most modern shopping complex offers tax-free shopping in air-conditioned comfort. You can find watches, clocks, china, jewelry, crystal, linens, sweaters, and liquor, together with souvenir items and tropical fashions. A restaurant is on the top floor of the building, and shoppers can stop for a cool drink and a snack at the little cafe downstairs. Open Monday to Saturday from 9am to 6pm.

Pelican Village
Princess Alice Highway, Bridgetown. ☎ **809/426-1966.**

While in Bridgetown, go to Pelican Village on Princess Alice Highway leading down to the city's deep-water harbor. A collection of island-made crafts and souvenirs is sold here in a tiny colony of thatch-roofed shops, and you can wander from one to the other. Sometimes you can see craftspeople at work. Some shops here are gimmicky and repetitive, although interesting items can be found. Open Monday to Friday 8am to 4pm, Saturday from 8am to 5pm.

Queen's Park Gallery
Queen's Park House, Bridgetown, St. Michael. ☎ **809/427-2345.**

The visual arts are flowering in Barbados, as many painters, photographers, potters, and sculptors work in a wide variety of styles and media. Queen's Park Gallery, in an 18th-century building and operated by the National Cultural Foundation, is open to the public. Hours are Sunday and Monday from noon to 3pm and from 4 to 8pm; Tuesday to Thursday from 10am to 8pm, and Friday and Saturday from 10am to 1pm and from 2 to 6pm.

The Shell Gallery
Carlton House, St. James. ☎ **809/422-2593.**

For the shell collector, this is the best place to shop in the West Indies: Shells for sale come from all over the world. The outlet features the shell art of Maureen Edghill, considered the finest artist in this field, who founded this unique gallery in 1975. One of Maureen's designs was commissioned by the Barbados Museum as a gift to Queen Elizabeth II. Also offered are hand-painted chinaware, shell jewelry, local pottery and ceramics, and imported batik and papier-maché artwork depicting shell and aquatic life. Open Monday to Friday from 9am to 5pm and Saturday from 9am to 2pm.

Walker's Caribbean World
St. Lawrence Gap. ☎ **809/428-1183.**

Close to the Southern Palms, this outlet offers many locally made items for sale, as well as handcrafts from the Caribbean Basin. Here you can buy the famous Jill Walker prints. There is also a gallery devoted to tropical prints. Open Monday to Saturday from 9am to 5pm.

8 Barbados After Dark

Most of the big resort hotels feature nightly entertainment, often dancing to steel bands and occasionally Bajan floor shows. Sometimes there are beach barbecues.

For the most authentic Bajan evening possible, and to top off your trip to Barbados, head for **Baxters Road** in Bridgetown, a street that reaches its peak of liveliness on Fridays and Saturdays after 11pm. In fact, if you stick around 'til dawn, the joints are still jumping. The street is safer than it might seem to visitors; Bajans come here to have fun, not to make trouble. Entertainment tends to be spontaneous. You might hear jazz on scratchy records—certainly the voice of Billie Holiday. Some old-time visitors have compared Baxters Road to the back streets of New Orleans in the '30s. If you fall in love with the place, you can "caf crawl" up and down the street. Just as in the days of Rachel Pringle in the 1780s (see "Miss Rachel & The Prince" in Chapter 8), nearly every bar is run by a Bajan woman. Prices are about the same from place to place, but each has its own atmosphere.

The most popular "caf" on Baxters Road is **Enid's** (she has a telephone, "but it doesn't work"), a little ramshackle establishment where Bajans devour fried chicken at 3 in the morning. Her place is open daily from 8:30pm to 8:30am, when the last satisfied customer departs into the blazing morning sun and Enid heads home to get some sleep before the new night begins. You can also stop in for a Banks beer. In fact, if you want a totally Bajan experience, why not come here and sit yourself down at one of the oilcloth-clad tables in the dilapidated back room? You can order a complete dinner for about $6.

Beach Club
Sunset Crest, St. James. ☎ **809/432-1309.** No cover Sun–Fri; Sat free for diners, $5 for nondiners.

The Beach Club is a bar and restaurant that serves as a social focal point for Sunset Crest. Many island residents happily hobnob here with friends and colleagues. Happy hour at the Beach Bar is from 6 to 7pm nightly, when drinks are half price. Fish fries, barbecues, or buffets are offered from 7 to 9pm daily, priced from $10 to $12.50.

There's live entertainment every night, including bands, amateur talent shows, films of Barbados, and local folk chorales. Sunday night is show night, when the entertainment is bigger and more theatrical than usual. Open daily from 11am to 2am.

Club Xanadu

In the Ocean View, Hastings, Christ Church. ☎ **809/427-7821.** Cover $42.50 with dinner; $12.50 show only.

In this small Ocean View (see "Where to Stay" in Chapter 10), musical revues are written, choreographed, and presented by American David McCarthy. Call to inquire about the shows as they are different every year. Open Thursday and Friday; buffet at 7:30pm, show at 9:30pm.

Coach House

Paynes Bay (on the main Bridgetown-Holetown road, just south of Sandy Lane, about 6 miles north of Bridgetown), St. James. ☎ **809/432-1163.** Cover $5 (includes $3 in drinks).

The Coach House, named after a pair of antique coaches that sometimes stand outside, is a green-and-white house said to be 200 years old. The atmosphere is a Bajan version of an English pub, with an outdoor garden bar. Business people and habitués of nearby beaches come here to order buffet lunches of Bajan food Monday to Friday from noon to 3pm. The price is $11 for an all-you-can-eat lunchtime assortment that includes local vegetables and salads prepared fresh daily. If you visit from 6 to 10:30pm, you can order bar meals, including flying fish burgers, with prices from $8 and up. There's also a more formal evening dining room where meals, served from 6 to 11pm daily, begin at $23.50 and include homemade soups and pâtés, shrimp Créole, and local fish, steak, and chicken dishes. Live music is presented most nights, featuring everything from steel bands to jazz, pop, and rock; an attentive crowd assembles here nightly from 9pm to closing.

John Moore Bar

On the waterfront, Weston, St. James Parish. ☎ **809/422-2258.**

This is the most atmospheric and least pretentious bar on Barbados. Established in 1958 in what had been a storefront, it was rebuilt in 1970 about 100 yards northwest of Weston's only fire station. Although its namesake John Moore died in 1987, the place is owned and managed by Mr. Lamont "Breedy" Addison, whose tenure here began as a teenager, working as an employee of Mr. Moore almost since the bar's original opening. If you think this bar functions only as a watering hole, think again: It's probably the most influential nerve center in this waterfront town, filled throughout the day and evening with the widest and most congenial group of residents in the neighborhood. Most visitors opt for a rum punch or beer, but if you're hungry, platters of local fish can be prepared—after a moderate delay—for between $5 and $7 each. Open daily from 9am until the last patron leaves.

Harbour Lights

Marine Villa, Bay Street (about a mile southeast of Bridgetown), St. Michael. ☎ **809/436-7225.** Cover $6–$10, depending on the performers.

In theory, at least, the heart and soul of this club is a dignified seafront villa, originally built directly above the beachfront about a century ago. In reality, however, the party and its participants sprawl over the surrounding land, dancing and reveling to the sounds of the live bands or recorded music that fill the nighttime air. Dancing might break out anywhere, especially on the patio overlooking the surf or at a Harbour Lights beach party. No one under 18, and no one wearing shorts, is admitted. Grilled meats and hamburgers are available from a barbecue pit/kiosk on the premises. Open daily from 9:30pm to 4:30am; live music Friday through Monday.

✪ 1627 and All That

Sherbourne Center, St. Michael. ☎ **809/428-1627.** Cover $50.

Nothing else in Barbados so effectively combines music with entertainment and dancing as does this establishment. It's the most interesting place in Barbados to visit on a Thursday night, when the format combines a cocktail hour, a large buffet of Bajan food, and a historic and cultural presentation. The site, Sherbourne Centre, is a conference facility. The ticket includes transportation to and from your hotel. Dinner is served at 7pm every Thursday, with show time at 8pm, concluding at 9:30pm.

Plantation Restaurant and Garden Theatre

Main Road (Highway 7), St. Lawrence. ☎ **809/428-5048.** Unlimited drinks, dinner, and show $50; show only $25.

This is the island's most visible showcase for evening dinner theater and Caribbean cabaret. Dinner and a show are presented every Wednesday and Friday. Dinner is served at 6:30pm, and one of two different shows (*Barbados by Night* or *Plantation Tropical Spectacular II*) is presented at 8:15pm. Both involve plenty of exotic costumes, and lots of reggae, calypso, and limbo. Advance reservations are recommended.

The Ship Inn

St. Lawrence Gap, Christ Church. ☎ **809/435-6961.** Cover $5 after 8:30pm.

Previously recommended as a restaurant (see "Where to Dine" in Chapter 10), this inn is now among the leading entertainment centers on the South Coast. Its pub is *the* island hot spot. Top local bands perform every night of the week, and patrons gather to listen to live reggae, calypso, and Top 40 music. The entrance fee to the Ship Inn complex is redeemable in food or drink at any of the other bars or restaurants in the complex. That means that guests are actually only paying $2 for the live entertainment. Open daily from noon to 2am.

The Waterfront Café

Cavan's Lane, The Careenage, Bridgetown. ☎ **809/427-0093.** No cover.

By anyone's estimate, this is the busiest, most interesting, and most animated nighttime watering hole in Bridgetown. Contained in a turn-of-the-century warehouse originally built to store bananas and freeze fish, it welcomes both diners and drinkers to its reverberating walls for Créole food, beer, and pastel-colored drinks. Live music (reggae, ragtime, rock 'n' roll, and jazz, depending on the performers) is presented Monday to Saturday from 8 to 11:30pm. Full Créole meals average $22.50. Careenage Coffee, laced with various after-dinner potions, is a longtime favorite. Food service Monday to Saturday from 9am to 10pm; bar service from 9am to midnight.

Index

FROMMER'S COMPLETE TRAVEL GUIDES

*(Comprehensive guides to destinations around the world, with
selections in all price ranges—from deluxe to budget)*

Acapulco/Ixtapa/Taxco
Alaska
Amsterdam
Arizona
Atlanta
Australia
Austria
Bahamas
Bangkok
Barcelona, Madrid & Seville
Belgium, Holland & Luxembourg
Berlin
Bermuda
Boston
Budapest & the Best of Hungary
California
Canada
Cancún, Cozumel & the Yucatán
Caribbean
Caribbean Cruises & Ports of Call
Caribbean Ports of Call
Carolinas & Georgia
Chicago
Colorado
Costa Rica
Denver, Boulder & Colorado Springs
Dublin
England
Florida
France
Germany
Greece
Hawaii
Hong Kong
Honolulu/Waikiki/Oahu
Ireland
Italy
Jamaica/Barbados
Japan
Las Vegas
London
Los Angeles
Maryland & Delaware
Maui

Mexico
Mexico City
Miami & the Keys
Montana & Wyoming
Montréal & Québec City
Munich & the Bavarian Alps
Nashville & Memphis
Nepal
New England
New Mexico
New Orleans
New York City
Northern New England
Nova Scotia, New Brunswick & Prince
    Edward Island
Paris
Philadelphia & the Amish Country
Portugal
Prague & the Best of the Czech Republic
Puerto Rico
Puerto Vallarta, Manzanillo & Guadalajara
Rome
San Antonio & Austin
San Diego
San Francisco
Santa Fe, Taos & Albuquerque
Scandinavia
Scotland
Seattle & Portland
South Pacific
Spain
Switzerland
Thailand
Tokyo
Toronto
U.S.A.
Utah
Vancouver & Victoria
Vienna
Virgin Islands
Virginia
Walt Disney World & Orlando
Washington, D.C.
Washington & Oregon

FROMMER'S FRUGAL TRAVELER'S GUIDES

*(The grown-up guides to budget travel, offering dream vacations
at down-to-earth prices)*

Australia from $45 a Day
Berlin from $50 a Day
California from $60 a Day
Caribbean from $60 a Day
Costa Rica & Belize from $35 a Day
Eastern Europe from $30 a Day
England from $50 a Day
Europe from $50 a Day
Florida from $50 a Day
Greece from $45 a Day
Hawaii from $60 a Day

India from $40 a Day
Ireland from $45 a Day
Italy from $50 a Day
Israel from $45 a Day
London from $60 a Day
Mexico from $35 a Day
New York from $70 a Day
New Zealand from $45 a Day
Paris from $65 a Day
Washington, D.C. from $50 a Day

FROMMER'S PORTABLE GUIDES

(Pocket-size guides for travelers who want everything in a nutshell)

Charleston & Savannah
Las Vegas

New Orleans
San Francisco

FROMMER'S IRREVERENT GUIDES

(Wickedly honest guides for sophisticated travelers)

Amsterdam
Chicago
London
Manhattan

Miami
New Orleans
Paris
San Francisco

Santa Fe
U.S. Virgin Islands
Walt Disney World
Washington, D.C.

FROMMER'S AMERICA ON WHEELS

*(Everything you need for a successful road trip, including full-color
road maps and ratings for every hotel)*

California & Nevada
Florida
Mid-Atlantic
Midwest & the Great Lakes
New England & New York

Northwest & Great Plains
South Central &Texas
Southeast
Southwest

FROMMER'S BY NIGHT GUIDES

(The series for those who know that life begins after dark)

Amsterdam
Chicago
Las Vegas
London

Los Angeles
Miami
New Orleans

New York
Paris
San Francisco